Britain and America

D0755518

This book is one component of the Open University course AA303 *Understanding Comparative History: Britain and America from 1760*. Details of this and other Open University courses can be obtained from the Course Reservations and Sales Centre, P.O. Box 724, The Open University, Milton Keynes, MK7 6ZS, UK. For availability of other course components, including audio-cassettes, contact Open University Educational Enterprises Ltd, 12 Cofferidge Close, Stony Stratford, Milton Keynes, MK11 1BY, UK.

Britain and America:
Studies in Comparative History,
1760–1970

Edited by David Englander
at The Open University

Yale University Press
New Haven and London
in association with The Open University

First published 1997

Grateful acknowledgement is made to the following for permission to reproduce material published previously elsewhere: the authors and Cambridge University Press for chapters I.1, II.1, IV.1, IV.2 and V.3; the Historical Society of Western Pennsylvania for chapter III.1; Frank Cass and Co. Ltd for chapter II.2; Blackwell Publishers for chapter III.4; Routledge Ltd for chapter V.1; the American Sociological Association for chapter V.2. Chapter IV.1 first appeared in a volume sponsored by the Committee on States and Social Structures of the Social Science Research Council of the United States.

Set in Linotron Bembo by Fakenham Photosetting, Norfolk
Printed in Great Britain by The Bath Press

Library of Congress Cataloging-in-Publication Data

Britain and America: studies in comparative history, 1760–1970/
    edited by David Englander at the Open University.
        Includes bibliographical references and index.
        ISBN 0–300–06977–4 (cloth).—ISBN 0–300–06978–2 (pbk.)
        1. United States—History—1783–1865.   2. United States—History—1865–   . 3.
    Great Britain—17th century.   4. Great Britain—History—18th century.   5. Great
    Britain—History—20th century.   I. Englander, David. 1949–   .   II. Open
    University.
    E179.U59   1997
    303.48′273041—dc20   96–36470
                                                                                     CIP

A catalogue record for this book is available from the British Library.

10 9 8 7 6 5 4 3 2

Contents

Preface

Books like credit cards create debts that are easy to acquire but difficult to repay. In the making of this volume I have drawn freely upon the expertise and good nature of friends and colleagues. I have benefited from the advice and assistance of Bernard Waites, Clive Emsley, Bill Purdue and Rosemary O'Day in the Department of History at The Open University and from the exceptional generosity of Professor Anthony Badger of the University of Cambridge. Debts of gratitude are also owed to Nicky Merridan who typed the manuscript and to Andrew Horner and Wendy Simpson who provided administrative support.

David Englander,
Department of History,
The Open University

Introduction

DAVID ENGLANDER

Events strikingly similar, but occurring in a different historical milieu, lead to completely different results. By studying each of these evolutions separately and then comparing them, it is easy to find the key to the understanding of this phenomenon; but it is never possible to arrive at this understanding by using the *passe partout* of some historical philosophical theory whose great virtue is to stand above history. Karl Marx, 1877.[1]

All history is comparative history; for without the drawing of comparisons the relationship between the unique and the general could never be known and history, as a discipline, would be impossible. In short, the comparative method applies the logic of experiment to the study of human society in the past. As such it assists in posing new questions, defining historical problems, separating necessary and contingent factors, identifying broad patterns and testing the validity of both specific and general hypotheses.

Comparison, as a mode of historical understanding, expresses the desire for a methodologically and conceptually more rigorous discipline. That desire has become more pronounced over the past fifty years or so as historians have become increasingly aware of the assumptions underlying their investigations and of the need to define clearly the questions and hypotheses with which they approach their subject matter. Scholars who are keen to increase the explanatory value of historical studies have found in the comparative approach a strategy that seems better able to reveal the structures, movements and processes that underlie the surface of events. One of them, the eminent German scholar, Hans-Ulrich Wehler, indeed, writes of comparison as the 'highest form of historical research'.[2] Whatever the status of his claim, there is no denying that comparative research is among the most innovative and exciting areas of recent historical inquiry.[3] Its preference for the analytical and systematic over the intuitive and descriptive, and for the challenging generalization over the closed conclusion, are sources of strength and distinction.

There is no approved way of doing comparative history. In their aims and objects, methods and procedures, writing and reporting styles, comparative historians are as varied as any other type of historian. So, too, are their research orientations. Some applications of the comparative method are concerned primarily with the search for variance. Here the emphasis is upon that which is particular to a particular historical experience. Comparative research, in these cases, is designed to illuminate the difference between structures and processes in order to understand better the specific arrangements that are found within each. Alternative research strategies will be preferred by those interested in establishing causal regularities applicable to more than one instance. Studies in this vein usually proceed from a well-defined general theory which is then tested in different historical contexts in order to provide empirical support for universal propositions. Both approaches have their dangers. The first tends to exalt historical contingency; the second tends to the elevation of an abstract causality.[4] Scholars who are sensitive to context and yet committed to the development of generalized historical explanations, have – following Ragin – turned to a case-oriented holistic approach that can better accommodate problems of multiple causation (i.e. the situation in which several different combinations of conditions produce the same outcome) and of conjunctural causation (i.e. outcomes resulting from the intersection of a set of conditions in time and space).[5] Such methodologies have been particularly effective in the study of the growth of modern social welfare policies. The development of the welfare state, it will be seen, cannot be understood simply by reference to socio-economic factors, but must take account of the determining influence of political institutions and processes that are the legacy of state formation and expansion in particular nations.

The articles collected here are offered both as an illustration and as a fair representation of creative comparative research. All have been chosen in connection with the Open University course, 'Understanding Comparative History: Britain and America from 1760'. Each item has been selected as an exemplar of the comparative method. Several pieces have been specially commissioned for this volume; others bring together the fruits of research and reflection in convenient format.

Britain and America: Studies in Comparative History is concerned to broaden and deepen our understanding of the development of liberal capitalist society in two different settings. It is organized on the principle that cross-national comparison is most effective when the focus is upon specific aspects of particular social phenomena. Thus there are five thematic sections, each preceded by a short introduction.

Section I, Political Culture and Development, is concerned with the organization of democratic politics and the sources of variation between the two national polities. Section II, Economic Development, addresses issues of comparative economic development and examines cross-national differences in the invention and adoption of mechanical methods in production. Section III, The City, takes up aspects of urban growth in the nineteenth century, the social relationships arising therefrom and the comparative responses in terms of transport, policing and planning arrangements. Section IV, Class and Class Conflict, comparing cross-national structures and experiences among workers, explores the interaction between technological and economic development, changes in jobs and the labour market, union formation, social conflicts and industrial participation. Section V, Gender, Citizenship and Welfare, looks at the tensions arising from the contradiction between certain sociological theories of citizenship which presuppose equality of rights and the operations of a capitalist market in which social inequality is assumed. The section includes a cross-national study of the denial of voting rights to women and other sex-based legal disabilities and an examination of gender and the origins of modern social polices in Britain and the United States. In this section, too, there is a comparative institutional analysis of how state-supported pensions for the elderly developed in Britain and America and a study of the influence of state capacity upon welfare reforms in Britain and the USA during the 1930s and 1940s.

The conditions in which the comparative method is most effective were indicated more than fifty years ago by the French historian Marc Bloch, one of its greatest practitioners, when he wrote of

> a parallel study of societies that are at once neighbouring and contemporary, exercising a constant mutual influence, exposed throughout their development to the action of the same broad causes just because they are close and contemporaneous, and owing their existence in part at least to a common origin.[6]

Although distant, Britain and the United States were never remote. In every other respect Bloch's prescription fits them exactly.

Until the second half of the eighteenth century Britain and America were united under the British Crown. At that time Britain was primarily an agricultural country, inhabited by some six million people, with a low standard of living, an hierarchical social system, and an aristocratic oligarchy in political control. America at this time was made up of thirteen colonies spread across the eastern seaboard of a vast and unexplored continent, with a population of less than one and a half million, engaged in agriculture, and administered by a government 3,000 miles away in London. A hundred years later things had changed radically. Britain had become the workshop of the world, with a large population (25 million), great urban and industrial centres, vastly increased wealth, greater social mobility and political democracy. America, in consequence of the Revolution of the colonies, had become an independent nation. By 1870 it had a population of 38.5 million, which had expanded to fill the continent. It had developed its own distinctive form of political democracy, and one person in four was urban. By the close of the century the United States had replaced Britain as the world's leading industrial power.

Industrial and social transformation occurred most dramatically in Britain between about 1760 and 1830. Industrialization in the USA came later. The Industrial Revolution, on both sides of the Atlantic, was more than a series of technological innovations and economic changes. It was a new way in which people looked at themselves, at society and the world at large. It offered, for the first time in human history, the prospect of controlling the environment instead of being at its mercy. The possibility of material abundance for all was no longer an idle dream, although it took time before the full implications of the new freedom were widely understood (and in this respect the Americans were far ahead of the British).

But if the term 'Revolution' suggests that a series of inventions in the textile, iron and engineering industries transformed the whole of economic and social life as suddenly and completely as political change was effected by the French Revolution, then it is somewhat misleading. Although contemporaries in Britain and the USA were constantly amazed at the pace of the changes going on around them, in fact the changes were largely confined to certain sectors of the economy, though these tended to be the pace-setters for the rest. Industrialization was a non-linear process, growing unevenly and varying according to time and local context. Much remains puzzling. British priority, for example, continues to engage historians, as it has done for several generations. What is clear, though, is that the Industrial Revolution was a complex and interlocking series of changes which resist any mono-causal explanation. Its shadow falls heavily across many of the phenomena that our cross-national comparisons are designed to illuminate.

The temptation to use industrialization as a sort of umbrella motif under which to account for other development, must, however, be resisted. Class and political democracy, two further themes with which this volume is concerned, are instructive. Certainly the language of class first began to be used in Britain at the time of the Industrial Revolution. Until the end of the eighteenth century people talked of ranks, orders or degrees. By the 1830s it was common to refer to the working classes, the lower class or the middle class. But class is a term with a dual meaning: it can be used either to describe social strata or to refer to the sense of class-consciousness. The working class in Britain, for instance, was a socio-economic group separated from the middle class by differences of income and power. But the working class was also distinguished by a sense of its own identity, an awareness or perception of itself – in fact, a class-consciousness.

The exact nature of that consciousness, how and when it emerged, and what significance to place upon it, have been subjects of argument. Historians of the United States have generally resisted interpreting their national history in terms of class-consciousness. Quite the contrary, many have gone so far as to deny that classes in the British or European sense have really existed at all in the United States. American 'exceptionalism', it is argued, can be accounted for by a combination of factors: the greater degree of citizenship, opportunities for high levels of geographical and occupational mobility, the absence of a homogeneous working class, the divisive influence of slavery and racism and the broad diffusion of capitalist values through the population. Historians of the United States have thus, for the most part, preferred to talk of status groups rather than classes.

On this basis, certain cross-national institutional differences can be (at any rate partly) explained. The labour movement is a case in point. The emergence of a strong trade union movement in nineteenth-century Britain was a consequence of the development of a large and distinctive working class. The formation of the Labour Party was the outcome of the alliance between the trade unions and socialist political leaders. By 1924 this alliance was strong enough to form a government. In the USA trade unions developed similarly in the nineteenth century and the American Federation of Labor was modelled on the British Trades Union Congress. The US labour movement, however, was weaker than its British contemporary. A smaller percentage of workers was organized and independent labour politics did not develop to anything like the same extent as in Britain. This was not because American workers were less militant than their British counterparts, neither were socialist groups lacking in the States. Workers in the United States were not only jealous of their republican heritage; they also embraced socialism, independent labour politics, Labor-Populism and the Knights of Labor. But from similar beginnings the two labour movements developed along different lines.

Such variation may owe something to differences in the development of political democracy. In the eighteenth century neither Britain nor America was a democracy in the modern sense, although both possessed representative institutions. Political rights were tied to property, and politics revolved around 'interests' rather than persons. The growth of popular democracy is the story of how political power in the British Parliament and in the American state assemblies and the federal Congress extended from aristocratic and commercial elites to include widening sections of the population. The process occurred in America earlier than in Britain. Many of the elected assemblies in pre-Revolutionary America had wide franchises, which, in New England, came close to universal male suffrage. Subsequently, the development of political democracy was generally dependent upon the extension of this suffrage in individual states. In Britain the broadening of the franchise followed fifty years of agitation culminating in the Great Reform Bill of 1832. But the working classes were still excluded, and it required Chartism and long years of popular agitation before the Reform Acts of 1867, 1884 and 1918 made popular democracy a reality.

In Britain, as in the USA, women were denied the right to vote. In both countries, too, women were active in the development of a suffrage campaign that raised more general questions about their status in society. Female activism, much of it middle-class in character, was also considerable in voluntary associations, abolitionism and temperance. The sources of feminism were various. In both countries the influence of evangelical Protestantism was pronounced. A pietistic environment which favoured religious individualism seems to have been conducive to the growth of feminism. The evangelical revival facilitated the emergence of women from domesticity, offered them a public role and involved them in questions of moral and social reform. Equally important was the inspiration drawn from the natural rights doctrines of the American and French Revolutions. On both sides of the Atlantic natural rights philosophy served to minimize differences and underscore the similarities between the sexes, and to highlight the importance of ideas of self-realization, freedom and autonomy. Structural changes in society, too, account for the rise of feminism: the separation of home and work compelled middle-class women, in particular, to redefine their role in society. The possibilities for the feminist movement depended in no small part upon the ways in which its various fragments combined, but also upon the ways in which it related to forces and groups which, although congruent with feminism, were not part of it. British women, like their American sisters, received qualified but not constant support from progressive elements in the trade union and socialist movements. British women who had been involved in Chartism and the anti-Poor Law struggles were subsequently relegated to a marginal position in a mid-Victorian labour movement that was increasingly patriarchally-minded and taken with ideas of 'the family wage' and 'separate spheres'. Middle-class women in Britain obtained walk-on parts or were permitted to perform prescribed roles by the mass political parties that were created in the wake of the 1867 Reform Act, but that was all.

Socialists, though generally more accommodating, particularly in the United States, hesitated to grant women full intra-party equality and remained ambivalent about women's emancipation where it challenged the deeply-rooted beliefs of the dominant sexist culture.

The extension of democracy in Britain and the USA was similar, though the form and pace of change was different. Industrialization came earlier in Britain, enfranchisement later. The social and cultural environment in which industrial society was born in the two countries differed significantly. Britain entered the Industrial Revolution as an hierarchical society, within which a landed aristocracy exercised social and cultural hegemony and paternalist supervision over a pyramid of ranks. The United States, by contrast, entered its industrial revolution with an open and egalitarian model of the social order. This affected labour's prospects and helps to explain some of the differences in the development of radical movements in Britain and the USA.

Still, it does not explain them all. Account must also be taken of other factors, such as immigration and settlement. America is a nation of immigrants. Immigration has touched every aspect of American life, creating fundamental problems and possibilities which are still working themselves out. When the first settlers arrived in 1607 they found a sparsely populated land – well under a million native Americans living in the area of what is now the United States. Native Americans were pushed westwards during the next three hundred years and their land taken by the newcomers. The filling up of the great continent proceeded by expansion from east to west, with an ever-advancing frontier of settlement. In the course of the nineteenth century the steady stream of immigration from Europe became a flood: successive waves brought English, Scots and Irish, followed by Germans, Italians and Poles and then mass migrations from Eastern and Southern Europe. Close on 40 million immigrants came to the United States between 1820 and 1950. This unprecedented movement of population has dominated the character of American history. The American working class, for example, reconstituted by mobility and immigration, assumed a social character that is quite dissimilar from that of its counterpart in Britain.

In both countries workers were concentrated in fast-growing industrial cities which, increasingly, became the controlling influence in national life. Cities, with their vast concentrations of propertyless people beyond the reach of the benevolent classes, were considered to be fearful places on both sides of the Atlantic. In both countries, too, similar strategies were applied to the maintenance of order. Differences in central–local relations and in access to power, however, meant that cops and bobbies did not operate in a uniform manner, and that transport developments and planning improvements likewise varied. These differences also owed something to the social character of the urban population. The recomposition of the American working class consequent upon mass immigration gave personal allegiances and ethnic loyalties a defining role in the civic culture in a way that had no parallel in Britain.

The relative weakness of American labour is sometimes identified as a key influence upon the unusual character of social welfare provision in the United States. Received views frequently suggest that in both timing and coverage Britain is pre-eminent in its social legislation and that, indeed, the welfare state is a British invention. Cross-national differences, when presented in this form, confuse rather than clarify or explain the variation in modern social welfare polices. In both Britain and America the assumptions of laissez-faire capitalism were abandoned slowly. State intervention to secure individual protection against the effects of unemployment, injury, old age and sickness, though it gained ground from the 1880s onwards, did not displace belief in individualistic notions of progress and improvement. With the twentieth century came an increasing commitment to welfare expenditure. The United States lagged behind Britain until the close of the 1920s, but progressed rapidly in the 1930s and 1960s. The implications of this change have been far-reaching. The role of the state and the expectations it arouses have shifted dramatically. In Britain and America the state is expected to assume a strategic role in welfare provision through the social security system and responsibility for the provision of services and benefits to satisfy its citizen's needs for housing, health, education and income. Questions arise as to the effect of welfare provision. Has it been merely to sustain capitalism and dilute demands for more radical reform? But, if, as seems possible, welfare policies are a necessary part of advanced industrial societies, it remains the case that the programmes enacted have differed considerably from state to state. The source of such variation are explored in several of the contributions. It will be seen that welfare policies are shaped not only by socio-economic factors but also by their specific historical context and the ways in which social policy initiatives are rooted in particular political, administrative and ideological contexts.

Britain and America: Studies in Comparative History, 1760–1970 will have failed in its purpose if it does not raise more questions than it answers for the aim of its contributors is as much to provoke thought and stimulate inquiry as to broaden and deepen our understanding. 'The comparative method', it has been written, 'is a method, a set of rules which can be methodically and systematically applied in gathering and using evidence to test explanatory hypotheses. It does not supply us with explanations to be subjected to test: this is the task for the historical imagination.'[7] Application and enthusiasm, a sensitivity to period and place, a gift for putting the pertinent question and, yes, a love of the past – all will still be required to make sense of historical inquiry. The comparative approach lends perspective and proportion to this enterprise. As Kipling once remarked, 'What should they know of England who only England know?' The comparative approach will serve equally to correct a similar tendency to view British history through the distorting lenses of American spectacles. Things which formerly escaped attention and were taken for granted will henceforth become problematical, even clear.

A NOTE ON EDITORIAL PROCEDURE

Articles which have been specially commissioned for this volume include full references. Otherwise, it has been our policy to omit all original footnotes except where a note qualifies a reference in the text. These notes have been collected at the end of each article.

Notes

1. Quoted in E. H. Carr, *What is History?* (London: Macmillan, 1961; Harmondsworth: Penguin, 1964), Penguin edn p. 6.
2. See introductory remarks of Hans-Ulrich Wehler, *Geschichte und Soziologie* (Cologne, 1977), n. 74.
3. Examples of the kind of work I have in mind in the sphere of Anglo-American studies include Richard Carwardine, *Transatlantic Revivalism, Popular Evangelicalism in Britain and America, 1790–1865* (Westport, Connecticut: Greenwood Press, 1978); Jeffrey Haydu, *Between Craft and Class: Skilled Workers and Factory Politics in the United States and Britain, 1896–1922* (Berkeley, Los Angeles and London: University of California Press, 1988); Sally McMurray, 'Women's work in agriculture: divergent trends in England and America, 1800–1939', *Comparative Studies in Society and History*, 34 (1992), pp. 248–70; Ann Shola Orloff, *The Politics of Pensions: A Comparative Analysis of Britain, Canada and the United States, 1880–1940* (Madison-Wisconsin: University of Wisconsin Press, 1993); Howard M. Woch, 'Unitarian philanthropy and cultural hegemony: Manchester and Boston 1827–1848', *Journal of Social History* (spring, 1993), pp. 539–57; Neville Kirk, *Labour and Society in Britain and the USA*, 2 vols (Aldershot: Scolar Press, 1994); Rosemary O'Day, *The Family and Family Relationships, 1500–1900, England, France and the United States of America*, Themes in Comparative History series (London: Macmillan, 1994); Frank Dobbin, *Forging Industrial Policy: The United States, Britain and France in the Railway Age* (Cambridge University Press, 1995) and Christine Bolt, *Feminist Ferment: 'The Woman Question' in the USA and England, 1870–1940* (London: UCL Press, 1995).
4. Those with an interest in methodological issues will find the following works particularly rewarding: A. Przeworski and H. Taume, *The Logic of Comparative Social Inquiry* (Malabar, FA: R. E. Krieyer, 1970); Charles Tilly, *Big Structures, Large Processes and Huge Comparisons* (New York: Russell Sage, 1984); Else Oyen (ed.), *Comparative Methodology* (1990) and Charles C. Ragin (ed.), *Issues and Alternatives in Comparative Social Research* (London and Newbury Park, CA: Sage, 1990).

5. Charles C. Ragin, *The Comparative Method* (Berkeley, CA: University of California Press), pp. 25–44.
6. Marc Bloch, 'A contribution towards a comparative history of European societies' in *Land and Work in Medieval Europe: Selected Papers by Marc Bloch*, translated by J. E. Andersen (London: Routledge and Kegan Paul, 1967), p. 46.
7. William H. Sewell Jr. 'Marc Bloch and the logic of comparative history', *History & Theory*, IV (1967), p. 217.

Part I Political Culture and Development

Both modern Britain and the modern United States claim to be democracies and, in spite of attempts to 'break the mould' in Britain, both have political structures which for long have centred on two major political parties. The origins of these democratic systems can be traced back to the seventeenth century (or even earlier if we follow the Whig tradition of the inexorable rise of Parliament), but they emerged as something readily identifiable during the nineteenth century. The sources of congruence and divergence are explained in the two extracts below.

J. C. D. Clark, in a highly controversial account, argues that, contrary to received opinion, the American Revolution has to be understood in terms of the transatlantic sectarian conflicts, particularly as they unfolded in the colonies. The traditional institutions of monarch, court, church and aristocracy and an ordered conception of society, he maintains, were far more salient to society and politics in the pre-Reform period than has previously been allowed. Pre-Reform-Bill-England, in his view, was an 'ancien regime' or a 'confessional state' in which church, crown and nobility was hegemonic. The implications of these arguments in relation to the Anglo–Atlantic world are developed in the extract that is reprinted below. To law and religion is reserved a special place in creating a distinctive colonial political discourse and in the transformation of the resultant antagonisms into a generalized opposition to British rule.

Rather different in its approach is the contribution by Mary K. Geiter and W. A. Speck. The sources of American identity in their account are altogether more varied. Their rich and suggestive article is primarily concerned to trace the growth and expression of a collective consciousness of a cultural identity and the extent to which 'America' changed from being a geographical expression into common cultural phenomena even before the inception of the new Republic. Their essay helps to explain the rapidity with which a new political identity could be invented once the Revolution began.

1

I.1

The structure of Anglo-American political discourse

J. C. D. CLARK

LAW, RELIGION AND SOVEREIGNTY

By the mid-eighteenth century, Englishmen on both sides of the Atlantic proclaimed their faith in liberty: they appealed to a common constitutional tradition even as they disputed its ownership and its application. They claimed the 'rights of Englishmen' and revered the texts in which they believed them to be embodied, like Magna Carta and the Bill of Rights. They commemorated a similar Protestant calendar of momentous anniversaries, including the Spanish Armada, the Gunpowder Plot, the execution of Charles I, and the birthday of the reigning monarch. They celebrated, and suspected a minority who were ambiguous about, the Restoration, the Glorious Revolution, the Act of Settlement, and the accession of the House of Hanover. They structured the political lives of their communities around representative institutions, and had the Westminster Parliament in mind as a model. As the Scots and Irish in the New World and the Old were progressively caught up in this hegemonic English myth, they too were drawn to subscribe to it and loudly profess it in order to exploit its libertarian implications: they were implications to which their very different sectarian and political traditions also pointed. Law and religion dominated men's understanding of the public realm.

Englishmen on both sides of the Atlantic received, and idealized, the common law. Law was, nevertheless, an area in which transatlantic discourse broke down and this book* explores, on a theoretical level, one of the pathways along which this process developed. On a theoretical plane, it will be argued that the pathway by which the hold of common law over

An abridged extract from J. C. D. Clark, *The Language of Liberty 1660–1832: Political Discourse and Social Dynamics in the Anglo-American World* (Cambridge University Press, 1994), pp. 31–45, 352–791.
* i.e. Clark's, *The Language of Liberty*.

America was weakened was by a growing polarization of a shared legal tradition into antitheses of common law and natural law. Natural law, as Lord Bryce remarked, 'which had been for nearly two thousand years a harmless maxim, almost a commonplace of morality, became in the end of the eighteenth century a mass of dynamite, which shattered an ancient monarch and shook the European Continent'. He wrote of France, but his insight applies to the American Revolution also.

Natural law and common law were, it will be argued, closely related in the English-speaking world. The mythology of the common law contended that it had always existed as a self-contained system, uncontaminated by any other legal code, rugged and immemorial, resisting foreign intrusions. This myth had some foundation, but needs to be importantly qualified. From the earliest times, the system known as the common law embraced a delicate interplay of English custom and Roman law principle in which, though the first predominated, the second was never extinguished. [. . .] Reformers in England, as in America, could therefore sometimes emphasize the natural-law element with the common law tradition. [. . .] This eclectic quality of the common law preserved a role for Roman law concepts within it, and the tactical need to find arguments to limit the unified King-in-Parliament who was created in the 1530s and who more securely ruled after 1660 kept an Anglican version of natural law near the political centre of attention. In this sense American colonists were merely emphasizing one strand in a common tradition; but they emphasized it to the point where 1776 may be understood as a revolution of natural law against common law. This constitutes the first of the main theses of the present book.

The American Revolution was mainly 'about' law: that is, the legal aspect of political authority, taxation and trade was at the centre of political controversy and determined the timing of the outbreak of armed resistance. But it was 'about' religion too, not only because religion created intellectual and social preconditions of resistance, but also because religion shaped the way in which British and colonial legal thinking developed and came to define certain practical problems as non-negotiable, beyond that sphere of pragmatic adjustment in which, for much of British and American history, legal disagreements had been addressed.

A second thesis of this book therefore concerns religion. The English-speaking peoples of the North Atlantic world were, by a large numerical majority, Protestants; and they defined themselves against Rome at a time when Protestantism was loud in claiming that it alone promoted civil liberty. Yet Protestantism in the Anglophone world had from the outset been marked by its proliferating diversities, and even the Church of England had been torn by conflict and schism over the interpretation of its status and its theology. The denominations which had separated from it in turn – Congregationalists, Presbyterian, Baptist, Quaker and others – competed for members with each other as well as with their parent. The uneasy and insecure existence of the sects, as well as their need continually to justify their separation from a parent both powerful and attractive, acted as perpetual irritants which kept vivid the memories of ancient grievances and encouraged Dissenters to wage a guerrilla war, sometimes desultory, sometimes militant, against the Church. In this war, they were often prepared to employ against Canterbury many of the charges that Canterbury itself still levelled against Rome. Within England, Wales and Ireland, the Church of England maintained an uneasy hegemony; but within the thirteen colonies these denominational problems, often exported versions of Anglican England's difficult relations with the religious traditions of Scotland and Ireland, grew in intensity; they lay behind many episodes of violent insurrection like those of 1689 in which James II's authority was overthrown in the colonies, and finally exploded in 1776.

The Church of England was not, itself, theologically homogeneous, any more than were the denominations which separated from it. With the decline in numbers and energy of 'Old Dissent' in the century after 1660, the most significant conflicts were increasingly played out within the Church rather than between the Church and the sects: High Churchmen and Low Churchmen, Trinitarians, Arians and Deists could all be found to assert that theirs was the authentic voice of Anglicanism. If Anglicans could increasingly win over Dissenters attracted to what was depicted as the immemorial and firmly established doctrinal orthodoxy of the Church, the opposite was also true: Low-Church Anglicans could be profoundly influenced by developments within Dissent, especially by the political mobilization of libertarian Nonconformists, playing on the claim that the Church too embraced a right of private judgement and had been founded at the Reformation in protest at the same forces of 'Popery and arbitrary power' that eighteenth-century Nonconformists on both sides of the Atlantic came to imagine were threatening them also. In this study the American Revolution is analysed theologically, as a rebellion by groups within Protestant Dissent against an Anglican hegemony, a rebellion which played on divisions within the Anglican Church itself.

Law and religion were profoundly related, however; the third main thesis of this book seeks to explain one of their points of contact. A rebellion of natural law against common law and a rebellion of Dissent against hegemonic Anglicanism were the same rebellion, since their target was the unified sovereign created by England's unique constitutional and ecclesiastical development: King, Lords and Commons, indivisible and irresistible, credited (according to Blackstone) with absolute power by the common law, dignified with divine authority by the Church. It is argued here that the English doctrine of sovereignty, classically but explosively expounded in Sir William Blackstone's *Commentaries on the Laws of England* of 1765–9, was neither his recent invention nor a legal doctrine only: it was and was seen to be quintessentially Anglican, worked out in the process of England's relations with Scotland, Ireland and Wales, and still asserted in a context that Dissenters in the British Isles as well as America recognized as an ecclesiastical one. Appropriately, therefore, the Blackstonian conception of sovereignty has been described as 'the single most important abstraction of politics in the entire [American] Revolution era'. [...]

CONSTITUTIONAL INNOVATIONS AND THEIR ENGLISH ANTECEDENTS

It has been argued by some scholars that the conception of sovereignty most memorably expressed by Blackstone was new, either in 1688 or with the accession of George III, and that colonists reacted swiftly against this innovation in the 1760s because they perceived its incompatibility with their local, long-established and acknowledged conception of constitutional law as custom rather than as command. [...]

Nevertheless, however novel the policies embodied in the Stamp Act or the Townshend duties, the dominant British definition of sovereignty had been evolving for a very much longer period. Colonial resistance to metropolitan assertions of authority, too, was at least as old as New England's arguments against the regime of James II's Governor, Sir Edmund Andros. Yet that same British definition of sovereignty had long been internalized by many colonial theorists, so far indeed that, under the pressure of tactical necessity in the 1760s, they found it almost impossible to frame an alternative despite the pressing need to do so. Why they finally did so, and why long-standing legal disagreements led at last to armed rebellion, is chiefly to be explained by new developments in the colonies.

The Revolution of 1776 was slow to happen partly because Englishmen on both sides of the Atlantic were locked into the belief that they were already living in a libertarian polity. The spheres of law and religion were not spheres of dictatorial power: in both the ideal of liberty was variously maintained, and in both the principles of consultation and representation were of long standing. Yet of all the transatlantic analogies the representative assembly was the most surprisingly ineffective and proved least able to evolve to resolve transatlantic problems. Whig regimes in England after 1688 progressively destroyed adjacent assemblies in the name of unified authority: the Edinburgh Parliament with the Union of 1707;

Convocation, the Church of England's representative assembly, in 1717; the Dublin Parliament in the Union of 1801. Even English parliamentary reformers, elaborating schemes for the renovation of the House of Commons, neglected to include plans for the incorporation of Members from the colonies, and the Scots and Irish allowed the Edinburgh and Dublin Parliaments to be snuffed out without producing alternative schemes for an imperial federal parliament. Similarly, eighteenth-century colonial assemblies steadily strengthened their positions in a series of daily conflicts with governors and imperial authorities without extrapolating their aims into a persuasive theory of representative democracy or a goal of a presence in the House of Commons. The demand of the 1760s for 'no taxation without representation' seemed to echo an ancient English constitutional principle; it was not a forward-looking blueprint for Jacksonian democracy or for seats in an imperial parliament.

Whatever the functions of colonial assemblies, these did not include the mobilization and expression of public opinion: no debate of any colonial assembly was ever published in a colonial newspaper, and the assemblies in general retained rules and assumptions safeguarding the secrecy of their proceedings that characterized the Westminster House of Commons in an earlier age. [...]

The theory which grounded the legitimacy of government on the consent of the governed did not arise primarily as a comment on the practice of representation in the colonies: it drew its main force from the idea of covenant in colonial religion. [...] English visitors to the colonies could easily imagine that they were stepping back into a world still preoccupied with ancient quarrels. From an English perspective, colonial rhetoric often displayed three marked characteristics. It represented a throwback to political alignments which Englishmen thought had been settled, at least within the British Isles. It addressed those old fears in the idiom of conspiracy theory. Finally, conspiracy theory was given its strangely intense significance by the immense power of denominational phobias. [...]

Englishmen in England and America were united in a shared political tradition, but it was not a sufficient bond of union to prevent breakdowns in 1688 and 1776, and it did not evolve to defend transatlantic ties against those other forces which threatened that tradition on both sides of the ocean.

THE GENESIS OF POLITICAL DISCOURSE

Constitutional challenges were articulated within the idioms of political discourse. [...] The two dominant idioms of discourse, daily reiterated, practically applied and prominent partly by reason of being lastingly con-tested, were law and religion. Each idiom had its own dialects. The English common law spoke with a different accent from canon law or the civil law applied in admiralty and ecclesiastical courts; in religion, Anglicanism stood defined between Roman Catholicism and the harsh variety of Protestant Dissent. The conflicts and unities of these idioms are a major theme of this book. Not only was colonial religious discourse much more plural than its English counterpart; the colonial legal idiom similarly placed much more emphasis on the traditions that rivalled the common law. [. . .]

The dominance of these two idioms meant that the insurrections dis-cussed in this book owed little to forces which later historiography has associated together as agents of 'modernization', like individualism, radi-calism or liberalism. The structure of Anglo-American debate in the two decades before the Revolution heavily and increasingly emphasized the corporate and collective element in American life. Colonists resisted British policy and finally demanded independence not as individuals but as parts of a collective voice in town meetings, colonial assemblies or supra-colonial gatherings like the Stamp Act Congress; they were mobilized not as individuals but in groups, whether local or denominational; the inde-pendence they seized was that of their colony corporately; the cosmic scenario in which their theology pictured them engaged was played out not by rebellious individuals but by a triumphant 'people', the children of God, the new Israel. The increasing use of the language of contract, and increasing claims that contracts had been broken, did not contradict the fact that one of the parties to the contract was assumed to be 'the people' of each colony collectively. Coke's doctrine of the God-given, perpetual allegiance of subject to sovereign was not broken up by the 'rise of the in-dividual' but by the drafting of individuals into an atavistic crusade against what sectarian theology identified as a Godless monarch. [. . .]

American exceptionalism, if it is to be a viable explanation, has to be re-located on the territory of American religious experience, and, especially, with regard to that profound shift in the composition of the colonial popu-lation which meant that while less than a tenth of Englishmen in 1776 were Dissenters, more than three quarters of Americans were enlisted in other denominations.

TRANSATLANTIC TIES AND THEIR FAILURE

Many other cultural sources of transatlantic union suffered from not being reified, turned from ideas and attitudes into things, concepts with capital letters which could be commemorated, celebrated and exploited.

Englishmen in England and America prided themselves on their modernity, on their rejection of ignorance, superstition and barbarism, their commitment to the values summed up in the phrase 'liberty and property' – the values of a polite and commercial society. Yet this still had few political implications at odds with the existing order. No-one in the English-speaking world then referred to 'the Enlightenment' or supposed that such a thing was shared on both sides of the Atlantic. [. . .] The Enlightenment is an explanatory device of historians; the men of the eighteenth century could not define it as antithetical to any political or social order, for 'it' had not yet been organized out of what were later to be its component parts.

Many studies of politics in Britain and America in the late eighteenth century have been premised on a view of the Enlightenment as a process of secularization embracing as a necessary unity aristocratic scepticism, bourgeois materialism and proletarian emancipation from patriarchal social relations. Yet each of these component parts has been challenged separately, and finally the ensemble itself is progressively questioned. National differences, too, were more important than Europe-wide similarities. Whatever may have been the case in France, and however much the French intelligentsia was influenced by materialist atheism, the English and colonial American scenario conformed to a different pattern. The elite's support for religion in the form of the established church was strong, and periodically reasserted in political crises from the Restoration through the Revolution of 1688 to the French Revolutionary challenge of the 1790s and beyond. The middle ranks of society markedly failed to develop a group consciousness, whether as a commercial bourgeoisie or a middle class, and their attachment to church or Dissent was even more evident than that of the elite. Finally, if rates of church attendance did decline among the populace after 1689, it is now clear that this cannot easily or simply be interpreted as emancipation into a new social order. Patriarchal forms were undoubtedly modified, but the structures of authority and order still engaged with a mental world very different from that of nineteenth century utilitarianism. The writing conventionally assigned to the Enlightenment in England, far from being secular, was suffused with theological and ecclesiastical argument; and heterodoxy was not a high road to secularization. [. . .]

It may appear paradoxical that eighteenth-century English society, increasingly picturing itself in terms of religious toleration, politeness and commerce, should have been increasingly pictured by its own dissidents and by American colonists in terms of sinister feudal, monarchical and clerical anachronisms. Part of that paradox is resolved by the discovery that the rebellions of the 1640s and 1688 did not constitute a revolutionary watershed, a complete break with the past; that many social forms and institutions of ancient lineage survived into a Whig present to be the targets of attack, or objects for revival. Part of the paradox is resolved, too, by the recovery of religion as a central component both of daily, grassroots communal practice and of the various discourses of political theory in which transatlantic relations were discussed. Since the term 'feudalism' did not appear in English until the 1830s, the hated phenomena had to be attributed as characteristics to other causes, especially religious; they could not be reified, and isolated, as a separate and secular historical force.

These continuities illuminate the survival also on both sides of the Atlantic of a powerful trope within legal and historical discourse, that of the ancient constitution. This retrospective idyll of a Gothic and pre-feudal libertarian polity of robust yeomen of freeholders and law-giving, law-abiding patriot kings was actively exploited and developed in seventeenth-century England, survived the Restoration and, though weakened, was quickly adapted for use after the Glorious Revolution. [...]

Under the impact of a strengthening doctrine of unitary sovereignty, and of the omnicompetence of that unitary sovereignty, the fundamental law which was often held to underpin the English constitution came after 1688 to be identified more with natural law than with the ancient constitution as immemorial and inviolable custom. The natural law tradition then steadily abolished itself in eighteenth-century England by its very success in producing an identity of religion between nation and monarch, so opening the way for the common law to modernize itself in the unhistorical idiom of Benthamite utilitarianism. The ancient constitution was increasingly unnecessary to those who took their stand on the principles of 1688 and 1714, and largely irrelevant after 1832. Reformers, however, could use that idea to appeal beyond the Revolution settlement to some pre-existing polity and what were supposed to be its original principles. [...]

If Englishmen in England and America were ignorant of the term 'Enlightenment', they had equally never heard the word 'nationalism'. Yet among the most powerful negations of eighteenth-century transatlantic discourse was its rejection of the foreigner and, especially, of the Roman Catholic religion. Nationalism, and the clash of clearly-formed national identities, do not however provide an easy answer to the problems of transatlantic relations. The old assumption that nationalism was a single, homogeneous phenomenon which, once established, contained a strong inner logic of development has been overset by the discovery that early-modern societies could sustain different, and varying, self-images; that these were often difficult to devise and preserve; and that they could be broken up rather than promoted by the advance of what is conventionally termed the Enlightenment. The colonies were too diverse in composition, too dependent on Old World historic myths, early to evolve a clear sense of their necessary distinctness as individual colonies, still less a sense of the common identity of all colonies. The early formulations of many colonies as religious experiments led them to seek a revitalized, purified homeland, not to reject their origin; their later insistence on claiming 'the rights of Englishmen' locked them into the historical scenario and national myth within which those rights were carried.

However much the symbols later vital to the nationalism of the United States were available in the colonial period, they were not yet given their nineteenth-century significance and until the Revolution were never assembled under the pressure of tactical necessity into coherent wholes. In France, it took the cataclysmic events of regicide and revolution to weld together the symbols of liberty into a representation of national identity. In colonial America similarly, the celebration of collective symbols of identity lacked a referent before 1776; it could only take the form of a stern and austere defence of the ancient constitution, the liberties of Englishmen. [...]

THE COMMONWEALTH PARADIGM

If the Enlightenment, the 'ancient constitution' and nationalism offer only ambiguous clues to the nature of transatlantic links, a fourth option appears more promising. It has been maintained that Englishmen in England and America were united in a single idiom of political discourse, native in England but universally adopted in the American colonies. The history of the American Revolution in particular has been dominated by a paradigm established in the 1960s, 'the assertion that the effective, triggering convictions that lay behind the Revolution were derived not from common Lockean generalities but from the specific fears and formulations of the radical publicists and opposition politicians of early eighteenth-century England who carried forward into the age of Walpole the peculiar strain of anti-authoritarianism bred in the upheaval of the English Civil War'. By the unmodified application, that is, to colonial America of the tradition brilliantly evoked as that of the Commonwealthmen, men writing in the idiom of John Milton and James Harrington, a tradition placed in a grander historical setting by the elucidation of its Florentine, civic humanist roots, and extended, especially for the early years of the American state, into an historiographical paradigm based on the idea of republicanism.

This study seeks to pluralize our map of political discourse by the addition of other, no less crucial, frameworks and political idioms. It has been suggested that Caroline Robbins's 'Commonwealthmen' are not to be understood as standing within a single tradition of thought, given different expression by three clearly-related generations of authors; that their common feature lay in their theories of religion, even in their theology, rather than in any secular speculations on civic virtue or in Harringtonian enquiries into the basis of power in landownership and trade, important though these things were. Yet if a common theme can be found in the works conventionally ascribed to this idiom, this common theme did not unite its authors: their identity and polemical purposes become fully evident only when they are placed in the denominational traditions to which they consciously subscribed or from which they passionately dissented. As a corollary, this study argues that religion was a vital concern both of the political elite and of populations at large in this period as private practice, as public morality, and as political symbol. Political discourse in England's North Atlantic possessions in the 'long' eighteenth century was plural, not homogeneously 'Commonwealth', and this pluralism is here traced chiefly to the sectarian diversity of those possessions. In the rivalry and antagonism of religious sects is to be found a crucial component of imperial politics and a central theme in the history of political thought, hitherto largely the province of church historians, but deserving of a more central place in the historical arena.

Our confidence in identifying an idiom of discourse should be qualified by the fact that eighteenth-century 'Commonwealthmen' were not, at the time, identified as a school, either by themselves or by others; the term was used, infrequently, to disparage individuals by an analogy with the 1640s rather than by asserting present membership of a recognizable group. It is now evident that these writers have been retrospectively assembled into a tradition by a distinguished work of history. [. . .] 'Commonwealth' doctrine was not recognized as an idiom of political discourse in the late seventeenth and eighteenth centuries, and in order to be understood in its contemporary tactical setting it needs to be resolved into its component parts.

The most salient feature of the 1770s and '80s for the historian of ideas on both sides of the Atlantic is that opinion was profoundly divided; the conflict of ideas as of armed forces took the form of a civil war. [. . .] The military conflict between patriot and loyalist militias was bitter but indecisive. Americans achieved independence because they avoided defeat for long enough, despite widely varying degrees of enthusiasm and support for the war among the colonists, until the international conflict and French military and naval intervention made Britain's position impossible. Yorktown did not symbolize the triumph of the American yeoman or prove his wholehearted consent to a single body of values; indeed it was the culmination of a campaign in which Catholic French regular forces (the navy included) outnumbered their colonial allies.

These features of the military conflict emphasize that the Revolution was not made by a previously-existing nation, united around a shared ideology, which threw off a foreign yoke in a decisive act; rather, the revolutionaries were left the victors in a fragmented civil war after their opponents had been compelled to give up the struggle. They were the survivors of an internecine conflict in which colonial opinion, like opinion in the British Isles, had been profoundly divided. This characteristic, emphasized by military historians, has been obscured for other disciplines by the dominance of successive unitary paradigms, especially the Commonwealth paradigm. Its dominance led one historian to omit opponents of the Revolution from his history on the grounds that 'the future lay not with them', a decision which created the very homogeneity which the Commonwealth paradigm presumed. Yet even the position of the victors cannot be correctly recreated without reference to what they were arguing against, and it is the reinstatement of these neglected themes, first in the history of Britain, then in the history of colonial America, that has moved our understanding of the Revolution closer to contemporary perceptions of it. [...]

The public ideologies widespread in the Anglophone world by the late eighteenth century warned against 'slavery', denounced 'tyranny', pointed out the ways in which men could be defrauded of their ancient liberties, recorded the threat posed by standing armies, and lamented the enervating effects of vice and luxury. All these themes were prominent in the rhetoric of American revolutionaries, but it was rare that they were greatly owed to a reading of authors like Henry Neville, Walter Moyle or Robert, Viscount Molesworth. Most were standard themes of the folk memories of Protestant denominations; they formed part of their myths or histories of their origins, of their reasons for dissent from the Church of England, and of their principled resistance to episcopacy or 'Popery'. Moreover, the goals of the Revolutionaries of 1776, like the goals of other champions of insurrection in the English-speaking world, went far beyond the negative rejection of the threats that 'Commonwealthmen' identified. Some of the Americans who rebelled in 1776 sought to found a new and timeless social order, *novus ordo seclorum*, in which material prosperity would naturally attend moral and religious purity, in which peace and righteousness would be, without further exertion, the inheritance of their descendants, in which human nature would be freed from its ancient disease and released into a new age of creative fulfilment and innocent emancipation. The translation of this millenarian vision into worldly terms entailed not secularization but a holy war. [...] Only if the divisions of denominational discourse were overlooked could a 'Commonwealth' school be created by the assembly of a list of able but diverse authors. Their writings undoubtedly reached the colonies in imported English editions, though in very limited numbers. [...]

The almost complete absence of reprints of the Commonwealthmen in America is not consistent with the thesis that their 'ideas acquired in the colonies an importance, a relevance in politics, they did not then have – and never would have – in England itself'. Moreover, this neglect is even more telling evidence by comparison with the reprinting in the colonies of many other English works which clearly did engage closely with colonial concerns. These included works defending the English parliamentary and legal tradition, and the chief summary of Scots resistance theory; they included also tracts denouncing the Jacobite menace to shared transatlantic freedoms. Colonial memories were long: they extended to recollections of Catholic atrocities in Ireland as well as the crimes of the Stuart family in England. They included theological works which spoke to growing colonial heterodoxy, but they included also classic works of Anglican theology, moral teaching and polemic. They naturally included works in which other denominations justified their separate status in the Old World, and did so, evidently, in ways relevant to their co-religionists in the New. For such an audience, evidence which seemed to point to Anglican intolerance was avidly seized and quickly disseminated: minor issues could have an immense strategic significance for the relations of denominations. Nor were all works in these idioms necessarily colonial reprints: colonial authors could articulate them equally clearly. The 'Commonwealth' tradition, if a tradition it was, was native to England. American political discourse was preoccupied with its own issues, often denominational. The idea of the existence of a universal secular idiom of politics for colonial Americans by 1776 is difficult to reconcile with the richness, diversity and sectarian nature of colonial American publishing. [...]

DENOMINATIONAL DISCOURSE

Americans derived their perceptions of England's corruption from denominational sources. These were the reverse of homogenous. [...]

American theology shared the three overriding preoccupations of reformed Protestantism: 'the depravity of man, the sovereignty of God, and the necessity of worshiping God and ordering the church strictly in accordance with Biblical prescription'. In the early seventeenth century, it was different conceptions in the third area that split Protestants into Episcopalians, Presbyterians and Congregationalists. [...] All these components were carried together in the denominations' sense of their past, and given intensity by contemporaries' understanding of ecclesiastical history not as the private life of a sect but as the cosmic drama of God's dealings with man throughout time. The fate of mankind in this divine scenario, not just the institutional fortunes of a sect, was the prize which subscribers to this discourse perceived to be at stake and which gave the fortunes of their sect its significance. These questions of ecclesiastical polity, fading in eighteenth-century England, remained vivid in Scotland and Ireland, intensified in the American colonies, and engaged with newly developing controversy on key points of theology. [. . .]

THE IMPLICATIONS OF THEOLOGICAL CONFLICT

Religion meant many things in early-modern society; all must take their place in a map of political discourses. [. . .] Religion meant, most obviously, formal public worship; but its extent at different periods in Britain and America is still a subject for quantification, and the significance of the figures available is still a matter for interpretation. It meant, secondly, informal meetings for worship where church buildings or ordained ministers were not available. It meant the practice of private piety and family observance. It meant the form taken by or the expression given to deep psychological needs and aspirations. It meant a set of doctrines concerning theology and ecclesiastical polity. It involved each denomination in patterns of daily life which, to greater or lesser degrees, distinguished them from other denominations. Religion thus acted as a definition and a symbol of group identity, often extrapolated from the denomination to the state. It embodied a society's or a sect's sense of its historical trajectory, both its past experience and its future expectations. Sometimes this forward-looking perspective included a vision which was covertly or overtly millennial. Often the remembered past sustained a negative image of rival denominations, bitterly resented for ancient crimes and denounced for these iniquities in a context which denominational conflict made apocalyptic.

The simultaneous presence of all these elements made early-modern societies far more theoretically articulate than the societies which succeeded them, and their social relations were expressed to a much larger degree in terms of grand theory. Among ordinary men and women, the degree of religious awareness in the early-modern transatlantic world was high. It was a culture in which the laity 'sustained churches by adhering to theological and ecclesiastical principles, and ... destroyed churches by overturning theological and ecclesiastical traditions'. The ideological imperatives which drove men to overturn those traditions are therefore of some importance, and are one recurring theme of this book. [. . .]

Its chosen period includes episodes of extreme theological ferment which may validly be set beside the 1530s or 1640s; indeed the 'long' eighteenth century witnessed extended contests over doctrinal issues which had not been central, and sometimes had been virtually overlooked, in those earlier episodes. [...] The correlation between theological heterodoxy and a preference for political reform was strong, but not exclusive. [...] Heterodox doctrines of the Trinity had wide implications, as Dissenters were aware. [...] To Socinians, the doctrine of the Trinity was not merely false theology, unknown to the Jews, to Christ himself and His apostles; it was, as Gilbert Wakefield announced in 1794, 'a doctrine, which will happily prove a mill-stone of destruction to all *political* establishments of Christianity'.

Other forms of heterodoxy had their political impact also. Profoundly influential in eighteenth-century Europe was 'the comprehensive moral philosophy of deism, which concealed itself under the title of *ius naturale* and, after first disregarding the eternal law, finally culminated in the complete moral autonomy of reason (Kant)'. The 'high degree of correlation in the early eighteenth century between neo-Harringtonian republicanism and deism' has rightly been observed; the correlation between Deism and anti-monarchical politics was to survive and indeed culminate in 1776 in the most effective of all Deist political tracts, Paine's *Common Sense*. Arianism and Socinianism shared with Deism one novel consequence. The more unnecessary the doctrine of the atonement, the more it could be presumed that man was inherently benevolent; it followed that he was corrupted, or enslaved, only by outside forces (that is, by other people). Nurture rather than nature was prioritized; and the more that the human condition or the workings of divine Providence were excused, the more the blame for society's ills had to be laid at the door of minorities of wicked individuals. The tyranny of sin was subtly transformed into the tyranny of kings and bishops. It was a trope of eighteenth-century historiography that detailed, inner knowledge of public affairs disclosed how great events were the result of small and personal causes; the heterodox imagination seized on this insight and inflated it into self-sustaining conspiracy theories. As much as the 1640s, the late eighteenth-century era of revolution was (in modern terms) an age of paranoia. Even in the absence of formal theological millenarianism, the discourse of late-eighteenth-century heterodox Dissent became increasingly preoccupied with threats of persecution in its perceptions of slavery and corruption, increasingly strident in its invective against civil and ecclesiastical tyrants. To interpret this construction of a social demonology as part of a process of the secularization of politics is to miss the doctrinal origins of these secular commitments and the theological context in which these social dramas were played out.

To an Anglican, the doctrine of original sin implied that natural liberty, the liberty enjoyed by man in a state of nature, meant for each person 'the uncontrouled Power of doing *as much Evil as he can*'; hence, by the social contract, man is 'necessarily restrained by particular *Obligations*'. A '*Law of Nature*' should therefore be understood not as a blueprint for frictionless perfection but as a regulatory law imposed by the Creator on an imperfect creation. This 'Law, call it of Nature or of God' was to be identified with ˙Revelation. 'I insist so much upon the Rule given in the *divine* Law', explained one author, 'because many of the American Leaders have attempted to sanctify their Revolt by a specious Appearance of *Religion*.' Emancipation from Calvinist doctrines of predestination, however, did not necessarily or easily release men from the consequences of the Anglican and orthodox Dissenting understanding of original sin. The progress within Anglicanism and Dissent of an Arminian doctrine of universally offered redemption did not of itself predispose men to rebellion: something different was needed to trigger that commitment. Nor was Providence banished from human affairs; rather, politically mobilized Dissent redirected the hitherto-confused Deity to become a warrior against kingly and episcopal authority. The role newly designed for God in punishing transgression actually assumed a far greater immediacy in the context of just resistance, or impious rebellion, against the Anglican symbols of Church and State. Far from being secularized, spiritual commitments, zeal and hatreds were transferred to the political arena in the 1770s to greater effect than at any time since 1688–9. [...]

It is a major contention of this book that early-modern societies were essentially sectarian in their dynamics: traditions of political thought and action were carried within and articulated by the mosaic of religious denominations which made up the British Isles and, still more, the North American colonies. Those denominations – Anglicans, Presbyterians, Congregationalists, Baptists, Quakers, Catholics and a host of less numerous sects – were sometimes influenced by revivalism and millenialism, sometimes not; but at all times they necessarily bought to the public arena long-rehearsed and still keenly-debated doctrines about their origins, purposes and destinies, and about what these entailed for the kingdom or empire within which they found themselves.

DENOMINATIONAL DYNAMICS AND POLITICAL REBELLIONS

If eighteenth-century England was relatively free from profound political upheaval, this must be attributed to the increasing hegemonic efficiency of the regime of peer and bishop, squire and parson, rather than to the presence of a Lockeian consensus about the justice of the settlement of 1689 or a passively deferential submission to the rule of the elite. [...]

In the thirteen colonies, however, the position was markedly different. [...] [T]he colonies displayed a level of political conflict significantly higher even than that of the British Isles. [...]

In the daily exchange of politics denominational dynamics provide an essential explanatory key, especially at those times of crisis when rebellion lifted the lid and allows a special access to the tensions and conflicts usually negotiated, or disguised, within the constitutional structures of representation and law. If a particular political discourse was a shared possession of Englishmen on both sides of the Atlantic, why did England increasingly avoid insurrection while America increasingly experienced it, with cataclysmic but still not final results in the 1770s? This book offers the outline of an answer by questioning the assumption that England *was* wholly immune from violent threats and by disaggregating the political discourse of England's possessions on both sides of the Atlantic. If the 'Commonwealthmen' were largely English, or operated within the English political arena, they had less to say to the Scots, Irish and Welsh, and less still to the even more resolutely diverse populations of the American seaboard. Moreover, ethnic unity was relatively weakly conceptualized in the early-modern world. What counted was denominational diversity, since the identity, rationale, historical origins and future mission of religious denominations were as clearly articulated and repeatedly stressed as ethnic identity was vaguely presumed and seldom raised.

In the early-modern period it was religious sects which, more than any other social groups, possessed international networks of communication which both mobilized their supporters and kept them informed of the activities of friends and enemies on two continents; by letters industriously written and sought, published journals, evangelical newspapers and magazines, and unwearied itinerancy, the degree of cultural contact surpassed anything yet available in a secular context. It was the ministers of these sects who were able to draw together popular audiences, sometimes of many thousands, and exhort them to a frenzy of collective commitment that secular politicians did not begin to approach until the Chartist mass movements of Victorian England. [...]

Denominations were not equal in their political roles. The significance of the inner dynamics of Congregationalism was greatly enhanced by that denomination's numerical preponderance in the colonies: 'By 1776, Congregational ministers in New England were delivering over two thousand discourses a week and publishing them at an unprecedented rate that outnumbered secular pamphlets (from all the colonies) by a ratio of more than four to one.' The contributions of these ministers were, moreover, well attuned to their hearers. For local New England audiences, their message was couched 'totally' in covenantal terms, 'nothing less than the preservation of Sola Scriptura and New England's privileged position at the center of redemptive history'. For those other colonies to which New England exhortation was massively exported, the message used the 'secular vocabulary of "rights and property" that all colonists shared in common'. One reason why the nature and purpose of the Revolution could be reinterpreted in merely secular terms was that the diverse sectarian composition of the colonies dictated the search for common denominators, indeed for a rhetoric which would disguise the ulterior motives of the Revolution's New England leaders. For those leaders, it has been well observed, 'Republican governments, like earlier half-way covenants, religious toleration, and revivals, were merely means to the end of maintaining pure churches and a virtuous people of the Word.' It was this mission which was destined to disillusion in New England's denominational and theological transformation during the next half-century. [. . .]

Americans did not, in the 1760s, suddenly adopt the ideas of John Locke; 1776 was not the outcome of an upsurge of what was later termed 'radical liberalism'. Denominational discourse had been familiar for more than a century in Britain and America; what principally changed was that it was reinterpreted in retrospect, following the Revolution, as secular natural rights discourse. 1776 was a 'Lockeian moment' chiefly in the sense in which Locke himself had been an anti-Trinitarian, preoccupied by the political menace (as he saw it) of orthodox religion, firmly located within a denominational and theological context. The American Revolution opened a new era; but its origins had little to do with visions of a hitherto-unrealized future, much to do with ancient divisions and hatreds. The Revolution of 1776 was, therefore, not unique: like many of the crises which had convulsed the early-modern world, it still retained many of the characteristics of a war of religion. [. . .]

CONCLUSION

British and American society retained much in common in the centuries after 1783: more, indeed, than they were now concerned to assert or willing to admit. Both explored models of democratic politics, were swept by evangelicalism and unbelief, were dominated by the urban-industrial experience. Yet, inexorably, the two societies' self-images and interpretations of their histories drew apart in fundamental ways, so that the demonstration of a 'special relationship' required a reinterpretation of the perceived past as much as an evocation of it. Law and religion continued to shape this process by which both America and Britain devised partly incompatible theories of their own exceptionalism. American understanding of the purpose of the Revolution quickly came after 1776 to turn on religious liberty as the antitheses of tyranny, and on law as the guarantor and definition of liberty; yet, paradoxically, the conflict of denominations steadily increased the authority of the group over the conscience of the individual, and the reconstruction of American law led the courts of the new Republic to develop a far more interventionist and innovatory attitude to their role. Common lawyers in England, in the same half-century after American independence, were increasingly bound by the doctrine of strict construction: Benthamite utilitarianism, not Jeffersonian natural rights, came to describe the truths the English saw as self-evident.

The military outcome of the American Revolution had a profound impact on its interpretation. Its character as a civil war on both sides of the Atlantic was obscured and replaced by an image of a war of national or colonial liberation in which a morally united America fought a morally united Britain: American loyalists and British republicans were systematically excluded from their own society's vision. Within America, the course of the war meant that a national mythology was built around the ideology of triumphant New England, not devastated Virginia or marginalized Quaker-pacifist Pennsylvania: the Anglican model, which had come closest to realization in the southern colonies, was not merely displaced but erased and forgotten as a possible pattern for a future America. Until at least the First World War, Americans from all backgrounds acknowledged that the values, stereotypes and aspirations of what the nineteenth century understood as the Puritan legacy were built into the minds of the rapidly multiplying citizens of the new Republic. Within the United Kingdom, the Anglican heartland of the south east of England retained its overwhelming cultural hegemony until 1832 and considerable (if less than hegemonic) power thereafter.

Gradually, Americans' understandings of the essence of their Great Experiments were modified. The separation of Church and State soon entailed that the new Republic's sense of its crusading mission to reform the old world was summed up not in Deism or Arianism but in the inclusive and seemingly secular term 'democracy'. Democracy was now held to be the essence of the American experiment; other states were divided into 'democracies' and the objects of reform. Yet whatever the diverse and often helpful meanings of the term, it is clear that democracy – in the sense of debates over the franchise, the distribution of seats, or the representative machinery in general – was not central to the conflicts which rent the English-speaking world in the early-modern period, and was not at the heart of the self-image of any of the societies which made up that world. Its key term had been not 'democracy' but 'liberty', and liberty was a term which had its ramifications chiefly in the vast intellectual territories then occupied by law and religion,

As a result of the genesis of the Revolution in these bodies of thought, the new Republic was built 'centrally on utopian millennial expectations'. Britain, avoiding revolution, crucially prolonged certain features of her public ideology until the millenarian challenge of the French Revolution had receded. In the last three decades of the eighteenth century America acquired a national myth of origins, built up from component sectarian myths; Britain in the same period turned her myths of origins into a saga of survival. America, having repudiated the homogenizing Anglican-aristocratic mores integral to British rule, built its sense of national identity in part through the elaboration of the myth of the 'melting pot', a natural and beneficent process which would assimilate residents and immigrants in a rational modernity: beneath this myth, religion and ethnicity survived in a dynamic relationship and eventually experienced an explosive recrudescence. Unreformed Britain remained set on a path towards a profoundly secular society with relatively little ethnic consciousness.

Where Britons began to dwell on (indeed sometimes to invent) immense continuities in their historic experience, and British ideals increasingly praised the stoic understatement of catastrophe, the American republic, freed from historical stabilities, embarked on a pattern of moral alternation: phases of moral endeavour which strengthened the persecutory and in-quisitorial elements in society, succeeded by phases of broken covenants, corruption and despair. In Britain the sacred trappings of the state were pro-foundly redefined but not wholly abandoned in 1832; British society found ways of sustaining its existing programmes of meliorative reform within the framework of the old moral order. In America a new and programmatic civil religion provided an evangelical impetus for a society unlike any the world had seen before: at once more ethical and more materialistic, more libertarian and more deferential to the sovereignty of collective opinion. With the passing of the old intellectual nexus of Church and State, British public life quickly lost its old preoccupations with tests and oaths; in America these formal affirmations of group integrity took on new life. British formulations of liberty remained stubbornly specific, resisting incor-poration into the generalized natural rights theoretic of 1789, they conse-quently proved far more open to augmentation and expansion than those of the new Republic. Where the Republic's inbuilt crusading ideology led to a second and equally devastating civil war, Britain's led anticlimatically to a series of Acts extending the franchise in parliamentary elections.

If the colonies' misconceptions about and grievances against British rule were fossilized in the Constitution of the United States. Britain's constitution was more stridently defended also. The independence of so many of her European-populated colonies allowed the public structures of law and religion in Britain to survive with little change, at least until 1828–32 and in many ways thereafter. The common-law doctrine of sovereignty was left untouched in successive waves of domestic reform, in the 1780s, 1830s, 1860s and later decades. Response to political challenges remained pragmatic, aimed at the efficiency of the bureaucratic machinery ('economical reform'), the armed forces or the electoral system; but the Anglican, common-law drive to uniformity remained, and the Irish rebellion against it of 1798 was met in classic fashion by the Union. The passage of that Act in 1800 marks the high point of state formation in the British Isles within that idiom.

The unified, absolute sovereign of the Anglican ascendancy meant that Britain's future after 1832 was to be one of sweeping, centrally-directed reform in all areas of national life; America, rationalized into the modernity of the 1780s, thereafter found it intensely difficult to restructure its machinery of government. The British constitution was a collection of contingencies: its contradictions were therefore seldom important. The American constitution, nationally a set of harmonious ideas, was equally the product of tactical imperatives; as such, it was involved in damaging internal contradictions from the outset. Rejection of a monarchical polity compelled the adoption of a republican democracy, despite the familiar colonial warnings that democracy entailed majoritarian tyranny. Montesquieu had observed that 'It is in the nature of a republic to have only a small territory; otherwise, it can scarcely continue to exist', but it was necessary to argue after independence that a republic was, uniquely in the case of America, a formula for stable government in a large state. The English euphemism of a checked and balanced constitution was developed by Americans to the point where the rejection of monarchy required a division of sovereignty among the institutions of federal and state governments; but the rejection of monarchy also entailed the vesting of sovereignty in a new and different abstraction, 'the people', and this unitary conception threatened the confederal ideal of avoiding tyranny by dividing and sharing authority.

The impact of seven years of fighting on American society was profound. Where British society was progressively disciplined by the demands of war overseas into a more austere, more hierarchical, more evangelical mode, America's experience of violence, disease, betrayal, impoverishment, deceit and insecurity were destructive of that polite and commercial culture, at once patrician and transatlantic, into which the colonists had sought to integrate. [. . .]

Colonists seldom derived from the Revolution exactly what it was that they had sought; rather, the realities of rebellion and war created a profoundly different society, different in ways hardly foreseen or sought in 1776. Episcopalians had sought to perpetuate the social order of which they were part by resisting its subversion by 'popery and arbitrary power'; they inherited a polity in which the Anglican model had been wholly effaced as an option for future American society. Presbyterians and Congregationalists were the most numerous sects in the America of 1776; by 1800 the Baptists, closely followed by the Methodists, had outstripped them all. Revolutionary intellectuals like Benjamin Franklin and Tom Paine had looked forward to a Deistic republic; by 1800 Deism had been swamped in many states by a massive evangelical revival. Even New England did not secure the sort of society for which its sons had fought, for Calvinist Congregationalism was soon profoundly modified by the proliferating Unitarianism of the early nineteenth century. [...]

Secular texts came to take the place of the covenants of colonial sects. The Constitution as a document itself became the centre of a 'popular cult'; it was widely regarded as 'fraught with supernal wisdom'; scepticism of its powers became 'the mark of political atheism'; it generated a 'ritual of the worship of the Constitution' as a system of law, endorsed in time by Woodrow Wilson as 'an indiscriminate and almost blind worship of its principles ... The divine right of kings never ran a more prosperous course than did this unquestioned prerogative of the Constitution to receive universal homage.' [...] The Declaration of Independence and the Constitution, as one political scientist observes, became 'sacraments'; Congress assumed a 'theocratic' role; the Supreme Court became 'a kind of secular papacy'. Irreverent nineteenth-century Britons increasingly pictured politics as a game. Since their religion was still not generally covenantal, even mass democracy did not transform British social relations into contractual ones.

Once the Old World sources of authority – elite social status or royal commission – were unavailable, new sources had to be sought in the fervour of nationalist zeal. The Founding Fathers, and especially their military leaders, became the objects of a strange reverence: one military historian has observed that the 'rhetoric surrounding Washington suggests that Americans did not want a new king or benevolent ruler so much as a high priest of the revolution, an exemplar of the qualities that would achieve the continent's promised future'. [...] In Britain, Wellington and Nelson symbolized stoic imperturbability and professional brilliance, but their private lives were widely discussed and they performed no function as moral icons during their lifetimes.

Once the Revolution had been firmly identified as the first crusade of the American civil religion, it became necessary to canonize the zealots who had brought it about. The Founding Fathers, where possible, were turned from political opportunists, propagandists or self-seekers of tepid or heterodox religious belief into the Luthers and Calvins, the Melanchthons and Zwinglis of the *Novus ordo seclorum*. With some exceptions, like the now-notorious Tom Paine, each became the subject of a secular epiphany. [...]

By the first centennial, the image of the Revolution as a holy war had expanded within the folk memories of the American sects to the point where the divisions and ambiguities within those denominations were forgotten. Presbyterians pictured the war as a Presbyterian crusade which sanctified martial heroism, turned the heterodox rhetoric of the Founding Fathers into the idiom of revivalist preaching, traced in the 'apparent chaos' of armed rebellion 'the will of God ... working toward order and organization', and found the culmination of order, reason and organization in a constitution depicted in terms reminiscent of the millennium. [...]

Yet, paradoxically, this retrospective homogenization of the positions of colonial denominations acted to secularize the historical interpretation of the Revolution and to drain the role of the sects of its immense significance: if most men, regardless of denomination, eventually seemed to have endorsed the Revolution, then the Revolution's values and causes must by definition have been irrelevant to religious differences.

This trick of perspective did not eliminate the problem, but obscured it. Thanks to the historical episodes explored in this book, a modern American scholar could observe the paradox that despite the high level of formal religious observance in the United States, 'practically every species of traditional orthodoxy in Christendom is intellectually at war with the basic premises upon which the constitutional and legal structures of the Republic rest'. Heterodoxy, revivalist enthusiasm and millenarianism were marginalized in mainstream historiography and became the study of specialists; American ideals of liberty and moral regeneration took shape within this framework of ideas nevertheless. It ensured that the dynamic given to the idea of liberty before and during the Revolution would not be lost thereafter, despite its secular translation. Many were persuaded. John Adams wrote from Amsterdam to his wife on 18 December 1781:

> the great designs of Providence must be accomplished. Great indeed! The progress of society will be accelerated by centuries by this Revolution. The Emperor of Germany is adopting, as fast as be can, American ideas of toleration and religious liberty, and it will become the fashionable system of all Europe very soon. Light spreads from the

dayspring in the west, and may it shine more and more until the perfect day.

Others interpreted the shared transatlantic inheritance differently, and deplored its division. Witnessing the fighting for New York, Lord Howe's secretary Ambrose Serle, moved to despair by the zeal of republican preachers, was driven to echo the harsh indictment of Lucretius: 'Such conduct in such persons affords too much Room for the Taunts of Infidels: Tantum Religio potuit suadere malorum.'

I.2

Anticipating America:
American mentality before the Revolution

MARY K. GEITER AND W. A. SPECK

The United States of America was no doubt a political construct. Yet the speed with which Americans changed from being subjects into becoming citizens, and their colonies were transformed into states, begs many questions about the fashioning of an American identity. At what point did both Britain's image of its North American territories, and the colonists' view of themselves, change from regarding the plantations as provinces, and the settlers as provincials, to viewing the eastern seaboard as a separate entity and its inhabitants as Americans? At what point were the connections of individual colonies to the mother country cut across by intercolonial ties? While this was clearly demonstrated in the disputes of the 1760s, particularly over the Stamp Act, in which questions concerning representation and sovereignty brought the colonies together, can it be traced back further? Did generations of colonists born in North America develop a different attitude to the continent from that of the first settlers? At what point did they cease to be colonists and become instead colonials (or, in the current jargon, creoles)? When did they consider themselves to be not only Virginians, or New Englanders or Pennsylvanians but also Americans? How far was there an American consciousness or mentality before it became a national identity? This paper seeks answers to these questions. In doing so it concludes that awareness of a collective identity emerged earlier than has previously been suspected. For while other historians have detected its emergence before the breach with Britain, notably during the war with France in the 1750s, this investigation pushes it back into the 1740s.

Before investigating the emergence of an American mentality it needs to be defined. For there are various ways in which a collective consciousness of a cultural identity can manifest itself. Thus German or Italian culture found expression long before Germany or Italy became nation states in the nineteenth century. Italy and Germany were not just geographical expressions in the early modern period. It is true that politically the areas they covered included myriad principalities and city states, which at times commanded stronger loyalties than the greater entity, setting Lombardy against Tuscany and Prussia against Saxony. But, however strong these centripetal forces might have been, the centrifugal forces which combined to produce the Italian Renaissance or the German Enlightenment ident-ified common cultural characteristics. Similarly, it is worth investigating whether 'America' changed from being a geographical expression into a common cultural phenomenon, despite strong regional identities such as those of New England or the Middle Colonies, before the United States was ever dreamed about.

Until recently historians tended to assume that an American conscious-ness of being other than European existed long before independence. The notion is implicit in the very title of Daniel Boorstin's highly influential book *The Americans: The Colonial Experience.*[1] Emigrants from England ex-perienced a sea change as they crossed the Atlantic. Their previous lives had not prepared them to cope with the problems of carving out a civi-lization from the wilderness. They had to jettison assumptions acquired from English society and adopt fresh ideas to survive in a new and hostile environment. The first generation of settlers thereby became the first Americans.

Of course the continent on which the colonies were settled was re-garded as a 'new world' and referred to as America, and its characteristics as American, from is first discovery by Europeans. Early in the seventeenth century John Donne could refer to his mistress as 'my America, my new found land', while later Hobbes and Locke could compare the state of nature with the American. 'It may peradventure be thought', wrote Hobbes, 'there was never such a time, nor condition of warre as this, and I believe it was never generally so, over all the world: but there are many places where they live so now. For the savage people in many parts of *America*, except the government of small families, the concord whereof de-pendeth on naturall lust, have no government at all, and live at this day in that brutish manner.' 'In the beginning', observed Locke, 'all the world was America.'[2] The two political philosophers placed their states of nature vaguely in 'America', and might not even have had English North America in mind, while they were clearly referring to the alleged conditions ex-perienced by native north Americans. Others, however, used the term more specifically to refer not only to the area settled by the English but also to the settlements themselves. Thus Nathaniel Ward referred to his town of Aggawam in 1647 not as being in Massachusetts but 'in America'.[3] William Penn even used the term 'Americanise', writing to Thomas Lloyd in September 1686: 'I aim at Americanising my family'.[4] What Penn meant by this term, however, is ambiguous – the *Oxford English Dictionary* records no usage of the word 'Americanise' before 1816. Three years earlier he had written to Lord Culpeper from Pennsylvania:[5]

> I am mightily taken with this part of the world: Here is a great deal of Nature, wch is to be preferrd to base Art, & methinks Simplicity wth enough, is Gold to Lackre, compared to European cunning. I like it so well that a plentiful Estate & a great Acquaintance on th'other side have no Charmes to remove, my family being once fixt wth me; & if no other thing occur, I am like to be an adopted American.

Here the ambiguity is more tantalizing. Penn could be referring to America as a cultural concept 'other' than Europe. On the other hand he could have intended by it to indicate no more than an intention to move his family to a different geographical environment.

Recent historiography leans towards the latter explanation. For of late historians have tended to play down American exceptionalism in the colonial period, and to argue that the colonists were too heavily dependent upon England to acquire a completely separate identity.[6] English men and women took across the Atlantic mental as well as physical baggage, creating colonies 'in English ways'. Their 'cultural hearths' were in the mother country. The colonies were provinces of England rather than separate American communities until the political breach with Britain. Indeed, it has even been argued that folkways imported into America from the mother country survived independence and can be detected as salient cultural characteristics today.[7]

Such an extreme version of the persistence of British culture has not been generally accepted.[8] It implies a static view of the past rather than history as process. The development of the colonies, for example the interaction of Europeans with native North Americans and Africans imported as slaves, created a society very different from that of the mother country. Yet curiously, as the colonies developed economically and socially, they did so along lines which bought them closer to the societies from which they were derived. Thus the cities along the eastern seaboard came to resemble British ports. The Boston of the tea party was much more akin to Bristol than to Winthrop's city upon a hill. Philadelphia was compared with Newcastle upon Tyne by a visitor in the 1740s.[9] The Reverend Michael Slatter observed in the middle of the eighteenth century:[10]

> From my own experience I can truly testify that often, when contemplating the towns, the level country, the climate, and the sensible inhabitants, living in the same manner, enjoying the same culture, pursuing the same business, and differing but little from Europeans, I

could scarcely realise that I was in reality in a different quarter of the world.

Paradoxically as the colonies came to replicate British society they became more independent of the mother country. While they were still settlements in the wilderness they needed the umbilical cord of supplies from England to sustain them. As their own economies and societies grew so they became more self-sufficient. Though they still imported English culture in the form of books, furniture and other artefacts, they also produced their own. Politically they were to remain provincial until the eve of the War of American Independence; but culturally they developed a consciousness of their own collective identity as Americans, by contrast with Europeans, by the 1740s. When William Livingston's poem *Philosophical Solitude or the Choice of a Rural Life* was published in 1747 the Governor of New Jersey sent several copies to England 'to shew them that America produces some Geniuses little inferior to the most Eminent Europeans'.[11] In 1752 'Mr Urban of North America' published a poem in the *Gentleman's Magazine* extolling the virtues of 'a lovely American'. As he explained 'by an American I do not mean an Indian, but one descended of British parents, born in America; many of whom, whatever those unacquainted with North America may imagine, both in Point of Beauty and Merit, are an Honour to their Mother Country, and seem rather (with due deference to the British Ladies be it spoken) to have improv'd, than degenerated by being transplanted into another climate'.[12] The writer was alluding facetiously to a serious debate about whether the American environment was detrimental to European species imported into it. This dispute divided the scholarly community on both sides of the Atlantic. Europeans tended to support the theory of degeneration, while Americans refuted it and even boasted that America was more congenial to the evolution of healthier more robust species than was Europe.[13]

There were, however, some Englishmen who were prepared to admit that decadent European learning would be superseded by an American renaissance. George Berkeley wrote a poem in 1726 'On the prospect of planting arts and learning in America'. In it he contemplated 'the rise of empire and of arts ... not such as Europe breeds in her decay' and concluded that 'westward the course of empire takes its way'.[14] Such views seem to have become widespread by the middle of the eighteenth century. 'An idea', observed Andrew Burnaby in 1760, 'has entered into the minds of the generality of mankind, that empire is travelling westward; and every one is looking forward with eager and impatient expectation to that destined moment when America is to give law to the rest of the world.'[15] An American who felt the call of destiny most strongly was Nathaniel Ames, who predicted that 'Arts and Sciences' would 'change the face of nature in their tour from hence over the Appalachian mountains to the Western seas'.[16]

'Mr Urban of North America' clearly subscribed to the view that America was superior to Europe, even breeding more attractive women. How far women born in America shared his views is unclear. At one time it was held that women fared better in the colonies than in England and that this made the colonial era a 'golden age' for them. If this were the case then perhaps they themselves judged life in America to be superior to their lot in the mother country, and that this in itself would induce an awareness of an American feminine culture different from the European.[17] However, recent historiography has thrown grave doubts on the notion that women were better off in the colonies, and has stressed continuities rather than contrasts in their experience on both sides of the Atlantic, at least until the revolutionary era.[18] During the Revolution, however, women were at the forefront in inculcating feelings of a new American political identity.[19] Whether the role of founding mothers emerged out of earlier sentiments of American cultural defences in the feminine experience is worth investigating. It seems likely that women felt themselves to be more cut off by the Atlantic ocean from their European kinsfolk than did men. Many male colonists crossed the sea to do business or to be educated in Europe, while overseas commercial transactions which held the two continents together were conducted overwhelmingly by men. Once in America women by and large seem to have stayed there. Moreover by the middle of the eighteenth century a great number had been born there, and never experienced Europe at all.

Indeed, by then most people of European descent in North America were not so much colonists as colonials. Every colony except Georgia contained several generations of native-born Americans. What has been dubbed the 'creolization' of the colonies is discernible at many levels.[20] At the top of colonial society the behaviour of the gentry, though superficially aping English models, was in fact significantly different. Thus the plantations of Virginia appear at first sight to be colonial replications of estates in the mother country. Houses such as Berkeley, Carter's Grove and Westwood, though more modest than the ducal palaces of Blenheim, Chatsworth and Castle Howard, bear comparison with such mansions of the English country gentry as Beningborough, Dyrham and the Vyne. Yet the economies of these estates varied greatly. Where the landed gentry in England drew rents from tenant farmers, the Virginian planter's income derived largely from the sale of his tobacco crops. This involved them directly in the cultivation of their lands, something which their English counterparts would have considered to be demeaning.[21] Their financial transactions with London, as well as those of the business classes below them, were conducted not only in sterling but in paper currencies which, though issued by the individual colonies, were collectively known as 'American money'. Even the labouring classes seem to have developed peculiarly American traits. Newspaper advertisements for runaway servants provided details of their birthplaces to help their identification. More and more in the 1730s were described as 'American born', as distinct from those who were 'Irish, Welsh, English, Scotch' or from 'the West Country, Staffordshire, Devon' and other English counties. It seems that they might have been recognizable by a distinctly American accent, since other notices observe the distinct characteristics of speech, e.g. 'a Scotchman by birth, speaks much of that tongue and speaks thick'.[22]

Slaves as well as servants appeared frequently in advertisements placed by masters asking for assistance in apprehending runaways. These did not need to have their physical features described, since they were identifiable by their colour, although distinguishing characteristics such as their clothes or their demeanour were employed to help identification.[23] How far black colonists developed an American mentality is very difficult to determine. Clearly they never had a European identity. Nor did they share a common African culture since there was no such thing. The areas of Africa which supplied slaves to North America varied greatly in their customs, language, religions and other cultural manifestations. Moreover, as blacks became acculturated in the colonies so they distinguished themselves from the fresh arrivals from Africa with their outlandish ways and 'Gulla' languages.[24] Instead they adapted to the culture of their white masters, acquiring English speech and skills.

The extent to which their African origins influenced black society depended upon region and, in the case of the South, the size of the plantation. In areas where the black to white ratio was high, as in large plantations, the African customs and beliefs would undoubtedly influence native-born blacks. In smaller plantations, where there was a lower proportion of blacks to whites and a higher ratio of native blacks to African-born people, the chances for assimilation were higher. Northern urban centres, such as Philadelphia, were more conducive to assimilation by blacks into white society.[25] Not only was there a lower black to white ratio, but the black population included more skilled free blacks than did the south. The learning of a skill was a path to freedom. It also acted as a mechanism that helped to inculcate a sense of separateness from their origins. Consequently, adaptation was critical to survival. However, assimilation was not complete. A century later, W. E. B. Du Bois described the feeling of 'twoness'.

For instance, blacks in colonial America could not participate in colonial

politics, though for that matter neither could women or indentured servants. Unlike most white colonists, moreover, their political allegiance was
susceptible to outside exploitation. Thus the authorities in Spanish Florida
could offer asylum to slaves who fled there from British colonies. This was
one incentive behind the Stono rebellion which broke out in South
Carolina in 1738, the most serious slave uprising in British North
America.[26] It perhaps set a precedent for Governor Dunmore of Virginia's
appeal to slaves to stay loyal to the Crown on the outbreak of the
American Revolution. By then, though, American consciousness had
taken on a political dimension. Before the 1760s, as cannot be too strongly
stressed, it did not develop a national identity. Nevertheless there was a
growing awareness of a common American culture.

At the same time blacks retained sufficient of their own customs to
develop what Allan Kulikoff has described as 'an Afro-American culture'.[27]
Although he traces its origins in the Chesapeake, this was not specific
to one colony or even to the South, though most blacks were concentrated in the southern colonies. Even in Philadelphia some vestiges of
black culture survived, for example in rituals associated with the burial
ground.[28] A verse description of an evening walk through the town in
1729 began

> Passing those fields where negroe slaves are found
> At Rustick Gestures to a dismal sound
> I into a place arrived in which is laid
> Poor Negroe's ashes when his debts are paid.[29]

The survival of African elements added a distinctive black contribution to
the emerging American culture.

Its emergence is apparently reflected in more frequent employment of
the world 'American' in the eighteenth century. A search of the *Eighteenth
Century Short Title Catalogue* yielded several printed examples. Thus Cotton
Mather signed a sermon published in 1701 'by an American'.[30] The first
American Almanac appeared in 1704, to be printed every year thereafter and
even to spawn rivals such as *The Loyal American's Almanac*, *The Universal
American Almanac* and Franklin's *American Country Almanac*. A newspaper,
The American Weekly Mercury, began publication in Philadelphia in 1728.
The American Instructor or Young Man's Best Companion appeared in 1748,
'containing spelling, reading, writing and arithmetick . . . and how to qualify any person for business without the help of a master . . . the whole better adapted to these American colonies than any other book of the like
kind.' There was a very short-lived *American Magazine* launched in
Philadelphia in 1741, which only lasted for three issues, although another

with the same title which commenced publication in Boston in 1744 lasted for three years. In 1757 the *American Magazine or Monthly Chronicle* began a longer run in Philadelphia. The following year the *New American Magazine* made its appearance.

Another electronic database available to colonial historians is the Accessible Archives edition of the *Pennsylvania Gazette*. This produced a yield of 106 usages of the word American in the years from 1728 to 1750, and 278 from 1751 to 1765. Many were inconsequential, but some indicated a cultural resonance. In 1747, for example, there appeared an advertisement for 'the most excellent and famous new invented American Balsam; it is of such extraordinary preparation, the like was never known to be produced in America'. On 17 July 1752 'the ingenious Mr Tom Bell the famous American traveller made his publick appearance' in Williamsburg, Virginia. In 1758 Ebenezer Kinnersley wrote to commend Franklin's scientific achievements as 'preferable to the united merit of all the electricians in America'.

A trawl through manuscript materials would no doubt produce many more instances of contemporaries using the term 'American' to describe features of the continent including themselves. James Logan's correspondence in the Historical Society of Pennsylvania contains several. 'Your power of Attorney is not sufficient to make titles by', Logan wrote to Daniel Worlin in May 1704, 'in which we are now grown nicer than you may think suitable to Americans.' In 1718, when there were rumours that he was in dispute with the Governor of Pennsylvania, he denied them, saying, 'I dare challenge all America to say whether they ever directly or indirectly heard one syllable of any difference between us that I either did or could know of . . .'[31]

However, these examples of the employment of the term are ambiguous. They could be dismissed as a mere geographical rather than a cultural expression. Then again they could be describing peculiar attributes of American as distinct from European culture.

The case of the American Philosophical Society was rather different. Benjamin Franklin proposed in 1743 the 'promoting of useful knowledge among the British Plantations in America'. As he explained, the intention of the scheme was 'that one society be formed by virtuosi or ingenious men residing in the several colonies to be called the *American Philosophical Society*'.[32] The use of the word 'American' rather than 'Philadelphian' or 'Pennsylvanian' suggests a consciousness of a continental identity over and above the colonial. Franklin envisaged it as a forum for showing that American science was on a par with that of Europe. As he wrote to a fellow member in 1753 about European criticism of his notions concerning electrical conductivity: 'I see it is not without reluctance that the

Europeans will allow that they can possibly receive any instructions from us Americans.'[33]

Now it is true that Franklin, like most of his colonial contemporaries, saw himself as an English subject. At one time he even considered settling in England. Where he and Cotton Mather had been born in America, James Logan, who also called himself an American, had actually been born in Ireland. But these identities were not necessarily contradictory. People on both sides of the Atlantic were experiencing identity crises in the eighteenth century. The very term 'European' apparently only came into common currency towards the end of the previous century, in preference to the word 'Christendom' which had previously characterized the continent.[34] Not only were English, Scottish and Welsh subjects adjusting to the new terminology of Europe rather than Christendom; they also had to cope with the idea of themselves as Britons after the Anglo-Scottish Union of 1707. As Linda Colley has shown, this national identity had to be sedulously fostered under the Hanoverians.[35] Although Colley's analysis suggests a top-down, deliberate approach to inculcating national awareness, colonial American identity was a subconscious evolution from a cultural awareness towards a national character. However, the point at which these two developments met was in the emergence of multiple identities. As Colley puts it, 'identities are not like hats. Human beings can and do put on several at a time.'[36] Thus it was possible to be simultaneously British, English and European. Similarly it was possible for Franklin to be an American, a Pennsylvanian and an Englishman. Hector St John Crevecoeur made this quite explicit when he contrasted the European arriving in the colonies with the 'new man' he became after becoming a freeholder: 'he is now an American, a Pennsylvanian, an English subject.'[37]

Crevecoeur is often regarded as a post-Revolution writer but, as the quotation indicates, his *Letters from an American Farmer*, though they were not published until 1782, dealt with the colonial situation. They were, after all, begun in 1759. Indeed his account of the transformation of a European into an American could be taken as endorsing the exceptionalist view that the colonial experience was different from the start. 'An European when he first arrives is limited in his intentions as well as in his views, but he suddenly alters his scale: two hundred miles formerly appeared a very great distance; it is now a trifle.' Again, '*they* no sooner arrive than *they* immediately feel the good effects of that plenty of provisions *we* possess'.[38] These are not political but cultural sentiments. They are not dependent upon events but seem timeless. However, a closer reading of the passages cited indicates that the changes could only occur when the colonies had developed into mature societies. Two hundred miles was a more considerable distance than in Europe in the early stages of settlement, when virgin forests had still to be cleared. Only with the construction of a road system linking the colonies could it become 'a trifle'. Even the abundance of provisions was the result of economic growth as well as a product of the natural resources of the continent.

These conditions, leading to the awareness of American differences with Europe, came about early in the eighteenth century. Jack Greene, who has recently re-emphasized the exceptionalist case in *The Intellectual Construction of America*, dates 'the behavioural articulation of British America' from 1690 onwards, and sees 'the conceptual identification of British America' developing after 1715.[39]

Co-operation in a common cause against the French seems more than anything else to have raised American consciousness during the mid eighteenth century. As Linda Colley has shown, the development of a British consciousness was inculcated by stressing its antitheses: France and popery. Britons were reminded repeatedly that they were not French or, for the most part, Catholics, who were regarded as virtual aliens in their midst. This negative propaganda reached its zenith during the Jacobite Rebellion of 1745. The victory at Culloden was the culmination not only of an anti-Jacobite but of a pro-British campaign.

Similarly American consciousness was inculcated by the negative sentiments of opposition to France and to popery. The French were seen as a threat to the very survival of the colonies from the 1730s on. During the wars of the 1740s and 1750s the threat became very real, and great efforts were made to unite the colonies against it. These efforts culminated in the 1740s with the capture of Louisburg by colonial forces. The acquisition of Cape Breton occurred in the same year as the battle of Culloden and in many ways was the American equivalent of that victory. Nathaniel Ames extolled the victory in his almanac for 1747. This publication had begun in Boston in 1726, but, apart from the place of publication, was virtually indistinguishable from British almanacs, which Ames plundered for copy. In 1747, however, he published a doggerel poem celebrating the success of American arms, and prophesying further victories:[40]

> Ten thousand bold *Americans* will join
> With cheerful hearts to extirpate a Race
> Of superstitious Papists false and base.

The capture of Cape Breton thus boosted the confidence of the colonists in their own abilities to take on the French independently of the British. The implications of this were not lost on the authorities in Whitehall. The Duke of Bedford, Secretary of State, warned the Duke of Newcastle that an attempted colonial conquest of Canada would be undesirable, since it would arouse feelings of independence in the colonies 'when they shall see within themselves so great an army possessed in their own right by conquest, of so great an extent of country'.[41] The subsequent surrender of Cape Breton to the French by the British at the peace of Aix la Chapelle was regarded by many colonists as a betrayal, and created rancour which helped the growth of American consciousness.

The coincidence of the war with the Great Awakening helped to foster the image of the French in Canada as anti-Christ, and by contrast imbued the American cause with the attributes of Liberty and Protestantism. This view of France as the embodiment of popery and arbitrary power created an attitude which could be seen as embodying tyrannical and intolerant power.

However, this awareness of a common culture developed prior to any consciousness of national identity and the process of state building. Although some historians have detected the origins of American independence before the final break with Britain, aspirations to autonomy by individual colonies cannot be regarded as anticipating a future nation.

There have been several investigations of moves towards independence prior to 1763.[42] There were indeed prefigurations of colonial independence, some as early as the seventeenth century. Edward Randolph, an agent for the Crown under Charles II, observed that Massachusetts acted in many respects as though it was independent of royal authority. Similar accusations were made in the eighteenth century against other colonies, which were also accused of seeking ultimate autonomy. In 1708 Lord Dartmouth, a member of the Board of Trade, observed that Lord Treasurer Godolphin stressed to them that 'no government could subsist without an absolute power lodged somewhere; and at the distance the plantations lay, it was necessary to place it in the governor and council, as acting by the Crown's authority ... all complaints against them from other people should be discouraged, as much as possible, or the plantations would soon be independent of England.'[43] Such support was not always forthcoming, and in 1747 Governor Clinton complained of New York that the assembly there denied 'dependence and subjection'.[44] A Swedish observer in the 1740s claimed to 'have been told by Englishmen, and not only by such as were born in America but also by those who came from Europe, that the English colonies in North America in the space of thirty or fifty years would be able to form a state by themselves entirely independent of old England'.[45] This sees to have been a remarkably prescient prophecy. If indeed Peter Kalm was right, then the separation of the American colonies was inevitable. It was, as another contemporary put it, 'in the womb of time'.[46] Thomas Paine was therefore merely mouthing a commonplace when he maintained that he had 'never met with any man, either in

England or America, who hath not confessed his opinion that a separation between the two countries would take place one time or another'.[47]

The phrase 'one time or another' is, however, a vital qualification to any whiggish view that the two sides in the War of American Independence were on a collision course long before it broke out. To rake over the history of the colonies looking for anticipations of independence is to indulge in what has been dubbed 'source mining'. Source miners invariably find what they are looking for; but they wrest it from its context. In fact most of those who raised the prospect of independence did so only to deny it. When the assembly of New Jersey told their Governor in Anne's reign that his notorious predecessor Lord Cornbury had accused them of seeking independence from the Crown, they remarked 'whoever can seriously think this and with deliberation assert it ought very seriously and without deliberation to be confined to the society of madmen'.[48] 'During the [Seven Years'] war', observed Joseph Galloway, 'no part of his Majesty's dominions contained a greater proportion of faithful subjects than the thirteen colonies ... The idea of disloyalty at this time scarcely existed in America.'[49] As late as 1774 Benjamin Franklin maintained that he had represented 'the people of America as fond of Britain, concerned for its interests and its glory, and without the least desire of a separation from it'. He even protested that he 'never had heard in any conversation from any person drunk or sober the least expression of a wish for separation, or hint that such a thing would be advantageous to America'.[50] Even those like Paine who vehemently disagreed, and thought that independence was inevitable, nevertheless anticipated that it would not happen immediately, but would come about 'one time or another'. George Grenville was blamed by his political opponents for having 'brought on a crisis twenty or possibly fifty years sooner than was necessary'.[51]

Moreover moves by individual colonies to achieve autonomy, such as Massachusetts was accused of seeking under Charles II, do not necessarily indicate a movement for *American* independence. Andrew Burnaby noted in 1759 that the Virginian gentry 'are haughty and jealous of their liberties, impatient of restraint and can scarcely bear the thought of being controuled by an superior power. Many of them consider the colonies as independent states, unconnected with Great Britain otherwise than by having the same common king and being bound to her with natural affection.'[52] There is nothing here to suggest that the colonies would get together to assert their autonomy. On the contrary, before the reign of George III it was notorious that they were reluctant to co-operate on any issue, including mutual defence. Attempts to get them to do so by the government in London were generally abortive.

Efforts by the imperial authorities to persuade the colonies to get their act together in war time show that the mother country tended to treat the colonies collectively as much as individually. This was graphically depicted in the representation of Britain's trans-Atlantic settlements as a female native north American. As Lester C. Olson has shown, this was easily the most frequently employed image of America used in eighteenth-century British prints and drawings.[53] It also took more concrete form in the figure representing the colonies at the base of the statue of Queen Anne outside the west door of St Paul's cathedral. The Indian Amazon stands for British America as a whole. This was how the Crown and its servants viewed it too. They were concerned about imperial defence, revenues and trade. In the first century of colonization imperial authorities were more concerned with the Caribbean than with the North American continent. The sugar islands were regarded as the jewel in the Crown. To look for the development of an American consciousness solely on the mainland, indeed, is to perpetuate an erroneous whiggish view of the concept. Certainly people living in the islands regarded themselves as inhabitants of America along with those on the continent. The *Jamaica Courant* printed an amusing story in 1751 of a merchant who left London to settle in one of the British West Indian islands. He allegedly applied to a correspondent in London for a bride along with other commodities covered by a bill of exchange. The correspondent procured one and sent her to the Caribbean along with other goods. 'The letters of advice, the bales, and the gentlewoman came safe to the port', reported the paper, 'and our American ... happen'd to be one of the foremost upon the pier at the lady's landing.'[54] Simon Taylor wrote from Kingston Jamaica in 1765, 'I hope we shall have a more favourable administration for America than the last has been for if they go on in the same methods as the last ministry we shall be utterly ruined.'[55] Only when the controversy between the colonies and the British government degenerated into open war on the North American continent did he start to distinguish between West Indians such as himself and the rebellious 'Americans'.

Continental colonists, however, had distinguished themselves from those in the West Indies long before then.[56] In 1731 'the gents of the northern colonies', representing all the seaboard settlements from Nova Scotia to South Carolina, petitioned parliament to protest against the proposed duty on sugar from sources other than British islands.[57] The petition did not restrict itself to the economics of protecting West Indian interests to the detriment of those of the 'northern colonies', but drew a moral distinction between the two. Thus it claimed that 'the northern colonies are a laborious industrious people [who] live with great frugality' while the inhabitants of the sugar colonies 'live in wantoness and luxury'. This sense of being morally superior to other peoples was a crucial factor in the development of a separate American consciousness. The comparison was eventually to be made between Americans and Britons. A key ingredient in the move towards independence was the conviction that the British were decadent and corrupt, by contrast with the virtuous Americans. The distinction had already been drawn by American colonists on the continent of North America to distinguish themselves from those in the West Indies.

As the eighteenth century progressed Whitehall officials also came more and more to distinguish between the West Indies and the North American colonies. By the middle of the century continental concerns required a discrete defensive strategy, with attempts to persuade the mainland colonies to co-operate in their own defence. Benjamin Franklin tried to capitalize on these initiatives with his Albany plan of union which proposed a constitutional association of the seaboard colonies with no reference to the islands. Indeed, the proposed Grand Council was to be elected by the twelve colonies from New England to the Carolinas. Georgia was not included, perhaps because it had only recently become a Crown colony when the plan was mooted in 1754. But then Nova Scotia was excluded too. It appears that Franklin was thinking in terms of the English colonies settled in the seventeenth century. His celebrated drawing of the seaboard colonies as a snake cut into several segments with the caption 'join or die' vividly encaptures the scope of his Albany scheme. The Albany plan fell through, mainly due to fears in Whitehall that it would promote a cohesive continental unit. However, it also failed partly because political relations between the colonies were still characterized more by competition than by co-operation. This competitiveness had been ingrained in the colonial situation from the start, as infant settlements struggled for settlers.

The promotional literature of the colonies was directed towards the advantages which they could bring to the mother country. Thus the investment potential of an individual colony was stressed over that of other colonies. Advertisements followed a pattern of exaggerating the limitless commodities of a settlement, from land itself to the exotic and truly fabulous lions, tigers, unicorns and fish as big as men, which were alleged to inhabit Florida in the sixteenth century.[58] In the following century John Smith and Francis Higginson boosted the produce of New England, where they claimed 6 or 7,000 beavers', otters' and foxes' 'furs of value may be had in a year'.[59] Later the promotional literature for South Carolina by Thomas Nairne and John Norris, as Jack Greene has pointed out, allured people to the colony with 'prospects that its extraordinary material promise would enable them to live there without want in ease and abundance and perhaps become rich'.[60] The allurement continued in 1709 with John Lawson's *A New Voyage to Carolina*. Lawson describes the Carolinas as a land flowing with more milk and honey than colonies to the north. Even the natives were more friendly![61] Meanwhile William Penn could not help expressing the economic potential of Pennsylvania in somewhat exaggerated terms. Not only is the geographical position of the colony ideal – a claim made by all the colonies – but the abundance of produce was phenomenal. Thus the sheer volume of fish in the rivers was such that the noise they made at night kept him awake.[62] As late as the 1730s 'Georgia's depiction in the promotional literature as a land of promise, a new Eden, was not significantly different from the early portraits of other colonies in regions south of New England'. It was confidently predicted that it would produce silk, which they had tried and failed to manufacture in significant quantities.[63]

Where the planting of the seaboard colonies was seen as an enterprise of the mother country, with the individual settlements competing with each other, the expansion into the Ohio region after 1750 was regarded more as an American endeavour. In a scheme submitted to the Board of Trade by Samuel Hazard, settlers were to be recruited largely from the colonists already living in North America.[64] They were allured by claims that the region was potentially much more fertile then the existing colonies, the veritable garden of America. 'Any person who knows the nature of the soil and the extent of our settlement', claimed Lewis Evans, 'will confess that all the land worth the culture from N[ew] H[ampshire] to Carolina and extended far back as there are planters settled within three or four miles of one another . . . is not equal in quality to half the arable land in England.'[65] This astounding assertion was made in order to boost the agricultural attractions of the new territories. Efforts were made to launch an Ohio company, with shareholders in existing colonies. Britain's backing was needed only for security against the French and their Indian allies. Samuel Hazard was sanguine that it would be forthcoming even in the 'troublesome time' of 1757. Indeed he thought that 'what relates to America may now be easily obtained since the genius of the nation in general is to support America'.[66] Unfortunately for Hazard the disruption caused by the Seven Years War prevented his scheme from going ahead despite the enthusiastic backing of Lord Halifax, the President of the Board of Trade. After the hostilities ended in Britain's favour, however, plans to colonize the Ohio region could be renewed. In 1763 a proposal was made 'for settling a very extensive colony upon the finest part of Ohio'. As with the previous colonizing scheme, the attractions of the region were boosted in the publicity. 'The situation, fertility of the soil, navigation and innumerable other advantages that attends this colony', it was claimed, were 'over and above any that can be mentioned in the American Empire.' Again the settlers were to be recruited from the eastern seaboard, not from Europe.[67] It was no longer envisaged that British troops would be needed to protect the settlers, as had been the case in Hazard's scheme.

British support of America during the Seven Years' War involved not only the dispatch of professional troops from Britain across the Atlantic but the raising of forces in the colonies, including the newly formed Royal American regiment. The initial experience of joint military manoeuvres seems to have disillusioned colonists brought up to believe that British soldiers were among the most effective in the world. Braddock's expedition and defeat in particular caused both resentment at the arbitrary and high-handed actions of his officers and men, and astonishment at the failure of British arms against the French and Indians. Lord Loudoun's behaviour thereafter did little to repair the damage done to the reputation of the mother country and its treatment of American colonists. Military historians have recounted many horror stories of interaction between British regulars and colonials, which did little to foster admiration for the mother country and much to enhance an American mentality.[68] The feelings were mutual. 'I am heartily tired of America,' Colonel Henry Bouquet complained in 1757, 'If I can once get rid of it, no consideration in the world would make me come again.'[69]

Much has been made of these reactions on the American side. Thus the immorality and swearing of the British troops is said to have shocked soldiers influenced by the religious zeal of the Great Awakening. It has even been suggested that these encounters fostered republican sentiments among Americans. Standing armies were upheld in Commonwealth rhetoric as dangerous to liberty. Such theoretical considerations were re-inforced by the actual experience of regular troops in their midst by the colonials.

Most of the anecdotes, however, appear to relate to the early stages of the conflict, when things went badly for the British in America. The insecurity and anxieties which were the predominant characteristics of North Americans in the mid eighteenth century were transformed in the later stages of the war with the elimination of the French threat though the joint endeavours of the colonists and the British.[70] At the end of the war in 1763 the colonists were paradoxically more aware of themselves as Americans and as subjects of the king of Great Britain than at any time in their previous history.

There were by then other developments which aroused awareness among colonists of a wider world beyond the colonial boundaries. Timothy Breen has emphasized how this process produced as he puts it 'an expanded cultural core'.[71] Increased commerce not only between the colonies and the mother country but also inter-colonial trade strengthened internal communications.[72] This in turn promoted an awareness of common American interests different from, and even in tension with, those of Britain. Hence the almost immediate rejection by most Americans of the

British claim that they were virtually represented in the parliament of Great Britain.

The Great Awakening, which swept along the eastern seaboard from Georgia to Maine, was another phenomenon transcending geographical and cultural boundaries. Jonathan Dickinson commented in 1742 on 'the conviction and conversion of sinners, so remarkably of late begun and going on in these American parts'.[73] The catalyst of these events was George Whitefield, who has been called 'the first American'. He has been seen as creating a public space which extended throughout the seaboard colonies, a continental marketplace for the commercialization of religion. The impact which the religious movement had in the colonies was twofold: on the one hand it crated a schism within denominations over disputes about salvation; but in another sense it united the colonies by crossing geographical and cultural barriers. Although, to quote Jon Butler, 'the denominations were hierarchical, not democratic institutions', the sheer size of the continent inhibited them from constructing a controlling organization which could impose a single doctrine.[74] As Patricia Bonomi shows, in practice dissenting ecclesiastical organization was informal: 'the word that came to be applied by the colonists themselves to the Dissenters' form of church government was *republican*.'[75]

Popular participation in the state as well as in the church was also more marked in America than it was in England. There has been a debate over the extent of the franchise in the colonies.[76] Some historians have claimed that in colonies such as Massachusetts and Virginia it extended to virtually all white adult males, making them 'middle-class democracies'. Others have challenged these findings, arguing from the property qualifications and voting records that it was restricted to only 50 per cent of the white adult male population.[77] But even the most conservative estimate is twice that of the most generous calculation of the English electorate in the eighteenth century, which concluded that it comprised one in four adult males. In this sense colonial America was far more 'democratic' than the mother country. Moreover, whereas electoral activity was frequent in all colonies, and annual in some, in England the frequency of general elections dropped from an average of one every two years between 1694 and 1716 to one every six between 1716 and 1784. Thus appeals to the people of England became rarer than in the colonies. It also became notorious that in Britain the government could exert more influence over the outcome of elections than the electorate at large, whereas the executives in the colonies were too exiguous to offset the popular vote.

These practical considerations, quite apart from conflicting ideologies, might account for the clash between the British concept of parliamentary sovereignty and the colonial insistence upon popular sovereignty which emerged in the revolutionary era. When the imperial authorities insisted that the king in parliament was sovereign, and could legislate for all subjects, they were merely expressing the realities of a system in which popular participation in the political process had become minimal. When the aggrieved colonists riposted that the people were the ultimate sovereign power they were not merely reiterating the commonplaces of country propaganda, but were articulating American electoral experience.

Perhaps such considerations can also be discerned in differences over what constituted the common good. According to Peter Miller, the crisis between Britain and the American colonists marked a turning point in this concept. Previously it was felt appropriate to leave the definition of communal welfare to governments. Afterwards many urged that the people should have a say in it. As Miller puts it:[78]

> It took a long time for the Americans to cease feeling British. But at a certain point this sense of community was pushed to the margins of debate. Friendship and reciprocity, or, as so many contemporaries described it, filial feelings, were swamped by the overwhelming sense of diverging interests. At this stage an incipient and vague North American identity, itself only the broadest possible rubric for a host of more particular loyalties, seemed a more obviously true description than he simple 'British colonist'. The government's claim that necessity warranted taxation was rejected. The metropolitan definition of the common good was no longer persuasive.

As this essay has sought to demonstrate, the development of an American mentality before the Revolution helps to explain the rapidity with which a new political identity could be invented. All the psychological elements were in place except one, the national. That last lever was not thrown until 1776. Before that colonists stubbornly adhered to their rights as Englishmen in their dispute with the British government. Indeed Joseph M. Torsella has observed that ironically they tended to be called Americans by their critics in Britain, while they protested their Englishness.[79] Mr Torsella concludes that 'a vibrant American identity and a national consciousness did not emerge until 1790'. While national consciousness could not develop until the United States had become a nation, an 'American identity' had emerged, as this essay has shown, at least three decades before that. As Carl van Doren put it: 'nothing should be clearer about the Revolution than that the English colonists had ceased to be British before they realized it.'[80]

When the confrontation became violent the negative sense of not being British was replaced by a positive American political identity.

Independence was far more compelling as a war aim than abstract English rights. To get men to fight and die as American citizens was more potent than appealing to them to stand and fall as freeborn English subjects. That was the *common sense* of Paine's celebrated tract. Its astonishing success, however, can only be explained by the development of an American cultural consciousness in the three decades before it appeared.

Notes

1. D. Boorstin, *The Americans: The Colonial Experience* (1958). This book has never been out of print!
2. John Donne, 'To his mistris going to bed'; Thomas Hobbes, *Leviathan* (Everyman, 1914), p. 65. John Locke, *Two Treatises of Government*, ed. P. Laslett (1960), p. 343.
3. Nathaniel Ward, *The Simple Cobbler of Aggawan in America* (1647). Aggawan became modern Springfield.
4. R. S. and Mary Maples Dunn (eds), *The Papers of William Penn*, Vol. 3, (Philadelphia, 1986), p. 350.
5. Ibid., Vol. 2 (Philadelphia, 1982) p. 350.
6. One exception is Michael Zuckerman, who sustained the exceptionalist thesis in 'The fabrication of identity in early America', *William and Mary Quarterly*, 34 (1977), pp. 183–214. This employs modernization theory to argue that the people who chose to emigrate from England to North America in the seventeenth century were exceptional, and felt the competing demands of individualism and collectivism most acutely. Consequently 'modernization proceeded most unimpededly in America' (p. 194).
7. W. Grayson Allen, *In English Ways: The Movement of Societies and the Transferral of English Local Law and Custom to Massachusetts Bay in the Seventeenth Century* (Chapel Hill, 1981); David Hackett Fischer, *Albion's Seed: Four British Folkways in America* (Oxford, 1989).
8. See the symposium on *Albion's Seed* in the *William and Mary Quarterly*, 48 (1991), pp. 223–308.
9. *The Infortunate: The Voyage and Adventures of William Moraley, An Indentured Servant*, ed. Susan E. Klepp and Billy G. Smith (Philadelphia, 1992).
10. *The Life of the Reverend Michael Slatter*, ed. Henry Harbaugh (Philadelphia, 1857), pp. 126–7.
11. W. Livingston, *The Independent Reflector*, ed. Milton Klein (Cambridge, Mass. 1963), p. 10.
12. *Pennsylvania Gazette*, 2 November 1752.
13. Antonello Gerbi, *The Dispute of the New World: The History of a Polemic,* translated by J. Moyle (1973).
14. *The New Oxford Book of Eighteenth-century verse*, ed. R. Lonsdale (Oxford, 1984) p. 175, where it is noted that although the poem was written in 1726 it was not published until 1752.
15. Andrew Burnaby, *Travels through the Middle Settlements in North America in the Years 1759 and 1760, with Observations upon the State of the Colonies* (1775), p. 149.
16. Nathaniel Ames, 'A thought upon the past, present and future state of North America' (1757), *Essays, Humour and Poems of Nathaniel Ames*, ed. S. Briggs (Cleveland, 1891), p. 286.
17. Roger Thompson, *Women in Stuart England and America: A Comparative Study* (1974).

18. Mary Beth Norton, 'The Evolution of white women's experience in early America', *American Historical Review*, 89 (1984), pp. 593–619.

19. Mary Beth Norton, *Liberty's Daughters: The Revolutionary Experience of American Women* (1980).

20. This ugly word has crept into usage in recent works on colonial culture. It has, however, some justification from contemporary parlance. Thus royal officers who went native in the eighteenth century were held to have degenerated 'into Creoles'. B. L. Add. MSS 33029: 'Extract of a letter from New England', cited in T. Barrow, *Trade and Empire: The British Customs Service in Colonial America 1660–1775* (1967), p. 322.

21. See Timothy Breen, *Tobacco Culture: The Mentality of the Great Tidewater Planters on the Eve of the Revolution* (1985).

22. The *American Weekly Mercury*, passim during the 1720s; the *Pennsylvania Gazette*, 18 May 1738.

23. See Shane White and Graham White, 'Slave clothing and African-American culture in the eighteenth and nineteenth centuries', *Past and Present*, 148 (1995), pp. 149–65. This article draws on *Runaway Slave Advertisements: A Documentary History from the 1730s to 1790*, 4 volumes, compiled by Lathan A. Windley (Westport, Connecticut, 1983). It examines 'how eighteenth-century slaves tested the boundaries of the system not only by appropriating items of elite apparel, but by combining elements of white clothing in ways which whites often considered startlingly inappropriate' (p. 150).

24. G. W. Mullin, *Flight and Rebellion: Slave Resistance in Eighteenth-century Virginia* (1972).

25. Gary B. Nash, *Forging Freedom: The Formation of Philadelphia's Black Community 1720–1840* (1988), pp. 11, 16–17.

26. Peter H. Wood, *Black Majority: Negroes in Colonial South Carolina from 1670 through the Stono Rebellion* (1974).

27. A. Kulikoff, *Tobacco and Slaves: The Development of Southern Culture in the Chesapeake 1680–1800* (1986), pp. 345–51.

28. Nash, *Forging Freedom*, p. 13.

29. *The American Weekly Mercury*, 5–12 June 1729.

30. Cotton Mather, *American Tears upon the Ruins of the Greek Churches* (1701). Mather also entitled his most famous work *Magnalia Christi Americana* and called John Winthrop 'Nehemias Americanus'. This suggested to Sacvan Bercovitch *The Puritan Origins of the American Self* (1975). This widely acclaimed study somewhat exaggerated the 'otherness' of seventeenth-century America, for instance by claiming that Mather's styling Winthrop ' "Americanus" indicates his service to the New World state' (sic; p. 2). It also prioritizes the formative function of puritanism in a way which few historians would now accept.

31. Historical Society of Pennsylvania, *Logan Letterbooks*: Logan to Worlin, [May] 1704; Logan to Col. Hunter, 5 January 1718.

32. L. W. Labaree (ed.) *The Papers of Benjamin Franklin*, Vol. 3 (1960), pp. 380–1.

33. Ibid., p. 463.

34. H. D. Schmidt, 'The establishment of "Europe" as a political expression', *Historical Journal*, 9 (1966), pp. 172–8.

35. Linda Colley, *Britons: Forging the Nation 1707–1837* (1992).

36. Ibid., p. 6.

37. J. Hector St John de Crevecoeu, *Letters from an American Farmer*, ed. Albert E. Stone (1986), p. 83.

38. Ibid., pp. 81–2.

39. Jack P. Green, *The Intellectual Construction of America: Exceptionalism and Identity from 1492 to 1800* (Chapel Hill, 1993).

40. Nathaniel Ames, *Almanac* (1747).

41. Arthur Buffinton, 'The Canadian expedition of 1746: its relation to British politics', *American Historical Review*, 40 (1939–40), p. 555.
42. J. M. Bumsted, ' "Things in the womb of time": Ideas of American Independence, 1633 to 1763', *William and Mary Quarterly*, 31 (1974), pp. 533–64.
43. Gilbert Burnet, *History of His Own Time* (6 vols, Oxford, 1833), Vol. 5, p. 362 (Dartmouth's note).
44. Cited in Bumsted, ' "Things in the womb of time" ', op. cit., p. 545.
45. *Peter Kalm's Travels in North America*, ed. Adolph B. Benson (1996), Vol. 1, p. 139.
46. Henry McCulloh, *The Wisdom and Policy of the French* (1755), quoted in Bumsted, ' "Things in the Womb of Time" ', p. 549. The phrase was also used by William Burke in *A Copy of a Letter from a Gentleman in Guadeloupe*, quoted in ibid., p. 561.
47. Thomas Paine, *Common Sense* (1776), p. 61.
48. 'The representation of the General Assembly of New Jersey relating to the administration of Lord Cornbury', 9 February 1711, *Documents Relating to the Colonial History of the State of New Jersey*, ed. William A. Whitehead (1992), Vol. 4, p. 36.
49. Joseph Gallowsay, *Letters to a Nobleman on the Conduct of the War in the Middle Colonies* (1780), pp. 8–9.
50. Carl van Doren, *Benjamin Franklin* (1938), p. 490.
51. P. D. G. Thomas, *The Townshend Duties Crisis: The Second Phase of the American Revolution, 1767–1773* (Oxford, 1987), p. 99.
52. Burnaby, *Travels through the Middle Settlements . . .*, p. 20.
53. Lester C. Olson, *Emblems of American Community in the Revolutionary Era* (1991), pp. 75–123.
54. *Pennsylvania Gazette*, 20 June 1750.
55. Cambridge University Library Vanneck correspondence. An edition of these letters is being prepared for publication by W. A. Speck and Betty Wood.
56. Thus an advertisement in the *American Weekly Mercury* for 13–20 December 1720 asked for 'any prints or written advices either from Europe or the West Indies'.
57. *Pennsylvania Gazette*, 15 July 1731.
58. John Sparkes, *The Attractions of Florida* (1564).
59. John Smith, *A Description of New England* (1616); Francis Higginson, *New England's Plantation* (1630).
60. Jack P. Greene, 'Early South Carolina and the psychology of British colonization', *Imperatives, Behaviors and Identities: Essays in Early American Cultural History* (1992), p. 100.
61. John Lawson, *A New Voyage to Carolina* (1709).
62. *The Papers of William Penn*, Vol. 2, p. 395. Penn to Aubrey, 13 June 1683.
63. Greene, *Imperatives, Behaviors and Identities*, pp. 115–16.
64. Pennsylvania State Archives, Harrisburg: MG8/361: Sammuel Hazard's letterbook 1757–8.
65. Lewis Evans, *Geographical, Historical, Political, Philosophical and Mechanical Essays* (Philadelphia, 1755) p. 4.
66. PA State Archives MG8 361: Hazard to Josiah Smith, Philadelphia, 13 October 1757.
67. *Pennsylvania Gazette*, 21 April 1763.
68. Alan Rogers, *Empire and Liberty: American Resistance to British Authority 1755–1763* (1874); Douglas Edward Leach, *Roots of Conflict: British Armed Forces and Colonial Americans 1677–1763* (1986).
69. Leach, *Roots of Conflict*, p. 94.
70. This gradual transformation is well documented in a series of letters from Colonel John Bradstreet to Charles Gould in the Morgan of Tredegar manuscripts in the National Library of Wales (Tredegar Park Mss, Box 128). Bradstreet began by being contemptuous of the colonial military effort, writing on 1 June 1755 from Oswego that he was

'endeavouring to make the worst of troops upon earth useful' (128/7). The following spring he was even more critical, writing sarcastically from Boston on 9 March 1756 of 'the mighty preparations of the British Americans to drive the French from Crown Point ... their conduct is worse (if possible) this year than last ... all proceedings on this side the water confirm me more and more in my first opinion that whilst the Americans are left to themselves in military operations nothing more will come of it than immense expence with loss & dishonor to his Majesty's arms.' (128/26) Yet Bradstreet relied on colonial arms to assist in the taking of Frontenac and was ready to raise an American regiment afterwards (128/passim).

71. T. H. Breen, 'Creative adaptations: peoples and cultures', *Colonial British America: Essays in the New History of the Early Modern Era*, ed. Jack P. Greene and J. R. Pole (1984), p. 220.

72. How far communications along the eastern seaboard had improved by 1720 can be inferred from advertisements placed in the *American Weekly Mercury* for 21 July and 18 August by William Hill of Philadelphia, offering 'to serve any gentleman as a swift and trusty messenger on foot or horse to any of the king's colonies on the continent'.

73. Jonathan Dickinson, *A Display of God's Special Grace: in a familiar dialogue between a minister and a gentleman of his congregation, about the work of God, in the conviction and conversion of sinners, so remarkably of late begun and going on in these American parts* (Boston, 1742).

74. Jon Butler, 'Coercion, miracle, reason: rethinking the American religious experience in the revolutionary age', *Religion in a Revolutionary Age*, ed. Ronald Hoffman and Peter J. Albert (1994), p. 8.

75. Patricia Bonomi, 'Religious dissent and the case for American exceptionalism', *Religion in a Revolutionary Age*, pp. 46–7.

76. Robert E. Brown and Katherine Brown, *Virginia 1705–1786: Democracy or Aristocracy?*; Katherine Brown, 'The controversy over the franchise in Puritan Massachusetts', *William and Mary Quarterly*, 33 (1976), pp. 212–41; J. R. Pole, *Political Representation in England and the Origins of the American Republic* (1966); Robert J. Dinkin, *Voting in Provincial America: A study of Elections in the Thirteen Colonies* (1977).

77. Dinkin, *Voting in Provincial America*, pp. 41–9.

78. Peter N. Miller, *Defining the Common Good: Empire, Religion and Philosophy in Eighteenth-century Britain* (Cambridge, 1994), pp. 15–16.

79. Joseph M. Torsella, 'American national identity 1750–1790: samples from the popular press', *Pennsylvania Magazine of History and Biography*, 112 (1988), pp. 167–87.

80. Van Doren, *Benjamin Franklin*, p. 360.

Part II Economic Development

In the early part of the nineteenth century Britain could justifiably boast of being the workshop of the world. In the last quarter of the century, however, her economic dominance was being undermined and one of her chief competitors was the United States. Economic historians have for long been interested in comparing British and American economic development. This is the subject of our second section, which begins with the seminal work of H. J. Habakkuk. Habakkuk asks: What determined the nature of nineteenth-century technological change? Why did Britain and America adopt the new technology at differing rates? Why, in particular, did Britain respond so tardily to the new technological opportunities? His argument centres on the high cost of labour and the problems of labour supply in nineteenth-century America in contrast to Britain. His assumptions about the rewards and advantages of independent agriculture in America and the need for skilled labour have been challenged; other historians have drawn attention to the different expectations in the domestic market for protected American goods as opposed to the worldwide market for British goods: Nevertheless, Habakkuk's work remains an essential basis for a study of the two economies during the nineteenth century. The other essay in this section, by S. B. Saul, focuses on the American impact on British industry in the years before the First World War. British industry was, and has subsequently been, criticized for its performance compared to that of its competitors during this period. Saul's analysis calls for a reassessment, for he demonstrates that some British firms were quick to take up American methods and to make rapid strides both in producing American machine tools and in designing and improving their own. Decline there was, but there was no universal failure within British industry or among British entrepreneurs.

II.1

Britain and America:
The economic effects of labour scarcity

H. J. HABAKKUK

THE SUPPLY OF LABOUR IN THE USA AND ENGLAND

Industry started to develop in the United States at a time when industrial money wages were substantially higher than they were in England, according to some estimates for the early nineteenth century perhaps a third to a half higher. This was fundamentally because the remuneration of American industrial labour was measured by the rewards and advantages of independent agriculture. [...]

Land was abundant and, except possibly in Virginia before the abolition of entails, it was accessible to purchase by men of small means. In the 1820s it could be purchased from the federal government at $1.25 per acre, which was well within the reach of a skilled labourer, who might at this time earn between $1.25 and $2.0 per day. 'The men earn here (in the cotton textile factories at Lowell) from 10 to 20 dollars a week', wrote an English observer in 1842, 'and can therefore lay by from 5 to 10 dollars, after providing for every want, so that in two or three years they accumulate enough to go off to the west and buy an estate at 1¼ dollars an acre or set up in some small way of business at home.' In England, by contrast, land was scarce in relation to labour, and the supply of land on the market, particularly of small properties, was restricted by the existence of large estates supported by legal restraints on alienation; the return on the cultivation of land in England up to 1815 was high since new techniques were available, and food prices were rising; but to set up as a tenant-farmer required considerable capital, and, even if an English artisan had been able to acquire the capital, the supply of farms to be let was limited, and absorbed by the demand of the sons of existing tenants. In England, therefore, a man could, generally speaking, enter agriculture only as a labourer commanding low wages.

The abundance and accessibility of land plus the fact that much of it was

An abridged extract from H. J. Habakkuk, *American and British Technology in the Nineteenth Century* (Cambridge University Press, 1962), pp. 23–76.

fertile meant that output per man in American agriculture was high. Moreover, since the cultivator was often also the owner, and his family supplied the labour, the advantage of the high output accrued to the cultivator. His income included: (1) an element of rent, which would in England have been a heavy charge on output and payable to the landowner, (2) agricultural profits, which in England accrued to the tenant-farmer, as well as (3) the wages, which in England went to the agricultural labourer. Furthermore the new land was brought into use in such a way that the returns to settlement on the frontier sometimes included elements of exceptional gain. Many American farmers had heavy debt charges; but there were no tithes, and taxes were low. Finally since the total earnings of the family in American agriculture tended to be divided among its members, there was less disparity between average and marginal earnings. In order to attract labour, therefore, industry had to assure the workers in industry a real wage comparable to average earnings in agriculture. English industry, by contrast, could acquire labour from agriculture at a wage equal to the very low product of the marginal agricultural labourer plus an addition to cover the costs of transport and of overcoming inertia. Thus, while in England industrial wages equalled the marginal product, in the USA the reward of the marginal labourer in industry was above his product, unless the manufacturer took steps to increase the product.

Moreover the course of agricultural technology in the early decades of the nineteenth century may well have accentuated the disparity between the terms on which labour was available to industry in the USA and England. In America improvements in agriculture took the form primarily of increasing output per head, the abundance of labour made it difficult for the labourer to enjoy the increase. In America agricultural improvements raised, and in England prevented, a rise in the terms on which labour was available to industry.

Comparison of industrial wage-rates does not of course measure precisely the difference in labour-cost, in terms of output, in the two countries. For, on the one side, the hours of work in America were generally longer, and conceivable effort was more concentrated. It may also be, as some contemporaries said, that better nutrition and more spacious working and living conditions, made the American a more efficient worker. On the other hand it might be supposed from the alternatives open to labour in America that the workers recruited into American industry were inferior, in relation to agricultural labour, when compared with the English; it is possible that is, that the pull of agriculture showed itself in the quality as well as the price of industrial labour in America. Then again, American employers had to endure higher costs than the English on housing and working-facilities of a kind which made the worker more agreeable but added little, if anything, to labour productivity. Probably also the rate of turnover of workers was higher in America, and therefore the likelihood smaller that they would acquire industrial discipline. Finally, England at the start was technically superior and this must have reflected itself in higher labour productivity. Since we cannot measure these conflicting influences, it is impossible to be precise about the differences in labour-costs in the two countries, but there is no reason to doubt the opinion of contemporaries that American industrial labour was substantially dearer than the English.

But American industrial labour was not dearer than the English; its supply was less elastic. It was more difficult to obtain additional labour for the industrial sector as a whole. This was partly owing to the abundance of land and the difficulties of internal transport, which required technical solutions and heavy capital outlays before they could be overcome. It was also partly owing to America's geographical remoteness from the areas of abundant population. [...]

Dearness and inelasticity are logically distinct; the consequences of a high level of wages prevailing over time are not the same at all points as those of a wage-level which rises when demand for labour increases. There have been situations where the floor set to industrial wages by *per capita* productivity in agriculture was low but the supply of labour was inelastic, for example, in England for much of the eighteenth century. There have also been situations where the floor set to industrial wages was high but where abundant labour was forthcoming at this wage – in some respects this was the case in the USA in the second half of the nineteenth century when there was a large amount of immigration. But in the first half of the nineteenth century, with which we are here mainly concerned, there was a contrast on both points, and a more marked contrast than existed either before or since; industrial labour was dear, and its total supply inelastic in the USA, and it was cheap and elastic in England. Since the general level of labour-costs was so closely connected with the elasticity of the supply of labour, it is difficult to discuss their effects separately except at the cost of repetition. In most of the following discussion, therefore, they are treated together.

THE INDUCEMENT TO MECHANIZE

It seems obvious – it certainly seemed so to contemporaries – that the dearness and inelasticity of American, compared with British, labour gave the American entrepreneur with a given capital a greater inducement than his British counterpart to replace labour by machines. The real problem is to determine how the substitution took place. Where the more mechanized method saved *both* labour and capital per unit of output it would be the preferred technique in both countries. It was where the more mechanized method saved labour but at the expense of an increase in capital that the American had the greater inducement than the English manufacturer to adopt it. (The term capital-intensive will henceforward be used to describe such a method.) [...]

There is little readily available information about the labour requirements of various techniques or about the price of different types of labour, and the following discussion is therefore conjectural. But a plausible case can be made for supposing that in the early nineteenth century in the USA an increased demand for labour raised the wages of skilled labour *less* than the wages of unskilled labour, and that, in many cases, the capital-intensive technique required, for its construction plus operation, more skilled labour per unit of output than the labour-intensive technique. [...]

The distinction between skilled and unskilled labour is, of course, constantly shifting; technical progress creates new categories of employment and calls for continual redefinition of skills. Skilled labour at the beginning of the nineteenth century was very different from skilled labour at the end. At the end of the century there was a whole spectrum of degrees of skill. At the beginning of the century there were three broad categories of labour. First there was the undifferentiated mass of unskilled adult labour. The money wage of such labour was a third or a half higher in America than in England. Secondly there were workers who performed tasks which required dexterity and aptitude but which, granted these qualities, could be performed after a short period of training and experience, for example some of the tasks performed by women in the textile industry. For such labour the American wage was rarely more than 20 per cent higher than the English. Finally there were the craft skills which were so technically complicated that they could be acquired only after a long term of training. Craft operations were so diverse that, more than in other types of labour, it is extremely difficult to make direct comparison, especially as rates varied widely according to season and from place to place, and we have no independent tests of the degree of skill being priced. Only a very detailed analysis of labour capabilities and of the relative values placed upon them in the two countries would establish the differences in this respect between America and England. But the random selection of rates given by Clark[1] suggests that the premium on artisan skills was generally lower in America than in England in the early nineteenth century.

How far differences in the premium on skill between the two countries represent difference in supply and how far differences in demand it is impossible to say, but there are some general reasons why we should expect the supply of skill, in relation to common labour, to have been more abundant in America than in England:

(1) As has been evident since 1939, a general shortage of labour is most acutely felt in the unskilled grades, in a shortage of recruits for heavy tedious work; workers in low-paid activities are more prepared to leave their jobs and seek better ones when labour is scarce, in relation to demand, than when it is abundant. A general shortage of labour raises the labour-costs of instrument-users more than those of instrument-makers. Where there is a persistent surplus of labour, it is those who are without skill, particularly the newcomers to the labour market, who have most difficulty in finding work; it is on the wages of the unskilled that the surplus has most effect.

(2) The pulling or retaining power of American agricultural expansion was felt most on unskilled labour. It was, of course, easier for the skilled worker to accumulate the capital necessary for settlement; but at the opening of the nineteenth century the costs of settlement were probably sufficiently low in relation to industrial earnings not to restrict the possibility to the highest-paid workers, and it was the worker without special industrial skills who stood to make the largest relative gain from agriculture. Furthermore, investment in social overhead capital, particularly transport systems, made heavy demands on general labour, that is labour not trained for particular operations, and the construction of canals, roads, and railways seems to have been more attractive to such labour than the factories. This type of investment was a more rapidly increasing proportion of total investment than in England.

(3) Literacy was more widely diffused in America and popular education developed earlier. [...] Thus a higher proportion of the population than in England was capable of being trained to skilled operations.

(4) There was much more international mobility of skill than of general labour, and a high proportion of English migrants to the USA before the start of mass migration were skilled workers. In the early decades of the century therefore, immigration did more to alleviate the shortages of artisan skills than of unskilled labour.

(5) Mechanical abilities of a rudimentary sort were widely spread in the USA at the opening of the century. [...]

(6) The up-grading of unskilled to skilled labour was less impeded in the USA because, though skilled workers were in fact organized earlier in the USA, trade union restrictions, conventions, apprenticeship rules, were less effective than in England.

We may reasonably conclude, therefore, that in America an increase in the demand for labour raised the cost of the methods which required a great deal of unskilled labour more than it raised the cost of the methods which required a great deal of skilled labour.

It is not always the case that the capital-intensive methods require more skilled labour per unit of output than the labour-intensive. But in the technology of the early nineteenth century there are likely to have been several cases where it did so. The *manufacture* of power-looms required more skill than the manufacture of hand-looms; and the same was probably true of the 'superior' as compared with the 'simpler' machines of all kinds. In the USA when demand for labour rose, the labour-costs of the machine-makers rose less than the labour-costs of the machine-users, and the costs of the machines which were expensive in terms of output rose less than the cost of the cheaper machines. At the very start, of course, 'power-looms' may have been more expensive in terms of 'hand-looms' in America than in Britain, because American deficiencies in engineering skills, compared with the British, were more marked in the making of complicated than of simple machines. The point is that, with the increase in industrial capacity, the ratio between the costs of manufacturing the equipment fell more rapidly in America than in Britain, quite apart from any possibility that the Americans were catching up on the English in engineering skills.

The position of the *operating costs* of capital-intensive and labour-intensive techniques is not so clear. There may have been industries in which the operation of the capital-intensive machine required a *lower* ratio of skilled to unskilled labour, which, to a greater or lesser degree, offset the higher ratio in the costs of its manufacture. But the probability is that, in a significant number of cases, the manufacture plus use of the more capital-intensive techniques required more skilled to unskilled labour than the labour-intensive. Where this was so, the fact that unskilled labour, in relation to skilled labour, was dearer in America than in England gave the American an inducement to make a more capital-intensive choice of technique. There is also the additional point that the type of labour which was relatively dearest performed the simple, unskilled operations which were, from a technical point of view, most easily mechanized.

Thus there were at least four circumstances in which a rise in the cost of American labour provided the American manufacturer with an incentive to adopt the more capital-intensive of known techniques, in order partly to check the rise in wages and partly to compensate for it. As, from experience, it became more evident that labour was the scarcity most likely to emerge during a general attempt to expand capacity, we should expect an increasing number of American manufacturers to have this in mind when choosing equipment and to become conditioned to adopting the method which did most to alleviate this particular scarcity. It is not, however, strictly necessary to assume that all, or indeed any, manufacturers consciously reflected in this way on the resource-saving characteristics of different techniques. Investment may have adapted itself to relative factor-scarcities by a process of natural as well as of conscious selection. If some manufacturers, for whatever reason, adopted improvements which were more appropriate to the factor-endowment of the economy, these men fared better than those which made a contrary choice. They competed more successfully in product- and factor-markets and by expanding their operations came in time to constitute a larger share of their industry. Moreover they brought influence to bear not only via the market but by force of example. Their success inspired imitators, and shaped entrepreneurial attitudes toward the most likely lines of development.

In England, where the supply of labour to industry as a whole was elastic, there was no reason, so far as labour-supplies were concerned, why accumulation should not proceed by the multiplication of machines of the existing type. Thus even if the general level of labour-costs had not been higher in America, the difficulty of attracting additional labour might have pushed the American entrepreneur over a gap in the range of techniques and induced him to adopt one which was not only more capital-intensive than he had previously employed, but was also more capital-intensive than those currently adopted by his English counterpart. But the fact that American labour was also dearer than the English provided the American entrepreneur with an incentive to adopt more capital-intensive techniques than the English, even had the supply of labour been equally forthcoming.

For this argument it does not seem essential that the cost of finance in industry should have been lower, in relation to labour-costs, in the USA than in Britain. It is enough if machines were cheaper in America in relation to labour, either because they could be imported or because they were made with the type of labour which was relatively most abundant. But the bias towards capital-intensity would obviously have been greater if in fact finance was cheaper in relation to labour in America.

The cost of finance to a manufacturer who reinvested his profits is more ambiguous than the cost of labour, because we do not know what, if any, imputed rate of interest was used. It follows from the assumptions of the simplified version of events to which we have previously referred that the country with the higher wages in terms of output has the lower rate of profit on capital, and this can be regarded as, in some sense, the relevant rate of interest. But this is not a very helpful guide to what actually happened. For although there are many quotations of profits for particular firms in particular years, it is rarely clear what definition has been employed and it is difficult to derive any general rate of profit. In any case accounting methods in early nineteenth-century manufacturing were extremely rudimentary, and it is wildly unlikely that, in comparing alternative techniques, anyone ever applied a notional rate of interest equal to the anticipated rate of profit.

For many of the simple techniques of the period it probably did not matter much if the entrepreneur neglected to impute a rate of interest on his locked-up capital. When the capital per unit of output was substantial, as it may have been in the construction of cotton mills, the need to impute some rate of interest would have been more evident, and probably rule-of-thumb methods were devised which corresponded well enough in general effect with more rigorous accounting principles. It is possible that manufacturers reckoned the cost of their capital by the alternative uses to which they could put their savings. Over a country so large and diverse it is impossible to say much in general terms about the consequences of proceeding in this way. The opportunity-costs of industrial finance in America were clearly higher in the USA as a whole than in Britain. But the extremely high rates of interest which are sometimes quoted, for example on business paper, reflect a considerable degree of risk and other market imperfections, and therefore greatly exaggerate the disparity between the two countries. While finance as well as labour was dear in America, the scarcity of finance attracted English funds more readily and earlier than the scarcity of labour drew out migrants. There were so few impediments to the import of British capital into America that the yields on long-term obligations in the two countries cannot have differed by very much more than the risk premium. An American textile manufacturer, asked by the Select Committee on Manufacturers of 1833 to describe his methods of calculating capital-costs, said that he reckoned his interest upon the purchased price of the machinery and for this purpose took a rate of 6 per cent in America, and of 5 per cent in England. The choice of these rates would have biased the American choice of technique towards the more capital-intensive methods.

In many cases, however, early manufacturers neglected to take account of interest except when they had to borrow from outsiders; each year they withdrew from the business enough to live on and ploughed back the rest irrespective of the yield on alternative methods of employing their funds. In effect, they behaved as if their capital cost them nothing. If entrepreneurs in both countries behaved in this way finance would certainly have appeared to be cheaper, in relation to labour, in America, than in England.

THE NATURE OF THE SPECTRUM OF TECHNIQUES

The practical importance of the inducements in the USA to adopt capital-intensive methods depended on the nature of the techniques available, and the possibilities they afforded for substitution between labour and capital. There clearly were several occasions on which one technique was manifestly superior for any likely range of factor-prices, and would therefore have been the most appropriate choice in England as well as America. The new techniques for spinning which were invented in the later eighteenth century were so much more productive for all factors than the old spindle that they were the best choice at any conceivable level of wages. But there were other situations in which the possible methods of production were sufficiently competitive, one with the other, for the manufacturers' choice to have been influenced by relative factor-prices. It is difficult to say how far the various new methods of spinning were substitutes for each other – Hargreaves's jenny, Arkwright's water-frame, and Crompton's mule – and how far the suitability of each type of machine for the production of particular types of yarn specialized their uses; but, at some stages of development, some manufacturers may possibly have been influenced, in choosing between them, less by the market for particular grades of yarn than by the relative costs of the methods in the production of similar grades. In the years immediately after its invention the power-loom was not so decisively superior to the hand-loom that its adoption was uninfluenced by relative factor-prices; and even as late as 1819 it was not clear that in England the saving of labour was sufficient to outweigh the increase of capital-costs of the power-loom: '... one person cannot attend upon more than two power-looms, and it is still problematical whether this saving of labour counter-balances the expense of power and machinery, and the disadvantage of being obliged to keep an establishment of power-looms constantly at work'. On balance it seems reasonable to suppose that in the textile industry in the first half of the nineteenth century, the range of possible methods of production was sufficiently wide and continuous in respect of the proportions in which they used capital and labour for the choice of techniques to be responsive to relative factor-prices. And though the point could be settled only by detailed investigation, there is a general reason for expecting that similar conditions prevailed in other industries often enough to make labour-scarcity worth considering.

In the first place technical progress was still more empirical than scientific, that is it depended more on the response to particular and immediate problems of industrial practice than on the autonomous development of scientific knowledge. Technical development was therefore likely to take the form of slow modifications of detail, as opposed to spectacular leaps to a new technique decisively superior from the start to its predecessors; most even of the 'great inventions' of the period resolve themselves on close inspection into 'a perpetual accretion of little details probably having neither beginning, completion nor definable limits'. (For the same reason the process of improvement was more likely to be sensitive to the factory-needs of the economy in which they were made.) In the second place a large sector of industry was organized on the domestic system. Under this system circulating capital was more important than fixed, and the commercial capitalist was always facing the question in what proportions to distribute his investment between fixed and circulating capital, that is, how much of his funds to lay out in raw materials to be worked up by domestic workers and how much on machines of his own. This choice was very sensitive to the cost of labour; and so long at least as the costs rose and indicated a shift *into* fixed capital, the commercial capitalist was in a better position to respond to the stimuli than his successors with a high proportion of their funds locked up in fixed capital. [...]

Moreover, even when the range of basic techniques likely to interest a manufacturer was very narrow or when one process was distinctly superior over a very wide range of relative factor-prices, it was possible to use them in a more capital-saving or a more labour-saving way, for example by varying the number of machines per worker, by running the machines for shorter or longer hours (by arranging workers in shifts) or at more or less rapid rates, and by variations in the amount of space per worker or per machine.

The existence of methods of varying the factor-intensity of the basic techniques meant that there was usually a fairly continuous range of methods and that the method which used a little more capital saved a little more labour. But relative factor-prices would still be influential even if there were discontinuities such that, at some point, the alternative technique saved a great deal of labour but required a great deal more capital. Indeed the most striking disparities between English and American technology were probably established in just such cases. The gap between the hand-loom and the power-loom, and again, towards the end of the nineteenth century, between the ordinary power-loom and the automatic loom, was wide. The capital-intensity of the 'superior' machine could be modified by running it longer, which some Americans did, but the need to make this modification is probably itself evidence that the new technique was much more capital-intensive than the old. The conditions of their labour-supply gave the Americans a much stronger incentive than the English had, to leap such a gap in the spectrum of techniques, with effects on subsequent technical progress which will be discussed later.

We have so far considered only the consequence for the choice of technique of the fact that labour was scarcer in America than in England, and have referred to natural resources only in so far as the abundance of agricultural land was a condition of the scarcity of labour. We must now take natural resources more explicitly into account.

The price of natural resources had an effect on the choice of techniques ranked by reference to the proportions in which they employed capital and labour. If natural resources were employed in the same proportions in the capital- as in the labour-intensive techniques, the price of natural resources would not affect the tendency of a rise in wages to shift the manufacturers' choice towards greater capital-intensity. If the supply of natural resources were inelastic, so that attempts to widen capital met rising costs for natural resources as well as for labour, the bias towards capital-intensity would be *strengthened* if the capital-intensive technique saved natural resources as well as labour, and *weakened* if it was more expensive in natural resources.

But this does not exhaust the possible effects of natural resources. For there may have been some alternative techniques, the principal difference between which was in their possibilities of substituting between natural resources and either capital or labour or both. Some techniques were important principally because of the proportions in which they used capital and natural resources: large blast-furnaces may have allowed a substitution of capital for raw materials, and the application of steam to water-transport may have involved the reverse sort of substitution – of power for capital; it is also possible that methods of building factories differed in respect of the proportions in which they used land and capital. There were also techniques in which there was substitution between natural resources and labour; in particular there were possibilities of using power from water and steam instead of man-power.

Because of the unhomogeneity of natural resources and variations in their price within regions it is impossible to make any general statement about their cost, in relation to labour and capital, in the two countries. Land was certainly more abundant in the USA in relation to both other factors, and this fact dictated the choice of American agricultural techniques, which substituted land for labour. The abundance of land, and the nature of the American climate also enabled some substitution of natural resources for capital. There was less need than in England for investment in farm-buildings – the maize-stalks were left standing in the fields and they provided winter shelter for the cattle who were sometimes not brought in at all; and because of natural pasturage there was less need for winter feed. In some regions the type of agriculture was influenced by the ability to substitute natural resources for capital and/or labour: maize growing, for example, was a labour- and capital-saving, land-intensive form of agriculture. American agricultural methods which 'mined' the soil in effect substituted natural resources for labour and capital and so did the use of wooden frame houses. In industry too the lower rents for sites enabled New Englanders to economize in labour and capital in the construction of cotton-textile mills and also to build mills which enabled more effective use to be made of the textile workers and textile machines by allowing them more space. Similarly the American railways were built in ways which, in effect, substituted land for capital, as contrasted with the English railways which were built with disregard for natural obstacles, a disregard which increased their engineering cost.

Almost certainly also, power was cheaper, in relation to capital and labour, along the Fall Line and its supply more elastic than that available to some areas in England, and it may be that the mechanization of the Massachusetts cotton-textile industry was a substitution not so much of capital for labour as of cheap water-power for labour. If, in order to use cheap power, it was necessary to use more capital per unit of output, the high cost of labour gave an additional inducement to the substitution, but if the power was very cheap the substitution might have been profitable even had American wages been at the English level; and in support of the argument it might be pointed out that mechanization was much slower in sectors of the American cotton-textile industry, for example in Rhode Island, where labour was no less dear but where power was expensive. Moreover, water-power was, in effect, substituted for capital as well as labour. The Americans ran certain types of textile machinery faster than the English, and this practice represented, to some extent, a substitution of natural resources for capital. 'Driving machinery at high speed', wrote Montgomery, 'does not always meet with the most favourable regard of practical men in Great Britain; because in that country where power costs so much, whatever tends to exhaust that power is a matter of some consideration; but in this country (that is, the USA), where water-power is so extensively employed, it is of much less consequence.'[2] The American cotton-textile manufacturers also obtained their raw cotton on somewhat better terms than did the English, and this enabled them to economize in labour by using a better grade of cotton; in Lancashire manufacturers economized cotton at the expense of wages, using a great deal of short-stapled cotton. In the construction of ships, clean timber enabled American ship-builders to economize in labour and capital.

This general line of argument is tantamount to the familiar view that the high productivity of American industrial labour was due principally to the fact that it was combined with richer natural resources rather than with more capital, though sometimes more capital per head may have been technically necessary to combine the labour with the resources.

But whatever force this argument may have for the later nineteenth century, in the period we are discussing it is not evident that, with the possible exception of cotton and wood, the natural resources relevant to industrial manufacturing were cheaper in relation to capital and labour in America than in Britain. [. . .] We feel justified therefore in proceeding on the assumption that the dearness of American labour is the most fruitful point on which to concentrate in an examination of the economic influences on American technology.

LABOUR-SCARCITY AND THE RATE OF INVESTMENT

In the immediately preceding subsection we have explained how the dearness and inelasticity of supply of American industrial labour gave American manufacturers an inducement to adopt methods which were labour-productive even though they were capital-intensive. But these characteristics which explain the *composition* of investment would impose a restraint on the *rate* of investment. The shift to the more capital-intensive techniques partly offset the effects of rising labour costs on the rate of profit, to an extent which depended on the adequacy of the existing range of techniques for the purpose. But the offset – in principle at least – could not be complete since, if the more capital-intensive method was as superior in productivity as this, it would already have been adopted in the USA before the rise in wages and in England at the lower wage-level. Once labour-costs had risen, the rate of profit would be higher with the more capital-intensive method than with the less, but it would nevertheless be lower than it was before the rise in the cost of labour, and, on reasonable assumptions, lower than in England; that is, other things being equal, the inducement to expand capacity would now be less than formerly and less than in England. Moreover, unless we assume (as was obviously not the case) that wage-earners were prepared to save the full increase in their earnings, the amount of a new capacity that could be financed was reduced. So long as the volume of investment depended on the profit-rate, investment in the USA must have grown more slowly than previously for, since the machines in the more mechanized methods were more expensive, in terms of output, than the simpler machines, it must now have taken longer for the American manufacturers to accumulate the capital to produce a given output; and on these assumptions investment would also have grown more slowly than in England. In so far as the more capital-intensive equipment employed in the USA was produced in the USA the move to the capital-intensive end of the spectrum lowered the rate at which capacity was expanded to an even greater degree, because the capital-goods industry had to devote itself to producing equipment which was expensive in terms of output. To this extent labour-scarcity was a disadvantage which might partially be offset by substituting machinery, so far as this was technically possible within the range of existing methods, but which was none the less a disadvantage.

To put the matter in slightly different terms, the desire to widen capital was more likely in the USA than in England to run up against rising labour-costs. Hence the desire to widen capital was more likely to lead to its deepening in the USA than in England, deepening being the method of partially offsetting the fall in marginal profit rates. But since, within the range of known techniques, the fall could not be completely offset, it imposed upon the desire of American manufacturers to widen capital a restraint to which English manufacturers were not subject.

This is the sort of situation envisaged by Marx. According to him, labour-scarcity – the exhaustion of the reserve army of labour – would lead the capitalist to substitute machinery for labour, that is constant for variable capital; this would lead to a decline in the rate of profit, a fall in accumulation and in the demand for labour and a consequent replenishing of the supply of labour. The size of the reserve army was maintained by variations in the total of accumulation and in the proportion between fixed and circulating capital. With a smaller reserve army of labour, the tendency to substitute machinery for labour was stronger in America; but by the same token, the rate of investment was subject to a more severe restraint.

In some industrial activities the dearness and inelasticity of labour did in fact exercise a powerful restraint on the rate of investment. This happened even in an industry like the manufacture of small arms where techniques were available which, at first sight, might be supposed adequate to compensate for the high cost of labour. 'High wages', wrote the Chief of Ordnance in a report to the Secretary of War in 1817, 'makes the business unprofitable to the contractors, and ultimately in many cases has occasioned their ruin.' The true rate of profit on the manufacture of arms, when the capital-costs were accurately accounted, was low; and many concerns remained in business only because their primitive accounting concealed the fact that they were, in effect, treating capital as income and failing to provide for depreciation. [...] For these, among other reasons, a very high proportion of the early small-arms manufacturers went into liquidation.

Nevertheless in a number of industries investment was rapid and in the industrial sector as a whole it is at least not evident that investment was slower in America in the first half of the nineteenth century than in England, despite the restraints of dear labour. It may be that the assumption which creates a problem out of this – the dependence of investment on the rate of profit on capital – is not valid; but for the moment we shall retain it, and try to consider what circumstances in America might have exerted a favourable influence on the rate of profit.

One possibility is that the natural resources were cheaper and their supply more elastic in the USA than in England to an extent which offset the effects of its dearer labour. In this case the restraint which labour imposed upon accumulation in America would have been matched by a natural-resource restraint in England. But, as has already been argued, it is not evident that the natural resources most relevant to manufacturing industries were in fact cheaper in the USA and they would have had to have been considerably cheaper to offset the dear labour, since in most industrial products labour was a higher proportion of total costs than natural resources. We must therefore inquire in what ways dearness and scarcity of American labour might have favourably influenced the *rate* of investment. We shall consider three main ways.

In the first place, the American manufacturers had a greater inducement to organize their labour efficiently. The dearness of American labour gave manufacturers an inducement to increase its marginal productivity in all possible ways, and not merely in ways which involved the adoption of more capital-intensive techniques. The shortage of labour in America from colonial times encouraged prudence and economy in its use – Washington, for example, calculated with care the proper output of various types of labour on his plantation. Americans from early times were often faced with a situation where a job had to be done – a house built or a river bridged – with the labour available on the spot, because the place was isolated and it was impossible to attract more labour. This gave them an enormous incentive to use their labour to most advantage, to make use of mechanical aids where this was possible, but in any case to organize the labour most effectively. Possibly lack of domestic servants led to an early rationalization of domestic duties and a corresponding increase in family efficiency; certainly the storage of labour led generally to longer hours of work, to a general emphasis on the saving of time and a sense of urgency about getting the job done. In his account of his visit to America in 1818 Cobbett observed that 'the expense of labour ... is not nearly so great as in England in proportion to the amount of the produce of a farm'.[3] The greater productivity of America, compared with British agricultural labour was partly the result of the fertility of the land; since labour was scarce, land which yielded a lower return per unit of labour was just left uncultivated. It may also have been due to the avoidance of the more labour-intensive crops (for example dairy produce) as well as to the avoidance of labour-intensive soils. The superior physique and education of the Americans may partly have been responsible. Probably also, even in 1818, the American cultivator not only co-operated with superior natural resources, but had superior equipment. But Cobbett seems to suggest that the high productivity of American agricultural labour was in some measure due to the fact that its operations were more efficiently organized. The use of labour in English agriculture was much more wasteful than in English industry, partly from inertia and habit, partly because farm labour was so easy to get.

This labour- and time-saving pattern of behaviour was established on the farm from the early days of settlement – it was an ingrained attitude and not simply an economic calculation – and it was carried over into other activities. 'In England', observed an English visitor to America in 1852, 'we cover our (railway) lines over with superintendents, police, guards, porters and a host of other officials; and relieve the passenger of many of these troubles which, in America, he contends with himself.' 'The American omnibus', wrote the same author, 'cannot afford the surplus labour of a conductor. The driver has entire charge of the machine; he drives; opens and shuts, or "fixes" the door; takes the money; exhorts the passengers to be "smart", all by himself – yet he never quits his box.'[4] This attitude to labour was also carried over into industry and led to the more efficient organization of operations. [...] The most conspicuous example of efficient use of labour is the training that the American manufacturers gave their workers so that each was able to handle more looms. Whereas, in England, the weaver spent some of his time doing unskilled ancillary jobs, the American weaver did nothing but weave. The American arrangement probably involved a somewhat lower output per loom, that is, an increase in capital per unit of output, but there is little doubt that the English manufacturer would have found it profitable to adopt the same method of economizing labour. The point was that his need to do so was less; abundant labour, like the salt on the edge of the plate, tends to be wasted. [...] In the manufacture of small arms, also, specialization of labour was carried much further in England than America, even before there were significant differences in technical processes; in England a workman specialized on one part of the weapons, but carried out all the operations on that part – in the USA several workmen each performed only one or two operations on the part.

Even, therefore, where there were no differences in technology or at least only such as involved the different dispositions of identical machines, differences in the organization of operations may have ensured that the intensity or effectiveness of an hour's labour was greater in the USA than in England, and this tended to make up for the fact that the price of an hour's labour was higher in the USA. It is not an accident that scientific systems of labour management originated in America. [...]

Secondly, dear labour not only provided an incentive to organize it more efficiently. It compelled American manufacturers to make a more careful and systematic investigation of the possibilities of the more capital-intensive of existing techniques. Thus labour-scarcity could have had a favourable effect on the rate of investment in inducing the Americans to adopt, earlier and more extensively than the British, mechanical methods which would have been the most profitable choice even at the lower wages prevailing in England.

Labour-scarcity might, in the third place, have stimulated technical progress. Technical progress, that is movements of the technical spectrum as opposed to movements along it, would, by increasing manufacturing productivity, raise or at least keep up profit-rates, whether the progress was manna from heaven or induced by rising labour-costs. But manna from heaven one would expect to drop more readily in England, since England initially had much larger supplies of technical knowledge. The point about labour-scarcity is that it constitutes a favourable influence on technical progress which was exerted more strongly in the USA than in England. Any manufacturer had an inducement to adopt new methods which made a substantial reduction of cost for all factors. But in their early stages, many of the methods devised in the nineteenth century could not be confidently assumed to effect such a reduction: before they had been tried out in practice for some time, estimates of their costs were highly conjectural. Where the best guess that could be made of a new method was that it promised a reduction of labour but some increase of capital, the Americans had a sharper incentive than the English to explore its possibilities. This is to say that labour-scarcity encouraged not only a careful and systematic investigation of the costs of the more capital-intensive of existing techniques, but the early adoption of any additions at the capital-intensive end which resulted from inventions of purely autonomous origin, even when they were made outside the USA. [...]

In the early decades of the century the principal effect of labour-scarcity in America was probably to induce American manufacturers to adopt labour-saving methods invented in other countries earlier and more extensively than they were adopted in their country of origin. The number of autonomous inventions was greater in the older industrial countries. But where their principal advantage was that they were labour-saving, they were more quickly adopted in the USA and labour-scarcity then induced further improvements, each additional improvement being perhaps small in relation to the original invention. And already in the early nineteenth century there were a number of important American inventions induced directly by the search for labour-saving methods and these became increasingly common as time went on.

Moreover, it was probably also easier for the Americans to adopt such methods. In England, where labour was abundant, labour-saving was likely to involve replacing, by a machine, labour that was already employed; in the USA it involved making a physically limited labour-force more effective by giving it machinery, but without displacing anyone, and with some increase in wages. There was, therefore, less opposition in America to the introduction of labour-saving practices and machines and of administrative methods for economizing labour: the fear of unemployment was less and the likelihood greater of gaining in higher wages from the increased productivity. In England, where there was a superabundant supply of hands and therefore 'a proportionate difficulty in obtaining remunerative employment, the working classes have less sympathy with the progress of invention'.

For the same reasons, more changes in production methods came spontaneously from the workers in America than in England; particularly when the worker had been self-employed earlier in life, and most of all when he had been a farmer, for he carried over into industry the inclination to seek his own methods of doing his job better. Thus in American canal-digging, the English methods were modified by the American farmers who devised a sort of primitive, horse-drawn bulldozer, similar to a device some of them had improvised on their farms. No improvement originated among the Irish navvies who dug the English canals.

If the methods adopted or developed by the Americans did no more than offset the initial disadvantage of high labour-costs, American entrepreneurs would have been on an equality with the English. In most cases, the methods must have done less than this. But in some cases they may well have done more. In exploring the borderland of blueprints, designs and embryonic ideas and hunches which lay beyond the end of the spectrum of existing techniques, it would not be surprising if the Americans hit upon some new methods which were so productive that they more than offset the high cost of labour, methods which reduced labour and capital per unit of output so greatly that they would have been the most profitable techniques even in the case of abundant labour. Very often the substantial reductions in cost came from ancillary developments and modifications made after the new technique had been operating for some time, and these benefits accrued most fully to those who had adopted the method earliest; and the process tended to be cumulative, since the successful application of machinery to one field of activity stimulated its application to another, and the accumulation of knowledge and skill made it easier to solve technical problems and sense out the points where the potentialities of further technical progress were brightest.

Furthermore, quite apart from the effect of labour-scarcity or the incentive and ability to develop superior methods, the shift of American industry towards the more capital-intensive techniques provided the American machine-making industry with an active market which stimulated inventive ability among the manufacturers of machines and machine tools and perhaps also afforded it some advantages of scale. Ability to produce a labour-saving machine in one field also made it easier to develop machines in other fields. Thus the United States developed the typewriter, not simply because in America 'copying clerks could not be bought for a pittance' but also because in Remingtons, the Illinois gunmakers, there were manufacturers available who could put ideas into practical effect. Standardization could be applied not only to final products but to the machines which produced them. [...] For these reasons there were cost-reducing improvements in the production of machines. Certainly by the middle decades of the nineteenth century there were some fields where the cost of the superior machines, relative to that of simpler machines, was lower in the USA than in Britain, and this was an independent stimulus to the adoption of more mechanized techniques in the USA. There were also fields in which a superior machine was available for some operations in the USA but not in England.

Once a number of industries had been established in the USA, a rise in real wages in any one of them due to technical progress exerted a similar effect on choice of methods as the initial high earnings in American agriculture. Where labour is scarce, any increase in productivity and real wages in one sector threatens to attract labour from other industries which have either to contract their operations or install new equipment which will raise their productivity sufficiently to enable them to retain their labour-supply.

In England where labour-supplies were abundant the technical progress in a single industry was not likely to stimulate technical progress in other industries by threatening their labour-supplies. It might, of course, stimulate technical progress in other industries by threatening their markets and in some cases their supplies of raw material; but not by threatening to draw off their labour. Any tendency for wage-earners within the technically progressive industry to establish a claim upon the fruits of their increased productivity was inhibited by the existence of a reserve army of labour, and the benefits of technical progress were likely to be diffused by means of lower prices over consumers as a whole, as in the case of the English cotton-textile industry.

In these ways the scarcity of labour gave Americans a keener incentive than the English had, to make inventions which saved labour. But it also gave them some reasons for being concerned with capital-saving. Throughout the previous argument the assumption has been made that the scarcity of labour biased the American entrepreneur's search for new methods towards those which specially saved labour; since this is what contemporaries seem to assert. But scarcity of labour, by exerting pressure on profits, did also provide some incentive to search for ways of econo-mizing other factors as well. Contemporaries only rarely suggested that dear labour was a reason for saving capital, but Montgomery seems to have been arguing in this way when he wrote: 'the expense of labour being much greater in this country (the USA) than in Great Britain, the American manufacturers can only compete successfully with the British by producing a greater quantity of goods in a given time; hence any machine that admits of being driven at a higher speed, even though it should exhaust the power, if it does not injure the worker, will meet with a more favourable reception in this country than in Great Britain.'

There is another link between labour-scarcity and attempts to save cap-ital. When, from a given range of techniques, the American choice was more capital-intensive than the British, this in itself provided the American entrepreneur with an incentive to reduce capital-costs, in order to modify the large amount of machinery per operative; particularly where there were indivisibilities in the equipment, he needed to get more out of his machines in a given period of time in order to bridge gaps in the spectrum of techniques. He could do this, without any significant change in the technical characteristics of the machine, by running it longer and faster. Both these were methods of paying for the machine in a shorter period of time, that is of diminishing the interest bill on the cost of the machine and increasing the speed at which the amortization fund was built up. Because of the capital-intensity of their output, the Americans saved more on interest charges per unit of output than the English would have. (Thus, though running machines faster and longer is in effect substituting labour for machinery, it is usually a sign of a capital-intensive technique.) Montgomery observed in the 1830s that the Americans ran their cotton-textile factories longer hours than the English and drove their machinery at a higher speed 'from which they produce a much greater quantity of work'. At the end of the century it was said of the American ironmaster that he 'wears out his furnaces much faster than the English ironmaster – in America furnaces require lining about every five years – and argues that the saving of interest on his fixed capital account justifies him in so doing'.

But running machines faster and longer was only one of the ways of re-ducing capital-costs per unit of output. When the capital-intensive labour-saving machines had been installed, there usually proved to be possibilities of technical improvement in their construction and use. For the economy as a whole, one important form of capital-saving consisted of labour-saving improvements in the manufacture of machines, and to such improvements we can apply the previous arguments about labour-saving improvements in general. The cost of machines in terms of output could also be reduced by improvements which increased their performance. Many of the inventions which were capital-saving in this sense were made as a result of attempts to improve machines whose principal advent when they were first introduced was that they were labour-saving. In the textile industries there were few specifically capital-saving inventions. The initial effect of most of the great inventions was to save labour per unit of output at the expense of some increase in capital or at least without much saving. The saving of capital came later from such improvements as the increase in the number of spindles on each mule and the increase in the speed of the spindle. It was the manufacturers who installed the more complicated capital-intensive techniques who were in the most favourable position to make the subsequent improvements of this type. [. . .]

American manufacturers were readier than the English to scrap existing equipment and replace it by new, and they therefore had more opportunities of taking advantage of technical progress and acquiring know-how. This is a convenient place to consider the relationship of labour-scarcity to this American habit. In its extreme form the readiness to scrap is represented by Henry Ford who is reputed to have said that he scrapped machines whenever a new one was invented. But to judge from scattered instances and contemporary comment, this readiness was a characteristic of American industry very much earlier than Ford. The Secretary of the Treasury reported in 1832 that the garrets and outhouses of most textile mills were crowded with discarded machinery. One Rhode Island mill built in 1813 had by 1827 scrapped and recalled every original machine. It would be difficult to parallel this from Lancashire. The English inclination was to repair rather than to scrap, and to introduce improvements gradually by modifications to the existing machines. John Marshall the Leeds flax manufacturer said in 1833 that his concern had 'reconstructed' its machinery twice in the forty-five years or so that he had been in business. In the English textile industry as a whole it is doubtful whether equipment was often scrapped except when a firm went bankrupt. The American readiness to scrap was noticed in other industries. One of the first English handbooks on woodworking-machines observed that 'there are throughout American factories but few wood-machines that have been running for ten years, and if any such exist there is a good and sufficient reason for abandoning them. The life of most machines used in joinery is not on average more than six years . . .' Contemporaries seem agreed on the general pattern of American behaviour: the American got something going, obtained his profits as quickly as possible, improved upon his original plant, and then scrapped it for something better. The problem is to explain his behaviour.

Scrapping is justified on strict economic grounds when the total costs of a new technique are lower than the prime costs of the old. The effect of high wages on decisions to scrap depended on the type of equipment being used and its age. The more mechanized and the newer American equipment was in relation to the English, the smaller incentive the Americans had to scrap in favour of a given new technique. This however does not exhaust the effects of dear labour on the incentive to scrap.

In the first place for a variety of reasons which we have already mentioned, the Americans tended to run machines faster and for longer hours than the English; they also built them in a more makeshift fashion. In these circumstances, though capital per unit of output would still be higher in the USA than in England (otherwise it would have paid the English to adopt the same methods), the capital would be physically used up in a shorter period of time, and the American manufacturer would be in a better position to buy a new machine embodying the latest technique.

In the second place, American manufacturers seem to have expected a higher rate of technical obsolescence than the English. An American friend of de Tocqueville told him in 1832: 'there is a feeling among us about everything which prevents us aiming a permanence; there reigns in America a popular and universal belief in the progress of the human spirit. We are always expecting an improvement to be found in everything.' While a rapid rate of achieved technical progress is favourable to scrapping, expectations about technical progress have a more complicated effect. If the entrepreneur expects technical progress to be rapid, especially if he expects it to be more rapid than it has been in the past, if, that is, he assumes that the latest available technique will have a very short economic lifetime, its high average costs may prevent its adoption. In these circumstances the entrepreneur will put off the decision to scrap until a major technical advance appears, unless he believes that, in order to acquire the experience to take advantage of such a major advance, he must keep up with all the intermediate stages.

But the expectation of rapid technical progress had other influences which were more favourable to scrapping. The entrepreneur who expected new equipment to become obsolete, not so soon as to deter him from installing it, but sufficiently soon for him to want to ensure against the possibility, would not pay for durability. This is another reason for the flimsiness of much of American equipment. [...] The less optimistic expectations about technical progress among the English is one reason for the durability and heaviness of English machinery; no doubt the professional pride of machine-makers was mainly responsible, but if their customers had calculated on a rapid rate of technical obsolescence they would surely have been able to modify the prejudices of the engineers. There is another point. Because the Americans made their arrangements on the assumption that better methods would soon be available, they were more concerned to get their money on new equipment as soon as possible. At the end of the century a French delegation to the Chicago Exhibition reported that American manufacturers invariably seemed to amortize their capital with the settled intention of replacing their machines by new and improved patterns. And this was probably the reason why earlier in the century Americans had the reputation of wanting their profits quickly. Thus technical, economic, and physical obsolescence were more likely to coincide in the USA than in England, at least in those branches of activity in which American expectations about the rate of technical progress were most closely realized.

In the third place, in so far as technical progress took the form of inventing machines which saved labour, but with some increase (or at least no demonstrable saving) in capital-costs it might pay the Americans to scrap when it did not pay the English. The same considerations which warranted the American manufacturer shifting towards the capital-intensive end of the spectrum of existing techniques when he was adding to his equipment might also warrant his replacing existing equipment when new methods were invented at the capital-intensive end. Where labour was abundant, and widening of capital could proceed at a constant wage, there was no inducement to replace existing equipment unless the new equipment yielded a higher rate of profit on the value of the old and new machines together. Where labour was scarce the preoccupation of the industrialist was with retaining or expanding his labour-force. His primary interest was with methods which would increase the productivity of labour and this was a more urgent concern than the return on capital, at least in the short run and so long as the return was enough to service any external finance and provide a conventional minimum return to the manufacturer. Accounting methods in the early nineteenth century were primitive – it was easier to calculate the likely labour-saving of a new process than its capital-costs. Manufacturers had to make their choice of technique on very rough-and-ready calculations on extremely inadequate data. The bias imported into the calculations by the nature of the labour-supply could therefore be a decisive factor. The American manufacturer was averse to retaining old equipment when more labour-productive equipment was available because the old equipment made poor use of his scarce labour. So long as the saving of labour was vouched for, the capital-costs were less important, at least within a fairly wide range, and in the absence of clear ideas and relevant data about the proper components of capital-costs, manufacturers were probably disposed to underestimate rather than overestimate them. But where, as in England, labour was abundant, and there was no pressing *need* to scrap, the calculations *had* to show, in order to warrant scrapping, a *higher* rate of profit on both machines than on the old equipment and the results of calculations in these terms were almost inevitably biased against scrapping. The crucial difference is where the onus of proof rested: in America the presumption was in favour of any equipment which raised labour productivity; in England the presumption was in favour of existing equipment – the onus of proof was on new equipment, it had to be demonstrated that it would yield a higher rate of profit.

The fact that maintenance-costs were mainly labour-costs, and that they tended to increase rapidly with the age of equipment, reinforced the American inducement to scrap; the costs of keeping a given piece of equipment intact were greater than in England.

Given the high costs of labour, and the inadequacy of existing accounting concepts and data, the readiness of Americans to give their labour-saving methods the benefit of any doubt about their capital-costs was a rational one. Even so, in particular cases, it may have led to scrapping in circumstances when it was not justified; the scrapping of old machines and the installation of new ones must sometimes have involved wastes which only capitalists who enjoyed superiority in respect of some other factor could afford to bear. [. . .]

But American readiness to scrap was partly irrational from an economic point of view. The expectation of more rapid technical progress was to some extent the result of the general optimism of the American character, and was initially independent of economic facts, rigorously defined. The Americans were, as Cobden said, a 'novelty-loving people'. In so far as the decision to scrap was taken from mere love of the latest method, it was even more likely to let down those who acted on it. Even in such cases, however, the decision, though 'unrational', may have turned out to be warranted by the eventual course of technical progress. Ford's readiness to scrap whenever a new machine was available might be reconciled with the orthodox criteria by assuming that, though it could not be reliably predicted of the new machines *before* their introduction that they would reduce costs to the requisite to justify scrapping, in more cases than not they proved to do so in practice. [. . .] Possibly also – a variant of the same explanation – the constant pursuit of the latest invention may have led to the adoption of machines which, though not themselves economic, ultimately put those who adopted them in a position to take advantage of later inventions which made spectacular reductions in cost. If the more capital-intensive of the existing range of techniques had the greatest possibilities of technical progress, a persistently optimistic view of the costs of new labour-saving methods led in the long run to the accumulation of experience and to further technical progress which outweighed the waste of capital into which it sometimes led American entrepreneurs.

This technical progress was not without its costs. The pursuit of the latest method must sometimes have dissipated a firm's resources without yielding a commensurate increase in experience. Possibly there was too much imitation of the successful leaders, and the capital-intensive methods were adopted by some concerns which would have been better advised to close down. Expectations about technical progress were not always realized, and equipment which could have been made more durable at modest expense when first installed had to be renewed at greater expense because it had fallen to bits well before new methods became available. Sometimes equipment was so makeshift that it quickly deteriorated, worked very inefficiently, and was costly in repairs. But it seems reasonably clear that on balance and over the economy as a whole, the American habit of not building the equipment to last and the closely-associated readiness to scrap were favourable to growth. For they meant that the American capital stock tended to be younger than the English and to embody more technical knowledge. Once achieved, technical progress in any line became more rapid in America than in England, and this in itself weighed strongly in favour of earlier scrapping; the point we have now been making is that the American propensity to scrap developed *before* technical progress was more rapid in America, and is therefore to be included among the independent sources of such progress. In this field, if not in others, what entrepreneurs expected came to pass because they expected it.

The scarcity of labour may therefore have exerted favourable influences on the rate of investment by inducing (i) a more efficient organization of labour, (ii) a more rapid adoption of autonomous inventions, (iii) a higher rate of technical progress and (iv) greater readiness to scrap existing equipment in order to take advantage of technical progress. There is also another way in which the composition of American investment might have exerted a favourable effect on its rate. The propensity to save out of profits may have been a function of the degree of capital-intensity. A plausible case can be made out for this view. A man who runs a machine is more likely to be interested in the possibilities of mechanization than the man who runs a sweat shop. The industrial capitalist whose capital was tied up in his factory and its equipment was more concerned with technical development than the commercial capitalist under the domestic system – and indeed the gain, in the early days, from any shift from the domestic system to the factory may have arisen principally from the increasing role it assigned to the type of capitalist who was interested in technical possibilities. [. . .]

We can now summarize the argument to this stage. The dearness of American labour and the inelasticity of its supply provide an adequate explanation of why, from a given range of techniques, the choice of the American manufacturer should have been biased towards those which were more productive per unit of labour because they were more expensive in capital per unit of output. The same circumstances might also have exerted favourable influences on the rate of investment by providing an incentive to devise new labour-saving methods, and because capital-intensity of investment increased the ability to devise such methods and also increased the propensity to save out of profits. The main point is the favourable effect of labour-scarcity on technical progress. This might resolve the sort of dilemma emphasized by Marx. It is often said that this dilemma was resolved by autonomous technical progress which sustained the rate of profit. The implication of the argument which we have been pursuing is that technological progress might itself have been the result of the exhaustion of the reserve army and not something introduced from outside the system.

The difficulty about this theory, as of any theory which regards 're-straint' as a net favourable influence on growth, is that it does not, in itself, explain why American manufacturers should have been able and prepared to continue investing in capital-intensive methods to the point where this investment yielded rapid and substantial gains in technical knowledge. Shortages frustrate as well as stimulate.

EXPANSION OF THE MARKET

In most of the preceding discussion we have assumed that the rate of industrial investment was limited by the supply of factors and depended on the rate of profit. We have assumed that, via the rate of profit, the level of investment in both the USA and in England was adjusted to the rate of increase of supply of all factors, and we have considered the consequence of the fact that, when investment increased at these rates, shortages of one particular factor, labour, appeared earlier in the USA than in England. But the rate of investment also depended on the expansion of the market. We must now consider the possibility that, in relation to the total supply of factors to industry, the demand for American manufactures in the first half of the nineteenth century was expanding more rapidly than the English.

This is prima facie probable. The major part of the demand for American manufactures came from the rise in agricultural incomes as cotton-exports from the southern states rose and as the country was opened up and population increased. In contrast, though a substantial part of the demand for English manufacturers also came from an increase in consumers' incomes in primary producing-areas, a considerable part came from a switch of demand from domestic-type industry to English factory industry, and depended on a fall in the cost of the English products. Thus the long-term growth in the demand for American industrial goods probably warranted a rate of investment, in relation to the supply of factors as a whole, which was more rapid than that in England.

Moreover, it is probable that any given increase in demand was likely to lead to a larger increase in investment in America than in England. In England an increase in demand was met from the existing centres of production where there were generally some possibilities of increasing output with small changes in existing equipment. In the USA, because of the imperfections in the product-market which we have already discussed, an increase in demand in a new area of settlement was likely to be met by the creation of new capacity and new concerns within the area, even though there may have existed some slack in the older areas, and without corresponding disinvestment in the older areas.

The rate of investment in relation to total factor-supplies is relevant to our argument in two ways. It is relevant, first, to the effect of factor-supplies on the invention and adoption of new methods. To the extent that investment was pressing more closely on total factor-supply in America than in England, the advance of technology would have been more sensitive to factor-endowment in America. Technology may be expected to edge along, adjusting itself to the relative resource-scarcities, only when there is, to begin with, rough balance between resources and investment – when the increase in capacity is constantly pressing on the available supplies of labour, natural resources and finance. It is in these circumstances that manufacturers are most likely to get clear indications of relative resource-scarcities, that those who adopt methods which are inappropriate to the relative resource-scarcities of the economy are penalized and that a new technique – whatever resource it saves – is likely, when introduced into one firm or industry, to have repercussions on other firms or industries and force them either to contract or innovate. Thus the firms in the USA which in the 1820s and '30s adopted labour-intensive techniques would have been placed in a disadvantageous position in competition with firms in the same or competing industries which had made a more appropriate choice and had adopted capital-intensive techniques. But this was not true to the same extent of firms which adopted capital-intensive techniques in England, the main effect of which would simply have been to depress wages. For the same reason new techniques which increased the productivity of all inputs had a more general effect in the USA than in England. If, in the early decades of the century, the actual rate of growth was higher in the USA compared with the possible rate of growth, this fact must be counted as a circumstance favourable to technical improvement, quite apart from the relative scarcity of labour *vis-à-vis* other factors.

The fact that investment in America was rapid in relation to the supply of all factors except agricultural land gave an incentive to improvements which were capital-saving as well as to those which saved labour. Where the existing techniques afforded no possibilities of alleviating the dearness of labour but the entrepreneur still persisted in the attempt to widen, the difficulty of getting capital would induce him to concentrate on making the most of his machinery in all ways which did not involve the use of additional labour per unit of output. Where the range of existing methods *did* allow the entrepreneur to compensate for dear labour by substituting capital, the adoption of more capital-intensive techniques would provoke the problem of finance even more acutely, especially if the techniques were very effective in saving labour. When investment is pressing against resources as a whole, the temporary resolution of the most severe scarcity is likely to be followed by the emergence of scarcity in some other factor.

A 'scarcity' of capital not only provided the user of machines with an inducement to get the most out of them: it gave the manufacturer of equipment an inducement to provide them as cheaply as possible. Many of the goods, the manufacture of which was most highly mechanized, were not single-use consumer goods but equipment designed to increase labour productivity or at least to meet a production problem (like the steel ploughs which were necessary to open up prairie soils). Where the cost of the minimum feasible piece of such equipment was large in relation to the funds available to the typical user, the demand was very sensitive to its price. This was said to be the case with woodworking-machinery and it was probably also true of some types of agricultural machinery, of such goods as sewing-machines and of such activities as ship-building. This was one reason for the flimsiness of much American equipment. According to the American friend of de Tocqueville, whom we have already quoted, 'one reason why our ships do not last long is that our merchants often have little capital at their disposal to begin with. It is a matter of calculation on their part. Provided that the ship lasts long enough to bring them in a certain sum beyond their expense, their aim is attained.'

Almost every observer pointed to this contrast between the durable English and flimsy short-lived American equipment. [. . .] For this general contrast there are many reasons. The flimsiness of American construction may have been partly the result of the technical inability of American engineers to make high-quality durable machines, and to the high cost of iron and the low cost of wood. It was partly the result of the fact that American engineers were not so long-established a profession, applied less rigorous technical standards and so allowed more weight to be given to economic considerations, in contrast to English engineers who were apt to subordinate economic considerations and who sometimes boasted of the fact. [...] If British purchasers of machines had consulted exclusively economic interests, unconfined by the technical prejudices of engineers, they might have preferred cheaper and less durable machines. But in addition there were quite rational economic reasons why Americans should have attached more importance than the English to building cheap machines of the sort which would bring quick returns. There was the need discussed earlier to modify the burden of the large amount of capital involved in the choice of capital-intensive techniques; though the American chose the more capital-intensive of existing techniques, any given technique was apt to be embodied in a less durable form in America than in England. This need made the American purchaser of machines readier to accept standard products, and less inclined to force upon machine-makers minor, but expensive, modifications. Then there was the expectation of more rapid technical obsolescence. But all these reasons had greater force in so far as investment in America was pressing closely on capital as well as on labour.

In building transport systems, too, the Americans attempted to economize capital more resolutely than did the English. Edward Watkin, a leading English railway-builder, put the contrast between the methods of the two countries at the middle of the century in the following terms:

> The cost of American lines has been brought down by the necessity of making a little capital go a long way, and by the sacrifice of many of the elements of permanent endurance which attach to our railways. We have deemed the inventions of railways a final improvement in the means of locomotion, and we have, therefore, constituted our works to last 'for ever' of bricks and mortar. We have made our rails strong enough for any possible weight of engine; our drainage capacious enough to remove any conceivable flood ... our bridges firm enough for many times the weight than can ever come upon them.

The Americans believed that the English desire for permanence was 'a bar to future improvement; while their [the American] plan for putting up with "what will do" leaves the door open for invention'. These were atypical of the views held by most people who had experience of the two countries. 'In making railways in the United States', said an American witness before the Committee on the Export of Machinery, 'we aim to economize capital, and we therefore are not so particular about reducing the gradients as you are.'

In the construction of railways [said another observer], economy and speedy completion are the points which have been specially considered. It is the general opinion that it is better to extend the system of railways as far as possible at once, and be satisfied in the first instance with that quality of construction which present circumstances admit of, rather than to postpone the execution of work so immediately beneficial to the country . . .

[. . .] The American canals seem also to have been built quickly and cheaply. 'They have built the longest canal in the world in the least time for the least money,' wrote one observer about the Erie canal.

At least in the case of railroads, however, there are some explanations of flimsy and rapid American construction which are independent of desire to economize on capital. Thus, over its entire lifetime, an American railway was likely to be less intensively used than an English railway and therefore did not need to be so well built. There was also in America a much greater disparity between intensity of usage in the immediate future and in the longer run. In America a system big enough to carry the load expected when the new region was fully opened up would be much too big for the traffic in the years immediately after building; and therefore the railways were built in ways which allowed them to be modified most easily when the increased demand came. The English, who could expect the load soon after building to be not dramatically below is maximum, had no reason not to build to last from the start. Rapid building was also prompted by the desire to obtain strategic advantage in relation to other competitors, which involved covering as much territory as possible despite limited resources; and by the wish to qualify for land-grants, which were a function of miles built. In these ways some of the differences between American and British railway-engineering can be explained without supposing that the Americans were more interested in saving capital per unit of output. But it is probable that an additional reason was that a higher rate of return on capital was expected of public utilities in the USA than in Britain, and this would result in lower capital-intensity. British canal- and railway-builders tended to project on the basis of 5 or 6 per cent rather than the industrial rate of profit. The Americans required more, and even 1 or 2 per cent more could make a substantial difference in projects in which capital is important in any case.

In a number of instances, therefore, the rapid rate of American investment, in relation to factor-supplies as a whole, was a reason for American interest in methods of economizing capital, over and above the reasons previously discussed.

The long-term growth of the market as a result of rising incomes in agriculture and the filling up of the country is relevant to the argument in a second way: it sustained the incentive to widen capital. According to the argument in an earlier section, the level of real wages in American industry was set by the absolute level of investment in relation to labour-supplies, subject to the minimum below which real wages in manufacturing could not go, a minimum determined by earnings in agriculture. The desire to widen capital – because of the production of tariffs and high transport costs and the filling up of the country – which determined the level of investment, came up against rising marginal labour-costs, and therefore led to capital-deepening, in order partially to offset the fall in marginal profit-rates. But, within these assumptions, the fall in marginal profit-rates could not be completely offset and would therefore reduce the desire to widen capital which was the impulse which set the whole process in motion. If one introduces technical progress, whether autonomous or induced by the fall in profit-rates, this would help to keep up profit-rates and might raise them, thus maintaining the desire to widen. The relevance of the long-term growth in demand is that it would help to sustain the level of accumulation for normal widening-purposes even in periods when technical progress was sluggish. The growth in demand, that is, contributes to resolving the problem of reconciling the rate of accumulation with the bias towards capital-intensity. This explanation would not be inconsistent with those offered at an earlier stage in the argument but it might render some of them otiose.

Notes

1. V. S. Clark, *History of Manufactures in the United States* (Washington, 1929).
2. James Montgomery, *A Practical Detail of the Cotton Manufacturer of the United States . . . Compared with that of Great Britain* (Glasgow, 1840), p. 71.
3. W. Cobbett, *A Year's Residence in the United States of America* (1818), p. 320.
4. E. W. Watkin, *A Trip to the United States* (1852), pp. 130, 139.

II.2

The American Impact on British Industry, 1895–1914

S. B. SAUL

It has long been customary to discuss the condition of British industry immediately before the First World War in gloomy tones, to stress the weaknesses and shortcomings and to indicate how rapidly its rivals were moving ahead. In this paper I want to suggest that the situation was more complicated than is sometimes made out; that there is much evidence of an awakening in certain vital sectors during these years and that this recovery owed not a little to the spread of American ideas in the engineering industry in particular. Amongst other things such a view is a matter of considerable moment to any analysis of the debate over tariff policy which began to rage at the turn of the century. That campaign had military and imperialistic connotations of course, but from a purely economic point of view it is important to discover exactly where the advantages of free trade lay and how serious were the encroachments of other countries. I propose, therefore, to discuss the American impact upon British industry with this more general theme constantly in mind and in the final section to try to draw the two strands together.

There is no space here to trace in detail the successes of American goods in overseas markets before 1914; largely they were due to a new technology in which the major elements were standardization and mechanization, the use of interchangeable parts and the development of the art of management to plan and co-ordinate these processes of mass production. Firearms, sewing machines, typewriters, agricultural machinery and watches were some of the products of this new approach. During the last few years of the nineteenth century more and more American goods began to appear on the British market; 'machinery of all kinds down to patent hair curlers; fresh meats to liver pills; oil stoves to mouse traps; cotton seed oil to shaving soap'. Financiers moved into Atlantic shipping and London transport, the meat trust into Smithfield. Some alarm and despondency was generated by the heavy imports of neat, beautifully finished American

Originally published in *Business History*, 3 (1967), pp. 19–38.

shoes which came to challenge an industry that had fallen way behind technically and commercially. Yet it is significant that British firms reacted with remarkable speed; shoe makers went to the United States and came back to introduce new methods, stylings, and fittings. Changes in manufacturing techniques were encouraged by the American United Shoe Machinery Company establishing a subsidiary to import and, after the Patent Act of 1907, to make the latest machinery. 'There can be no doubt that the boot and shoe industry is now in process of a more sudden and complete revolution from a hand to a machine industry than any other great English industry,' noted an American report in 1904.

Another surprising feature of the American 'invasion', as it was called, was the unprecedented import of locomotives. Though it was only short-lived, this episode aroused a most searching enquiry in the technical press over the relative merits of British and American engines and manufacturing methods generally. Here was an industry in which Britain considered herself supreme, but so fast were American engines making their way in overseas markets that many wondered if there were not certain fundamental weaknesses in British practice. The answer seemed to be that each country manufactured to suit its own needs. The British was a beautifully built, expensive engine, very rigid and requiring good track and ballasting. The American, though less perfect technically, was cheaper, more flexible and rode better on a poor track which the British engine had a tendency to jump. The crucial fact from the point of view of exports was that most overseas tracks were mediocre at best and American engines gave greater satisfaction, holding the line better, taking sharper curves and causing less wear. The Americans also had the advantage in that their locomotives were less complex, parts were made interchangeable and the design standardized so that it was possible to build for stock. The difference was one of technical versus commercial perfection which British engineers too often ignored. For this the locomotive builders sought to blame the consulting engineer who was the keystone in the organization of their trade.

The practice of employing an intermediary, unconnected with buyer or seller, was common in Britain whereas in the United States such an outside designer was rare. If used at all he simply issued general specifications to bidders who then offered such of their stock designs as were suitable. The British consultant, his detractors urged, ignored commercial factors because he had no stake in the matter beyond his fee; 'he was more concerned in maintaining a reputation for infallibility (or for being different) than in endeavouring to execute the work in the most economical manner. In short, money – other people's money – was no object.' Locomotive builders complained bitterly of the engines designed for the Indian and colonial railways which they said were too perfect technically, were subjected to unnecessarily strict testing procedures and were made yet more expensive to build since no attempt was made at standardization. Consequently colonial governments had to pay dearly for unsuitable engines and the makers had no firm basis from which to build up an export trade with non-colonial countries.

At this time too, several contracts for bridges in the colonies were awarded to American firms. The most famous of these was the Atbara bridge in the Sudan which was urgently required for military purposes. The Pencoyd works at Philadelphia actually delivered for shipping in six weeks – much earlier than any British offer – and though the price was a secondary factor, the best British offer was half as much again as the Pencoyd. Again the consultants were blamed for designing entirely new bridges for each occasion and rendering impossible the degree of standardization achieved at Pencoyd. In the United States many bridges were constructed to pattern as multiples of a given span, the builder being responsible for his own design. On the other hand, as the journal *Engineering* commented, 'In this country it has been the custom since iron bridges were first constructed for each engineer to design his own bridge with the main object of making them somewhat different to every other engineer's design.' Possibly some of these designs were more pleasing aesthetically, but they were certainly expensive and provided no good production base for an export trade. These practices were deeply rooted and would take long to change but at least the American successes brought their methods vividly to the fore and, behind all the cries of woe, there was much informed discussion which helped to initiate slow but definite progress towards greater standardization.

Possibly the sector of the engineering industry to come most powerfully under American influence was the machine tool trade. During the first half of the nineteenth century men such as Maudsley, Nasmyth and Whitworth had led the world with their lathes, planers, slotting and shearing machines. But after 1850 it was American builders who took the initiative with the machine tools and precision gauges which alone made interchangeability possible. None of these machines had more influence on productivity than the turret lathe. Probably first developed in England, the idea was taken across the Atlantic by emigrant craftsmen; such lathes were used for some time in the shops of tool builders and first sold commercially in the 1850s. The turret was a round or hexagonal block which rotated about its axis with a hole in the middle of each side into which tools were inserted and brought successively into contact with the work. In its automatic form it was often called a screw machine but in fact it was ideally suited to the production of many kinds of duplicated small parts, since drilling, boring, turning and facing could all be done in the same machine. Another radical change came through the milling machine in which the ordinary cutting tool of the planer or shaper, for example, was replaced by a rotating disc or drum with teeth cut in the rim. With its continuous motion the machine was technically more perfect than the reciprocating tools, which wasted power on the return stroke; it had a broader working edge than the traditional tools and, above all, unlike them could cut to any geometrical shape. Milling machines were used for many operations which had previously been carried out laboriously by hand, but one vital development was their adaptation for the cutting instead of casting of gears. It was most important to obtain accurate gears as the speeds of mechanisms began to increase so markedly and when the automatic machine appeared in 1877 it became possible to produce them cheaply and in quantity. The grinding machine largely displaced the more costly scraping and became indispensable in any shop working to fine limits. There was too the micro-caliper for machinists which played a major part in raising standards of accuracy. Pre-eminence in design and manufacture passed over the Atlantic; it was a serious matter, for the machine tool trade was a vital education for many others and by losing it Britain was falling behind in other directions as well.

These machine tools found their way only slowly in England outside the government arms factories, which gave a large order to Robbins & Lawrence of Windsor, Vermont during the Crimean War. In 1865 Charles Churchill, son of a New England engineer, became the first distributor in London to deal exclusively in American tools. His business began to prosper in the 1870s when the Brown & Sharpe milling machines first came to Britain and one of the first complete plants tooled by him was the gatling gun works, opened in Birmingham in 1889 under an American manager. Many saw and were convinced and for the next six years orders rose by 15 to 20 per cent a year. The real turning point, however, came with the bicycle boom.

During the 1890s a craze for the new safety bicycle swept the country and for the next few years the industry expanded rapidly. Considerable numbers of American machines were sold in Britain but most of them were so poor that they did little more than engender widespread distrust of the quality of all American goods. On the other hand, the boom itself had a varied and vitally important impact upon British manufacturing methods. One writer thought that its great contribution to mechanical engineering came in the machinery for making ball bearings, first introduced in Coventry in 1893. Another was the development of steel stampings by American manufacturers to replace the old heavy machined castings, but pride of place must go to the consequences of the bicycle boom for the machine tool trade. Here, almost for the first time in Britain, was an industry requiring numerous standardized parts in large quantities and many firm were starting business with no antiquated appliances or traditional ideas to hamper them. Hundreds of American machine tools were imported. Charles Churchill's were loaded with orders and were forced to increase their capital in 1897. Exports to Britain from four leading American machine tool makers rose from £86,165 in 1895 to £337,528 in 1897. The upshot was to give a great boost to the manufacturer of these tools in Britain and also to make industrialists throughout the whole engineering trade deeply aware of the significance of the new American methods.

British machine tool makers certainly had plenty of leeway to make good. Firms in the north had long dominated the trade and some continued to do so in the heavier class of tools. But it is clear that many had long been resting on their laurels and were utterly indifferent to new ideas. The view of a *Times* correspondent was:

> It must be admitted that the machine tool shops of Lancashire and Yorkshire have not maintained their early supremacy. They have remained at the head of certain classes of manufacture but in regard to others in which innovation has been most active the inspiration has nearly all come from America and has been caught on this side in the Midlands rather than the North.

In addition, whereas most American firms built one or two machines and could therefore employ mass production methods in their manufacture – moulding machines, for example, which were little used in Britain – and could better afford the initial outlay on jigs, cradles, etc., nearly every British firm attempted to produce the whole range of tools and many other things as well. Worse still, many British makers had come to regard themselves as professional men, above the hurly burly of commerce, and accustomed to instruct their customers as to what was good for them. Engineering firms were almost clients of particular makers, and made little attempt to bargain and compare one tool with another. With but few exceptions the machine tool industry in Britain had degenerated into the most unscientific of the mechanical engineering trades; rule of thumb methods and the minimum of calculation were the rule, catalogues were full of useless generalities and design was at a standstill. American machines were not accepted without criticism, of course, even among their most enthusiastic supporters. Their convenience for the worker, accessibility and numerous ingenious devices were all widely applauded, but many argued that they were too light, and certainly the poorer makes were often frail and unstable. The British tradition was for heavier and more durable tools – a doubtful advantage in a period of rapid innovation. Both sometimes went to extremes, but in the best American models the amount of metal required had to be carefully calculated, whereas the British method was said to be to give about enough metal and add 50 per cent to make sure!

Certain firms led the way in the revival, and of these probably the most notable was Alfred Herbert's of Coventry, now the largest machine tool firm in Europe. Alfred Herbert began business on his own by taking over a small engineering concern in Coventry with the help of capital from his father, a Leicestershire farmer. Soon he turned to making simple tools and components for the expanding cycle trade. Luck then played a part for, through his brother, Alfred acquired the sole selling agency in Britain for the weldless tubing made by a French firm. With this windfall as the financial basis he committed himself more deeply to machine tool making. In 1890 the first turret lathe was made, and seven years later the firm acquired the services of an American engineer, Oscar Harmer, who immediately reorganized the works and greatly extended the turret lathe output. At this time they also secured the agency for several American machine tool makers. Herbert's employed only 12 men in 1887; a decade late there were 500, and by the middle of 1903 the number had risen to 930. The machines were widely praised in the technical press and stood out at the cycle shows of the late 1890s which were otherwise dominated by American tools. In 1905 an office was opened in Paris and four years later another in Berlin to deal with enquiries for their machines, and an American report of that year noted that more of their machines were to be found on the Continent than any other British make. Their plant was described as one of the finest in Europe 'with methods that are essentially American' and of their hexagon lathe it was noted, 'it would seem that the best American features, coupled with a British sense of stability have been united in this design'. It is significant that in 1912 when an important American firm, the Fellows Gear Shaper Company of Springfield, Vermont, needed a new shop superintendent, they brought in a man who had been trained by Alfred Herbert's.

Progress in the industry was most marked in the Midlands but the revival was in fact very widespread. *The Times* was soon writing of 'stagnation having given way to many-sided developments'. More important is the testimony of overseas experts; the *American Machinist* observed in 1907 that the Olympia Exhibition of that year had shown that if American builders decided to inaugurate another campaign for trade with Britain, 'they will find a different condition of things from that which prevailed ten years ago'. Two years later it was reported that machines formerly almost wholly of American origin – universal grinders, special turret lathes, light and medium drilling machines – were now built regularly for stock by British makers, and in 1911 a correspondent referred to the rapidly narrowing gap between European and American methods. A French businessman told another American journal that though the French automobile industry had been built up on American machine tools, so great had been recent progress that French car builders could get all the tools they wanted from Britain, Germany and to some extent from France. One of the most penetrating observers of the trade, Joseph Horner, wrote of its vitality; 'existing conditions are such that no manufacturer, however eminent, can feel sure any one type of machine or machine tool ... may not be superseded if not rendered obsolete at no distant period'. The remodelling of lathe design he described as 'absolute, astonishing and amazing'. Many firms found it necessary to extend their shops; in 1901 Charles Churchill had bought a small works in Salford for 'tooling up' imported machines; five years later he opened a works at Pendleton and developed there a manufacture of precision grinding machines which did much to encourage their use in Britain. The older manufacturers of reciprocating machinery, now faced with the rivalry of milling machines, set about remodelling their planers and shapers for higher speeds and seeking ways to offset the loss of power on the return stroke. For them the electric motor was especially valuable and indeed there was an all round increase in the use of individual electric drive for machine tools. Undoubtedly the revival was much helped by the discovery of high speed steel by the Americans, Taylor & White, in 1898. Various Sheffield firms took up the new steel with great energy and soon achieved world pre-eminence in its manufacture. Enormous stresses were now carried at the point of the tool and demanded not merely that the drive be powerful but also that the carriage and indeed the whole machine be heavy. What had been a debatable fault in British machine tools now become an essential virtue. It was a great stroke of fortune, and firms such as Tangyes and Armstrong Whitworth were soon producing huge high speed lathes and dominating the market, causing the *American Machinist* to comment on the 'tremendous strides (that) have been made in the last three years'.

Of course all the deficiencies were not made good by any means. Exports from both Germany and the US were much greater than those from Britain. American statistics show that exports of 'metal working machinery' to Britain were well maintained, averaging £342,000 per annum from 1897/98 to 1901/02 and £368,000 from 1907/08 to 1911/12, though more than anything these figures indicate how eagerly British industry was modernising its equipment. Some highly specialized tools were not made in Britain because the market was too small – precision lathes and multiple spindle drilling machines for example. Chucks for holding the work in the lathe were still largely imported and there was room for considerable improvement in the use of gear cutting machines. Moulding machines were only making their way against great prejudice and were almost all imported. Nevertheless, the American impact had done its work and with the growing pressure of demand from the motor car and electrical industries, the years from 1900 to 1914 saw rapid if belated strides made by this vital sector of Britain's economy.

The rejuvenation of the machine tool trade was accompanied by a parallel awakening in many other trades. It was not before time for, with certain exceptions such as shipbuilding, the engineering industry was certainly desperately backward in its use and understanding of machine tools. This scathing comment was made by *The Engineer* in 1898:

> It is impossible to go through most shops in this country without finding a more or less large proportion of tools which are only fit for the scrap heap. Curiously there is nothing which an engineer grudges so much as money spent on machine tools, which are, so to speak, the very life blood of his establishment.

Years before the same journal had warned that British machine shops were too slapdash, spending huge sums on machines that were not kept up: 'surfaces meant to be flat are not flat, things that should be round are oval, that which should be straight is crooked ... Our duty is to warn our readers in good time and urge upon them more and more the imperative necessity of maintaining their reputation against the world.' Many overseas visitors were impressed by the poor relationship between masters and men which did so much to inhibit the development of more modern manufacturing methods.

> Nothing is more frequent than the remark that the working man does not need more than so many shillings a week ... This view among employers has prevailed for so long and is so nearly universal that their every effort is to obtain more work for a traditional wage rather than to decrease the cost of production by means which will justify a higher wage ... Workingmen have come to accept the view widely too and it is the acceptance of this theory of status which is at the bottom of the deadlock in British industry.

In these circumstances workmen, unlike their American counterparts, rarely offered new ideas and when they did were likely to be rebuked for 'cheek'. As for machine tools, managers often knew little and cared less what their men thought of them. 'We give a man a tool suitable for the work he has to do and if he don't like it there are others that will' was the attitude found by an American observer, and a Manchester journal wrote of the 'stinging reproof that rings through every shop in England – "you are paid for working, not thinking"'. Yet it was the view of a high official in a major American tool firm that their superiority derived above all from improvements suggested in the shops.

All this obviously could not be changed overnight by the American example but nevertheless there is much evidence of a widespread improvement in engineering practice even outside those industries in the Midlands and the South which had less trouble from these traditional shortcomings. In 1900 the *American Machinist* was remarking upon the changed atmosphere. Sneers and disgust at American ideas in the technical and daily papers had turned to open-mouthed admiration; 'only those who are acquainted with the facts know what a paralysis was taking hold of the engineering trades of this country as a result of unreasonable methods' but now had come recognition of the need for change 'and men who were foremost in opposing improved methods and tools have even been found abusing the English shops for lacking such things'. Some years later an American consul made this comment:

> No one who has not lived in England during the last seven or eight years can realise how great has been the awakening here nor how changed the British mental attitude is regarding new ways of doing things. There has been much wise and clever adaptation to British cheaper labour of American machinery ideas.

Other reports spoke of automatic machinery which had hitherto been unknown outside arms factories and a few cycle works finding its way rapidly into the leading engineering establishments. Electrical engineering, steam turbine, and gas and oil engine builders were particularly affected and hosts of machines were sold to produce castings and forgings, for cutting off, grinding, and sharpening in all manner of works.

One of the most important features of American establishments was the tool room, where tools of special sizes were kept for stock and constantly checked for accuracy. All kinds of machine tools were employed there for making and sharpening tools – work of great precision which was carried out by skilled mechanics, less skilled labour now being required for repetition work in the machine shops themselves. In itself the tool room was not a new idea but in Britain the practice had generally been for the machinist to sharpen and reset his own tools in the shop. There each machine soon became the centre for the accumulation of tools, many of which were eventually lost, and in any case many workers were not competent to carry out such skilled operations accurately. Even where a tool room had existed, it normally consisted of no more than a forge and a grindstone but with precision tools these were utterly inadequate for the task. With the new machines, tools could be set and kept up only by first class craftsmen, and the advantages of a tool room of the American type were so obvious that the method was widely adopted in progressive British works in the two decades before 1914. The development of interchangeable manufacture in the United States also encouraged the use there of new wage systems of which the Halsey Premium Bonus plan was probably the most famous. In a modified form it made its way rapidly in British engineering works from about 1898 onwards and in turn helped to bring about important modifications in machine tools themselves. Such payment systems made it more important than ever to ensure absolutely correct speeds for each operation and new kinds of variable speed mechanisms were introduced for this purpose.

Naturally the pace of change varied between one branch of engineering and another and between different areas. In the Midlands one reads of wide developments in the use of drop forgings, of cut gears being substituted for cast on a growing scale and 'in this industrial awakening more and more firms were seeing the value of an official whose sole job was to ensure a continuous flow of work to each tool'. On the other hand in 1912 *The Times*, though praising what had been done, castigated the engineering centres of the north for continuing to grudge every penny spent on improvement and for renewing nothing until absolutely obliged to do so. This malaise was to take longer to dissipate but clearly the lessons were being learned most thoroughly in the places which were to be the key centres of engineering in the future.

By the mid 1890s the electrical engineering industry in Britain was lagging way behind its competitors in Germany and the United States. Undoubtedly this was partly due to faulty legislation, which paralysed for a time the development of both supply stations and electric traction, but certainly too it derived from a general suspicion of the industry which followed the wild speculative boom and subsequent losses of the early days. Because of the slow growth of public supply, for some years the only field for heavy electrical engineering was for private supply to shops, hotels, large houses etc.; every installation was different, standardization impossible and as a consequence business tended to be ruled by the technician and not by the businessman. Electrical engineering took on a tinkering character; many of its leaders were telegraph and telephone men, inventors, wiring contractors, good enough in their fields but rarely engineers in the broad sense. The supply industry came to be organized as a collection of small stations with quite grotesque differences in practice and in equipment. Most of the machinery for these early stations was supplied by British firms, for it was plant of a simple nature, requiring no great engineering skills for its production, but the industry remained ill prepared to meet the challenge when much larger power stations and electric traction came along with far more complex demands. The industry had its bright spots of course. Mather & Platt, a Manchester general engineering firm, had obtained from Edison the first British rights to his dynamos and did considerable pioneer work for electric railways and industrial electrification. A Wolverhampton firm, the Electric Construction Corporation, makers of the Elwell–Parker motor and possibly the biggest works solely devoted to electrical engineering in Britain at the time, attracted the attention of an American manufacturer of dock machinery. In 1893 the Elwell–Parker Electric Company of Cleveland, Ohio, was incorporated and began making motors to the British design, the ECC taking 7½ per cent of the initial stock issue. The firm of Willans & Robinson had some 2,000 of their central valve engines installed in power stations in the decade after the first was built in 1885 and drew worldwide attention on account of their works organization and extreme use of interchangeability.

But even the best in Britain could not approach the growing technical and financial strength of foreign firms and by the mid 1890s their competition was being fiercely felt. American influences had been strong from the first. As early as 1880 the Anglo-American Brush Electric Light Corporation had been formed to acquire for £200,000 the Charles Brush arc lighting patents. American engineers and foremen were brought to the works at Lambeth and a nephew of Brush was made chief engineer. The Babcock & Wilcox safety water-tube boilers, which were widely used in power stations, were also of American origin. Boilers were manufactured in Britain in part of the Singer Company's works at Glasgow from 1881 onwards but not until 1891 was a British company formed to take over all Babcock & Wilcox's foreign business, and even so American shareholders still retained a substantial interest in the new company. In 1889, a Westinghouse subsidiary began to distribute their products in Britain; the Thomson–Houston Company three years previously had formed the firm of Laing, Warton & Down for the same purpose. They began to supply more and more equipment for ordinary generating purposes and when tramway construction belatedly got under way in the mid 1890s these two firms used their already wide experience to dominate that market both as regards the power stations and the cars themselves. The car bodies were usually, though by no means always, built in Britain but apart from the need to import motors and controllers, the difficulty lay in producing a suitable truck. In a horse tram this was a simple mechanism but in electric trams it formed an integral part with the motor, transmitted the driving power, and needed to carry greater weights at faster speeds. Up to 1900 every truck was imported from the American Brill or Peckham companies. The peak of this competition came with the building of the Central London Underground Railway. The electrical equipment was obtained from the American GEC for approximately $450,000 and the 49 electric elevators were supplied by the Sprague Company at a similar cost. In the generating stations six engines of 1300 hp each were purchased from the Allis Company of Milwaukee which had already taken many orders in Britain for its powerful slow speed engines. It was estimated that of the 300,000 hp of steam engines used in generating plants for lighting and traction purposes at this time 73,000 was American and of the 200,000 kw capacity of generators in use 71,000 came from American machines.

The recovery of British industry was certainly helped by one stroke of fortune. No sooner had the design of massive reciprocator-driven engines been brought to practical perfection by the Allis firm and others, than Charles Parsons transformed the situation with his steam turbine. The first turbine was used in a power station at Newcastle in 1888 but it was only in 1900 when the city of Elberfeld boldly ordered from Parsons two 1,000 kw units, that the capabilities of the turbine were demonstrated on a large scale. All this coincided with and much encouraged the campaign in Parliament for larger electric supply areas. Reciprocating sets, though magnificent feats of engineering, had almost reached the limit in size, and power station development as we know it could not have taken place but for the smaller dimensions and higher efficiency of the turbine. Soon after Parsons' patents expired in 1904, ten British firms were making Parsons-type turbines and several sold rights to American firms. The Parsons monopoly had already been broken when the American GEC began to build the Curtis impulse turbine and by 1914 most of the turbines made in Britain were of the impulse type. Even so, Parsons had made his great contribution towards recovering ground lost to American engine makers and still in 1914 supplied a turbine to a Chicago power station with four times the capacity of any built to that time.

In the electrical engineering industry proper there emerged, around 1900, several new works fully capable of meeting this overseas competition. Using American techniques, managers, engineers, capital and research to varying degrees, operating on a considerable scale with the most up to date machinery, they dominated the industry which had so recently been a pitiful collection of inefficient, unprogressive, small firms. The two

American companies which had previously only traded in Britain opened large new factories. The British Thomson–Houston Company began manufacturing at Rugby in 1902 and by 1911 could claim that they had supplied a third of the tramcar equipment then in use and three-quarters of the motors for Britain's electric railways (including London Underground lines). Even more spectacular was the huge Westinghouse factory erected at Trafford Park, Manchester. Despite strong promotional activities and many orders for power stations and tramways at home and abroad, however, the firm was never able to obtain sufficient orders to justify the size of the initial investment. One adverse factor was their strict adherence to American designs, which they tried with little success to force upon the customer – a mistake that machine tool makers avoided. British Westinghouse were never popular and their financial difficulties caused some jubilation in other sections of the industry for they were widely accused of responsibility for the bitter price cutting which plagued the industry after 1900 as they sought business for the vast plant at almost any price.

A third firm, though of British parentage, followed American ideas and methods closely from the first. Late in 1899, under the leadership of the Kilmarnock engineering firm, Dick Kerr & Co., the English Electric Manufacturing Company was formed and began manufacture at Preston with an American engineer, Sidney Howe Short, as technical director. Short had pioneered the conduit system of electric traction and several new types of electric motor and when the Walker Company, with which he was associated, amalgamated with Westinghouse, he was free to cross to England. Under his direction the works were laid out and equipped with the most modern American machinery and soon work was begun on generators for the London surface tramways, the largest machines made in Britain to that time. An American journal commented that 'it speaks volumes for the progressive policy of English Electric that they are enabled to do such work shortly after their reorganization'. In 1902 the new company was absorbed by Dick Kerr; shortly afterwards an electric car building works, also controlled by them, was amalgamated with two others and by 1905 the group was capable of turning out 1,000 complete cars a year. With its electrical engineering, general contracting and steam turbine manufacture as well, Dick Kerr became one of the most important and progressive firms in the industry.

Possibly the largest firm at this time was the General Electric Company, which had begun business in 1887 and moved into heavy electrical engineering on a large scale at a new works in Birmingham just before 1900. Here the influence came from Europe rather than the USA, and they manufactured in several vital fields under Continental licences – particularly the new polyphase motors and metal filament lamps. GEC fought a bitter and successful struggle to break the Continental monopoly of the supply of carbons to this country and undertook the manufacture of telephone equipment, which to that time had also been largely imported. Other developments included the building of a large new works at Stafford by the Siemens Company, which was then leased to the parent German firm. Rapid if unprofitable progress was made in the production of heavy equipment there, more especially electric locomotives for export and machinery for industrial electrification. The Brush Company had moved into an existing works at Loughborough in 1889 and much extended them, placing the shops, significantly enough, under an American engineer. In the supply of tramway equipment they were pioneers in many ways, being the first British firm to make their own trucks and the first to build all steel cars.

The overall effect of these changes is hard to measure. For tramways and for local supply station equipment foreign competition was largely eliminated. In the contracting field gains were made too. In 1900 the well-known New York firm, J. G. White & Co., established a subsidiary in London to handle all their extra-North American business; by 1906 they had completed tramway contracts worth over £3m and had others in hand worth £2m. The Sprague elevators which had won the large contract for the London Underground in 1899, developed serious faults in practice and disappeared from the market; later elevators for the underground were provided mostly by British firms.

Huge strides had been made, though this is not to deny that the industry faced serious problems. Internal competition was acute, for home capacity had expanded rapidly, foreign firms still had open access to the market and demand was not growing as had been hoped. By 1906 the basic tramway network was complete and the invention of the metal filament lamp effected such an economy in the use of current as to leave the supply undertakings temporarily with excess capacity. British railways, in many cases poorly managed and heavily overcapitalized, took advantage of the technical dispute over third rail or overhead transmission to delay plans for electrification. Great hopes were placed upon electric drive in textile mills but very little was done. The electrical industry was at fault for not studying more closely the special problems involved, but steam drive in many mills had been brought to such perfection that electric drive was normally only worth while in new mills, and the great boom in building had come in Lancashire between 1905 and 1907 before the necessary electrical equipment had been fully developed in Britain. Nearly every electrical engineering firm was in financial difficulties between 1906 and 1910, and many were forced to cut down already meagre research staffs and fall farther behind in new techniques and ideas. Yet while British firms struggled for the highly competitive work for public bodies, overseas firms concentrated on the less competitive contracts for industrial electrification where they had greater experience and a long lead in the manufacture of AC motors. In many shipyards, collieries and steel mills their machinery was paramount.

These difficulties of British industry were heightened by a disastrous lack of standardization and by the small degree of combination and co-operation which was achieved, almost insuperable obstacles in an industry where the economics of large-scale production were so great. The weakness in financial power was serious too. Foreign firms often had strong support from financial institutions and on several occasions were able to secure large contracts for schemes financed by their backers. Nor could British firms help to finance electrical engineering projects at home. Whereas textile machinery and steam engine makers, for example, were often prepared to accept payment in mill shares, few electrical engineering firms, in their parlous financial condition, could afford to emulate them. They were forced to form connections with tramway and contacting concerns but with many of these financially embarrassed too, the gains were distinctly limited.

In 1913 output in Britain remained well below that in Germany and the USA. British exports of electrical goods, apart from cables, did not compare with those of Germany, but all this should not be allowed to conceal the very real progress that was made. The table below shows that exports of electrical machinery, for example, were growing much more quickly than imports.

British Trade in Electrical Machinery
(annual averages. £000)

	1904–7	1908–10	1911–13
Exports	688	1,463	2,010
Imports	515	524	1,107
Imports from Germany	164	322	749
Imports from USA	417	159	285

(Note total imports are imports less re-exports, but imports from Germany and the USA are gross imports. Re-exports were something like 7 per cent of total gross imports.)

The establishment of American branch plants obviously helped to reduce imports of American machinery and the table indicates how successfully British industry pushed for overseas markets during the depressed years from 1906 onwards, when internal competition was so acute. Certainly the pre-war boom brought a considerable rise in imports from Germany but with home output of electrical equipment rising quickly in those years too, there is no doubt that from 1910 to 1914 industrial electrification was at least going forward very rapidly. The point reinforces our evidence of a renaissance in engineering generally at this time and indeed the electrical industry itself argued that it was after rather than before the war that British industry began to lag most seriously in its use of electricity.

This brings us back to our point of departure – the implications of American industrial competition for British tariff policy in the early years of this century, and the general interpretation of British industrial progress at that time. Certainly there were no grounds for complacency but we have argued that it would be equally incorrect to exaggerate the short-comings. Much progress had been made in following and adapting the American example but the latest advances in all too many industries continued to be made abroad, and for many products manufactured by mass production techniques Britain still depended on imports from the USA or upon assembling parts manufactured there. Precisely why Britain was lagging is difficult to say. Differences in size of internal markets alone will not suffice, though perhaps the argument gathers more weight when one includes the concept of 'social depth' of demand which made the US a paradise for the sale of standardized products. Without further detailed information it is difficult to know how far differences in factor prices played a part. Capital was probably cheaper in Britain, though it was not always readily available for new ventures. It is true that there was a relative abundance of skilled labour in Britain but this did not prevent the more forward-looking British firms from quickly adopting American techniques once they were well known, even though they had not pioneered the way. There is certainly much evidence to show how seriously the weight of tradition hindered industrial progress – in methods of working, in industrial relations and particularly in the form of a wanton disregard for the commercial aspects of business life.

Yet it would have been a serious mistake to have attempted to cure all this by restricting foreign competition. In all the industries we have discussed, imports from overseas helped to create new demands and to stimulate British industry to action. It was the absence of enterprise during the 1870s, '80s and early '90s in the engineering industry above all which set Britain behind, but when American and German exporters began to exploit this weakness, the response, especially in the newer trades, was immediate. As we have shown, their example began to bring changes in the more traditionally inclined industries too. Even had the reaction been slower, it would have been disastrous policy to deny British industry the opportunity of learning about and using the new tools and factory methods. It has been argued that imports made it difficult for British firms to reach a scale of production large enough to become viable, but in the electrical engineering industry at least this was a minor matter compared with their inability to organise into less numerous units. As it was, it still remained convenient to import machinery such as precision lathes and moulding machines where demand was not yet sufficiently great to justify laying down special plants to their manufacture in Britain.

There are serious pitfalls facing those who generalize too freely over the shortcomings of British industry at this time. Certain sectors obviously were more vigorous than others but it is extremely difficult to measure these divergencies, especially when they exist between different geographical areas of the same industry. The difficulty is heightened by the fact that, in the absence of such figures, progress is often analysed through foreign trade statistics, which are more readily available. These are at best ambiguous. As our analysis shows, imports may continue to rise, not necessarily because the producing industry at home is inefficient, but simply because industry in general is becoming more aware of the potentialities of the product. This happened with machine tools and electrical machinery just prior to 1914. One must remember, too, the growing importance at this time of licensing arrangements and the establishment of branch plants overseas, which could both much affect the pattern of trade. Parsons, for example, sold few turbines in Europe or the United States, though thousands of that type were soon in use there; on the other hand, almost every diesel engine and electric lamp made in Britain before 1914 was manufactured under foreign licence. Some economists have based their arguments on figures for imports of 'manufactures' into Britain but here even more confusion arises. At the height of the 'invasion' over 40 per cent of American exports to Britain under this category consisted of refined oils, copper, leather and wood manufactures, none of which competed seriously with any major British industry. True competition was largely confined to those industries using interchangeable methods – machine tools, sewing machines, typewriters, agricultural and electrical machinery. In 1913/14 these provided about a half of Britain's imports of American machinery.

These difficulties of measurement therefore make it all the more important to study complex industries such as engineering with the greatest care, sector by sector. Here we have concentrated upon machine tools, which were basic to the whole industry, and electrical engineering, which was to be so crucial for all future developments. The automobile industry would repay similar attention and older trades such as locomotive engineering obviously had problems of their own. It is clear that both the sectors we have studied and others, such as the footwear industry, gained immensely from the American 'invasion' – from the stir to action, from new tools and factory methods, from direct investment, from the experience of American engineers who came to work for so many British firms. And as these industries belatedly matured so their influence permeated back through the whole engineering trade and began a rejuvenation of old fossilized trades. Industrial change is always a complicated process, with growth and stagnation side by side between and within industries. It would be difficult to think of a period when this was so more than in those last two decades before 1914.

III   The City

The nineteenth century witnessed massive urbanization in the two societies. Our third section explores aspects of cities and their growth and starts with a short comparative survey of the urbanization process by Leon S. Marshall. Social history has come a long way in the years since this essay was first published and many of its conclusions are now questionable, but it still provides a valuable starting point for exploring the subject.[1]

Comparative studies of criminal law enforcement systems are well advanced. The development of professional police in London and New York, contrasting the impersonal authority of the former with the personal authority of the latter has, for example, been the subject of a book-length study which suggests that the difference sprang from the understanding of legal power and of government in the two societies.[2] Clive Emsley, by contrast, is concerned with a particular form of policing. His essay considers the dual role of the police in upholding the law and maintaining the peace during the industrial disputes. He explores police organization and the principles and authorities that guided the police in the performance of these duties in order to explain variations in police practice, above all, the greater disorder and violence of American as compared with British policing of strikes in the first half of the twentieth century.

The final two pieces are both concerned with the social implications of changes in the physical environment. Mark Clapson, in a specially commissioned essay, compares the growth of cities and suburbs to reveal aspects of urban development that are concealed by attending only to the experience of a single country. His essay examines both the sources of suburban dispersal and the myths, images and ideological representations of that movement in literature and empirical social inquiry in order to identity the comparative significance of suburbanization for social change.

David Ward's essay, the final piece in this section, takes up this transport theme by comparing the suburban development of Boston and Leeds. He explains the different conditions which determined the differing pattern and extent of such development in the two cities. The essay underlines, implicitly, the value of the skills of historical geography for the social historian.

Notes

1   For example, Marshall believed that crime and disorder increased with urbanization, but for arguments that crime at least levelled out from the middle of the nineteenth century in both countries see V. A. C. Gattrell. 'The decline of theft and violence in Victorian and Edwardian England', in V. A C. Gattrell, Bruce Lenman and Geoffrey Parker (eds), *Crime and Law: The Social History of Crime in Western Europe since 1500* (London, 1980) and Erick H. Monkkonen, *Police in Urban America* (Cambridge University Press, 1981). The comparative point might also be made that although Britain was an urbanized society well before the United States, she never appears to have been more violent, more disorderly or more crime-prone.

2   Wilbur R. Miller, *Cops and Bobbies: Police Authority in New York and London, 1830–1870* (University of Chicago Press, 1977).

III.1

The English and American industrial city of the nineteenth century

LEON S. MARSHALL

Cities throughout history have been the focal points of civilization; and the association of such cities as Babylon with the ancient Oriental empires, Athens with Greece, Rome with the Mediterranean empire of the Caesars and with medieval Christianity, and Venice and Florence with the Renaissance are commonplaces in history and literature. Although trite from frequent repetition, true and significant is the observation that, with all that cities have been, in no previous age has urban society had so complete domination over the life of mankind as at the present. To the student of English or American history, therefore, the rise of the industrial city of the nineteenth century is particularly important, for in that history may be found the origins of many of the critical problems troubling our own disjointed and embittered society.

The supremacy of earlier towns over their neighbouring countrysides was due to the domination of commerce over industry: that is, the facilities of the city for the distribution of productions beyond the means and requirements of household and simple agrarian economy stimulated the productive energies of the surrounding population and, in consequence, the economic needs of the city set up the pattern of economic life existing around it. In the present day, however, the economic system created by the industrial city has approached the solution of the problem of production, but has created a new set of problems arising out of that of distributing the wealth produced by this modern industrial system.

In an economic sense, an industrial city is one whose resources are almost wholly devoted or subordinated to the producing of *form* utility – the shaping of raw materials into goods for human use. London, Liverpool and New York, where manufacturing plants are only incidental to the principal business of the city, are commercial rather than industrial cities

Originally published in the *Western Pennsylvania Historical Magazine*, 20 (September 1937), pp. 169–80; reprinted in Alexander B. Callow Jr (ed.), *American Urban History. An Interpretive Reader with Commentaries*, 3rd edn (Oxford University Press, 1982).

since exchange (wholesale, retail, or financial) together with transportation is their chief activity. On the other hand, Manchester, Birmingham and Pittsburgh, even though they are not now so predominantly characterized by factories and mills, are industrial cities because their wealth, population and economic activities are largely devoted to the supplying of their factories and those of the surrounding communities with the essentials of industrial life, and their prosperity is dependent upon that of their leading industries.

In the first half of the nineteenth century, Manchester, Birmingham and other towns in England developed into industrial cities according to a pattern which recurred in Cincinnati, Pittsburgh and other American cities whose leading businesses were transformed by the industrial revolution. The adoption of a series of labour-saving inventions and of improved processes of manufacture led to the concentration in factories of the cotton industry around Manchester, iron industry around Birmingham and woollen manufacture around Leeds, where facilities for labour, power and capital were abundant. The increased prosperity and the demand for labour accompanying this concentration of industry brought in a flood of immigrants to these towns. The earlier balance in a town society composed of gentlemen, merchants and artisans was shaken to its roots by this influx of what soon became an urban proletariat badly housed, subject to extremes of temporary affluence and poverty, and not easily adapted to the discipline of town and factory life. On the other hand, self-made capitalists accumulated fortunes by amazing combinations of luck, foresight, determination and energy. Recognizing their importance in the community and in the nation, these frequently uncultured and ruthless factory owners seized political leadership from the older dominant interests, and ultimately forced government to protect and foster the system that had enriched them. At the same time, green spaces and quaint old buildings disappeared as land was needed for offices and warehouses, and beyond the new 'business districts' grimy factories pushed rows of jerry-built dwellings past the original limits of the town. Disease, poverty, crime, industrial conflict and social animosities broke down the traditional institutions that had controlled smaller and more orderly populations, while the bewildered and alarmed inhabitants strove to erect new political and social machinery to control and refine the social revolution that was going on around them.

Wherever this pattern of development recurred, its most striking effects appeared in the growth of urban population. By 1860 more than half the people of England lived in cities and factory towns, and by 1920 more than half the population of the United States lived in urban centres. In the first fifty years of the industrial revolution, the American, as had the English

cities previously, received the greatest impact of the population movement. Paterson, New Jersey, grew from 7,500 in 1840 to 68,000 in 1890;
Philadelphia from less than a hundred thousand to over a million in the
same period; and Pittsburgh and Allegheny from 31,000 to a third of a
million fifty years later. Chicago, Cincinnati, Milwaukee, Kansas City and
scores of other cities rivalled this growth, and the rise of the automobile
industry produced a recurrence of this phenomenon in the twentieth
century.

The influx of population was much more rapid than the expansion of
housing facilities. Congestion affected all classes, driving first the wealthy
and later the middle classes to the suburbs; but for the incoming workers,
too poor to afford better, the only accommodations were cheap lodging
houses, and run-down tenement buildings from which absentee landlords
derived as much rent with as little expense as possible while awaiting the
profits of rising real-estate values. Five families living abroad and con-
tributing little to the community in the form of taxes or improvements of
their property drew most of the rentals from Pittsburgh's slums, a fact that
accounts for much of the great following of Henry George's single-tax
programme in Pittsburgh.

Until epidemics of cholera, typhoid fever and smallpox terrified the
middle classes of townspeople into attempting sanitary reforms, the disease
and death lurking in the dark squalor of the slums was hardly known to the
general public. Whether in England or America the discoveries made by
sanitary reformers reveal a depressing similarity. Manchester, with 200,000
inhabitants, had scarcely a sewer, irregular scavengers' carts hardly touched
the filth that rotted in dumps to make it more marketable as fertilizer, and
until the middle of the century the town's water supply was not sufficient
for more than one-third of its population. Such facts as these explain why
in 1841 the average expectation of life at birth in Manchester was only a
few months over twenty-four years. In America, a little later, few cities
possessed half as many miles of sewers as of streets, and half the latter were
unpaved. Fully one-third of the houses in the 1880s relied upon private
vaults and household utensils for the disposal of human waste. A large part
of Philadelphia's million inhabitants drank water from the Delaware river,
into which had been emptied daily 13,000,000 gallons of sewage. Typhus,
typhoid and scarlet fever were the natural concomitants of such sanitary in-
adequacies, and Pittsburgh's share in this ghastly record consisted of the
highest mortality rate for typhoid in the world between 1899 and 1907, or
1.30 per thousand.

Public philanthropy tried first to stem this invasion of disease and death
by erecting hospitals, of which Pittsburgh added eight between 1882 and
1895. Street improvements because of the demands of traffic proceeded

more rapidly than improvement in sewage, which also involved scientific knowledge as well as expense to property. Although building societies for the erection of model cottages were common in the English towns as the result of experience with congestion, only a few such attempts were made in the United States, and only where industrial corporations erected model 'company houses' in the new industrial areas were these successful. Except in the new cities of the West, such as Salt Lake City, the United States lagged far behind England in city planning.

A report on a survey of Pittsburgh in 1908 pointed out another feature of industrialism: 'an altogether incredible amount of overwork by everybody, reaching its extreme in the twelve-hour shift for seven days in the week in the steel mills and the railway switchyards'. Although the report considered the proportion of women in local industries as 'menacing', Pittsburgh's mills were not so adaptable to the labour of women and children as were canning and textile factories, where light though fatiguing routine made possible their employment because of their cheapness and amenableness to discipline. In the single decade of the 1880s, the number of children employed increased from 1,000,000 to 1,750,000. In spite of ten-hour laws the usual working day in many industries, even where women and children were employed, was twelve hours. Although the labour of women and children was not new, the factory and the industrial city created new problems of family disintegration, fatigue, delinquency and industrial superannuation, and impressed the criticalness of these problems by the vividness of the industrial scene. The public reaction to these conditions were the factory and public-health movements in England in the 1830s and 40s, and state agitations in America for ten-hour laws and legislation for sanitary improvements.

Legislative protection for women and children in industry in response to the demands of public opinion was achieved more rapidly in England than in America. Using as an accepted principle Sir Robert Peel's Act of 1819, which attempted to remedy abuses in the employment of children in cotton mills, societies of English humanitarians and factory workers forced Parliament to pass the Factory Act of 1834, the Mines Act of 1842, and the Ten Hours Act of 1847 in spite of the mill-owners' appeal to the currently accepted theory of laissez-faire in the relations between the state and industry. In America the manufacturing interests entrenched themselves in the state legislatures behind the argument that regulatory legislation would enable industries in those states not having such regulations to ruin the manufacturers of the states where the employment of women and children was limited. In spite of this opposition the national Eight-Hour League succeeded in obtaining such laws in six states. Although the effect of these laws was greatly vitiated by lax enforcement, the enlightened opinion aroused by the agitation, the example of a few states, and the constant pressure of shorter-hours advocates brought a gradual reduction of the hours of labour and an improvement in health conditions in American factories.

The increase in leisure afforded by the shorter-hours movement and the belief that the open air of the country made the agricultural population healthier than the urban produced considerable activity in the founding of parks, and in the census of 1880 the acreage and description of such places received a prominent place in the report for each town. A Boston society in 1880 provided sand gardens for children, and by 1898 thirteen other cities in the East had established children's playgrounds. Philanthropic organizations such as the Women's Christian Temperance Union, the Society for the Prevention of Cruelty to Animals, the Society for the Prevention of Cruelty to Children, the State Charities Aid Association and the Red Cross were established to deal with other problems of industrial life.

The human animal appeared to be changing his habitat and his manner of living with all the effects known to biology of such changes in animal life. The entire effect upon human physiology of the transition in dwelling place and even in diet (particularly because of the widespread use of factory-made foods) has not even yet been determined, for historians of this period have given their attention principally to the alterations of the industrial environment by which the inhabitants of the city tried to make it a more suitable place for living. That improvements were possible was due in large part to the greater productivity of the new system of manufacture and distribution.

Startling as was the growth of population in the towns of the nineteenth century, it was far exceeded by the increase in productions. In the last half of the century American textile production increased sevenfold, agricultural implements twenty-five, packing fourteen, and iron and steel ten. In this increased productivity, labourers as well as capitalists shared. If Professor Clapham is correct, industrial wages in England advanced 40 per cent and the cost of living decreased 17 per cent in the sixty years after 1790; Miss Coman has estimated that in the United States wages increased 12½ per cent and prices decreased 40 per cent between 1867 and 1900;[1] thus there were approximate net gains of 70 and 86 per cent for the English and American workingmen, respectively, in the margin between earnings and subsistence as compared with the initial years. While capital gains from this improved position appear in the increase of savings-bank deposits and in insurance, the mass of wage earners did not invest in either of these but spent the difference upon a higher standard of living which the greater variety of manufactures made possible.

From the point of view of the city the significant fact was that this increased economic productivity and the improved economic position of the mass of its inhabitants with respect to subsistence did not bring economic security. The replacement of skilled labourers by machinery produced a series of crises in various trades. This and the constant lowering of the limit of industrial superannuation added constantly to the number of unemployed. The competition of women and children and of immigrants of low standards of living augmented suffering and discontent. Finally, incapacitation from industrial accidents and disease completed the demoralization of a large section of labour and made poverty a norm of existence even in prosperous times. Commenting on these conditions, a French visitor to Manchester in 1844 thus compared the poverty in the old with that in the new cities, 'At Paris, half the population go to the hospitals and almshouses to die. At Manchester, half the births take place in the public charities.'[2]

Cyclical depression, which appeared in both England and the United States almost regularly every decade after 1815, demonstrated the failure of the new system to provide economic security to the labouring population. During the depression of 1837 a charitable society in Manchester found 40,000 pawn tickets, representing an indebtedness of $27,500 at 16 per cent in 4,000 working-class homes. In the United States nearly half a million were thrown out of work on the railways alone by the panic of 1873, only 400 out of 666 furnaces were in operation in the following spring, bread lines were common in every large city, and wages fell on an average of 10 per cent and did not reach their former level until 1890. During the panic of 1907 the surveyors of Pittsburgh reported: 'Low wages for the great majority of the labourers employed by the mills, not lower than in other large cities, but low compared with prices – so low as to be inadequate to the maintenance of a normal American standard of living; wages adjusted to the single man in the lodging house, not to the responsible head of a family.' To Englishmen and Americans who remembered that under the domestic system the wage earner had owned a plot of ground to supply him with food in bad times and that in earlier days the West had offered homesteads to oppressed craftsmen, the pre-industrial era appeared as the golden age now replaced by suffering and chaos.

Of Manchester in 1844 Léon Faucher said: 'At the very moment when the engines are stopped ... moral order ... disappears in an instant. The rich man spreads his couch amidst the beauties of the surrounding country, and abandons the town to the operatives, publicans, thieves, and prostitutes, merely taking the precaution of leaving behind him a police force whose duty it is to preserve some material order in this pell-mell of society.' A visitor described Pittsburgh in 1880s as 'hell with the lid off'. Pittsburgh, Chicago, Detroit and Cincinnati were centres of organized crime, and in the nation the homicide rate quadrupled while the population doubled. The failure of the police to cope with this growing disorder was accompanied by a series of embittered industrial disputes, which appeared to be the first skirmishes of a social revolt.

Between 1816 and 1850 scarcely a year passed without a great strike in either the cotton industry or the building trades in Manchester, while these conflicts were increasingly supported by unions in other cities. The panic of 1873 produced a long strike in the New England textile mills. A 10 per cent cut in wages in 1877 precipitated the first nationwide railway strike marked by battles between soldiers and workmen in Baltimore, Reading and Pittsburgh. The workers of Baltimore foreshadowed the contemporary sit-down strike when they seized the railway yards and prevented the moving of trains, and in Pittsburgh the defeat of the militia gave control of the town to a lawless mob for two days. The bloody Homestead strike of steel workers in 1892 inaugurated an almost continuous series of strikes and lockouts lasting during the remainder of the century.

To restore order to a society that appeared near self-destruction, the philanthropically-inclined wealthy and other community leaders attempted to strengthen the church, the schools, charitable institutions, and the local government. In England, the distress uncovered during the cholera epidemic led six wealthy Manchester philanthropists to found the first statistical society in the world in 1833 'to assist in promoting the social improvement of the manufacturing population' by 'collecting facts concerning the inhabitants'. Clergymen, merchants and manufacturers supported monitorial schools under rival organizations in the 1820s; temperance societies, mechanics' institutions, and savings banks in the 1830s; and associations to promote public health, factory reform, public parks and national education in the 1840s. The leaders of the new British manufacturing communities neglected few opportunities to inculcate what they believed to be the virtues of urban citizenship: knowledge of the 'useful arts', temperance, industry and thrift.

So closely parallel were the problems of the cities within the industrial pattern that the counterpart of each of the foregoing activities might be found in the history of almost any American manufacturing city. Local and national scientific associations took up the task of fact-finding. Washington Gladden of Columbus, Ohio, and other clergymen supported the rights of labour in its battle with capital and reorganized their congregations into 'institutional churches' with charitable and educational agencies. American advocates of broader educational opportunities were more successful than the English in obtaining the assistance of the state to education, and illiteracy dropped from 17 to 11 per cent in the last twenty years of the century. In adult education the business genius of Redpath and Horner combined with philanthropy and local patriotism in an attempt to raise the general level of culture through the lyceum and the Chautauqua movement.

As philanthropy and mutual assistance proved at best only ameliorative, the pressure of these problems and of the interests affected by them was greater upon government. In the 1760s the residents of Manchester had congratulated themselves on their lack of a municipal corporation, but in 1790 they began to create a series of new governmental agencies to perform tasks too complex for the traditional institutions. Beginning with watching and poor relief, the local government added before 1850 the regulation of hackney coaches (the traffic and transport problem of the day), street improvement, water supply, gas lighting, fire protection, sewage disposal, and market and public park administration. As in American municipal growth, this progress was accomplished by struggle with vested interests and against corruption: Manchester had a 'boss Nadin' sixty years before New York experienced 'boss Tweed'.

There is not sufficient space within the limits of this article to present details illustrating the expansion of American municipal government, but the facts are sufficiently well known and depart but little from the Manchester pattern. Whether contemporary municipal government has restored the order and security demanded by its citizens is still an open question but not a new one, for the issue has been raised in each town as it has developed into an industrial city and is inherent in its life, as, indeed, are each of the problems that have been suggested as elements in the history of English and American industrial cities in the nineteenth century.

While the conception of a pattern of development is of invaluable assistance in the study of the rise of contemporary society, the student of this history must realize that four points of differentiation between the English and American industrial revolutions make parallels and analogies not only hazardous but if not carefully done very misleading. Briefly these differences are: first, the priority of the industrial revolution in England; second, the existence in England of privileged classes strongly intrenched in government and in social influence; third, the powerful influence of the agricultural West and South in America; and fourth, the enormous proportion of foreign-born population in the United States due to immigration. In these differences, however, lie additional reasons why the American social scientist should be intimately acquainted with the evolution of the English industrial city.

The first great advantage in the study of the English pattern in the nineteenth century is that in the earliest phases the basic processes of a society undergoing industrialization appear in relative simplicity, since the historian has but to consider the impact of a relatively few new developments upon a traditional background. With the passing of the West and the industrialization of the South, those purely American differentiations will be of less importance in analysing the continuation of the processes at the present time. Finally, the influence of foreign immigration upon the United States may not have exerted so differentiating an effect as might be supposed, and because of the present immigration policy and the rapid Americanization of the descendants of the foreign-born the greater part of this difference in conditions is bound to disappear.

The Industrial Revolution, it has been said, has been succeeded by a scientific revolution, industrial capitalism by finance capitalism, urbanization by metropolitanization, but the process is not yet complete, and as long as remain the problems created by the Industrial Revolution – the control of disease, poverty, and crime by urban communities, the raising of cultural standards necessary to urban citizenship, and the removal of economic insecurity – social scientists and historians will be interested in the American and English industrial city of the nineteenth century.

Notes

1. John H. Clapham, *The Early Railway Age, 1820–1850* (Cambridge, 1930), pp. 561, 601, 602; Katherine Coman, *The Industrial History of the United States*, rev. edn (New York, 1925), p. 306.
2. Léon Faucher, *Manchester in 1844: Its Present Condition and Future Prospects* (London, 1844), p. 145.

III.2

Police and industrial disputes in Britain and the United States

CLIVE EMSLEY

The maintenance of public order during industrial disputes is one of the most contentious and dramatic of the task of police forces. The New Police in England[1] were created in the midst of the massive changes in the economy which are commonly described as the Industrial Revolution. As a result of this, and as a result of other nineteenth-century states looking to the English police model at a time when they also went through an industrialization process, some historians and social scientists have been tempted to see the New Police largely as a body designed to discipline and hold in check the new working class. Such an interpretation is rather too mechanistic and over-simplistic; yet it is true to say that the New Police were created, at least in part, to establish a new perception of order on the streets and that, as the nineteenth century wore on, the police were increasingly recognized as the first line of defence against riot and disorder. The aim of this chapter is to explore how the police of England and the USA were employed during industrial disputes from the late nineteenth century to the beginning of the Second World War. The comparison is used as a means of highlighting differences and similarities between the organization and practice of the police in the two countries.

While English local government had prided itself on its independence since the late seventeenth century, England was, nevertheless, a unitary state within which the population clearly perceived itself as being English. The USA, in contrast, was a federal state; individual state legislatures were jealous of their independence from the federal government in Washington; the ethnic mix brought about by the enormous immigration of the nineteenth and early twentieth centuries meant that while there was an 'American Dream', it remained somewhat problematic as to what an American actually was. During the second quarter of the nineteenth

I wish to thank the ESRC for financial assistance towards my research on the police. An earlier version of this chapter appeared as 'Polizei und Arbeitskonflikte – England und USA im Vergleich (1890–1839)', in Alf Lüdtke (ed.), 'Sicherheit' und 'Wohlfahrt'. Polizei, Gesellschaft und Herrschaft im 19. und 20. Jahrhundert, (Frankfurt am Main, Surkhamp, 1992).

century the British Parliament had passed a series of acts establishing police forces; the County and Borough Police Act of 1856 was the climax of this legislation, making the creation and maintenance of police forces obligatory on all local authorities in both counties and municipalities. This act also provided for an inspectorate to supervise the different police forces and award certificates of efficiency. Such a certificate initially entitled a local authority to one quarter of the cost of the pay and clothing of its police from government funds; after 1874 the government grant for efficient forces was increased to one half of the pay and clothing costs. In the USA during the nineteenth and early twentieth centuries there was no federal legislation regarding police forces; there was no system of inspection and no government aid. Policing remained rooted in local government and quite independent of federal supervision.

While numbers fluctuated a little, between 1890 and 1939 there were just under two hundred police forces in existence in England and Wales in any one year. These forces were of three kinds. The largest was the London Metropolitan Police, and this was the only force completely independent of local government. The Commissioner of the Metropolitan Police was responsible directly to the Home Secretary, and while political radicals and some Liberals argued for local government control, the argument was always deployed that the Metropolitan Police had too many 'imperial' tasks – notably the protection of the royal family, of government – to be granted any supervision of the force. In provincial cities and towns, in contrast, the municipal police forces were under the direct control of civilian watch committees appointed by the elected town councils. It was possible for the watch committee to give direct operational orders to its chief constable. The chief constables of the county police forces had rather more independence. Before 1888 a county chief constable was responsible to the police committee of his county's bench of magistrates; but after the local Government Act of that year, which introduced elected county councils, the chief constable reported to the Standing Joint Committee (SJC) of a county. The SJC was made up of an equal number of magistrates and elected county councillors. But while the watch committee of a city or town could meet at least once a week, the SJC of a county might meet only quarterly, thus giving the chief constable much greater independence from civilian supervision. Moreover, the law itself granted the chief constable of a county much more freedom of movement; he alone was responsible for appointing and dismissing his men, while in the towns this authority was vested in the watch committee. The system of watch committees and SJCs was not static. There were increasing encroachments by central government as ministers and their civil servants found it easier to correspond directly with chief police officers rather than having to go through local government. Such encroachments gathered momentum in the industrial disorders immediately preceding the First World War, and during the war itself. At the same time the police increasingly saw themselves as experts and professionals in matters of crime and public order. This led both to the police seeking to distance themselves from local supervision, and also to some local authorities sanctioning a degree of this distancing in the belief that the police were indeed the experts and the professionals in such matters – this was especially the case with watch committees who, in theory, had much greater controls of discipline and supervision than SJCs.

In the USA during this period there were thousands of separate police forces. Those in the big cities, especially along the eastern seaboard, were similar to the municipal police in England; the police chiefs of these cities were appointed by, and generally subservient to, the elected mayors and municipalities. But while these police chiefs may, in some measure, increasingly have been regarded as professionals and experts, there was no national authority similar to the Home Office to encroach on local control and foster a degree of police independence. In the smaller townships and counties the police chief was himself a local politician who stood for popular election as sheriff and then swore in his own deputies. The early twentieth century saw increasing developments in state police forces responsible to the state governor: as will be explained below, these forces were often created primarily to deal with industrial disorder, but they also became deeply concerned with the supervision of the major highways, a task which expanded considerably as a result of the development and growth of motor vehicles.

The English police were never at the beck and call of an employer simply to maintain industrial discipline. However during the nineteenth century, in several instances, the law appeared to many to have been structured in the interests of the employer.[2] The police were never employed as strike breakers, but were deployed to prevent a breach of the peace. Legislation in 1875 authorized peaceful picketing by members of a trade union engaged in an industrial dispute and the Trade Disputes Act of 1906 confirmed this situation; but picketing remained a murky area in law and the discretion of the police on the spot remained paramount in determining its extent – it was, for example, alleged in Parliament in the summer of 1914 that in some instances members of the Metropolitan Police 'themselves have decided that not more than one picket shall be allowed'.[3] Ugly confrontations in strikes commonly began between strikers and men imported to replace them – 'free labour' (in the employer's parlance) or 'blacklegs' and 'scabs' (in the words of the strikers). Such confrontations generally resulted in the police being deployed to prevent violence, but in reality this meant the protection of the 'free labour', and in practical terms this could not help but contribute to strike breaking. There were also others who might need police protection in a trade dispute. During a miners' strike in County Durham in 1891 the county police were deployed to prevent disorder when 'Candymen', or bailiffs, were sent into the village of Silksworth to evict strikers from company housing. Evidence surrounding the affair is contradictory: there were allegations that some of the 'Candymen', disgusted with their job, tried to desert, and that the police were instructed to prevent this. There seems little doubt that a party of loyal 'Candymen' and their police protectors were pelted by a crowd; and there is no doubt that fifty police made a ferocious baton-charge into the crowd, inflicting injuries on men, women and children. The incident gave rise to a stormy parliamentary debate, but the Home Secretary could argue that the local control of the police meant that the whole affair was nothing to do with him: 'I beg ... to point out that these police are not in my hands.'[4] Allegations were also made in Parliament that partiality within the SJC prevented discussion of the affair, and that partiality on the part of local magistrates led to the dismissal of assault cases against the two superintendents in charge of the police on the occasion of the incident; all to no effect.[5]

Two years after the Silksworth affair a miners' strike in the West Riding of Yorkshire resulted in fatalities, and, in consequence, more precise instructions to the civil power about how to respond to industrial disorder in general, and to riot in particular, were prepared. Strikes and employers' lock-outs meant that by the beginning of August 1893 there were over 80,000 miners idle and 250 pits closed down in the West Riding; the West Riding Police had only 1,042 men with many other demands on their time, notably the Doncaster Races, which were thought to require the deployment of 259 men early in September. It was precisely at this juncture that the situation in the mining districts deteriorated as crowds began to enter colliery yards and demand the end to any continuing surface operations. The manager of Ackton Hall Colliery at Featherstone requested police protection for his surface workers; the Chief Constable informed him that, unfortunately, none was available, but he arranged for a magistrate to meet a squad of twenty-eight soldiers at the pit. The appearance of soldiers inflamed the situation; the soldiers were stoned and ultimately responded by firing on the crowd, leaving two dead and fourteen injured.

The shooting at Featherstone provoked an outcry; it had been believed that the police had, over the previous half century, generally replaced the army in dealing with disorder, and no-one had been shot by troops during a riot since the Chartist period. An enquiry was set up to investigate the events[6] and the following year an inter-departmental committee was appointed to define the responsibilities of policemen and soldiers in the event of riot and, particularly, to consider the circumstances in which the latter might aid the former. The committee concluded that troops should only ever be used as a last resort. It urged police forces to enter into mutual aid agreements with each other as a means of bringing greater constabulary force to bear in the event of civil disorder; police forces had aided each other since the mid-century, and the Police Act of 1890 had recommended that formal agreements be made for mutual aid, but few such appear to have been agreed before 1895. The committee suggested that, in the counties, the chief constable was the man best placed to recognize the need for requisitioning troops in an emergency; in the boroughs, however, given the authority of the mayors and watch committees, any such demand was to go through the mayor.[7] Local independence, and the structure of the Common Law, meant that these recommendations were not always followed in the next few years. Some county chief constables, often former military men themselves, appear to have preferred having troops readily available when confronting disorder rather than relying on their own, and their neighbours', police constables; and some magistrates, sometimes large-scale employers themselves, preferred to use their power under the Common Law to requisition troops when and where they considered it desirable. Perhaps also it was just too much trouble to organize mutual aid agreements; in 1908 only 30 county forces and 27 borough forces, out of a total of 187, had entered into such. In the same year the Home Office issued a circular to the police forces attempting to limit the use of troops; it instructed that any request for troops should go to the Secretary of State for War as well as to the local commanding officer, and it also suggested that the recruitment of temporary, special constables might be considered for an emergency.[8] But it was a wave of strikes between 1910 and 1912 which, thanks to a determined interventionist Home Secretary, Winston Churchill, brought about a marked erosion of the local direction of army and police.

In the spring of 1910 a new and aggressive shipping firm, Houlder Brothers, upset the well-established relations between unions and employers in the docks at Newport in Monmouthshire. An agreement reached between employers and unions was repudiated by Houlders who sought to bring 'free labour' into the port and demanded police protection. The Watch Committee feared serious disorder and even bloodshed; having sought the advice of the Home Office the committee refused police protection and threatened to use their police to prevent any 'free labour' being brought into the docks. The Home Office turned to the Crown Law Officers for advice; the latter replied that the grave nature of the situation justified the action taken since protecting the 'free labour' could have been provocative, but they warned that such emergencies were to be considered as very rare.[9]

A much more protracted dispute broke out in the South Wales coalfield in November 1910, and in the following summer the entire railway network was brought to a halt when railway owners, who refused to recognize the union, refused to negotiate with union officials. Churchill addressed Parliament in apocalyptic terms,[10] and acted vigorously. In the former instance he stopped the troops requisitioned by Captain Lionel Lindsay, the Chief Constable of Glamorgan, and sent 300 Metropolitan Police from London in their stead. These Metropolitan Police, however, were put under the command of the principal army officer in the area, General Nevil Macready. While the London policemen, and those troops already available to Macready may, in some ways, have worsened the situation, in others they probably eased it. Lindsay had a close personal relationship with the local colliery owners; he frequently dined with one of them, shared horses with him, and even took his advice on police matters. Macready, in contrast, refused all the invitations to himself and his officers that were received from the local coal owners.[11] In the railway strike Churchill again acted decisively by deploying troops in considerable numbers to protect railway lines and stations and, in some instances, to run emergency services. 'Talk about Revolution!' protested the Labour MP, Kier Hardie. 'The law of England has been broken in the interests of the railway companies . . .'[12] Churchill also urged the recruitment of a reserve of special constables so that mutual aid agreements between police forces could be fulfilled more easily; these special constables were to be considered alongside the permanent constables when assessing a force's efficiency and eligibility for the government grant. This suggestion infuriated several watch committees, who complained that the Home Office was seeking to encroach on their authority. Some eventually agreed to implement the suggestion; but others ignored it. In the counties too the recruitment of special constables was patchy, sometimes highlighting a sharp division of opinion between the chief constable and the SJC.[13] The use of troops in strikes was much more restrained under Reginald McKenna, who replaced Churchill at the Home Office in October 1911, but a significant shift had occurred from troops being requisitioned by local authorities as a back up to the police, to troops and, to a lesser extent, even police being directed by central government. The disorders of the pre-war years also demonstrated an increasing independence, particularly on the part of county chief constables, from their local police committees. William Ruck, the Chief Constable of Caernarvonshire, called in troops to help his force during a strike of quarrymen in the summer of 1901 even though only one member of the SJC (who also happened to be the owner of the quarry in question) agreed with him. Captain Lionel Lindsay was criticized by his SJC for borrowing local police without its authority; and while the SJC felt that 60 special constables would be sufficient for the county's needs, Lindsay thought in terms of 2,000 to 3,000.[14]

The chief constables of counties were usually drawn from the gentry and often had a military background; their men came from the semi-skilled and unskilled working class. However, there were significant differences in recruitment policies which appear to have been largely dictated by chief constables. Some deliberately excluded local men from their force, but others found a majority of their recruits within their jurisdiction.[15] Policemen from one force drafted into the jurisdiction of another to maintain order during a strike obviously had no relationship with the strikers; this may have given their superiors more confidence in ordering a baton charge, and it may also have reduced the inhibitions of ordinary constables in such a charge as well as in any other, less violent, confrontations with strikers. But there were many other factors which may have contributed to a shortness of temper among police on strike duty even where there were local men. Deployment during a strike could mean the suspension of leave, and married men deployed under mutual aid agreements were uprooted from their families.[16] Yet it would be wrong to confuse the police role in strikes with the attitude of individual police towards politics, or towards fellow workers and trades unions in general. Thomas Smethurst left his job as a miner to join the Bolton police in 1888; looking back on his police career he recalled that the police generally sympathized with strikers, though they were commonly seen as the enemy.[17] In 1908, while the Birmingham Police took a tough line on demonstrations organized by the local Right to Work Committee, the ordinary constables requested permission to contribute to a relief fund for the unemployed and the chief constable authorized meetings to discuss weekly subscriptions to such a fund.[18] Moreover the close of 1913 witnessed the creation of a trade union among police in London in defiance of the orders of the Metropolitan Police Commissioner; and very quickly the union spread into the provincial forces, in defiance of a directive from the Home Office.[19]

The First World War put enormous strains on the police. Their tasks were increased, while their ranks were periodically trawled and reduced by the demands for men for the army. The depleted ranks were partly filled by keeping on men who were passed retirement age and by using the special constables established during the pre-war strike emergency. It is at least arguable that the wartime decline in petty crime and drunkenness was due more to the new burdens on fewer policemen than to any improvements in morality. It is also probably that the pressures of the war contributed significantly to the two police strikes, commonly described at the time as 'mutinies', in August 1918 and in August 1919. But the war also developed the pre-war trends in the policing of strikes. Government control of the economy in wartime brought the government more directly into negotiating problems of labour relations. Strikes in wartime could not be allowed to last; either the strikers' demands were rapidly agreed to, or else the strike had to be broken. There was no pool of 'free labour' available in wartime and so the police did not find themselves having to protect 'blacklegs'. However, there was the fear of subversion, especially after the Russian Revolution, and this led to a growth in political policing hitherto unknown in England. The country was divided into special administrative areas each under the direction of an Authorized Competent Military Authority (ACMA) who was answerable to General Headquarters and responsible for enforcing the regulations made under wartime emergency legislation. Chief constables worked closely with the ACMAs, but were subordinate to them. The links with the ACMAs and the centralized intelligence services, both the Metropolitan Police Special Branch and MI5, bypassed the chief constables' links with their SJCs or watch committees and further eroded local control of the police.[20] With the restoration of peace the pre-war system was re-established in theory, but not entirely in practice.

In the immediate post-war years especially there was concern among ministers that industrial disputes were inspired by revolutionary activists. The tasks of ordinary policemen in most strikes remained largely unchanged; they were required to prevent a breach of the peace and they were assisted in times of major industrial conflict by special constables often sworn in for the duration of the emergency. Political policing by Special Branch and MI5 was continued at something approaching its wartime intensity, and the Emergency Powers Act of 1920 enabled the government to take powers undreamed of by Churchill in the strikes of 1910 and 1911. The new Act enabled a government to declare a state of emergency for the duration of one month at any time when action was threatened which would deprive the community of 'the essentials of life'. During the state of emergency the government was empowered to make any regulations which it deemed necessary to preserve the peace and to ensure public safety. Emergency regulations were introduced during the Miners' Strike of 1921 and the General Strike of 1926. Chief constables were informed, confidentially, of the government's emergency plans in October 1920,[21] another step which divorced them further from their local police committees and tied them closer to central government.

Not every chief constable sought to confront strikers. In Lincoln, for example, during the General Strike, Chief Constable William Hughes worked closely with the strike committee, and the Watch Committee authorized street collections by the local Trades Council and Labour Party for women and children in mining areas.[22] In South Wales, in contrast, the chief constables appear to have believed that they were engaged in a war, and the mining communities responded accordingly. The 'Battle of Ammanford' raged from mid-morning to mid-afternoon on 5 August 1925 as police defended Rock Colliery at Glyn Neath, Carmarthenshire, from strikers determined that a 'blackleg' electrician should be removed. The local Chief Constable was open in expressing his concern about the growth of Communism in the district, '[it] stands for the disruption of the British Empire, the end of Constitutional Government, hauling down the Union Jack and hoisting the "Red Flag" and the setting up of a Soviet Government'.[23] Suppressing strikes, in such reasoning, thus became a means of preserving the British way of life. Local SJCs with Labour representatives were incensed by such reasoning and by the actions of such chief constables, but the chief constables were able to rely on the support of the Home Office and central government. In the most extreme case, in July 1926, the SJC of Monmouthshire called on their Chief Constable to resign since 'his actions in times of emergency are calculated to disturb the peace of the county'. The Chief Constable refused to resign; and the Home Office refused payment of the police grant until the local authority gave in over the matter in December.[24] Confrontations of this sort led to increasing arguments on the part of central government ministers and their apologists that the police must be independent of local politics; though the growing central control and the increasing independence of chief constables were never translated into formal law.[25] The experience of the General Strike led some chief constables to question whether the idea of 'peaceful picketing' was actually a contradiction in terms: 'In my opinion', declared the Chief Constable of Bristol, 'there is no such thing as peaceful picketing and picketing of any kind is a menace to the transport of food supplies during a strike. The mere presence of pickets often amounts to a form of intimidation, especially when they stand outside premises and make written notes of the men at work, etc. Many instances of this nature did occur during the recent emergency, although the pickets themselves kept within the law.'[26] In 1927 a new Trade Disputes Act toughened the law by widening the meaning of 'intimidation' and forbidding mass picketing, and following this the police were, in general, encouraged to exert greater pressure on pickets.

These issues have never been seriously discussed in the traditional histories of English police which prefer to concentrate on 'the good humour ... impartiality and forbearance' of the bobby.[27] This perception was very much that of the middle class, who rarely perceived the police as oppressive, and generally acknowledged them as protectors; it was also the image projected in the essentially integrationist newspaper press and, during the 1930s, in cinema newsreels.[28]

There was violence in strikes in England; many of its worst manifestations were in those areas, like South Wales, where a tradition of worker syndicalism was confronted by aggressive chief constables, or else in those instances where young, middle-class special constables provoked strikers or were let loose on a crowd.[29] Much also probably depended on the immediate local situation: whether the police were local, or drafted in under the mutual aid system; whether they were particularly aggrieved at losing rest days; what kind of leadership they had on the spot. A few people were killed in industrial disorders but only when troops were deployed; police violence was generally confined to the wielding of truncheons during a charge, and while a blow from a police truncheon could kill, such fatalities were extremely rare. This violence pales into insignificance in comparison with that in the United States. Some of the violence in American strikes stemmed in part from the actions of aggressive police chiefs, but it also often involved private police recruited by detective agencies specifically for a strike emergency.

One key reason for the importance of the detective agencies was the different relationships between the American urban cop and his community and between the English bobby and his. For an earlier period Wilbur Miller has contrasted the impersonal authority of the bobby, generally perceived, at least by middle-class commentators, as an upright manifestation of the impartial and inflexible law, with the personal authority of the cop, who was tacitly allowed the discretion of ignoring the law to deal with the 'dangerous classes'.[30] Moreover if the bobby was an impersonal manifestation of the law, the cop was a fellow-citizen. The cop could be very close to his community and, in consequence, he might side with members of that community when they were on strike; indeed one historian has suggested that in the towns and cities during the late nineteenth century the local police functioned primarily as defenders of working class interests.[31] In Indianapolis in 1913, for example, some police refused to serve if it meant protecting 'blacklegs' during first a streetcar strike and then a teamsters' strike.[32] The same thing happened in the Knoxville streetcar strike of October 1919, where part of the problem was that the police themselves were unionized having affiliated to the American Federation of Labor (AFL) in July of that year.[33] Such incidents could also get the support of the local mayor, especially if the employers in the strike were not local. 'The Vincennes Traction Company', explained the mayor of Vincennes, Indiana, during a streetcar strike,

is owned by non-residents and the line is run with little consideration for the rights and conveniences of the people of the city. The company does not live up to its franchise obligations and persistently ignores the communications of the city officials upon these matters. When this strike threatened I told the superintendent of the line that I would preserve order, but I would not, under any circumstances, man the cars with policemen.[34]

The same kind of thing could occur in the small towns policed by elected sheriffs and their deputies. In March 1914, for example, the management of the Gould Steel Works, Depew, New York, complained that the deputy sheriffs were not guarding them properly during the strike because they were local residents in sympathy with strikers. Sheriff Becker, however, challenged this claim; he insisted that the management of the Steel Works were primarily interested in having private detectives sworn in as deputies, and that these detectives, if sworn, would only start trouble.[35]

In contrast it could also happen that the local police were closely linked with local employers. In Chicago during the streetcar conductors' strike of 1885 the police were used to ride on the cars and to protect non-strikers; in the following year a third of the city force were deployed to protect strike-breakers at the McCormick Harvester Plant, the incident which led to the Haymarket Outrage.[36] In Buffalo, New York, at the close of the nineteenth century, the city was controlled by business interests who had no qualms about using the city police – largely recruited from German immigrants – to control their workers – largely recruited from Polish immigrants.[37]

The United States Commission on Industrial Relations, which was principally organized by a group of professors at the University of Wisconsin and which met from 1912 to 1914, received much information on police partiality in strikes. There was Sheriff Jefferson Farr, 'the King of Huerfano County', who was accused of running everything in his county from elections to brothels, and who also allegedly controlled the courts in the interests of the Colorado Fuel and Iron Company.[38] During a textile workers' strike in Paterson, New Jersey, it was reported that a local mill owner loaned his car to the police for transporting strikers to prison.[39] The Senate Committee on Education and Labour, better known as the La Follette Committee, which met from 1936 to 1940, heard similar evidence of partiality. It was while the committee was meeting that the notorious Memorial Day Massacre occurred, with the Chicago Police firing on unarmed strikers demonstrating outside the Republic Steel Factory; ten demonstrators were killed and over a hundred injured, and the whole event was captured for posterity by a cameraman from Paramount News. Sheriff Theodore Middleton of Harlan County, Kentucky, boasted that he would have no labour disturbances in his jurisdiction; he recruited tough ex-gaol birds as his deputies and used them in the interests of local mine owners. Sheriff John A. Miller of Contra Costa County, California, ran his county for the benefit of the local fruit farmers and he intimidated any labour organizations or activists who dared set foot there.[40] Counties like Huerfano, Harlan, and Contra Costa were remote. With little or no state police, and the physical problems of transporting big city police – even assuming that the legal authority and the agreement of municipalities for this could have been obtained – sheriffs like Farr, Middleton and Miller could become a law unto themselves, or unto the most influential and wealthy individuals or corporations in their jurisdictions.

Between the extremes of police sympathy for the strikers and police partiality on the side of the employers there appears also to have been a degree of what might be termed professional cynicism. The great muck-raker Lincoln Steffens detected such in his early years as a journalist in New York during the 1890s. Steffens set out to investigate the reasons for the high incidence of police clubbings, particularly during disputes in the garment trade. Standing on a picket line with the police he saw a strike-breaker struck down by a picket wearing brass knuckles; the picket, in turn, was bludgeoned by a cop's night-stick – the cop turning to Steffens to explain that the brass knuckles were 'the emblem of the [union] organization'. A debate followed between a cop and a picket

> on the law, the rights of man and especially strikers, which was as irritating to me as later the debates in the US Senate were on the constitutionality of some bill proposed – and for the same reason. The argument had nothing to do with the subject before the house. It was just a case of lawyers disputing not the right, wisdom, or justice of the matter in hand, but precedents and decisions; and the policeman and the picket knew, disputed and strained the law to their appointed uses. They irritated me, and they so irritated each other that I could see and understand why the policemen kept feeling of, weighing, and finally whirling nervously his long night-stick, like a lion waving its tail.

Steffens concluded his account by describing the cynicism of the cops on picket duty, particularly with reference to a workshop owner who was threatening to make a complaint to police headquarters about pickets under the eyes of the police.

> 'I remember this boss when he was a union organizer. I beat him up once myself for picketing, and now he's got a shop himself he's still a-fighting the police for the law and his rights.'
> 'Just like the workers!' I exclaimed.

123

'Oh, hell, They're all alike, workers and bosses, the same breed, the same rights to all th'law on their side and against all the law on th'other side.'

'The law is just a club then', I remarked. 'The police are a weapon to be used or denounced.'

'You have said it', one cop said heartily, and the other nodded, 'Sure'.[41]

It was possible to call on military assistance by characterizing the disturbances which sometimes accompanied strikes as 'insurrection'. This enabled a state governor to appeal to the federal president for federal troops. The numbers of the latter called upon in this way were relatively small; their appearance was generally sufficient to bring an end to disorder, and to strikers they appeared as a more impartial force than the state militia, or National Guard. Perhaps as many as half of the instances in which the National Guards were called upon by state governors in the last quarter of the nineteenth century involved labour troubles.[42] In the eastern states especially the National Guards became known for their links with business and industry, and for strike-breaking; in Pennsylvania businessmen dominated several of the state's National Guard units, discouraged the recruitment of workingmen, and ensured that any soldier who failed to turn out for strike duty was expelled; Luke Grant concluded, in one of his reports for the Commission on Industrial Relations, that, in general, 'the men in the ranks of the organized militia usually [were] recruited from occupations in which there [were] no labour unions'.[43]

The deployment of National Guardsmen in strikes was expensive and it required more of a commitment to militia duties than most volunteers were prepared to give. Furthermore, it was generally regarded as undermining the National Guard's readiness for more obvious military action. In the last quarter of the nineteenth century there were demands for a specialized police in Pennsylvania which could take over the Guard's role in strikes. The Anthracite strike of 1902 provided the opportunity for the state legislative, dominated by mine owners, to sweep through legislation providing for such a force. The Pennsylvania State Police received a poor press from labour organizations and socialists; they were stigmatized as 'Cossacks'. Nevertheless, in 1913 the New York State Chamber of Commerce proposed the creation of a similar force. There was an outcry from organized labour and the political left; but there was also a well orchestrated propaganda campaign employing both the written word and the new medium of the cinema praising the example of the Pennsylvania State Police as courageous, impartial Anglo-Saxon heroes protecting true Americans (and especially American women) from alien hordes. The New York legislative voted to establish a state police in March 1917.[44]

The remoteness of many business and industrial concerns in the United States also gave further opportunities for the development of the strike-breaking activities of the Detective Agencies. In the 1914 strike by Colorado miners, which resulted in the Ludlow Massacre, the Colorado Fuel and Iron Company was able to get its mine guards, some of whom were recruited through the Baldwin-Felts Detective Agency, incorporated into A Troop (cavalry) and B Company (infantry) of the Colorado Militia; it was the men of these units who were responsible for the killings.[45]

The first, and probably most celebrated of the detective agencies was that established by the Scots immigrant Allan Pinkerton in Chicago in 1850. From early on Pinkerton's men were engaged in checking on employees for their bosses and, following the Paris Commune and with the increase labour unrest of the 1870s, they became increasingly involved in infiltrating unions and strike-breaking.[46] The Pinkertons suffered a serious reverse following their bloody attempt to break the Homestead strike in 1892, but their example spawned scores of competitors; by 1914, when the detective agencies were past their peak, there were still more than 270 of them prepared to hire guards, at $5 a day to industrialists.[47] Strike breaking could become a career for men in the detective agencies, with the ultimate achievement being the creation of a man's own agency. There were distinct occupational types within the agencies: the 'Finks', whose task was to encourage strikers to return to work; the 'Nobles'. who protected 'free labour' and 'loyal workers'; the 'Missionaries', who mixed with strikers, propagandized against the strike and occasionally provoked violence.[48] The agencies boomed between about 1905 and 1910: in this period an economic upswing gave the unions the muscle to conduct strikes and the employers the money to hire detectives; large-scale production led to absentee employers who grew further estranged from the local union leaders and policemen; there was also a degree of laxity on law enforcement which enabled the free employment of non-resident police officers like the detectives.[49] While in some instances, where, for example, employers and local sheriffs were hand in glove, the detectives were sworn in as deputies, elsewhere they could find themselves opposed, and even arrested by the local police.[50]

In England Special Constables were deployed as an auxiliary to the police during the First World War and during major industrial confrontations like the General Strike of 1926; in the aftermath of the Russian Revolution especially some senior police officers saw themselves as guardians of 'Englishness' against the threat of what they perceived as an alien political creed manifesting itself in union activity. Towards the end of the nineteenth century in the United States there had been a growing belief among native-born Americans that violence in industrial disputes was the work of aliens, and this had probably contributed to the ferocity directed against immigrant strikers.[51] Such beliefs reached a new peak during the First World War with unpleasant and often fatal results for some strikers and labour activists, especially any such linked with the International Workers of the World, or 'Wobblies'. The American Protective League was founded in the spring of 1917; President Wilson had his doubts about the organization, but it received support from some at the heart of his administration, particularly the Justice Department's Bureau of Investigation (later the Federal Bureau of Investigation or FBI). By the following year there were reputedly 250,000 APL activists in over 600 towns and cities. Their principal concerns were to investigate disloyalty, unearth draft dodgers, and break up anti-war meetings, but their crude patriotic vigilantism also led them to persecute those who manifested 'disloyalty' by organizing unions and strikes. Copper miners in Arizona were rounded up by vigilantes and local sheriffs and transported out of the state; in the first instance, at Jerome, the miners were on strike, in the second, at Bisbee, the 1,800 victims were simply suspected of being Wobblies. In Butte, Montana, vigilantes brutally murdered a Wobbly organizer, Frank Little. In the immediate aftermath of the war a spate of strikes fostered a panic equating unions with Bolshevism and this, in turn, produced another wave of brutality directed particularly against immigrants, many of whom were deported.[52]

But not all workers and union activists were Wobblies; there was some improvement in industrial relations during the First World War which, in spite of the 'Red Scare' of the immediate post-war period, continued with a greater preparedness on the part of some employers to talk to some union leaders. The welfare capitalism, which had begun in the war years, continued in the 1920s and employers offered benefits to their workers as substitutes for unions. The New Deal policies of the mid-1930s, in particular the National Labour Relations Act (the Wagner Act of 1935), also eased the potential for, and the degree of, violent conflict. The American working class became more integrated with the decline of, and restrictions upon, immigration; this lessened the alienation of the workforce as well as much of its alien nature, and it also reduced the potential for ethnic friction, or even perhaps ethnic solidarity, between policemen and strikers. The police themselves were becoming increasingly professional in their approach to their tasks, though, of course, where the police and their superiors feared subversion or Communism on the part of unions there could still be partiality and violence. Finally, while there was no central state powerful enough, as in England, to threaten local control of law and order, developments in federal policing in the First World War and during the 'Red Scare' removed some of the functions of the detective agencies in seeking out subversives; such duties were taken over by the new Federal Bureau of Investigation, which was not prepared to sanction the activities of private detectives within its jurisdiction.[53]

In any attempt to compare the policing of strikes in England and the United States it will rapidly become clear the historian is not always comparing like with like. The greatest similarities are to be found between the English experience and the situation in America's big cities, particularly those along the north-eastern seaboard. While some English magistrates were large-scale employers who could be involved in strikes, and while some English chief constables could be rather too friendly with employers, the situation in the more remote areas of the United States, where the law could be largely what the local sheriff and employer decreed, and where armed guards could be recruited and used with virtual impunity, had no direct English parallel.[54] The close relation of many American cops with their communities at times made them more unreliable than their English counterparts during a strike, and this led the more aggressive employers to turn to detective agencies, while state governors looked to the military, and gradually new state police organizations. The individual American states maintained their independence from the centre, while local government in England increasingly lost out to the gradual encroachments of central government. These encroachments cannot be seen as part of a conspiracy, rather it seemed logical to ministers and the civil servants in the Home Office to correspond directly with local police chiefs without having to go through an additional tier of local government administration; the logic of this seemed irrefutable to these men as some strikes became national and appeared to require, in consequence, a response that was also national. The First World War and the fear engendered by the Russian Revolution accelerated these processes, especially where central government and police chiefs became concerned about the political reliability of local Labour and Left-wing councillors.[55] There was nothing comparable to the encroachment of England's unitary state in the United States, but it needs also to be remembered that distance and the organizational structure of American trades unions militated against the kind of national strikes witnessed in England. The 'Red Scare' of 1919, with the ensuring arrests of Communists and Communist Labour Party members in the so-called 'Palmer Raids', contributed to the development of the Federal Bureau of Investigation and this assumed some of the tasks of the detectives, but the American police forces remained tied closely to their localities.

The policing of strikes in the United States at the end of the nineteenth and in the early part of the twentieth centuries was far more violent and bloody than in England. Many Americans were worried about this, and such anxieties led to enquires like the Commission on Industrial Relations and the labour investigations of the La Follette Committee. For all the ferocity and violence on the picket lines there was an openness about American society and a desire to investigate apparent outrages. In contrast, in England there was little investigation into alleged incidents of police partiality or violence. Successive Home Secretaries insisted they had no control over local police and that therefore any investigation had to be local; it was also argued that any enquiry would really play into the hands of extremists who had an interest in undermining the police. Throughout the period English politicians, policemen, and commentators on police affairs, regularly asserted that the English police were the best in the world. The corollary of this assertion was that the English police did not require any serious investigation; but the assertion itself was based largely on the left-over prejudices and smugness of the Victorian age and not upon any honest comparison.[56]

Notes

1. I use the word England as shorthand for both England and Wales. Scotland had, and continues to have, a different legal system and while from the middle of the nineteenth century Scottish police forces grew to resemble those of England, I have omitted consideration of Scotland from this paper.
2. Clive Emsley, *Crime and Society in England 1750–1900*, 2nd edn (London, Longman 1996), pp. 135–6 and 200–1.
3. *Hansard*, LXIII, 23 June 1914, col. 1639.
4. For contrasting views of the affair see *Sunderland Daily Echo*, 21, 24, 25, 26 and 27 February and 2 and 6 March 1891, and *Sunderland Herald and Daily Post*, 2 and 6 March 1891. For the initial parliamentary discussions of the affair see *Hansard* CCCLI, 5 March 1891, cols. 237–9 and 269–97; quotation at col. 285.
5. Ibid., 13 March 1891, col. 925, and 16 March 1891, cols. 1058–9 and 1073–4.
6. Report of the Committee Appointed to Inquire into the Circumstances Connected with the Disturbance at Featherstone on 7 September 1893 *Parliamentary Papers*, 1893–94 [C.7234].
7. *Report of the Inter-Departmental Committee on Riots* (London, Her Majesty's Stationery Office, 1895).
8. Jane Morgan, *Conflict and Order: The Police and Labour Disputes in England and Wales 1900–1939* (Oxford, Clarendon Press, 1987), pp. 39–40.
9. Barbara Weinberger, *Keeping the Peace? Policing Strikes in Britain 1906–1926* (Oxford, Berg 1991), Ch. 2 *passim*.
10. *Hansard*, XXXIX, 22 August 1911, cols. 2286 and 2327.
11. Roger Geary, *Policing Industrial Disputes 1893 to 1985* (Cambridge University Press, 1985), p. 36.
12. *Hansard*, XXXIX, 22 August 1911, col. 2335.
13. Morgan, *Conflict and Order*, pp. 58–60. The occasional pressure on police forces with mutual aid agreements during these years can be gleaned from the following

letter from the Chief Constable of Huntingdonshire to the Chief Constable of Nottinghamshire, 21 Feb. 1912: 'I hardly like to promise to send you any of my force in the event of a coal strike as I am under obligation by written agreement to assist four of my neighbouring forces. If I am not asked for assistance by any of them, and should I not apprehend any trouble at home, I would endeavour on receipt of a wire from you [to] dispatch a Sergt and 15 men, and an Inspector if required, at 24 hours notice.' Cambridgeshire Police Archives, Chief Constable of Huntingdonshire, Letter Book, 1906–15, fol. 271.

14. Morgan, *Conflict and Order*, pp. 38–9, 48 and 59.

15. Clive Emsley and Mark Clapson, 'Recruiting the English policeman *c.* 1840–1940', *Policing and Society*, 3 (1994), pp. 269–86.

16. In December 1912 and in November 1913, for example, the Chief Constable of the East Riding suspended all leave in his force because men were needed under mutual aid agreements; on the first occasion it was because of a strike on the North East Railway, on the second, it was a strike by carters in Leeds. Humberside Police Archives, East Riding Constabulary, Memorandum Book, 1912–15, fols 26 and 67.

17. Thomas Smethurst, *Reminiscences of a Bolton and Stalybridge Policeman, 1888–1922* (Manchester, Neil Richardson, 1983), pp. 9 and 25.

18. Cyril Collard, 'Unemployment agitation in Birmingham 1905–1910', in Anthony Wright and Richard Shackleton (eds), *Worlds of Labour; Essays in Birmingham Labour History* (University of Birmingham, 1983), pp. 35–62; at p. 51.

19. V. L. Allen, 'The National Union of Police and Prison Officers', *Economic History Review*, II (1958–9), pp. 133–43.

20. For wartime developments see David Englander, 'Military intelligence and the defence of the realm: the surveillance of soldiers and civilians in Britain during the First World War', *Bulletin of the Society for the Study of Labour History*, 52 (1987), pp. 24–31; and idem., 'Police and public order in Britain, 1914–1918', in Clive Emsley and Barbara Weinberger (eds), *Policing Western Europe 1850–1940: Politics, Professionalization and Public Order* (Westport, Conn., Meckler, 1991), pp. 90–138.

21. Sir Arthur Dixon, 'The Home Office and the Police between the Two World Wars' (unpublished, 1966 copy in Police Staff College Library, Bramshill), p. 242.

22. Morgan, *Conflict and Order*, pp. 122–3 states that the events in Lincoln during the General Strike led to an inquiry by the Inspector of Constabulary and forced the resignation of both the Chief Constable and the Chairman of the Watch Committee. However both Hughes and Councillor Charles T. Parker remained in their posts, and Hughes was able to report to the Watch Committee on 17 June 1926 that the Home Office had agreed to pay one half of the police overtime bill amassed during the strike. Lincolnshire Record Office, Lincoln Watch Committee Minute Book, 1917 to 1926, fols 494–5. For the authorization of the street collections see fol. 491.

23. Morgan, *Conflict and Order*, pp. 199–201.

24. Barbara Weinberger, 'Police perceptions of labour in the inter-war period: the case of the unemployed and of miners on strike', in Francis Snyder and Douglas Hay (eds), *Labour, Law, and Crime: An Historical Perspective* (London, Tavistock, 1987), pp. 150–79, at p. 169.

25. Laurence Lustgarten, *The Governance of Police* (London, Sweet & Maxwell, 1986), p. 49.

26. Scotland Yard, 'Summaries of information regarding the strike furnished by chief constables in England, Scotland and Wales', Part II of *Aspects of the General Strike, May 1926* (June 1926).

27. T. A. Critchley, *A History of Police in England and Wales*, 2nd edn (London, Constable, 1978), p. 200. The words are repeated in individual force histories e.g. Richard Cowley, *Policing Northamptonshire 1836–1986* (Studley, Brewin Books, 1986), p. 76

and Douglas J. Elliott, *Policing Shropshire 1836–1967* (Studley, Brewin Books, 1984), p. 164.

28. Ken Ward, *Mass Communications and the Modern World* (London, Macmillan, 1989), p. 98. For information on the newsreels I am indebted to my colleague, Tony Aldgate, who has particularly drawn my attention to such items as British Movietone News, Vol. 8, No. 383, *A Tale of Two Cities*, which contrasts British and French police handling the street disorders in 1936.

29. Geary, *Policing Industrial Disputes*, pp. 65–6. See also, for a different comparative perspective, Clive Emsley, 'Police forces and public order in England and France during the inter-war period', in Emsley and Weinberger, (eds), *Policing Western Europe*.

30. Wilbur R. Miller, *Cops and Bobbies: Police Authority in New York and London, 1830–1870* (University of Chicago Press, 1977).

31. Bruce C. Johnson, 'Taking care of labor: the police in American politics', *Theory and Society*, 3 (1976), pp. 89–117.

32. Report of Selig Perlman, 10 March 1914, and Selig Perlman, 'The Teamsters' strike at Indianapolis in December 1913', both in unpublished reports of the Research Division of the Commission on Industrial Relations, 1912–15 [henceforth CIR] microfilm P71–1683 in the State Historical Society of Wisconsin.

33. James A. Burran, 'Labour conflict in urban Appalachia: the Knoxville Streetcar Strike of 1919', *Tennessee History Quarterly*, 38 (1979), pp. 62–78.

34. CIR, Appendix to Report on Street Railway Employees, Vincennes, Indiana, Traction Company, p. 3. It was common in such strikes for police to ride in the streetcars to protect 'blackleg' drivers and conductors.

35. CIR, 'Report of Daniel T. O'Regan, Depew, NY. March 30, 1914'.

36. Cyril D. Robinson, 'The mayor and the police: the political role of the police in society', in George Mosse (ed.), *Police Forces in History* (Beverly Hills, CA, Sage, 1975), pp. 277–315; at pp. 293–6.

37. Sidney L. Harring and Lorraine M. McMullen, 'The Buffalo Police 1872–1900: labour unrest, political power and the creation of the police', *Crime and Social Justice* (1975), pp. 5–14. See also, for a more general discussion of industrial cities in the Great Lakes area, Sidney L. Harring, *Policing a Class Society: The Experience of American Cities, 1865–1915* (New Brunswick, NJ, Rutgers University Press, 1982).

38. CIR, Inis Weed, 'The Colorado Strike', pp. 18–19.

39. CIR, 'Public hearings on industrial conditions and relations in Paterson, New Jersey, June 15–18, 1914', evidence of Rudolph Katz, p. 32.

40. Jerold S. Auerbach, *Labor and Liberty: the La Follette Committee and the New Deal* (Indianapolis, Bobbs-Merrill, 1966), pp. 117–18, 121–8, and 187–8. Middleton's activities were scrutized by the committee in 1937 when it was pointed out that, since 1934, he had recruited as deputies 3 men who had served sentences for murder and 8 who had served prison sentences for manslaughter; 37 of his deputies had been convicted of felonies and 64 had been indicted at least once.

41. *The Autobiography of Lincoln Steffens*, 2 vols (New York, Harcourt Brace & World, 1931), Vol. 1, pp. 211–14.

42. Barton C. Hacker, 'The United States Army as a national police force: the federal policing of labor disputes 1877–1898', *Military Affairs* (April 1969), pp. 255–64.

43. CIR, Luke Grant, 'Violence in labor disputes and methods of policing industry', n.d. pp. 39–47; Joseph J. Holmes, 'The National Guard of Pennsylvania: Policeman of Industry, 1865–1905', PhD. (University of Connecticut, 1971); Robert Reinders, 'Militia and public order in nineteenth century America', *Journal of American Studies*, II (1977), pp. 81–101; CIR, Luke Grant, 'Violence in labor disputes . . .' p. 42.

44. Gerda W. Ray, 'From cossack to trooper: manliness, police reform, and the state', *Journal of Social History*, 28 (1995), pp. 565–86.

45. George W. Pest, US Commission on Industrial Relations, *Report on the Colorado Strike* (Washington, DC 1915), pp. 101–4; CIR, 'The Colorado militia and the strike' (Report of the Military Commission, 1914), pp. 32–6.

46. Frank Morn, *'The Eye that Never Sleeps': A History of the Pinkerton Detective Agency* (Bloomington, Indiana University Press, 1982).

47. CIR, 'List of detectives', 1914; Daniel O'Regan, 'Conclusions derived from investigation of armed guards up to September 1914'.

48. Auerbach, *Labor and Liberty*, pp. 103–4.

49. Rhodri Jeffreys-Jones, 'Violence in American history: plug uglies in the Progressive Era', *Perspectives in American History*, 8 (1974), pp. 465–583, pp. 519–21.

50. Ibid., pp. 627–8.

51. John Higham, *Strangers in the Land: Patterns of American Nativism 1869–1925*, revised edn (New York, Atheneum, 1963), pp. 53–4 and 89–90.

52. David M. Kennedy, *Over Here: The First World War and American Society* (Oxford University Press, 1980), pp. 81–3 and 289–92; Neil A. Wynn, *From Progressivism to Prosperity: World War I and American Society* (New York, Holmes & Meier, 1986), pp. 51–2 and 211–15.

53. These conclusions owe much to the work of Rhodri Jeffreys-Jones, in particular 'Violence in American history', pp. 465–583, and 'Profit over class: a study in American industrial espionage', *Journal of American Studies*, 6 (1972), pp. 233–48. For the rise of the FBI and its first director's obsession with internal subversion see Athan G. Theoharis and John Stuart Cox, *The Boss: J. Edgar Hoover and the Great American Inquisition* (Philadelphia, Temple University Press, 1988), especially chapters 2–6.

54. There may, however, have been some parallels in the situation in areas of the British Empire. In Bombay, for example, employers called upon traditional community gangs in the working districts for their organized strike breakers; R. S. Chandavarkar, 'The police and public order in Bombay city, 1870–1940', unpublished paper read at the conference on 'Policing the Empire', Birkbeck College, London 19–20 May 1988. For the links between criminal gangs and the strike-breaking detectives in the United States see, *inter alia*, Donald Henderson Clarke, *In the Reign of Rothstein* (New York, Grosset & Dunlap, 1929) and Leo Katcher, *The Big Bankroll: The Life and Times of Arnold Rothstein* (New York, Harper, 1958).

55. See, for example, West Midlands police Archive, Superintendents' Reports and Confidential Letters, 1901–1923, fols 499–504, Chief Constable to Under Secretary, Home Office, 2 and 7 November 1919.

56. These arguments are developed at length in Clive Emsley, *The English Police: A Political and Social History* (Hemel Hempstead, Wheatsheaf, 1991).

III.3

Suburbanization and social change in England and North America, 1880–1970

MARK CLAPSON

INTRODUCTION

There are compelling reasons for a comparative historical assessment of the significance of suburbanization to social change in Britain and the United States. Both countries witnessed the growth of mass suburbia from the later nineteenth century, as mass public transportation systems reduced travelling times and brought the city and its outskirts closer together. From the 1920s the rise of the motor car and the relocation of industry, made possible by electricity, speeded up and expanded suburban sprawl. In both countries there was a romantic reaction against the perceived large size, ugliness and dangers of the industrial city, and an attempt to bring the best of small town and country life together in planned romantic or garden suburbs. The British and American middle classes, through their purchasing power, initiated the suburban dispersal from the city centres as they sought a safe, private, comfortable home in the rural fringes of the city, for which they were prepared to commute, to travel to work and back.

During the interwar years, however, but especially since 1945, the working classes broke the near middle-class monopoly of suburban living as affluence extended further down the social scale, and state housing policies and slum clearance programmes favoured outward relocation. This democratic residential transition, however, was not shared by ethnic minorities of colour in Britain or North America in the period under discussion here. Both countries have also witnessed in the postwar period, especially during and since the 1960s, a 'north–south drift': the migration from declining northern and mid-country industrial cities towards the booming and suburbanizing cities of the south. This meant, broadly, the 'sunbelt cities' of the USA, and the new towns and new estates of suburban south east England. The problems of the largely blue collar manufacturing industries and the growth of the mostly white collar sector provide the structural explanation for this drift.[1] As a consequence of this dispersal, both countries witnessed the rise of an inner city problem, the social, economic and environmental decline of many major cities. Finally, a powerful, often amusing, but obscurantist 'myth of suburbia' has been plied on both sides of the Atlantic, which mocks and caricatures the suburban way of life.

It is impossible, in one paper of this length, to treat these issues in detail. It is possible, however, to synthesize those key themes and questions outlined above within a general approach. This paper will discuss the following areas: first, the reasons for suburban dispersal in the two countries since 1880; second, why the suburbs in Britain and America attracted often bitter criticisms from novelists, journalists, critical sociologists, cultural commentators and other writers; and third, what sociologists in both countries found out about suburban lifestyles, as social investigators began to turn their attention to the suburbs during the 1950s. Finally, some broad conclusions about the significance of suburbanization for social change will be made. Before progressing to these substantive issues, however, we must recognize that 'suburbs' is a nebulous category whose meaning and scope requires definition.

DEFINITIONS AND SCOPE

The area of the town or city so often termed suburban has never been spatially static or demographically homogenous. Moreover, in terms of location and proximity to the employment centres or to the countryside, suburbs can vary enormously. For the purposes of this social history, 'the suburbs' may refer to residential areas superseding the commercial and dwelling areas of the central or inner, and usually historically older, hearts of the town. David Thorns' Anglo-America 'suburban typology' divides suburbs into, among other categories, planned middle-class and planned working-class residential, and unplanned middle-class and unplanned working-class residential.[2]

Around the towns and cities, the earlier suburbs were in turn often surpassed by further suburban growth, giving rise to inner suburbs and outer suburbs. Subdivisions of land, purchased by builders and then developed into residential blocks, refer to the majority of American suburban residential areas. In Britain, suburban growth since 1880 has been described as being made up largely of 'estates', a label which incorporates the Victorian and Edwardian exclusive estates of the wealthy middle class, and the more downmarket 'villadom' of the middle-class mainstream. During the inter-war years the lower middle classes moved out in droves to the suburbs in what is now viewed as classic semi-detached suburbia of unplanned residential estates. Simultaneously, hundreds of thousands of working-class families were decanted out to planned residential municipal estates built as a result of the interwar housing legislation. Since 1945 the suburbs have been made up of new estates built by private developers and local councils in government-promoted and planned town expansions, and in 'peripheral projects' initiated by local authorities attempting to accommodate the growth in populations of their towns, and the centrifugal force of urban migration.[3]

By 1970 almost all British and American cities and towns had undergone a continuous urban spread since 1880, which had resulted in an extensive bleeding from the centres as a result of suburbanization and, from the 1920s, a planned dispersal to new municipal estates whose rationale was exactly that of relieving the centres of overcrowding. (A similar rationale justified the postwar new towns, but a discussion of those is beyond the scope of this chapter.) To give just some of the largest examples: in Britain, Birmingham, London, Liverpool, Manchester and Newcastle underwent a considerable evacuation of the city centres, as did, in the USA, Chicago, Detroit, New York City, Boston and Pittsburgh.[4] These were the largest examples of a general socio-urban phenomenon. This was largely a white phenomenon during the period considered here. Those who did not possess enough money, or who were reluctant to move out, and Afro-Americans and Afro-Caribbeans were noticeable in both respects, were left in the decaying inner-city areas.[5]

THE CAUSES OF SUBURBANIZATION

The nineteenth-century cities and towns of both Britain and America had undergone often massive spatial and demographic growth as a result of migration from the land, and also, especially in the States, immigration. One important response to the overcrowded and degraded conditions of the poorest areas of the city was provided by model employers in both countries throughout the nineteenth century. The 1880s and 1890s, for example, saw a number of planned industrial residential communities for workers, notably Bournville and Port Sunlight in England, and Echota and Pullman in the USA.[6] These were the most famous exemplars of many similar schemes.

During the later nineteenth and early twentieth century, furthermore, planned residential garden suburbs, in America 'romantic suburbs', were originally developed with ideas of 'social mix' and 'social balance' in mind, as solutions to the overcrowding of the central areas. Workers would be siphoned off and distilled into civilizing and healthy environs, where they would improve by living nearby to urbane middle-class residents.

Most of these experiments, however, evolved rapidly into middle-class enclaves.[7]

The human scale of the housing and the street plans, however, in harness with a desire to alleviate both the overcrowding of the city centres, became a strong influence on the ideas of Ebenezer Howard, the 'father' of the garden city movement. The title of his book, *Tomorrow: A Peaceful Path to Reform* (1898) recognized the fears of urban and social degradation, and possible social collapse, that exercised so many reformers in both later Victorian and Edwardian Britain, and also in North America, notably the influential authority on urban affairs, Lewis Mumford.[8] Howard argued for planned new communities, neither city nor country, but a synthesis of both. These were to be clearly circumscribed concentrations of population, distinct from the *ad hoc* suburban outflow which had contributed to a spatial separation of the classes. Letchworth, built in Hertfordshire from 1903, was the first major fruit of his energies and ideas.

Letchworth, along with the middle-class planned garden suburbs, were characterized by low-rise, low-density housing, and were redolent with the trappings of the countryside: a garden, and closeness to the fields and woods. They provided an important template for suburban design in both countries, hence Britain and North America share a common heritage in domestic architecture: 'the Anglo-American suburb' of comely non-central, low-rise low-density residential districts.[9] The mass versions of the later suburban estates, however, were often a pale imitation of the best Victorian and Edwardian examples.[10]

The suburban formation of British and North American towns and cities, moreover, has been contrasted with the higher-density planning of the classic continental city. It is, for example, revealing to note that the central residential areas of French cities have in no small part been reserved for the wealthy bourgeois, whilst many workers and the poor were forced out to the suburbs.[11]

Urban historians are unanimous that nineteenth-century mass voluntary suburbanization was initiated by the middle class. In both Britain and North America, the growing chaos, squalor and perceived dangers of the unregulated town and city centres stimulated an escapist departure from a city centre home to rural 'bourgeois utopias' on the outskirts.[12] It is noticeable, however, that a small and relatively affluent section of the artisan and uniformed working class was able to afford to rent in the suburban 'dormitory' developments of north and south London. As David Reeder's work on Charles Booth's great survey of the *Life and Labour of the People in London* shows, by 1900 most suburban areas of the metropolis were predominantly middle-class, but were differentiated, economically and culturally, into 'inner' and 'outer' suburbs. There was a constant pressure on the inner suburbs from 'the centrifugal tendency of the better-off' as one of Booth's researchers phrased it. Hence, many inner suburbs underwent decline, allowing poorer working-class households to move in.[13] In the provinces, with local variations, these phenomena were general to many of the major industrial towns and cities of Britain and North America.

The move to the suburbs was only spatially possible via mass transportation systems. During the mid to late nineteenth century the railways and the horsedrawn carriages were a major stimulus to suburban growth, and from the later nineteenth century, streetcar suburbs, trams and the underground or subway trains facilitated speedier commuting in the British and American city.[14]

The motor car was to accelerate and expand suburban growth still further in the interwar years. In Britain, for example, the number of cars owned rose from 109,000 in 1919 to two million by 1939.[15] The 1920s and 1930s constitute the era of classic semi-detached suburban houses, over 2,500,000 of which were built. As Stevenson and Cook have argued, a time usually associated with the Slump and its hardships saw growing affluence for the lower middle class and the affluent working class in regular employment. A move to the suburbs expressed a sense of social and economic well-being, and embraced the new mobility.[16] Yet it was also an era of council estates: 1,300,000 council dwellings were built by local authorities, with the assistance of government subsidy, from 1919.[17]

In the United States, the 1920 census confirmed that for the first time more than half of all Americans were living in towns and cities. The interwar years consolidated and expanded America as an urban nation through the process of suburban growth. Between 1920 and 1929 the number of automobile registrations rose from 8,000,000 in 1920 to 23,000,000 by 1929, before the Great Depression curtailed this trend. By the end of the 1930s, however, the 'automobile suburbs' were again ascendant.[18]

In both countries, furthermore, housing policies facilitated suburban growth. In 1934, as part of the New Deal, the Federal Housing Administration and the Veterans' Association were set up to assist house buyers with mortgages. This proved particularly useful to ex-servicemen, and in the period 1948 to 1954, 44 per cent of all houses were bought with FHA and Veterans' Association support. Large-scale private buildings by developers constituted the supply side of this suburbanization. American public housing schemes were of lesser magnitude than in Britain, where the early postwar governments continued to favour subsidized dispersal into out-of-town peripheral projects and new towns, largely constructed by local authorities. There was also privatized extension to the suburbs, and private finance for mortgages, the financial backbone of owner-occupied suburbia, was provided by building societies throughout the period under discussion.[19]

Both the interwar years, and the postwar period, then, witnessed urban dispersal. Whether publicly or privately built, however, this was looked on with horror by many observers.

THE ANTI-SUBURBAN CRITIQUE

The growth of the suburbs and their myriad houses was regarded with loathing by many architects and planners who wished to contain urban England and America, in order to create a truly modern and urban town as opposed to rural nostalgia of the garden city and the bastatardized suburbs. They also wished to prevent the corrosive effect of sprawl on the countryside. So whilst the Modern Movement shared a desire to halt suburban sprawl, it was an alternative ideology to the garden city movement in British and American town planning. In 1933 a group of Leftist architects, planners and urban designers, influenced by the Swiss modernist Le Corbusier, denounced the suburbs as bourgeois, and 'an illusory and irrational paradise' which was 'scattered across the entire globe and carried to its extreme consequences in America'.[20] They preferred total new designs for urban living: higher-density, high-rise dwellings in brand new cityscapes.

What the Modern Movement exposed in its attitude to suburbia was a certain contempt for the chosen domestic destination of the masses. This was an important facet of a pessimistic and elitist approach to the majority in a developing era of mass consumption and mass communications.[21] The suburbs were accused of bringing about an alienation – an estrangement – of person from person. These accusations, and this contempt for the suburban landscape and its inhabitants, was not limited to the urban design professions. As John Carey's discussion of the British interwar literary elite has shown, literary representations of suburbia were frequently negative, even hateful. Graham Greene, George Orwell and Evelyn Waugh, for example, presented the suburbs as bland unstimulating tracts of housing peopled with crabbed, unfulfilled, and semi-literate sad cases. John Betjeman's famous poem called for the aerial bombardment of Slough, a new suburban growth town of the 1930s, with its 'tinned fruit, tinned meat, tinned minds' and 'bogus tudor bars'.[22]

Intellectuals who sought the popular ear on the wireless or the popular mind in writings, turned on the suburban sections of their audience. That 'man for all media' J. B. Priestley,[23] lamented the interwar suburbs as 'the third England', the first being the rustic countryside, the second being the

Victorian urban-industrial England. Like Matthew Arnold and William Morris before him, and in common with such contemporaries as Orwell and the Leavises, Priestley fretted about the influence of Americanism on 'organic' British culture, and was in no doubt that the original character of life in the new car-borne suburbs emanated from the USA. 'America, I supposed, was its real birthplace':

> This is the England of arterial and by-pass roads, of filling stations and factories that look like exhibition buildings ... where the smooth wide road passes between miles of semi-detached bungalows, all with their little garages, their wireless sets ... It is a large scale, mass production job, with cut prices.[24]

A number of important American intellectuals had similar responses. Writing in the 1950s, Lewis Mumford evinced the dangers of mass society elitism when he argued that the suburbs, brought into existence by the extension of the democratic ideal of material enrichment for all, was the conformist conclusion of social and economic mass production. For Mumford, suburban uniformity, conformity and passivity threatened the very forces of democracy: 'In the mass movement into suburban areas a new kind of community was produced ...

> a multitude of uniform, unidentifiable houses, lined up inflexibly, at uniform distances, on uniform roads, in a treeless communal waste, inhabited by people of the same class, the same income, the same age group, witnessing the same television performances, eating the same prefabricated goods, from the same freezers, conforming in every outward and inward respect to a common mould ...[25]

This quote exemplifies the classic denunciation of suburbia, and the superficial grasp of those social changes and of popular aspirations which had brought the suburbs into existence. The author is assuming that uniformity of environment means uniformity of experience, of values and orientation. In implying passivity, conformity and witlessness as characteristic of suburbia, Mumford echoed the view of the crowd shared by English novelists and Nazi dictators.[26]

In 1950s America, however, Mumford was not alone in his criticism of the suburbs. As the USA enjoyed unprecedented levels of affluence and full employment during the 1950s, writers warned of the dangers of complacency, corporatism, conformity and conservatism in Middle American society. William H. Whyte's study of the suburb of Park Forest ruthlessly depicted the 'organization man'. Bearing a number of sociological similarities to the Victorian Mr Pooter of north London,[27] the organization man was a white collar worker, trapped in an incremental and bureaucratic place of work, adopting an instrumental view of religion, school and neighbourhood, voting Republican, and living a life in fear or disdain of the poor or the ethnic minorities. Sociability was rampant, and took the form of home entertaining, trips with neighbours, church and school functions, and a variety of interest and hobby groups. This pattern of social interaction, however, was exclusive. It kept out the unwanted, and served to reinforce status distinctions both within, and between, subdivisions.[28]

That eloquent critic of American culture, David Reisman, in a book first published in 1950, argued that the affluent suburbanite lived a life of 'other-directedness' and inner unfulfilment, living at the behest of his intellectual and financial superiors, and of advertisements. Reisman was not just attacking the suburban way of life: he was adopting a polemical position which viewed the suburbs as the most profound condition of the 'new America'. In its growing love of the 'car culture' and of mobility in general, America was in danger of becoming a rootless and anomic society.[29] Writing in *Socialist Commentary* in 1961, Tosca Fyvel felt that similar changes, 'affected by American styles, by the insistent advertisers', were growing in Britain.[30]

Fyvel was not alone. Christopher Booker, the journalist and cultural critic, has shown how Reisman's and Whyte's analyses of the suburban condition found favour with a generation of disillusioned postwar intellectuals in Britain. The allegedly egregious suburbans featured in the gloomier prognoses of the 'what's wrong with Britain' school of cultural criticism and highbrow journalism.[31] As the blurb on the back of the Penguin edition of Whyte's *The Organization Man* put it: 'All of this is of direct interest to us, for what is happening in America is happening here.' In the broadsheet newspapers, and in journals such as *Encounter*, *The Spectator*, *Socialist Commentary*, and even *Punch*, many writers decried the death of 1945 optimism, and the sense of national community of the mid-1940s. From the hopes and communitarian dreams of 'utopia', England had apparently passed into 'subtopia'.[32] The hastily constructed suburban new estates and the allegedly more privatized life therein seemed to be a grim confirmation of that. Conformity and passivity seemed to be the tasteless fruits of affluence, as the most affluent sections of the working class penetrated suburbia in ever-increasing numbers, via the municipal estates, or the mortgage facilities of the building societies, and settled down to a life based around the television set and the car, ownership of both of which was increasing rapidly in that decade.[33] Poorer sections were encouraged to move to new towns, expanded towns or peripheral housing estates by slum

clearance and rehousing policies, where they also appeared to be developing a newly privatized lifestyle when compared to the slum.

A number of sociologists, for example Ferdynand Zweig, argued
that the British worker on the new estate was developing the 'other-
directedness' described by Reisman, and becoming middle-class.[34] Michael
Young and Peter Willmott, in their mid-1950s study of Bethnal Greeners
who moved to suburban new estates on the fringes of East London, added
to the sense of doom. The affluent working class, they argued, was
becoming middle-class: it was absorbing the domesticated, privatized, individualist and consumerist values of the bourgeoisie, leaving behind a
proud communitarian tradition and 'keeping themselves to themselves'.[35]
This phenomenon, dubbed 'embourgeoisement' by Left cultural critics,
appeared to confirm the social substance of the changes taking place.
Another of the most poignant effects of dispersal on community was the
demise, Willmott and Young argued, of women's informal primary caring
relationships: the mutual self-help system which existed between female
neighbours, and most strongly between the mother and her daughter, and
which came into its own as the daughter married and had children. It was
feared that the strength of this relationship was weakened by the distance
between Bethnal Green and the out-county estate.[36]

Women's feelings and experiences in the move, whether via a planned
migration from slum to suburb, or a 'voluntary' move as part of a household's mobility, was an important subject of debate in both countries in the
1950s and during the 1960s. The condition of 'suburban neurosis', a term
first used in the medical journal *The Lancet* in 1938 to explain the psychological problems of housewives on the Peckham estates in South London,
was re-examined in a number of socio-psychological studies, in both
countries. Some, for example the survey of relocation to West End Boston,
Massachusetts, concluded that women who were moved from the comparative closeness of the slum to a new block some miles away, were indeed torn by the move and the loss of the closeness of family and friends.
Other studies in Britain argued that the deep-rooted symptoms of neurosis were probably already present before the move, which was the catalyst
for the symptoms to appear. And some concluded that the move, with all
due recognition to the stresses and strains of moving, was ultimately beneficial to the mental and physical health of women. There was, then, no
consensus about the effect of the move on suburban women. It is, however, important to recognize that the majority of those undertaking these
studies were men.[37]

One of the more risible cultural by-products of this debate over
women's position in the suburbs was the power over the male imagination
exercised by a residential area which was largely devoid of male commuters

during the day. The image of the sex-mad and frustrated suburban woman, a variation on loneliness and allegedly neurotic behaviour, has played a powerful role in the popular culture, both in literature and on film and television, and has reinforced the suburban myth in both countries.[38]

At much the same time as the aforementioned studies were being made, other equally sensitive and empirical social investigations into the British and American suburbs were coming to different conclusions to those of Young and Willmott, Zweig, Reisman and Whyte. These sociologies have left the social historian with a richly detailed source of life in the subdivisions of America and the new estates of Britain in the later 1950s and during the 1960s.

THE SOCIOLOGY OF SUBURBIA

The need for a more level-headed and objective sociology of the suburbs, to confront some of the pessimism about subdivisions and new estates was called for, for example, by Berger, Dobriner and Gans in the United States.[39] In Britain, among others, Cullingworth, Mogey and Rankin shared, with their American counterparts, a questioning of the considerable critical generalizations made about suburban life from a few specific studies of Park Forest or suburban Essex.[40] An in-depth discussion of their findings is impracticable here, but some of the most important conclusions deserve an airing: most estates and subdivisions tended to generate an occupational and status pattern which attracted people from similar income levels, a consequence of both individual preferences and property prices. However, within each street there could be a considerable range of different jobs of the heads of household. There were, also, 'working-class suburbs' in both countries, and gradations within them, just as middle-class districts were divided up by income.

These sociologists explored the suburban idea of the good life more positively than its critics ever could. The good life was viewed in terms of a pleasant residential area populated by people of similar incomes and occupations, a suburban house as opposed to a flat or apartment enriched with the latest labour-saving devices, the ubiquitous television, a car – in America's case two cars – essential for mobility, a garden, easy access to the countryside and nearby parks. Generally, people wanted a mixture of sub-rural living with all the urban amenities near at hand, accessible both by car and on foot.

Safe streets and good schools for the children were essential. This made clear that the majority of people who were on the move to the suburbs were relatively young: they were couples about to begin a family or families with children about to begin school or already there. The stage of the life cycle was essential to an understanding of the patterns of behaviour in the suburbs, as they were relatively more heavily populated with young families than the inner cities. The nuclear family, moreover, was thrown back more fully on its resources in the suburbs, whereas the poorer urban centres were characterized by a higher level of nearby extended family networks. At the levels of occupation, educational attainment, town or region of origin, and interests, beliefs and values, however, the suburbs were quite heterogeneous. From those sociologies mentioned here it is possible to see that the relatively better-off suburban areas, when compared to inner-city locales, were the developing contexts for a more heterogeneous culture of leisure and pastimes, too. It is also important to note that in all these studies cited, the majority of people, whether they had moved of their own volition, or as a result of rehousing programmes, did not wish to return to their previous home district.

During the later 1950s, a comparative study of English new estates in Bristol, both council and private, and wealthy and not so wealthy subdivisions in Columbus, Ohio, the sociologist H. E. Bracey confirmed such findings, but also pointed to some important differences between the two countries. American houses were bigger. American suburbanites, both middle- and working-class, were more mobile because they were wealthier and had a higher per capital ownership of cars. Women, for example, drove much more than their English counterparts, and this allowed them to travel more easily to meet people. The English working-class suburbanite was the most 'static' of those samples studied by Bracey, and they were most vociferously critical of the lack of nearby shops and services, because they were most dependent, especially the older groups, on public transport.

There was a strong emphasis upon respectability in both middle- and working-class families, the phrase 'keeping myself to myself' signifying an overriding concern for privacy. Bracey also described the social roles of both informal neighbouring, and more formal recreational, religious and problem-solving groups, clubs and associations. American middle-class subdivisions, especially women, were most active in these respects, but this was a function of greater wealth, free time, and more freedom of choice and movement. He assumed that as the English suburbanites, both middle- and working-class, grew wealthier, they would increasingly converge with their American cousins.[41]

Bracey did not much deal with another common feature of the transatlantic debate about suburbia: 'embourgeoisement'. Bennet M. Berger, in his study of a working-class auto-manufacturing suburb in California, was explicit that the culture and politics of the American suburbanite were not transformed into an egregious and Republican middle-class culture.

Eighty-one per cent of his sample still voted Democrat, they still lived a life of instant as opposed to deferred gratification, and ideas and values of hard work and respectability were working-class values, not *a priori* middle-class ones. Most had no aspiration for office work. As one auto worker said: 'I got nothing against guys in white shirts, but I just ain't cut out for work like that.'[42] Berger also noted the disinclination of American workers and their families to become involved in the local associations and organizations of the middle class. Instead, they stuck with the union.

In Britain during the 1960s, the team of Goldthorpe, Lockwood, Bechhoffer and Platt, in their study of car workers and other blue collar workers of Luton, also found the idea of the embourgeoisement of the working class on the new estates to be a myth.[43] However, it is interesting to compare the seemingly more active culture of associations, clubs and groups which existed generally within British working-class suburban life as opposed to American suburban culture. The Community Associations movement, for example, had since the 1920s, and working in harness with statutory authorities, involved people living on working-class new estates, who agitated for better social and practical facilities.[44] By the late 1960s, however, the Community Associations movement in Britain was declining in working-class estates. Its high points had been the interwar years and the 1940s and 1950s. During the 1960s, however, as the sociologist David Donnison wrote, the Community Associations movement was forced to recognize that its facilities and activities required a wider scope than the localized definition of 'community' allowed. People were indeed increasingly coming together around shared interests, rather than on the basis of street identities, and this meant the movement had to widen its geographical parameters and re-think its ideas about community.[45]

Donnison's argument reflected a wider shift in the approaches of some key sociologists and town planners in the 1960s. The ideal of 'neighbourhood units' went out of fashion. This concept, so popular among planners in both countries before, during and after the Second World War, held that people of varying occupational backgrounds should live near to each other in socially mixed neighbourhoods which were within walking distance of the shops and facilities required to sustain them. As Peter Mann argued, in an article referring to both Britain and America, in the planning of neighbourbood units the town planners provided the geographical homogeneity, which rested upon 'a ready-made concept of neighbourliness which is foreign to [people's] nature'.[46]

So what had happened to the lower class suburbanite was not a process of embourgeoisement, nor a diminishing of any capacity for social interaction. Instead, there was a less active neighbourliness in the street-based sense associated with poorer areas, but a higher level of home-based pursuits, and a growing diversity in recreations, tastes and interests. A powerful equation seemed to be shaping the socio-urban behaviour of the two countries: affluence plus choice plus greater mobility led to a departure from the enforced sociability associated with poorer areas. An oral historian has referred to this as an 'erosion of community norms',[47] and writers on city life in America have made stark contrasts between the visible vigour and dignity of the city street and the seeming passivity and uniformity of the suburbs.[48] Oral historians have made significant contributions to our understanding of social change in the twentieth century, but few of them approach positively and in detail the widening of tastes, interests and patterns of social interaction enjoyed in the movement from poorer areas to residential suburbs, and the *limitations* of neighbourhood as a means of understanding change in working-class culture.

An understanding of suburbanization in both Britain and America teaches us the following lesson: suburbanites continually sought to achieve a balance between greater affluence, the comforts of home, neighbourliness and wider interactive networks which transcended localism for town-wide, regional, national and even international cultures of connection and association. Class and income continued to determine the access to new opportunities. Gans' conclusion stands for both suburban nations: 'if people have the discretionary income and skills to make choices, they will begin to express and to implement *preferences*. This can create a demand for greater diversity in housing, recreation, taste, and in many other aspects of life.[49] This view has wider implications for social change. As a 1969 paper by Norman Dennis argued, new estates and subdivisions merely threw into relief the major changes and continuities occurring in postwar society.[50] Like Ruth Glass before him, Dennis showed impatience with those who felt that a local collection of houses ought, intrinsically and externally, to be thriving local communities.

Such themes were taken up by the influential town-planning thinker Melvin Webber in the 1960s. Based in Berkeley, California, Webber argued that people were enjoying greater levels of choice and mobility than ever before, and could communicate, instantly, with others over hundreds and thousands of miles. Hence the idea of 'place' as a basis for the social organization of towns and cities required drastic re-thinking. To use some key phrases of Webber, the city was becoming 'a nonplace urban realm'. And 'community without propinquity' was a useful term for understanding social interaction in an age which was witnessing the decline of traditional urban-industrial communities, and the rise of 'post-industrial' social and communications networks based more upon formal association and secondary contacts via the telephone and the screen. English urban planners and social thinkers shared the gist of Webber's ideas, even if they could point to local differences between Britain and the USA. The Liverpool planner F. J. C. Amos, for example, argued in 1968 that English society was witnessing 'a transition from an urban society based on local industrial communities to a new urban associational society'.[51]

Webber is also significant for our discussion because he was appointed as a consultant to Llewelyn Davies, Weeks, Forestier-Walker and Bor, the planning team appointed by Milton Keynes Development Corporation in 1967, the year that most famous of English new towns was first designated.[52] Milton Keynes's 'grand suburban design'[53] of garden city gridsquares, held between fast roads on a Los Angeles style gridiron is of considerable importance in concluding our discussion. It is a suburban city, as noted; it represents the continuing discourse and practical exchange of ideas between British and American town planners which began with the planned suburbs of the late nineteenth century, mentioned above, through to the adoption of neighbourhood units as bases for the social design of postwar suburban neighbourhoods, and new towns. In Milton Keynes, 'localism as a basis for community was envisaged as but one variable in a culture which would be increasingly less territorial, and more mobile, city-wide, regional, national, and international'. Technology, the car, telephone, television and the computer, were central to Webber's vision, and also to the planning of Milton Keynes. It was, perhaps, a cogent coincidence that the 'university of the air', the Open University, was established in Milton Keynes in 1969. The home-based study materials, in alliance with the course tutorials and summer schools of this distance learning institution have brought people together upon the basis of shared enthusiasms for a wide range of academic interests, and across distances which vary from a few miles to hundreds.

CONCLUSION

Finally, it is interesting to note two related postwar developments. Both countries have seen a southward drift away from the declining manufacturing regions of the north to the booming, suburbanizing cities of the south. In England this means London and the south; in the US, the 'sunbelt cities'.[54] An historical analysis of the significance of this transition is beyond the scope of this chapter, but it does suggest still further a shared – if sometimes divergent – continuing pattern of socio-urban change in both countries. This may be all the more significant if the two nations are passing, as planners, socialists and economists have argued, from an industrial to a post-industrial socio-economic system.[55] We must note, however, the urban and regional differences within this historical trend, and warn against a simple view which sees a simple and total transition from a goods-producing to a service-centred system. A post-industrial and increasingly suburban future may not be an *inevitable* consequence of those changes discussed here, but that should not stop us recognizing the perception of these changes in both countries during the 1960s. All of these developments, however, beginning with nineteenth-century suburbanization, and culminating in a new phase of suburban or even post-suburban sprawl in the later twentieth century, deserve further comparative historical analysis.

Notes

1. Howard P. Chudacoff, 'Political, economic and spatial factors in the postindustrial city', in Howard P. Chudacoff (ed.), *Major Problems in American Urban History* (Lexington: D. C. Heath, 1994), pp. 379–80; A. H. Halsey, 'Social trends since World War II', in Linda McDowell, Philip Sarre and Chris Hamnett (eds), *Divided Nation: Social and Cultural Change in Britain* (London: Hodder & Stoughton, 1989), p. 23.
2. David C. Thorns, *Suburbia* (London: McGibbon & Kee, 1972), p. 83.
3. This definition is based upon Thorns, *Suburbia*, pp. 31–4, 83; Peter Willmott, 'Social research and the new communities', *American Institute of Planners Journal*, 31 (1967), p. 388.
4. Dennis J. Judd, *The Politics of American Cities: Private Power and Public Policy* (New York: Harper Collins, 1988), pp. 156–8; Bruce Wood, 'Urbanization and local government', in A. H. Halsey (ed.), *British Social Trends Since 1900* (London: Macmillan, 1988), pp. 325–7, 330.
5. Judd, *Politics of American Cities*, pp. 236–8; Peter Hall, 'Moving on', *New Society*, 24 November 1977, p. 412.
6. Robert A. M. Stern with John Montague Massengale, *The Anglo-American Suburb* (London: Architectural Design, 1981), pp. 52–7.
7. S. Martin Gaskell, 'Housing and the lower middle class, 1870–1914', in Geoffrey Crossick (ed.), *The Lower Middle Class in Britain* (London: Croom Helm, 1977), pp. 160–64; Kenneth T. Jackson, *Crabgrass Frontier: The Suburbanization of the United States* (New York: Oxford University Press, 1985), p. 68.
8. Wendy Sarkissian, 'The idea of social mix', *Urban Studies*, 13 (1976), pp. 236–7.
9. Stern, *The Anglo-American Suburb*, p. 12.
10. Gaskell, 'Housing and the lower middle class', pp. 179–80.
11. Michael Wagenaar, 'Conquest of the center or flight to the suburbs? Divergent metropolitan strategies in Europe, 1850–1914', *Journal of Urban History*, 19/1 (1992), pp. 63–6.
12. Robert Fishman, *Bourgeois Utopias: The Rise and Fall of Suburbia* (New York: Basic Books, 1987); David Reeder, *Suburbanity and the Victorian City* (Leicester; University of Leicester, 1980).
13. David Reeder, 'Representations of metropolis: descriptions of the social environment in *Life and Labour*', in David Englander and Rosemary O'Day (eds), *Retrieved Riches: Social Investigation in Britain, 1840–1914* (Aldershot: Scolar Press, 1995), pp. 329–30.
14. Stern, *The Anglo-American Suburb*, pp. 62–80.
15. Ian Davis, 'Dunroamin and the Modern Movement', in Paul Oliver, Ian Davis and Ian Bentley (eds), *Dunroamin: The Suburban Semi and its Enemies* (London: Pimlico, 1994), p. 16.

16. John Stevenson and Chris Cook, *The Slump: Society and Politics during the Great Depression* (London: Quartet, 1979), pp. 24–5.
17. Paul Taylor, 'British local government and house building during the Second World War', *Planning History*, 17/2 (1995), p. 17.
18. Chudacoff, *Major Problems in American Urban History*, pp. 299–325.
19. Thorns, *Suburbia*, p. 67; Jackson, *Crabgrass Frontier*, pp. 190–218.
20. Davis, 'Dunroamin and the Modern Movement', p. 40.
21. See, for example, Tony Aldgate, 'Mass society', in John Golby *et al.* (eds), *Between Two Wars* (Buckingham: Open University Press, 1990), pp. 195–201.
22. John Betjeman, 'Slough', 1938; John Carey, *The Intellectuals and the Masses: Pride and Prejudice among the Literary Intelligentsia, 1880–1939* (London: Faber and Faber, 1992), pp. 46–70.
23. D. L. LeMahieu, *A Culture for Democracy: Mass Communications and the Cultivated Mind in Britain Between the Wars* (Oxford: Clarendon Press, 1988), p. 317.
24. J. B. Priestley, *English Journey* (London: Heinemann Gollancz, 1934, 1937 edition), 1937 edn, pp. 401–2.
25. Lewis Mumford, *The City in History* (New York: Harcourt, Brace Jovanovich, 1961; Harmondsworth: Penguin, 1979), Penguin edn, p. 553.
26. Carey, *Intellectuals and the Masses*, pp. 182–3.
27. Mr Pooter is the 'Nobody' of *The Diary of a Nobody* by George and Weedon Grossmith (first published in *Punch*, then in book form in 1892; Penguin Modern Classics, 1965). He and his wife Carrie live at The Laurels, Brickfield Terrace, Holloway and Pooter's attitudes and doings exemplify English suburban life in its Victorian heyday.
28. William H. Whyte, *The Organization Man* (New York: Simon and Schuster, 1956; Harmondsworth: Penguin, 1965).
29. David Riesman, *The Lonely Crowd: A Study of the Changing American Character* (New Haven and London: Yale University Press, 1951, 1970), 1970 edn, pp. 17–23, for example.
30. Tosca Fyel, 'Thoughts about suburbia', *Socialist Commentary* (January, 1961), p. 22.
31. Christopher Booker, *The Neophilliacs: A Study of the Revolution in English Life in the Fifties and Sixties* (London: Fontana, 1970), pp. 144, 161.
32. Ian Nairn, *Outrage* (London: Architectural Design, 1955).
33. A. H. Halsey (ed.), *Trends in British Society since 1900* (London: Macmillan, 1972), pp. 551–2.
34. Ferdynand Zweig, *The Worker in an Affluent Society* (London: Heinemann, 1961), p. 206.
35. Michael Young and Peter Willmott, *Family and Kinship in East London* (London: Humanities, 1957; Harmondsworth: Penguin, 1979), Penguin edn, pp. 156–63.
36. Young and Willmott, *Family and Kinship*, pp. 61, 46–7, 55–6.
37. This discussion is based upon the following: Jane Lewis and Barbara Brookes, 'A re-assessment of the work of the Peckham Health Centre, 1936–1951', *Milbank Memorial Quarterly*, 61/2: (1983), p. 330; P. Hall, 'Some clinical aspects of moving house as an apparent precipitant', *Journal of Psychosomatic Research*, 10/1 (1966), pp. 54, 68–9.
38. In the USA the film *No Down Payment* (1957) is but one example. For Britain, see Leslie Thomas, *Tropic of Ruislip* (London: Fontana, 1974).
39. Bennet M. Berger, 'The myth of suburbia', *Journal of Social Issues*, 17 (1961), p. 49. This article was a distillation of Berger's *Working-Class Suburb* (Berkeley: University of California Press, 1960); William M. Dobriner (ed.), *The Suburban Community* (New York: Putnam, 1958); Herbert J. Gans, 'The balanced community: homogeneity or heterogeneity in residential areas?', *Journal of the American Institute of Planners*, 27/1 (1961); Herbert J. Gans, *The Levittowners: Ways of Life and Politics in a Suburban Community* (New York: Pantheon, 1967).

40. J. B. Cullingworth, 'Social implications of overspill: the Worsley Social Survey', *Sociological Review* 8/1 (1960), p. 77; J. B. Cullingworth, 'The Swindon Social Survey: a second report on the social implications of overspill', *Sociological Review* 9/2 (1961), p. 151; J. M. Mogey, 'Changes in family life experienced by English workers moving from slums to housing estates', *Marriage and Family Living* 17/2 (1955), pp. 124–8, which included some of Mogey's key findings from his *Family and Neighbourhood: Two Studies of Oxford* (Oxford: Oxford University Press, 1956); N. H. Rankin, 'Social adjustment in a north-west new town', *Sociological Review* 11/3 (1963), pp. 293–6.

41. H. E. Bracey, *Neighbours: On New Estates and Subdivisions in England and the USA* (London: Routledge & Kegan Paul, 1964), pp. 181–91.

42. Berger, 'The myth of suburbia', p. 49.

43. John H. Goldthorpe, David Lockwood, Frank Bechhoffer and Jennifer Platt, *The Affluent Worker in the Class Structure* (Cambridge: Cambridge University Press, 1969), pp. 157–65.

44. See, for example, Ruth Durrant, *Watling: A Survey of Social Life on a New Housing Estate* (London: P. S. King, 1939), pp. 39–50.

45. Raymond Clarke (ed.), *Enterprising Neighbours: The Development of the Community Association Movement in Britain* (London: National Federation of Community Organizations, 1990), p. ix.

46. Peter H. Mann, 'The Concept of Neighbourliness', *American Journal of Sociology*, LX/2 (1954), pp. 163–4.

47. Elizabeth Roberts, 'Neighbours: North West England, 1940–1970', *Oral History*, 21/2 (1993), pp. 43–44. In his review of Elizabeth Roberts' work, the oral historian Carl Chinn has argued that 'we have abandoned the communal space': *Social History Society Bulletin*, 20/2 (1995), p. 32.

48. Jane Jacobs, *The Death and Life of the Great American Cities* (New York: Random House, 1961; Harmondsworth: Penguin, 1984), Penguin edn, pp. 13, 83.

49. Gans, 'The Balanced Community', p. 183.

50. Norman Dennis, 'The popularity of the neighbourhood community idea', R. E. Pahl (ed.), *Readings in Urban Sociology* (Oxford: Pergamon Press, 1969), p. 84.

51. Frederick Amos, 'The planner's responsibility to the community', speech to the SSRC/CES Conference *The Future of the City Region*, July 1968; copy in possession of this writer.

52. Melvin M. Webber, 'Planning in an environment of change, Part 1: Beyond the industrial age', *Town Planning Review*, 38 (1968–9), pp. 179–95; 'Planning in an environment of change, Part 2: Permissive planning', *Town Planning Review*, 39 (1968–9), pp. 277–95; 'Order in diversity: community without propinquity', in Lowdon Wingo (ed.), *Cities and Spaces: The Future Use of Urban Land* (Baltimore: Johns Hopkins Press, 1970), pp. 23–54.

53. Terence Bendixson and John Platt, *Milton Keynes: Image and Reality* (Cambridge: Granta Editions, 1992), p. 167.

54. Halsey, 'Social trends since World War II', pp. 22–3.

55. Daniel Bell, 'The coming of the post-industrial society', in Charles Jencks (ed.), *The Post-Industrial Reader* (London: Academy Editions, 1992) pp. 250–66; Webber, see note 52.

A comparative historical geography of streetcar suburbs in Boston, Massachusetts and Leeds, England, 1850–1920

DAVID WARD

Some of the most striking contrasts in the appearance of British and American cities are inherited from regional differences in the type and scale of urban growth in the sixty years before the outbreak of the First World War. This period was characterized by the construction of improved dwellings in new suburban locations which were linked to the industrial and business sections of the city, at first by horse-drawn and later by electrically powered streetcars. Today these streetcar suburbs are surrounded by the more extensive, and often morphologically quite distinct, residential developments associated with the period after the First World War, when the internal combustion engine provided more flexible means of local transportation.

Innovations in local transport, however, were introduced more rapidly in North America than they were in Britain, and the streetcar tracks and services were also much more extensive. Accordingly the streetcar exerted a much greater influence upon the growth and upon the social and economic life of American cities. In considerations of nineteenth-century urbanism, regional variations in the effects of local transportation upon the growth and characteristics of cities have received only limited attention and it is proposed in this paper to explore some of the contrasts exhibited by the streetcar suburbs of Boston and Leeds and, further, to relate these contrasts to the different developmental experiences of British and American cities between 1870 and 1914.

With the exception of London, the late Victorian additions to British towns were limited in their areal extent and often represented only a modest advance on former housing conditions. Throughout this period much building took the form of the filling in of vacant areas near to the city centre. Terrace dwellings (Fig. 1) arranged in a rectilinear pattern in certain

Originally published in *Annals of the Association of American Geographers*, 54/4 (1961), pp. 477–89.

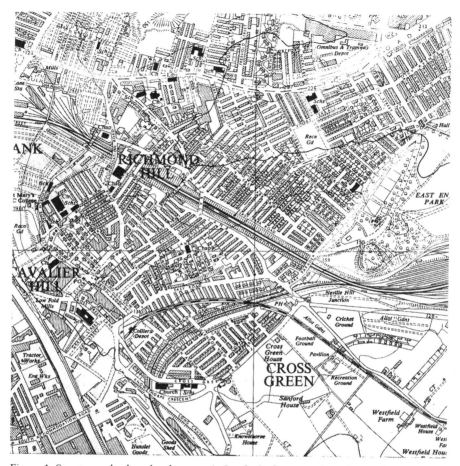

Figure 1 Streetcar suburban development in Leeds. Scale: approximately 6 inches to 1 mile. (Reproduced from the Ordnance Survey Map with the sanction of the Controller of Her Majesty's Stationery Office. Crown copyright reserved.)

peripheral districts near to streetcar services did, however, provide improved homes for a restricted number of middle-class people. In contrast, the detached or semidetached house set in its own lot (Fig. 2) was the dominant type of suburban residential building at this time in the United States. These houses were not only laid out in a more spacious fashion but they also represented a greater advance on former living standards than did the British terraces. Electrified streetcar services were introduced only slowly in Britain and, indeed, many early routes were specifically provided by municipalities to link isolation hospitals, parks, and cemeteries with the city proper. In the United States, at a much earlier date, street railway tracks were extended by private companies well beyond the continuous

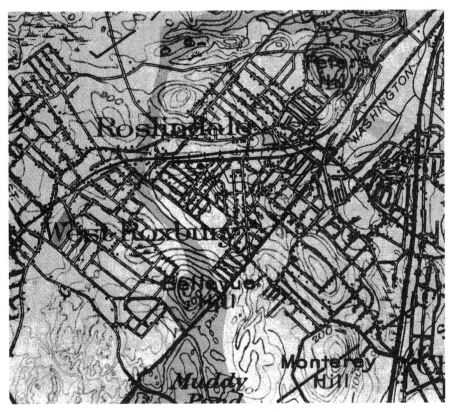

Figure 2 Street car suburban development in Boston. Scale: 1:24,000.

built–up areas and the electrification of much more extensive systems was almost complete before the first modest adventures in electrified services had commenced in most British provincial cities.

By the later decades of the nineteenth century the populations of American cities were increasing at their greatest rate whereas in Britain the rate of population growth in large cities was greatest in the earliest decades of the century. In the second half of the nineteenth century British cities grew more slowly partly because emigration depleted their populations in the 1880s and again in the first decade of the twentieth century. A proportion of this emigration was, moreover, partly responsible for swelling the populations of American cities in the same decades. In 1870 Boston and Leeds each contained about a quarter of a million people; by 1920 Leeds had doubled its population whereas Boston had increased threefold.

Table 1 Peaks and troughs in the British and American building cycles 1860–1920.

Great Britain		United States	
Peaks	Troughs	Peaks	Troughs
1863			1864
	1871	1871	
1877			1878
	1887	1890	
1899			1900
	1912	1909	
1920			1918

THE DIFFERENCE IN PHASE OF THE RESIDENTIAL BUILDING CYCLE IN BRITISH AND AMERICAN CITIES

The growth of the populations of American cities was greater than that of British cities whereas the periods of intensive residential building occurred in different decades on either side of the Atlantic. In general, building activity in British cities was most pronounced in the mid-1870s and at the turn of the century, whereas in American cities intensive building occurred in the late 1880s and early 1890s and also in the middle of the first decade of the twentieth century (Table 1). This difference in phase of British and American building cycles has been related to the migration of people and capital from Britain to the New World when economic conditions were attractive in the United States and a corresponding tendency for greater domestic investment and internal migration in Britain when economic conditions in America were less attractive. Residential buildings in the United States would thus reinforce the general boom in investment and immigration whereas in Britain residential building, as a major item of domestic investment, would occur when opportunities for foreign invest-ment were restricted and, therefore, stand in an inverse relationship to the trade cycle.

This complementary relationship between migration, investment, and residential building in Britain and the United States has been regarded as a fundamental characteristic of the Atlantic economy in the two generations before the First World War. More recently, reservations concerned with the degree to which investment in, and migration to, the New World could affect the secular trend of residential building in Britain, have been expressed and some observers have been inclined to attribute fluctuations in the British building cycle to local and domestic rather than to inter-national conditions. Nevertheless, the difference in phase of residential building on either side of the Atlantic, whether it was created by local or by international conditions or indeed by both, reflected the different chronology of the growth rates of British and American cities. The timing of such spurts and lags in the amount of residential building may well have been affected by, or, indeed, have had an effect upon the successful introduction of innovations in local transportation.

THE RESIDENTIAL BUILDING CYCLE IN LEEDS

Although residential building may respond to local conditions and exhibit marked regional variations, all the larger northern English industrial cities experienced a marked boom in residential building in the mid-1870s and in the late 1890s whereas in the 1880s and in the decade immediately preceding the First World War there were pronounced slumps. From gaining over 200,000 people by migration during the 1870s, the northern English industrial towns lost nearly 60,000 by emigration in the following decade. Leeds, however, received a substantial influx of Jewish immigrants from Eastern Europe during the '80s, and by 1890 there were as many as 8,000 Jews, largely occupied in the growing ready-made clothing industry of the city.

Indeed, Leeds gained more people by migration in the 1880s when foreign immigration was high than in the '70s and '90s when migration within Britain was more pronounced (Table 2). But over half of this gain by migration in the '80s, represented the substantial influx of Eastern European Jews, who were finding their way to American cities in even larger numbers at the same time. In Leeds, therefore, there was a counterpoise to the effects of native emigration and the prolonged period of depression in the building trade. The local building cycle, therefore, shows a minor peak in the late 1880s which punctuated the lengthy depression between the national peaks of the mid-'70s and late '90s (Fig. 3).

Although Leeds thus was somewhat insulated from the more severe

Table 2 Population growth in Leeds.

	Total population	Net increase	Natural increase	Gain or loss by migration
1871	259,212			
1881	309,119	49,970	42,503	7,404
1891	367,505	58,386	41,012	17,374
1901	428,968	61,463	47,098	14,365
1911	445,568	16,582	47,979	−31,397
1921	458,232	4,077	26,001	−21,923

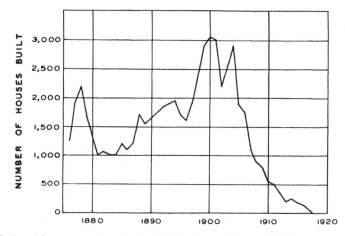

Figure 3 Annual amount of residential building in Leeds, 1876–1920.

effect of the building slump and emigration in the 1880s, the city lost over 30,000 people by emigration between 1901 and 1911 which, in one decade, eliminated the gain by immigration of the two preceding decades (Table 2). In spite of this heavy emigration, the boom in residential building which started in the late 1890s continued on into the early years of the twentieth century; between 1898 and 1903 the amount of building was greater than in any other preceding five-year period (Fig. 3). Since construction continued on into the period of emigration, the number of empty houses in the city rose rapidly and by 1904 amounted to over 5 per cent of the total number of dwellings.

This large number of empty houses, however, need not indicate a miscalculation of demand on the part of the building industry, for new tastes in the style and location of dwellings can also stimulate the removal of existing residents. The distribution and the rents of many of the empty houses in the city suggest that a large proportion represented the former

Table 3 The distribution and rents of empty houses in Leeds, 1905.

Distance from city centre	Total number of houses	Rents below five shillings	Rents above five shillings	Total number empty	Percentage empty
Within 0.5 mile	16,859	445	255	700	4.2
Beyond 0.5 mile Within 1 mile	28,546	734	1,007	1,741	6.1
Beyond 1 mile	34,841	874	524	1,398	4.0
Total	80,246	2,053	1,786	3,839	4.8

Note: Most of the new suburban houses were beyond one mile from the city centre (see Fig. 7).

homes of middle–class people who had taken advantage of the new street-car facilities to move on to improved terrace houses. Over half the empty houses were situated in a zone between a half mile and a mile from the city centre where the proportion of empty houses in 1905 amounted to 6.1 per cent. In the congested central districts and in the outer suburbs the proportion empty was about 4 per cent (Table 3); for the city as a whole it was 4.8 per cent. Some two-thirds of the empty houses were of intermediate rents (i.e., five shillings or more)[1] so that they would be beyond the means of most of the residents of the central slums.

Thus the boom in residential building at the turn of the century was associated with the movement of people, whose income had already enabled them to live at some distance from the city centre, to better residences in suburban locations. The larger number of empty houses, which were only slowly reoccupied as rents decreased and as building declined in the decade before the outbreak of the First World War, indicated an internal redistribution of an existing population. Since it was only in the late 1890s that the Leeds streetcar system was fully electrified and the track extended, the building boom which these developments sustained was hardly started before emigration began to drain the city of much of its natural increase in population. Under these circumstances the streetcar suburban developments must have been somewhat curtailed. In Leeds transportation innovations stimulated a pronounced boom in suburban residential building but both the dimensions of this boom and the scale of new local transport provisions must have been reduced by the coincidence of the application of the innovations with the beginnings of heavy emigration.

THE RESIDENTIAL BUILDING CYCLE IN BOSTON

Boston experienced fluctuations in the volume of residential building which were distinctly out of phase with those which occurred in Leeds. Boston experienced pronounced peaks in building activity in the early 1870s and in the late '80s and early '90s whereas the slumps in residential building occurred in the late '70s and early '80s and again around the turn of the century (Fig. 4). The relationship between migration and building activity is, as in Leeds, somewhat obscured in the first decade of the twentieth century. In Leeds building continued at a high level in spite of heavy emigration but in Boston, although there was exceptionally heavy immigration between 1905 and 1915 (Table 4), the increase in building activity was relatively subdued (Fig. 4).

Most of the immigrants into Boston in the decade before the First World War were from Italy, Russia, and the Eastern Mediterranean lands

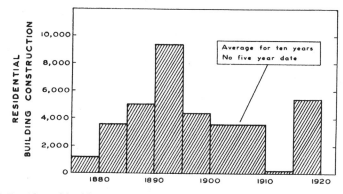

Figure 4 Residential building in Boston by five-year periods, 1875–1920.

and they mainly occupied the central tenement districts by the further subdivision of existing structures.[2] In 1900 there were 8.44 people per dwelling in Boston but by 1915 this index of congestion had advanced to 10.05 people per dwelling. As in Leeds, empty houses were the abandoned homes of middle-income people who had moved on to better dwellings and for long the rents of these dwellings were beyond the means of the newly arrived immigrant in Boston. For a decade contemporary American observers had been impressed by the effect of the streetcar in facilitating the dispersal of people from central areas but after about 1900 their impressions were rapidly revised as Boston was once again flooded with immigrants who had neither the income nor, in some instances, the desire to move to suburban locations.

The earlier confidence in the effect of street railroads in the improve-

Table 4 Population growth in Boston.

	Total population	Net increase	Natural increase	Gain or loss by migration
1870	287,532★			
1875	341,919	54,387	34,954	19,433
1880	362,839	21,021	23,230	−2,209
1885	390,394	27,556	9,057	18,499
1890	448,477	58,082	33,205	24,877
1895	496,920	48,443	26,217	22,226
1900	560,892	63,972	49,417	14,555
1905	595,380	34,488	19,690	14,794
1910	670,585	75,205	44,230	30,975
1915	745,439	74,854	50,908	23,946
1920	748,060	2,621	24,670	−22,049

★ Includes areas annexed in 1872.

ment of the conditions of urban life had, however, been based upon the impressive scale and successful application of innovations in local transport in the late 1880s and early '90s. Moreover, in Boston the electrification of the streetcar system occurred at a time when large numbers of immigrants from the Maritime Provinces of Canada were arriving in the city.[3] These Maritime Canadians, unused to urban congestion, had a predilection for the more open housing of the streetcar suburbs and, unlike later immigrants from Russia and Italy, the Maritimers had the economic means to take immediate advantage of suburban residences. Indeed, Maritime Canadians dominated the house building industry in Boston. Thus the residential building boom stimulated by the provision of improved means of local transport had the added impetus of heavy immigration of people of moderate means and with a preference for suburban living.

Innovations in local transport in Boston initiated a residential building boom but the dimensions of this boom must have been greatly enlarged by the contemporary arrival of large numbers of immigrants. This supplementary stimulus of population growth may well have encouraged the confident investment in local transport and residential building far beyond the proportions suggested by the tentative experiments in electrified streetcars in the 1880s. British investors in local transport at the same time had not this insurance of the effects of immigration[4] quite apart from any differences in real wage levels in the two countries and, in spite of experimentation with steam as well as electricity, the application of electricity to local transport and more particularly the extension of track awaited municipal initiative in the 1890s.

LOCAL TRANSPORTATION AND RESIDENTIAL BUILDING

The urban geographer is primarily concerned with the size, location, and characteristics of streetcar suburbs, for these properties represent the spatial consequences of the secular changes in the volume of residential building and of improvements in local transport. Accordingly, the different type and scale of suburban development in Britain and the United States between 1870 and 1914 can be related to the contrasts in the developmental experience of cities on either side of the Atlantic. The chronology of transportation innovation affected the timing of the residential building booms whereas the circumstances of migration affected the dimensions of the boom. In the last analysis, however, the differences in the standard of living and in the size of the British and American middle classes may have exerted the strongest influences of all on the development of streetcar suburbs.

Discussions of the different fluctuations of the residential building cycles in Britain and the United States only rarely have considered the relationship of these cyclical contrasts to the different chronology and scale of innovations in local transportation in the two countries. Certainly Walter Isard has endeavoured to relate not only the booms in residential building, but also those in immigration and general economic conditions in the United States, to the critical innovations in transportation which took place during the nineteenth century. Isard, however, does not elaborate upon the different chronology of building booms in Britain where the residential building associated with the introduction of electrified streetcars occurred several years later. It would appear that the earlier introduction of more comprehensive and extensive transit systems in American cities can be related to the demographic conditions in cities on the western side of the Atlantic at the critical period of innovation. It is, therefore, to the contrasts in the timing of transportation innovations and their effects on the type and scale of urban growth in Boston and Leeds that the analysis now turns.

THE DEVELOPMENT OF LOCAL TRANSPORT IN BOSTON

Local transport facilities in Boston had been well developed long before the introduction of the electric streetcar in 1887. The steam railroads had provided commuter services in the 1840s for wealthy merchants who lived in neighbouring towns but conducted their businesses in Boston. During the 1850s the introduction of the horse-drawn streetcar opened up land adjacent to the contemporary built-up area. It was the horsecar that facilitated the residential development of the South End in the '50s and '60s and of the inner parts of Dorchester and Roxbury during the '70s and '80s when costs were falling and streetcar tracks were extended into a sparsely settled countryside (Fig. 5).

Throughout this period the fare was five cents within the immediate Boston area so that the journey to work was restricted by time rather than by cost. During the 1870s and '80s the density of crosstown services and routes increased whereas the limit of such facilities expanded outwards so that people whose places of work were neither central nor fixed had adequate facilities. The extension of track opened up considerable areas of land so that residential development was relatively sparse and, as the area of possible residence was enlarged once more by the electrification of the streetcar services, the intervening areas within the horsecar suburbs were filled with less ostentatious buildings.

The slow pace of the horsecar placed definite limits on the distance from which people could commute each day. In 1880 it was reported that:

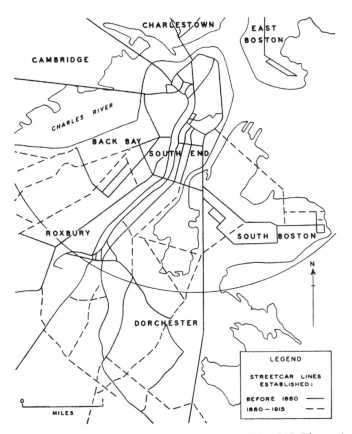

Figure 5 The growth of Boston's public transport system, 1880–1915. The arc is 2.5 miles from the city centre.

> ... between two and a half and five miles from the city center, there was abundant underdeveloped land, since it was as quick and convenient to travel by steam railroad from five miles or more as by horse railroad for three or four miles.

Seven years later the problem was alleviated by the rapid electrification and amalgamation of almost all the private horsecar services in the Boston area under the single management of a new company known as the West End Street Railway Company. The success of experiments in the use of electric power for streetcar services conducted by the original West End Company prompted the owners to purchase, coordinate, and electrify most of the then existing streetcar services in and around Boston. In 1894 the Boston Elevated Company was formed to provide rapid transit facilities in the form of elevated tracks and subways and in 1897 this company obtained a lease of the West End Company so that the future developments of

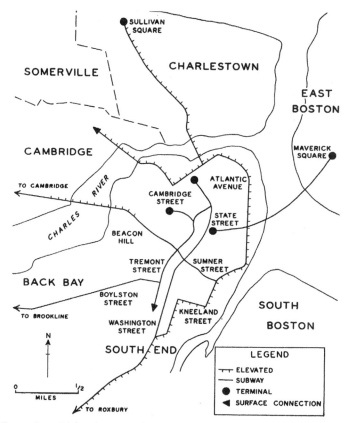

Figure 6 Boston's rapid transit system in 1915.

elevated and subway services would be integrated with the surface system (Fig. 6).

In 1887 the West End Company had acquired 91.8 miles of track and a system which catered for over 90 million passengers each year (Table 5). In 1897 the Boston Elevated Company acquired 316.05 miles of track of which over 300 miles were already electrified and a system which catered for about 180 million passengers each year (Table 5). By the outbreak of the First World War the Boston Elevated Company operated over 500 miles of surface track and over 30 miles of rapid transit track (Figs 5 and 6) but passenger traffic especially after 1905 increased at a rate faster than that of the population of the city as a whole and faster than the company could install more adequate facilities. By 1914 the company was handling almost 350 million passengers each year (Table 5).

At the turn of the century, just as the electrified streetcars appeared to be creating the possibilities of universal suburban living and thereby fulfilling the hopes of so many optimistic observers of the 1890s, the financing

Table 5 The expansion of public transport facilities in Leeds and Boston, 1870–1920.

	Boston*			Leeds	
	Number of passengers (in millions)	Total track (in miles)		Number of passengers (in millions)	Total track (in miles
1871	34				
1881	68				
1887	92	212			
1895	155	275	1894		27.5
1899	191	338			
1904	242	445	1902	48	71
1909	281	484			
1914	343	515	1916	94	114
1919	325	535			

* The Boston system also served several adjacent towns which together with Boston contained a total population of about one million people in 1900 and about 1.2 million people in 1920.

and management of American street railroads became one of that group of urban problems which to many reformers expressed the generic condition of city life. The heavy capital investments in elevated track and subways came at a time when labour and material costs were rising and it became increasingly difficult for the already overcapitalized company to attract further capital or to yield an operational profit at the uniform five-cent fare to which it was committed by its charter. Certainly construction works were often designed to milk the operating company but in Boston the municipality actively participated in the construction of some of the subways and allowed the company merely to lease them.

Regardless of these later difficulties, which were to force the Boston Elevated Company into the hands of receivers by 1919,[5] the facilities provided and the volume of traffic which they handled was on a scale unprecedented in any English city except London. Equally impressive was the reduction in the time of the journey to work made possible by both the electrified and rapid transit services, and between 1885 and 1895 the boom in residential building was heavily concentrated in areas beyond two and a half miles from the city centre (Fig. 5). It was during this period that the positive effects of the street railroad in improving the conditions of urban living were extolled. Much of the achievement of the early electrified streetcars was obscured by the preoccupation on the part of later reformers with the abuses and problems of railroad management in the decade before the First World War.

The commissioners appointed by the Massachusetts Legislature in 1898 to investigate the street railway conditions in Europe found that European experience in local transportation was surprisingly limited and suggested that:

> ... to institute a comparison ... between the street railway transportation of Boston as at present developed and that of Birmingham or Glasgow, is so absurd as to suggest ignorance. The appliances in use in the European cities so named may, and probably do answer the demands made upon them, but they pertain to conditions of urban life and of urban movement wholly different from those which now prevail in Massachusetts.

In England in 1898, 618 miles of track served the seven and a half million people who lived in the largest cities and the annual number of passengers carried amounted to 474 million people. In the Boston district alone there were 316 miles of track serving the needs of only a million people and handling 181 million passengers a year (Table 5).

THE DEVELOPMENT OF LOCAL TRANSPORT IN LEEDS

In the early 1890s observers in Boston were still optimistic about the benefits to urban living which would be derived from the streetcar, but a Sanitary Congress held in Leeds could suggest only the sober procedure of the compulsory purchase of peripheral estates, the construction of public housing, and the provision of municipal transport. Apparently there were not enough middle-income people to encourage the private builder and consequently little encouragement for the streetcar company to expand its services beyond the existing built-up area. Indeed, in the 1890s the horse omnibus, which had been forced off the streets of Boston in the '50s by the horsecar, still remained the most flexible and extensive form of public transport in Leeds.

It was in 1870, some twenty years later than in Boston, that a street railway company had been formed in Leeds. This new Leeds Tramway Company was granted a twenty-one year lease by the City of Leeds to lay tracks and to operate horsecar services on condition that cheap fares were provided for artisans, mechanics and labouring classes. The horsecar services were neither extensive enough nor speedy enough to encourage commuting by working men. The first improvements in speed came with the introduction of steam power in the '80s but this form of power proved inappropriate to congested city streets. In 1891 experiments in the use of electric power proved successful, and in 1894 the Corporation of Leeds took over the system and proceeded to implement the conversion of the whole system to electricity. In spite of these changes the system was still confined to the main roads out of the city, and the crosstown routes were still dominated by the horse-omnibus companies. Even when the city decided to operate and electrify the street railways, it inherited only 27.5 miles of track (Table 5).

Thus, in 1884 a witness reported that in Leeds: 'there was no tendency, active or passive, for sections of the population to move from the centre to the outskirts. There was no difficulty in obtaining good houses at a short distance from the city centre . . .' Five years after the municipality began to operate and electrify the system, however, a contemporary observer commented that:

> . . . there were wide excellent roads and along them for about three and a half miles from the centre of the city, tramways with horse, steam and electric traction offered ready and cheap locomotion; giving to many householders the opportunity of residing away from their shops, offices and factories and rendering building land more valuable than it otherwise would be.

By the turn of the century the municipality had doubled the length of track and electrified most of the system (Table 5). Although the demand for suburban and improved housing was growing in the late 1890s and the town was making substantial gains to its population by immigration, most of the extensions to the streetcar system were designed to serve such amenities or services as parks, isolation hospitals, and cemeteries located on the edge of the town (Fig. 7). In this way the public streetcar system moved into areas in which the private company had feared to operate in view of the sluggish demand for suburban houses in the late '80s and early '90s.

Thus the application of innovations in local transport was sustained in the mid 1890s by the provision of services to public institutions on the edge of the city, and only later in the '90s and in the early years of the present century were suburban residences, related to the new streetcar services, built in large numbers. The boom in suburban residential building, however, occurred at a time when Leeds was beginning to feel the effects of emigration in retarding the growth of the city's population. Many of the new routes provided by the municipal transport system were designed to replace the horse omnibus on cross-city services or to link the Leeds system with that of neighbouring towns (Fig. 7); and the demand for suburban housing was not large enough to affect the development of the large areas of land bought within daily commuting distance of the city by the electrified streetcar. Unlike Boston, only limited areas beyond two and a half miles from the city centre were developed by suburban builders (Fig. 7).

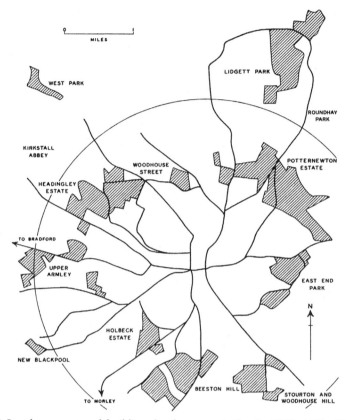

Figure 7 Local transport and building developments in Leeds, 1890–1919. Circle is 2.5 miles from the city centre.

In Leeds the suburban residential development associated with the new streetcar services was, in fact, confined to certain well defined districts. These suburban developments had a more spacious and regular layout than terrace rows in more central locations and consequently, in a large city dominated by small landholdings, were located in those areas where large estates could be purchased for building purposes (Fig. 7). Land suitable for suburban building thus had not only to be accessible to the business district by means of streetcar services but also to be of suitable dimensions to accommodate the larger scale of building. In Leeds the demand for improved dwellings, whether dependent upon the level of real wages or upon taste, was so limited that only some of the restricted number of estate lands available were actually utilized for building purposes before the First World War.

The expansion of the built-up area of Leeds under the stimulus of improved local transport facilities was then decidedly modest before the

First World War. By 1916 Leeds was served by 114 miles of track which handled 94 million passengers each year or less than one-third of the capacity of the Boston system (Table 5). The limitations of demand in a city which was losing population by emigration, at the very time that the electrified services began to stimulate suburban residential development, must have affected the dimensions of the streetcar suburbs. Similarly demographic factors had been unfavourable during the late 1880s when the critical innovations in local transport were made; whereas, in Boston, heavy immigration provided a stimulus to the more confident application of electric power.

MUNICIPAL CONTROL AND THE RESIDENTIAL BUILDING PROCESS

Differences in the scale of suburban growth in Leeds and Boston were also conditioned by the contrasting methods devised by the local authorities to direct and control building in the new suburbs. In Boston the scale of individual building operations was quite small and the constant changes in the alignment and orientation of the grid arrangement of streets are a result of a great number of developers who contributed to the construction of streetcar suburbs. The impression of great uniformity and monotony within the streetcar suburbs was a consequence of the lack of originality in house design and street layout on the part of developers and suburbanites.

In the process of buying farms and building homes, restrictions were at a minimum but since developers often stressed the material superiority of their new subdivisions, a necessary minimum of utilities and paving was often provided to attract the middle-class clientele. Inadequate utilities in a subdivision usually reflected the intention of the developer to cater to low-income groups. Although Boston introduced a rigorous code governing the construction of tenements, the control of subdivisions was always limited and designed to facilitate the process of suburban growth. Some suburbs were indeed destined to become shantytowns because of lack of adequate municipal direction in the provision of utilities and labour; most of the streetcar suburbs, however, suffered little contemporary disadvantage from the limited degree of municipal control.

In Leeds the control of new building was quite comprehensive in the second half of the nineteenth century. As early as 1866 local laws dictated the arrangement of houses, minimum street widths, maximum continuous house frontage, structural dimensions, and, above all, the approval of the plans of all new building by a special committee. This legislation was later codified and applied to most large British towns with the approval of the

Public Health Act of 1875. An underlying assumption of this legislation was that further building would take the form of terrace rows and, therefore, the problem of congestion could be controlled by geometry. In Leeds the more regular and better spaced terraces which, at first, filled in vacant spaces in central parts of the city and, later, characterized the streetcar suburbs, represent the consequences of this legislation. In Leeds, however, most of the improved terrace houses were still built back to back[6] and it was 1901 before the problem of cul-de-sacs was encompassed by the legislation.

Clearly the adoption of the detached or semi-detached house by the American middle class removed many of the imperative needs to control building which exist when dwellings are arranged in the form of terraces. The single house set in its own lot represented a nostalgia for the farm-house or the single houses of the main streets of small towns and also indicated the close relationship between improved living conditions and owner occupancy. Although the number of middle-class Bostonians who lived on lots of any size and who were able to pay off their mortgages was quite small, the intention and the achievement of this aim was well represented by the detached house and its small-town architecture. Ownership of a segment of a terrace has not quite the symbolic and actual quality of separateness possessed by a detached or even a semi-detached house. Even when multi-family structures began to appear on the inner margins of the streetcar suburbs, they took the form of 'three-deckers' in which three families on three separate floors would enjoy the separateness of a small lot.

CONCLUSION

The different conditions of urban growth in Leeds and Boston between 1870 and 1914 greatly affected the application of innovations in local transport, the degree and type of control over building exercised by local governments, the physical extent and appearance of the improved dwellings of the streetcar suburbs, and the popular confidence in and imagery of the possibilities of suburban life. In the late nineteenth century innovations in local transport and the rising incomes and changing tastes of middle-class people sustained the growth of streetcar suburbs. But the decisions to build improved dwellings in new locations were made under somewhat different conditions of urban growth.

In the United States the confidence in the possibilities of suburban living and the rapid population growth of the period around 1890 sustained the rapid application of innovations to, and the rapid expansion of, the street railway systems and thereby ensured the rapid growth of streetcar suburbs within the framework of extremely limited control of building by local authorities. In Britain urban growth was somewhat sluggish at this time and innovations were applied only later in the nineties when population growth was more sustained. This belated application of improvements in local transport, however, was largely accomplished by municipal enterprise and in scale was infinitesimal in comparison with developments in American cities. Improved dwellings were the result of the modification of the old terrace form of housing and conceptions of improved living were rather based on the more idealistic and comprehensive solution of new 'Garden Cities'.

Notwithstanding the current controversy concerning the cause of the differences in phase of residential building cycles in Britain and the United States, these differences do, however, express the important distinctions in the chronology of population growth and of the introduction of improved local transportation. The secular and quantitative differences in residential building cycles in Leeds and Boston are clearly recorded in the contrasting characteristics of their respective streetcar suburbs. Even today the late nineteenth-century streetcar suburbs survive as part of the contemporary urban scene and their different appearances and dimensions in Britain and the United States are the result of regional contrasts in the conditions of urban growth some fifty years ago.

The effect of technical innovations and especially of transportation upon the spatial structure of cities and economies is a recurrent theme of economic geography but the spatial consequences of the same innovation may well be quite distinct because of the conditions and rates of urban or economic growth in a particular place at a particular time. Local transportation did not refashion the internal spatial structure of cities in precisely the same way or for precisely the same reasons even within the Western world. Indeed, if the cultural geographer is to analyse the distributional aspects of industrial capitalism and, in particular, one of its most enduring memorials, the industrial city, there will need to be a more systematic investigation of the regional variations in the chronology and rate of economic growth, and also investigation into the aspirations and organization of social groups which are affected by and which at the same time also stimulate the process of social change. As Meinig has recently suggested the necessary and exhilarating task of the geographer is to reconstruct the 'geographical context' of that constellation of situations, objectives, and possibilities with which decision-makers are faced. Certainly to understand those parts of our cities created by nineteenth-century growth requires not only an understanding of the temporal setting but also the varying conditions of regional growth.

Notes

1. Contemporary observers regarded a rent of five shillings per week or more as beyond the means of working-class wage earners.
2. In fact, at this time efforts were made to check the overcrowding in tenements by legislation. The result, however, was that no further tenements were built and the existing tenements provided the only large supply of low-rent housing.
3. From 1890 to 1900 Canadians formed 50 per cent of the total number of immigrants arriving in the port.
4. The Jewish immigrants into Leeds in the 1880s were concentrated in the Leylands district near to the city centre and consequently had only a small effect on the demand for suburban houses.
5. In 1919 the state of Massachusetts organized the street railways of the Boston District as a Metropolitan Agency.
6. A back-to-back terrace was one in which dwellings extended only halfway through the terrace and consequently different dwellings fronted onto the two streets enclosing the row of houses.

IV   Class and Class Conflict

Since the emergence of the Labour Party in Britain at the end of the nineteenth century it has been possible to perceive parties as representatives of class interests – although empirical evidence would not always support such an interpretation. Such a view is scarcely possible in the United States where the most unlikely alliances are found within parties; it was, for example, a broad coalition of big city bosses, southern conservatives and liberals from northern and western states which helped secure the presidency for a succession of Democrats from Andrew Jackson to Harry Truman.

Class in political economic and social terms, is seen as irrelevant to the course of their nation's development by many Americans. Yet 'class' is as clearly identifiable in American society as in British, where it has formed a key element in political debate for at least a century. Furthermore, class conflict in American society, as manifested in the shape of labour disputes, has generally been more brutal and bloody than its British counterpart.

Questions of class and class conflict are explored in the fourth section of this volume. The first extract underlines the essential differences between the American and the British working class during the nineteenth century. Ira Katznelson explores the ways in which class issues are, directly and indirectly, conditioned by the structures and activities of states. His account shows how state-centred factors – the priority of universal suffrage (for white men) in relation to capitalist industrialization, integration promoted by patronage-dispensing political parties and local machine politicians rather than a national bureaucracy or political 'establishment' – served to create a pattern of class understandings quite unlike that of Britain.

In consequence of the early extension of the franchise in the USA, its decentralized government and locally based mass parties, American workers entered the political arena as members of neighbourhoods and ethnic groups rather than as members of an economic class. American workers, it is argued, thus developed a dual personality. At work they defined themselves by reference to class, but their political consciousness was based on ethnic and residential solidarities. Jeffrey Haydu's equally arresting analysis is concerned with the metal trades and the difficulty of mobilizing workers across lines of status and skill. Haydu is concerned with worker responses to industrial change at the beginning of the twentieth century, above all with the comparative reaction of skilled metalworkers to new methods of production that challenged their jealously guarded craft traditions. The question Haydu seeks to answer is how was it that British and American workers came to concentrate on economic demands rather than on the control of work itself. He looks at heavy industry in Coventry and in Bridgeport, Connecticut, during the First World War, to explain the striking similarities of union tactics, management policy, and government intervention in the era of total war.

IV.1
Working class formation and the state: nineteenth-century England in American perspective

IRA KATZNELSON

When the House of Representatives investigated election fraud in New York City in 1868, it uncovered a massive scheme organized by Tammany Hall to sell counterfeit naturalization papers in order to register immigrants, who were not yet citizens, to vote. The committee report revealed that neighbourhood saloons provided the locations for most of this activity. The testimony of Theodore Allen, the owner of St Bernard's on Thompson Street in Greenwich Village, was quite typical:

> I keep a public house, and a man by the name of James Goff and his brother, who were engaged in procuring naturalization certificates, used to come to my house a great deal. ... I suppose 1000 were sent to Brooklyn that I saw them have. They contracted for these papers, they said, at 50 cents a head.

Each Sunday evening, from the mid-1850s to the late 1880s, a debating society met at the Hope and Anchor Inn on Navigation Street in England's Birmingham. Some twenty to forty speakers would argue their cases on a set topic. From the vantage point of the middle classes, Brian Harrison has noted,

> there was much to frighten the outsider observer: the motion of 23 January 1859 for working class enfranchisement was unopposed, and the monarchy lost by thirty-nine votes to sixteen in a debate on republicanism on 22 March 1863. On two occasions, 26 August 1866 and 21 April 1867, the Society was visited by prominent London Reform Leaguers: these included George Howell who joined in the debates. ... By twenty-three votes to fifteen, on 11 June 1871, the Society supported the Paris Communists. Nor was its radicalism exclusively

Originally published in Peter B. Evans, Dietrich Rueschemeyer and Theda Skocpol (eds), *Bringing the State Back In* (Cambridge, London and New York: Cambridge University Press, 1985), pp. 257–84.

political. On 21 August 1859, the strikers in the London building trade were supported by twenty-two votes to two; on 16 October 1864 the midlands miners, on strike at the time, were supported by forty-five votes to eighteen.

The puzzle I wish to identify and explain can be discovered in the working-class saloons and pubs of nineteenth-century city neigbourhoods in England and the United States. In both countries drinking places were important centres of transportation before the widespread introduction of steam-powered streetcars and trains; and after, they were places of refreshment for short- and long-distance commuters. Sometimes plain and sometimes extravagantly decorated, public houses were places of entertainment, especially for men. Some were music halls, some underworld hangouts, some houses of prostitution. All were places of dense sociability, embedded in the fabric of street and community. And, especially after midcentury, most were gathering places for crowds that were increasingly homogeneous in terms of social class.

In both England and the United States public houses became the most common location of working-class political activity. In the United States, saloons provided hospitable gathering places for political parties. Saloonkeepers often acted as political entrepreneurs who built modestly durable and intensely local partisan machines capable of delivering votes in a predictable way in exchange for patronage. As an important study of party organization in the nineteenth and early twentieth centuries concluded, 'The saloons were the nodal points of district organization of both parties. In the back rooms the bosses met to discuss their plans for carrying the districts, while out in front before the bar the captains were building up good-will among the patrons.'

These political parties [. . .] were organizations the political mobilization activities of which were disconnected on the whole from the trade union and work dimensions of working-class life. The manifest content of saloon politics was not that of class but of ethnicity and territoriality. It was concerned with the links between the citizens of a specific residential area and the local level of government.

Working-class pubs in England, by contrast, were part of a network of values and organizations that reflected and promoted the view that class pervades all social relationships, not just those at the work place. For the middle classes, pubs came into their own, much like American saloons, as places of mobilization of voters at election time, but for the great majority who could not vote, the meeting rooms of *their* pubs provided refuge for a host of oppositional political activities, including, most notably, trade union and Chartist groups.

The contrasting political content of working-class activity in pubs and saloons in England and the United States is indicative of a general pattern that has been overlooked in most treatments of working-class formation in England. Implicit in much of this scholarship is a Continental contrast that makes problematic the cautious, reformist quality of workers' collective expression and actions, especially after the demise of the Chartist movement. By contrast, the class character of working-class dispositions, organization, and activity is taken for granted as the virtually inevitable product of capitalist-industrial development. The important, but in this respect typical treatment of the emergence of class in the early nineteenth century by Asa Briggs thus begins by reminding us (no doubt correctly) that 'the concept of social "class" with all its attendant terminology was a product of large-scale economic and social changes of the late eighteenth and early nineteenth centuries' and stresses that 'the change in nomenclature in the late eighteenth and early nineteenth centuries reflected a basic change not only in men's ways of viewing society but in society itself.'

A comparison with the United States demonstrates the dubious quality of even such an innocuous formulation and its confusion of necessary and sufficient conditions. As in England, American workers eschewed class struggle outside of a gradualist, constitutional framework. In the United States, however, a split consciousness came to divide the working class: as labourers at the work place and as ethnics or residents of this or that territory in their residential communities. In England, by contrast, there was no equivalent divided consciousness, nor was class as a category of social understanding limited to the realm of work and labour. 'Class' joined rather than divided the realms of work and off work. Especially characteristic of working-class struggles in early industrial England, Stedman Jones has argued, was 'the closer intertwining of industrial demands. ... It is difficult to separate political and industrial demands in the thirties and forties because working-class leaders themselves rarely did so. Universal suffrage, according to Doherty, the spinners' leader, "means nothing more than a power given to every man to protect his own labour from being devoured by others." ' Such rhetoric would have been quite unusual in the United States, and the talk of suffrage gives us a first hint as to how to think about why.

These differences in the degree and character of class understanding and activity, captured in microcosm in the differences between the rhetorical and organizational content of political gatherings at the drinking places of working people, indicate how the dominant tradition of English working-class historiography debilitates our understanding by assuming what must be explained and, in so doing, makes comparative studies of England and other instances of working-class formation very skewed. At the extreme, this perspective simply treats England as the paradigmatic case of class formation: As the first working class to be made *and* to make itself, it re-vealed the ineluctable logic of the capitalist mode of production. In this way, historical analyses of the English working class have tended to mimic Marx's identification of England at the economic level as heralding the path of Western capitalist development more generally.

Historical treatments of American working-class formation have suf-fered, not without irony, from an imitation of this approach. A good num-ber of radical social historians in the United States (who are better described as neoprogressives in the Beardian sense than as neo-Marxists) have sought to recapture and reconstruct the long-neglected past of the working class. The large, suggestive literature they have produced too often assumes the aptness of the 'making' teleology in English work. The important issue is not whether class was made at all in America or in England or elsewhere, but rather the *terms* on which a working class was formed.

How shall we go about the task of explaining the puzzle of variation between English and American patterns of working-class formation? My starting point is an aphorism of Irving Howe's: 'The working class is a reality, the proletariat an idea.' Approaches to problems of class formation that are too structural and too teleological are unable to deal with real working classes, precisely because they address theoretically constructed proletariats expected by imputation of interest to appear and act in history in particular ways.

But which concrete *historical* factors shall we place our explanatory bets on? This essay develops a state-centred explanation. I argue in a brief examination of 'labour aristocracy' approaches to English working-class formation that economy- and society-centred explanations tend to make unwarranted teleological assumptions, overemphasize the place of work, and underestimate the significance of spatial arrangements, especially as they concern the connections between work and home. I next show that even when we compensate for the shortcomings of such explanations by stressing the reorganization of city space under the impact of industrializa-tion, by underscoring activities in working-class residential communities, and by making contingent what some theorists assume to be 'natural', they still fail to account for the kind of variations we find in the politics of the neighbourhood and the saloon. On key dimensions, especially the conse-quences of capitalist and urban development for working-class residential spaces, the United States and Britain were very similar. The differences in English and American patterns of working-class formation, I try to show, are best accounted for by the impact of the organization and public poli-cies of their respective states.

This is an essay, in short, about how states and their policies shape and inform the creation of meaning about class expressed in language, dispositions and organizations. At issue is how the political contexts created by state authorities established the vocabularies and institutional forms that workers would develop to shape and represent their demands directed both to employers and to the state in the early industrial period. In explaining the contrasting cases of England and the United States, I stress the importance of variation in patterns of interest representation and repression rather than the similarities between the two states (porous bureaucracies, constitutional continuity, and the significance of the law), which are often lumped together too crudely under the macrocomparative rubric of the 'weak' state. Without attention to the differences between these states' organizations and public policies, I argue, it is not possible to understand the key differences in class formation. How and why the state provided a major source of variation in key features of the development of the English working class, considered in contrast to the American, is the analytical centrepiece of the essay.

SOCIETY- AND ECONOMY-CENTRED EXPLANATIONS

If working classes are expected to develop 'naturally' in certain militant or revolutionary ways but do not, historians are tempted to search for alibis.[1] Since most treatments of working-class formation in England take working-class moderation as the object of their explanations, they characteristically try to explain why the counterfactual of a revolutionary class has not been realized. Although this puzzle and this approach are very different from my own, I begin here for three reasons: it is the dominant approach; attention to it will help us to clear some important analytical ground; and some works in this tradition will help us to reformulate a precise, if dissimilar, object of analysis.

'Labour aristocracy' explanations of both a crude and subtle variety are the most common 'alibi' approaches. Using such diverse criteria as wage levels, regularity of work, trade union membership, styles of consumption and culture, and commitments to distinctive sets of norms and values, scholars have sought to find a fault line dividing the working class. The analytical payoff is a political one. As Henry Pelling has observed, 'It is an essential feature of the Marxist theory of the labour aristocracy that this supposedly small section of the working class was conservative in politics and imposed its conservatism upon working-class institutions, thereby concealing but by no means eliminating the underlying militancy of the mass of the workers.'[2]

This approach is beset by a number of fundamental empirical and analytical flaws. The term 'labour aristocracy' is inexact. It shifts in meaning from one treatment to another. A number of microlevel treatments of the relations of craft and manual workers in specific industrial settings indicate just how difficult it is to specify work locations where aristocrats of labour actually confronted a mass of workers. Contrary to expectations of the theory, empirical evidence, especially for the late nineteenth century, suggests that 'it was the more prosperous workers who were the more politically militant and radical, while the lower ranks displayed either apathy or conservatism'. And if the leadership of unions did display a certain narrowness of focus, stressing immediate gains in wages, working conditions, and in public policy rather than more fundamental social transformations, what were their strategic alternatives?

The labour aristocracy approach invites comparison with continental Europe rather than with the United States. This orientation highlights certain questions and obscures others, especially those with which this essay is concerned. Leaving this problem aside for the moment, we might note that the construction of a European foil for the English case depends on an entirely problematic vision of what actually happened across the English Channel. Reformism is not just an English issue. There are quite remarkable similarities in all the capitalist societies of Western Europe and North America with respect to the limits in practice of working-class challenges to the existing order. The implicit Continental contrast in much scholarship about the English working class operates on an entirely misleading model of sustained, heroic, protorevolutionary activity by European working classes.

Perhaps an even more basic problem in the labour aristocracy position (one stressed in an important critique by H. F. Moorhouse) is its tendency to assert *a priori* the significance of a segment of the working class. Such a designation is not possible to assess unless working-class culture as a whole is examined. At most, an explanation stressing a privileged stratum of labour would have to be the outcome of a historical analysis of causes of variation in patterns of working-class formation in specific settings rather than a model of cooptation and sellouts imposed on historical analysis.

This reading and critique of the labour aristocracy approach, and, by extension, other equivalent answers to the question of why the working class did not behave as an essentialist class model predicts, begins to clear the ground to an alternative approach. It beckons us to shift focus away from the gradualist *problématique* of the Continental contrast toward a focus on the emergence of a holistic, or global, kind of class consciousness in England that an American comparison implores us to explain. It insists that we look in the first instance not at a fragment of the working class but at the language and activity of the group broadly conceived, and it demands that we reject the notion that there is one most likely course of working-class development. Instead, we must turn to history and its variations, even as we understand that each case of working-class formation is one of a family sharing common traits – but what history and what traits?

Let us return to St Bernard's saloon on Thompson Street and to Birmingham's Hope and Anchor for some guidance about how to proceed. These public houses shared a number of traits that highlight basic features of capitalist industrialization and urbanization that are directly connected to the variations in patterns of working-class formation we have identified in the English and American cases. These public houses were located in neighbourhoods that were predominately residential. Such local places of work as existed were outside the home. The communities in which they were found were segregated by class. The pubs – like local fire companies, gangs, burial and insurance societies, and other neighbourhood-based organizations – were part of the fabric of new kinds of working-class residential communities. Unlike preindustrial city neighbourhoods, where people tended to work in home-based settings and where the social classes were jumbled together, the new urban space separated work from home and the classes from each other.

The significance of this spatial reorganization is apparent when we realize that what distinguishes the early development of the English from the American working class concerned primarily patterns of culture and activity, not at the place of work, but at the place of residence. In both countries working people constructed tools where they lived in response to the bewildering environments in which they found themselves. Although the forms assumed by working-class organizations in the two societies were virtually identical, however, their rhetorical and institutional contents diverged radically. The contrast between the American pattern of divided consciousness and the English pattern of a more holistic understanding of the significance of class is, at its core, a difference in understanding about the meaning and role of working-class neighbourhoods and their links both to work places and to the political process. For this reason, before we attempt to account for this divergence we need to look closely at the spatial reorganization of the early industrial city.

First, however, I should like to make a small detour. An important book, Patrick Joyce's *Work, Society, and Politics: The Culture of the Factory in Late Victorian England* (Hassocks, Sussex: Hunster Press, 1980), provides a coherent alternative to the labour aristocracy position on post-1840s working-class gradualism by focusing on the working class as a whole. His treatment differs fundamentally from this essay not only in the puzzles it explores but also in its explicit rejection of the spatial dimension I think so important. By detouring briefly through Joyce's book, I will be able to clarify my argument and meet the most cogent objections I know to it.

Joyce focuses on the factory rather than on the residential community in Lancashire and the West Riding. Building on a distinction originally proposed by Stedman Jones between artisans subject to the formal control of capitalists and factory workers subject to 'real' substantive control in the work process, he tries to show how the consolidation of the industrial factory system created a common reality for workers and how their experience of work shaped their institutions and mentalities outside of work. A culture of deference forged in the factory, he argued, was extended to all facets of social and political existence.

Joyce acknowledges that the factory and the neighbourhood had become separate entities, but he maintains that the factory and its social relations were at the heart of neighbourhood feelings and that the class segregation of working-class housing areas was nestled into a larger, well-ordered system of deference. In this view, working-class subcultures were but an aspect of an elaborate network of exchanges between the classes presided over by manufacturers who dominated not only the politics but the cultural expectations of their town and whose sway over working-class life was the product of their deeply rooted, factory-based hegemony. He maintains that as the industrial process became more developed factory life penetrated more deeply into other spheres of life; the less complete the mechanization of production, the less powerful was the hold of the paternal culture of the factory.

In advancing this claim, Joyce challenges not only the view, which I hold, that the growing separation of place of work from place of residence made possible an autonomous working-class cultural and political life, a matter I shall return to, but also the core argument of the labour aristocracy position, which he turns on end (and in so doing reproduces its corporeal shape). 'Far from being the "moderates"', he writes, 'the labour aristocrats were in the forefront of radical politics in this period ... The politics of labour ... were chiefly the concern of those outside the cultural environment of the factory, and especially the craft and skilled sectors in the working class. If these were a labour aristocracy then it was independence rather than reformist "collaboration" that was their political legacy.'

In turning upside down the labour aristocracy position, Joyce adopts its tendency to overstate the divisions between craft and factory workers at the work place (writing about France, William Sewell has shown how factory transformations may in fact provide for new definitions and extensions of craft labour) and leaves unaccounted for the immense number of workers, like those in the engineering trades, who fall neatly into neither broad category. Furthermore, although it is clear that the 'aristocrats' *by definition* provided leadership to the trade union and party politics of the late nineteenth century, it is by no means clear that they were 'radical' as opposed to 'gradual', neither is it obvious that they represented an elite without a mass, factory-based following. For the trade unions such a claim borders on the ridiculous, and for the electoral process the question must remain opaque because most factory workers could not vote until the end of the First World War.

From the perspective of the argument I am developing, Joyce's mimetic treatment of the aristocracy thesis is not merely a matter of secondary interest. It points to the failure of both positions to make crisp distinctions among three axes of differentiation of working-class members: (*a*) workers relatively privileged at work (whether because of their wages or the character of the labour process); (*b*) workers with different styles of life in residential communities segregated by distinctions not only between the working class and other classes, but within the working class itself; and (*c*) workers who provided the political leadership for trade unions, pressure groups, and political parties. The various attempts to collapse all of these axes into one grand axis of internal working-class division obscure the interesting contingent questions about the relationships among these three (sometimes overlapping) sets of actors. From my point of view these distinctions are crucial, because without them it is impossible to ask why, and under what circumstances, political leaders make demands at work directed at employees and, off work, directed at the state in the same terms (as broadly was the case in England) and when they press their demands in utterly different terms in each arena (as broadly was the case in the United States).

TRANSFORMATIONS OF URBAN SPACE

What of Joyce's challenge to the stress on the spatial separateness of work and community and its implications? He takes some pains to deprecate the significance of this separation. The factory town of the mid-nineteenth to late nineteenth century, he writes, 'retained more of the village than it acquired of the city. Understood as the "walking city" the factory town grew by cellular reproduction, the town slowly absorbing factory neighbourhoods in its expansion.' Until the introduction of tramways and bicycles at the turn of the century, he continues, 'the link between home and work remained firm until these severed it'.

If Joyce is correct, then a state-centred explanation of the single, rather than divided, quality of class understanding in England is not necessary. We might then argue that differences in class formation between the United States and England simply are reflections of different patterns in the objective orgnization of spatial relations. In this approach the split consciousness of the American working class would be explained by changes in city space in the antebellum period. [. . .] The more unitary English pattern, by contrast, would be accounted for by the more tight integration of work space and home space.

It is not possible to sustain this line of reasoning, because Joyce is wrong. There was a major reorganization of space in the very large and middle-sized industrializing cities and towns in the middle decades of the nineteenth century. The most dramatic changes came about in the largest cities; indeed, one cannot help but wonder if the exclusion of Liverpool and Manchester (Lancashire's most important centres of working-class concentration) did not bias Joyce's view of the relationship of work and off work; But even in smaller cities (we shall look at the Lancashire factory town of Chorley later) it would be difficult to overstate the importance of changes in and about space.

The large-scale urbanization of British society is one of the most striking features of the nineteenth century. None of the ten largest cities less than doubled in population between 1801 and 1851 (compared with only one of the top French cities in the same period). At this moment of astounding growth, Leeds and Birmingham tripled in size; Manchester and Liverpool quadrupled. All of the ten largest cities had populations of over 100,000 by 1851, with Liverpool and Manchester well over 300,000. By midcentury Liverpool's upper and middle classes 'who could afford to do so had moved from their place of work or business or even beyond it into adjacent townships'. Their residential areas in new suburban rings were divorced from both the work and the residence places of workers. Within the heart of the city there were 'distinctive zones of different economy and society'. Dividing the city into eight areas, Lawton has shown with great clarity how Liverpool space had become sorted out into spatial divisions of the classes from each other. Other research has carefully established that most of the housing constructed in early nineteenth-century Liverpool was built for the new working classes in class-segregated residential neighbourhoods. By midcentury, workshop houses had become domiciles of the past for the majority of Liverpool residents and those of other industrializing cities.

Joyce might suggest that the big-city pattern is atypical, but very fine recent studies would put such an assertion in question. A. M. Warnes, for example, has studied the Lancashire town of Chorley between 1780 and 1850. In the manner of Sam Bass Warner's study of Philadelphia, he takes three 'snapshots' of the town in 1780, 1816, and 1850. Before 1780 the town was an agricultural township, serving the market and commercial functions of its rural environment. Its growth began to accelerate around

1780 as a result of the weaving trade stimulated by the mechanization of spinning. Even so, its landscape continued to be defined by its preindustrial functions: 'Nowhere had large employing units been formed; most people still lived at or immediately adjacent to their place of employment.'

Between 1780 and 1816 the town's population increased by 50 per cent to 6,000, a growth stimulated mainly by employment in early, small textile mills. At this date factories and clusters of houses around them became part of the town topography, but the growth of the textile industry can be accounted for more by the enlargement of existing workshops than by their replacement by factories, and 'residential location was still to a great extent determined by the location of employment and not usually by the social differences among the population'.

Nevertheless, the 1816 social geography of the town was rather more complicated than that of 1780. A somewhat more differentiated pattern had developed, characterized by a more well-defined commercial core, a more rapid pattern of growth in outlying parts, and scattered but discernible clusters of settlements associated with specific new occupations, including calico works and cotton-spinning factories.

By 1850 the town had been radically transformed. In the years since 1816 Chorley had become a factory town. Reporting on the same transformation stressed by Joyce, Warnes notes that handloom weavers, once the majority of the population, were reduced to under 10 per cent of the work force. Using the enumerators' books of the 1851 census, he estimates that 'over one half of the economically active were engaged in branches of the textile industry that necessitated a journey to work'. Furthermore, he finds not only that there was a dramatic shift from domestic employment, but that 'by 1851 the proximity of home and workplace was breaking up, at least for certain sections of the workforce', and 'the conditions for a recognizable pattern of social segregation were beginning to develop.'

It is important not to overstate the modernity of this pattern. Only a negligible number of workers (about 4 per cent) lived more than a mile from their work, and over half of the 1,813 people Warnes examined lived within a quarter-mile of their work places. Of the two in three workers who no longer laboured where they lived, the majority had to move only short distances to overcome the separation. 'Nevertheless there is no doubt that the average distance travelled to work had sharply increased since 1816, not only because more workers lived away from their work but also because of the increasing variety of employment.' In a striking finding Warnes reports that, the newer the factory, the farther away were the locations of residence of its workers.

He also hypothesizes (contra Joyce's emphasis on tied loyalties) that with the diversification of work places there may have been a reduction of commitment by workers to a particular factory or employer, as well as a diversification of family employment in different factories. These changes probably increased the average distance of family members from work. Residential differentiation based on occupation was being replaced by a 'tendency for those with similar incomes, educational levels, or other status variables, to congregate in limited parts of the town'. Paradoxically, belonging to certain occupations (spinning, printing, and bleaching) made such a divorce between occupations and residence possible.

Joyce concludes his treatment of the residence community with a caution. The impersonality and class segregation of the twentieth-century town are so often read back into the nineteenth century that we forget just how unlike the towns of these two centuries were. As words of prudence these imprecations are well taken, but for the purposes of our discussion they largely miss the point. Writing about the industrial revolution more generally, Sewell has shrewdly observed that 'what now appears as the hesitant beginnings of a long and slow development seemed to be a major departure to contemporaries: even a few steam engines or blast furnaces or spinning mills could make a powerful impression on people who had never seen them before. From their point of view, modern industry was a distinctive feature of their age; theirs was an industrial society as no previous society had even seen.'

So with the spatial concomitants of industrialization. What mattered not at all to contemporaries of the nineteenth century was the degree of difference between the nineteenth- and twentieth-century city; impressed on their lives and consciousness was the new urban form that introduced patterns of separation between work and off work not just for the very wealthy but for the majority. In some towns places of work and residence may have been only a short walk away, but they were places *apart*, and except in the case of employer-provided housing (by best estimates only a small fraction of working-class housing, even in single-factory towns) workers came to cluster in communities separate from the locus of work, from other classes, and from other workers with different (Weberian) class attributes.

This revolution in space produced a fundamental change in relationships of authority and in forms of local organization. With the exception of company towns, where factory masters held sway over the totality of working-class life, the role of capitalists was constricted to the work place, freeing workers to live without direct supervision by their bosses in their neighbourhoods. This new freedom was undergirded by a new division between markets for labour and markets for housing. In the workshop structure of employment and residence, the two had moved together to the same rhythm. With the sundering of this link, working-class communities came to be shaped more and more by real-estate speculations and by the strategies of builders and landlords. They became stratified by income and styles of life. And they came to be conscious environments that people of all classes sought to shape and control.

In these new environments, working-class people created new institutions, new relationships, new patterns of life. The *contingent* connections between these and broader patterns of politics and class formation have too long been neglected in favour of such explanatory shortcuts as the labour aristocracy hypothesis.

There is, however, one major exception to the rule of the neglect of space in this approach to class formation. It is worth our attention, because it gives us important clues about how to shape our analytical questions and our approaches to answering them. This exception is John Foster's *Class Struggle and the Industrial Revolution* (London: Weidenfeld & Nicolson, 1974), the most explicit (I would say rigid) Leninist version of the aristocracy thesis. Its great merit is to have introduced social space into its arguments about working-class reformism. Foster's study of Oldham is rich with hypotheses about cross-class alliances, demographic and production patterns, and the formation of a specific kind of labour aristocracy. I shall leave most alone, but I do wish to highlight Foster's unusual sensitivity to the implications of spatial transformations in the early industrial town and his attempt to incorporate space as a constitutive element of the social structure.

The transformations of the textile industry in Oldham were not merely changes in the organization and techniques of production. When production was organized in cross-class households, where work and off work were tightly integrated, a patriarchal model of class and authority based on face-to-face paternal relations and the direct supervision of the various spheres of social life integrated the social order. The material and ethical claims of this system could not survive the industrial process that shattered household patterns of production.

Foster shows that during the first half of the nineteenth century Oldham's workers came less and less frequently to live where they worked. As the town's districts came to be designated increasingly either as places of work or as places of residence, members of the working class came to live apart from their employers and their supervision. By devising their own social and cultural institutions where they lived, working people fashioned an independence from the patriarchal claims of their employers. These institutions, rooted in the relatively free space of the working-class community, provided the potential basis for the construction of relatively independent sources of class and group dispositions and collective action.[3]

Although Foster's contribution more than shares in the dubious features of the labour aristocracy position, his joining of space, class, and politics has the particular merit of making *conditional* the role that working-class neighbourhood institutions might play in the larger story of working-class life.

Because of his focus on the traditional historiographical problems of working-class reformism, Foster stresses the contingent aspects of these social and cultural institutions with respect to whether they became autonomous organizations capable of building working-class solidarity against capitalists and the state in spite of divisions among workers or whether they became differentiated between the community institutions of the 'aristocrats' and the rest of the working class (with the former becoming closely tied to bourgeois ideology, politics and authority).

What Foster does not deal with are the related, but different contingent questions of whether and under what circumstances workers will utilize their newly autonomous institutions in the residence community to mount demands not only against their employers but against the state in class terms. Put another way, what will be the relationship between the politics of labour and the work place and the potentially separate emerging politics of community?

Of all the Western industrializing countries, the urban–spatial histories of the United States and England in the nineteenth century were the most alike.[4] So too was the array of territorially based working-class institutions that provided a dense infrastructure to community life. As workers in both countries experienced the separation of work and community, they developed ways of construing and acting on these experiences in their new residential spaces and institutions. Precisely because of the relatively tight controls that employers continued to exercise in the post household factor (a point stressed by Joyce), the residence community came to loom so important as the place where workers could create meanings and practices in partial freedom.

Let us return once again to some of these local institutions. Historians of American neighbourhood and political party life have long been impressed by the combination of sociability and political action of the local party machine. The same dual role of leisure and instrumental activity characterized Chartist meetings in workingmen's clubs, friendly societies, and public houses. Rowley writes, for example, of annual dinners held to 'commemorate the birthday of Tom Paine, enlivened by radical songs, toasts, and recitations', and, more generally, of heavy drinking during business meetings. Whereas such activities underscored a divided working-class consciousness in the United States, they helped promote a more global consciousness of class in England.

Quite unlike the American patterns, where even early trade unions developed meeting places at or very near work places, English trade union branches, many secret and illicit, usually met in working-class neighbour-hoods, most frequently in pubs. The organization of industrial disputes was often pub-based, and pub landlords frequently acted as strike co-ordinators or union treasurers. Many unions were identified with specific public houses, and some important Chartist pubs (like Nottingham's Seven Stars and the King George on Horseback, the landlords of which acted as treasurers of their local Chartists cells) simultaneously were prominent meeting places for industrial and political organizers.

Friendly societies, the main self-help community organizations of English workers, also gathered in ale houses. Intensely local in character, many of these societies were trade unions by other names that sought to protect their funds and their members from legal recrimination. The qual-ity of the 'trade union consciousness' created by this compressed set of working-class organizations in the residence community obviously is rather different from the 'trade union consciousness' that came to prevail in the United States, where from the very earliest moments of trade union history labour unions were disconnected from other institutions and locations of working-class life and political activity.

From the vantage point of the United States, the key issue for studies of English working-class formation is whether we can account for the broad cultural pattern identified by Pelling as a combination of political and social 'conservatism, associated however with a profound class consciousness and quite commonly a marked sense of grievance'. This distinctive mix of pol-itical caution, stressed by most historical analysts, and a keen, pervasive sense of the relevance of class divisions to all spheres of life (a situation described by Eric Hobsbawm in the language of 'high classness') was very different from the American pattern with respect to the second, but not the first, characteristic. Obviously, the English pattern was the result of a his-torically contingent process. What were its causes?

One way to approach this question is to ask why both trade union and political agitation in England but not the United States were pressed into institutions of residence community. There, in the voluntary organizations created in the 'free space' of communities separated from work places, English workers learned to put claims to their employers and to the state in a rhetoric and idiom of class.

What accounts for this development? Obviously, the industrial urban, spatial, and organizational patterns that English workers shared with their American counterparts cannot explain the divergence between the two histories of working-class formation. Equally clear is the inability of society- and economy-centred explanations, rooted more in what these societies share than in their differences, to account for these variations. In the remainder of this essay I propose that important differences in the organizational structures and the public policies of the states in the two countries account for the key divergences we have identified. The claims I shall make, I hasten to add, are provisional – in Charles Tilly's words, 'more solid than working hypotheses, perhaps, but less firm than theses one nails up to challenge all the world, at the end of a long inquiry'.

STATE STRUCTURES AND STATE POLICIES

A focus on the state as a major source of variation in patterns of class formation in the English and American cases at once confronts an important feature of the macrocomparative literature on the state: the tendency to lump these two countries together under the rubric of the Anglo-American 'weak state'. J. P. Nettl's seminal essay proposing that 'stateness' be treated as a variable cites Marx favourably for observing that the United States and England were excluded from the 'necessity of violent overthrow of the state because there was no state as such to overthrow'. In neither country is the state 'instantly recognizable as an area of autonomous action', and in both, the law, rather than being an emanation of the state, has a great deal of autonomy.

Most analyses of the 'weak' American state, from Tocqueville's *Democracy In America* to more recent treatments such as Huntington's well-known analysis of the diffusion of the Tudor polity, root the US experience in the British for the obvious historical reasons. In this largely persuasive line of analysis, England is understood to be an aberrant case of state formation in early modern Europe. The Glorious Revolution of 1688, though radical from a Continental perspective, ratified the traditional prerogatives of Parliament against those of an absolutist alternative. Sovereignty was defined not by a conflation of the civil and the civic within the state but in terms of representation and, ultimately, a system of political parties linking state and society through electoral mechanisms.

Although English sovereignty crystallized in a single representative body, indicating a pattern of centralization very different from the American federal system, where sovereignty ultimately resided in the 'people', both countries shared a very clear contrast with the state patterns of continental Europe. These states, unlike those of Prussia or France, did not have a monopoly of access to technical, professional information. Furthermore, for reasons Barrington Moore explains, 'England's whole previous history, her reliance on a navy instead of an army, on unpaid justices of the peace instead of royal officials, had put in the hands of the central government a repressive apparatus weaker than that possessed by strong continental monarchies.' Colonial America, of course, shared in and inherited the characteristics of the British state, whose Crown bordered on an abstraction and which was relatively undeveloped as an autonomous entity demarcated from civil society.

Although one might be tempted to point to an apparent correlation between strong states and militant working classes in continental Europe and to the seeming correlation between weak states and reformist tendencies within the working classes of England and the United States, the consequences of the weak states in both England and the United States compared with the absolutist and bureaucratic regimes of the Continent are not self-evident. Propositions along these lines would have to depend on caricature to the point of distortion. Continental working classes have hardly displayed a uniform propensity for revolutionary or protorevolutionary activity, just as the English working class has known moments of militant contention (E. P. Thompson, for one, thinks that in 1832, as in 1819, the year of Peterloo, 'a revolution was possible' because 'the government was isolated and there were sharp differences within the ruling class'), and American workers have challenged capital at the work place with great courage and at high risk and cost.

If it is difficult to move directly from an assessment of a given state as 'strong' or 'weak' to statements about revolutionary versus reformist working-class orientations to the regime, it is even more difficult to make this kind of causal claim if we want to explain whether class, as a category of understanding and action, joined the spheres of work and community or was limited to the sphere of work.

The main attempt I know of to apply this line of reasoning to the English case, that of Kenneth Dyson, is flawed in ways that an American comparison reveals. In his view, England's weak state 'helped to cement polarization in the industrial and political systems. ... Accordingly, the experience of a relatively "unbridled" capitalism gave it a bad reputation, created a powerful and isolated working-class culture, and undermined willingness to cooperate both in industry and in politics. Britain acquired a peculiar class structure: the obstinacy and distrust associated with attitudes of "them" and "us" were not directed at the state but at bastions of privilege and exclusiveness associated with society.' We shall see, from an American vantage point, that it is misleading to say that working-class dispositions and structures of feelings in England were not honed in opposition to the state. The American experience, moreover, in which 'we' – 'they' distinctions based on class were restricted largely to employee–employer conflicts at the work place, appears to belie this line of argument.

But appearances can be deceptive, for if we inquire about the precise organizational forms that the 'weak state' took in England and the United States; if we examine the different clusters of political rights the two working classes possessed in the early industrial period; if we look at other bundles of public policies; and if we explore the effects that these differences had on the content of working-class organizations located where workers lived, we shall be able to make more persuasive connections between the characteristics of these states and their activities and divergent patterns of working-class formation.

The most important political right in the nineteenth century, of course, was the right to vote. Here the differences between the United States and England were marked. Virtually all adult males in the United States could vote by the early 1830s, but in England only one in five adult males composed the eligible electorate after the reforms of 1832, one in three after 1867, and only three in five even after 1885. How important was this difference for our puzzle?

Accounts of the genesis of the franchise and the story of its expansion have long been familiar themes in treatments of the formation and civic incorporation of Western working classes. Reinhard Bendix, elaborating the scholarship of T. H. Marshall, has suggested that there is a common sequence of the extension of voting citizenship in the West that helps to explain the shared political gradualism of the various national working classes. By contrast, H. F. Moorhouse explains English reformism (the standard object of analysis), not so much by civic incorporation through the franchise, but by the long period of exclusion of workers. The differences between the protagonists of this debate, however, represent two sides of the same coin, since all the participants in the discussion agree on what is not in doubt: that franchise extensions, and their timing have had an important effect on working-class propensities to act in certain ways. They disagree only about how. Here, too, a comparative American perspective is chastening, for the history of the franchise in the United States reminds us that gradualist outcomes do not depend only, or necessarily, on a protracted period for the extension of citizenship rights to individuals.

What is so striking about the familiar discussions of the franchise and class is their avoidance of the question about class formation that are at the heart of the comparative puzzle with which we are concerned. The quick, nearly conflict-free extension of the franchise to men in the United States and the much more protracted, conflict-ridden expansion of the right to vote in England are central to explanations of the differences between the global consciousness of class on one side of the Atlantic and the divided consciousness of class on the other.

But the impact of the variation of political rights on class formation was not a direct or simple one. To understand it, we have to take up the franchise in combination with another key difference between the two countries concerning the organization of the state: that of a federal versus a unitary state.

Nettl, it will be recalled, who introduced the concepts of 'weak' and 'strong' states into contemporary comparative-historical political sociology, stressed that the United States and England shared relatively diffuse state organizations, but he paid insufficient attention to the differences in the ways their states were organized. The diffuse federal organizational structure of the United States took much of the charge out of the issue of franchise extension, for there was no unitary state to defend or transform. Once suffrage restrictions were lifted (in tandem with other democratizing reforms, such as an increase in the number of public offices and in the regularity and frequency of elections), the United States had the world's first political system of participatory federalism.

Within this framework of state organization and democratic political rights, new kinds of political parties with a mass base were constructed. These political organizations, reaching into virtually every ward and neighbourhood in the country, put together the spatial, ethnic, religious, and political identities of the various subgroups of the American working class. This act of organization and social definition took place where workers and their families lived. It created direct links between the political system and voting citizens, who were organized into politics on the basis of many identities but rarely those of class as such, and this pattern created an institutional and participatory structure that was set apart from the organizations workers created to put their demands to their employers.

American participatory federalism was not just a system of voting based on intensely local solidarities. It was also a system of governance, taxation, and delivery of services, During the antebellum years in the cities, where the bulk of working people lived, municipal services provided the main content of a local politics of patronage and distribution. This period saw the interaction of professional police forces, the bureaucratization of municipal charity and poor relief, and the establishment of mass public school systems, as well as a massive programme of publicly licensed construction. Political parties focused on the connections between these services and the various neighbourhoods of the city. Local politics became a segmented and distributive politics of community. In this politics, workers appeared in the political arena not as workers but as residents of a specific place or as members of a specific (nonclass) group. Although there were many class-related economic issues on the national and state political agendas, including internal improvements, tariffs, control of banking, and slavery, the process of voting for most workers was insulated from these concerns, because it was focused elsewhere.

By contrast to the United States, the interplay of state and class in

England was radically different in each of the respects I have quoted. The unitary (not federal) English state concentrated distributive public policies at the centre as a result of the passage of such public acts as the Poor Law of 1834; the Public Health Acts of 1848, 1866, 1872, and 1875; the Police acts of 1839 and 1856; and the Food and Drugs Acts of 1860 and 1872. Whether this growth was mainly the result of the initiatives of humanitarian and Benthamite civil servants and parliamentarians or the result of attempts to defuse class-based opposition of industrial capitalism (these are the two main poles of a lively historiographical debate), the growth of the *central* government was staggering. In 1797 most of the 16,000 employees on the central government payroll were customs, excise and post office personnel. By 1869 this number had grown to 108,000, reflecting the new activities undertaken by the administrative agencies of the state. For the century as a whole, public expenditure grew fifteen times in real terms.

If patronage and property were the two hallmarks of the pre-nineteenth-century civil service, by midcentury patronage had been sacrificed to 'save the main pillar, property'. The professionalization of governmental administration at the centre, a process that marked the period from 1830 to 1870, further focused attention by members of all social classes on the centre of the state apparatus in London. As Parliament and Whitehall took on new responsibilities for social policy and the regulation of working conditions and as they reorganized their affairs to rationalize the enforcement of regulations and the delivery of services, they potently reached into and affected working-class life, at the work place but especially in the residence community. Each new parliamentary act and each new wave of administrative expansion and reform focused ever the more sharply the attention of the working class on the state and its activities.

From the perspective of a working person (and from an American perspective), the state that he or she confronted was not a 'weak state'. The comparative intensity of the tie between the working class and the central state was powerfully reinforced by the second aspect of what Harold Perkin has aptly called the nineteenth-century 'battle for the state': the struggle for the franchise.

Just as the services and the regulations of government penetrated working-class life and thus reinforced class identities at the residence place as well as at the work place, so the demand by English workers for the right to vote could have been constructed on no other basis than that of class, for the working class was excluded on explicit class criteria. Only with universal suffrage, Heatherington wrote in the *Poor Man's Guardian* in December 1831, would 'the term *classes* merge into some comprehensive appellation, and no bloodshed will ensue'. Although working-class reform organizations before and after 1832 were local in organization, unlike

American political party machines they directed their claims of citizenship *to the centre*, that is, to Parliament.

One effect of the interplay between the state and the workers where they lived was the creation of a common fault line, based on class, in all parts of English society:

> One of the distinguishing features of the new society, by contrast with the localism of the old, was the nationwide character of the classes, in appeal if not always in strength. At some point between the French Revolution and the Great Reform Act, the vertical antagonisms and horizontal solidarities of class emerge on a national scale from and overlay the vertical bonds and horizontal rivalries of connection and interest. That moment ... saw the birth of class.[5]

When every caution has been made, the outstanding fact of the period between 1790 and 1830 is the formation of the working class. This is revealed, first, in the growth of class-consciousness: the consciousness of an identity of interests as between all these diverse groups of working people and as against the interests of other classes. And, second, in the growth of corresponding forms of political and industrial organizations. By 1832 there were strongly based and self-conscious working class institutions – trade unions, friendly societies, educational and religious movements, political organizations, periodicals – working-class intellectual traditions, working-class community patterns, and a working-class structure of feeling.

English working-class voluntary organizations turned outward in two respects. Rather than reinforcing local particularities based on intraclass differences of territory, income, or craft, they linked the activities and sensibilities of workers to each other across these lines. Furthermore, they joined to the concerns of the residence community the class issues of political participation, public policy, and trade unionism. In this respect, the Chartist movement provided the most important post-1832 concretization and deepening of these tendencies, which contrast so sharply with the role played by neighbourhood-based working-class voluntary organizations in the United States.

Chartism provided the unifying pivot of English working-class dispositions and organization. This movement took a working class that had oscillated from the turn of the century between economic and political action and fused both kinds of action in a national network of community-based associations. For some two decades, Chartism created a distinctively English global consciousness of class harnessed not only to the campaign for votes, but to poor law agitation, to trade unionism, to factory reform, to Owenite socialism, to an unstamped press, to millenarianism, and to machine breaking.

In all these activities Chartism reflected the great diversity of a differentiated working class. Where there was a substantial number of artisans, Chartist associations tended to stress values of self-help and independence. Where handloom weavers predominated, as in Lancashire and the West Riding, the form and content of agitation tended to be more strident. Where domestic industry predominated, as in the East Midlands, workers were more likely to seek allies and guidance from middle-class reformers.

Overall, however, there were consistent themes to Chartism. These included the attempt to build an independent political voice for labourers based on class understanding, as well as the regular elaboration of links between economic problems and political representation. At its most vigorous, Chartism swallowed up other working-class movements and gave them a common definition. Its key feature, J. F. C. Harrison has argued, was 'its class consciousness and temper. ... Chartists of many shades of opinion emphasized their movement was concerned to promote the interests of working men as a class.' They 'assumed the need for class solidarity and their leaders talked the language of class struggle'.

From the point of view of the historiographical *problematique* of gradualism, Chartism seems to be another instance of working-class reformism. From the vantage point of the American comparison, the important feature of Chartism is its scope and depth as a class institution and its posing of a democratic, egalitarian alternative to the existing political and economic order based on a class analysis. As Trygve Tholfsen has stressed so tellingly, the Peoples' Charter was not just a political document but a coherent class-based set of demands connecting all spheres of society. 'Implicit in the Charter was both a demand for the transformation of the structure of politics and the broader principle that working men ought to exercise control over every aspect of their lives. ... What set Chartism ideologically apart from middle-class liberalism ... was the conviction, often only tacit, that class was the crux of the problem of progress and justice.' This view was reflected at the level of organization. Unlike American political parties which were class-specific in the neighbourhood but were otherwise inter-class institutions, the Chartist 'party' was entirely independent of the Whigs and Tories, and over time, the Chartists drew away from middle-class allies.

If Chartism disconnected the working class from other classes, it joined the political to the economic aspirations of workers, and it was affected as a movement by economic conditions and struggles. The dominant classes and politicians who successfully managed to use the state to deny workers the vote in 1832 tried to crush trade unions both before and after. As a consequence, it was possible for Chartism to become the common core of the working class and thus to impose itself as the common sense of a holistic rather than a divided kind of class-consciousness, in tandem with a trade unionism quite different from its American counterpart. Just as the absence of political citizenship pressed political agitation into the autonomous institutions of working-class localities, so the state's stance with respect to union activity produced relatively weak unions and compelled workers to bring their work-place organizational efforts into the protected space of the residential community.

The Combination Acts of 1799 and 1800 made union organization very risky and thus drove labour organization underground, to the pubs and friendly societies of hospitable neighbourhoods. Even after the acts were repealed in 1825, the state used the common law to interdict strike activity.

After 1825 trade unions were harassed, though not legally suppressed; unions, as such were no longer unlawful, but action in restraint of trade was. The Combination Act of 1825 did not by itself make strikes illegal, but it left to judicial opinion whether a strike was in restraint of trade. This legal situation did not prevent the development of unions; on the contrary, there was an explosion of public unionization attempts, sometimes on a grand scale, in the late 1820s and 1830s. But the fact that 'after 1825 the common law was involved against trade unions to an unprecedented extent' produced a situation that compelled unions to keep their planning and activities as secret as possible, hidden from the authorities in community-based associations. Moreover, the legal climate of repression combined with the pressures on union continuity provided by the operation of business cycles made unions especially fragile institutions. At moments of economic depression, the state could leave to economic forces the role of restraining unions, but when the cycle proved favourable and unions grew more bold, the state could invoke the doctrine 'to the effect that any overt positive action by groups of workers was likely to be a wrong in the nature of Conspiracy, even where the strike was quietly conducted'.

As a result of these political forces, English organized labour was too fragile to provide an independent basis of action against capital. English workers were pushed out of the arena of work into politics and into the residence community at the same time. Although the trade unions themselves never joined Chartism, 'the greater number of trade unionists', Slosson found, 'declared for the Charter.'

In the United States, by contrast, the comparatively mild character of state repression against trade unions made a clearly defined, public, workplace-based organization of works possible. There, too, workers were liable for combinations under the common law, but in the American federal system there was no national legislation or central direction to anti-union prosecutions. Charges brought in one locality were not brought in another, and prosecutors found convictions difficult to obtain in a system of trial by peers rather than by magistrates. American unions were buffeted by economic crises throughout the nineteenth century and, in the century's later decades, were faced with a wave of public as well as private attempts to repress labour organization. In the early period of class formation, however, the problems that unions had with the law were quite secondary. In times of economic prosperity workers were not inhibited on the whole from joining unions at the work place; in the middle 1830s, for example, some two in three craft workers in New York City were unionized.

The organzational forms of the American and English states and their constitutional and public policies, in short, had very different consequences for the political content of local working-class associations and, by extension, for patterns of working-class formation in each country. In the United States, political agitation for the vote was unnecessary, and the community provided the location for the organizations at the base of interclass political parties that appealed to voters by mobilizing nonclass solidarities. Unions, in turn, were allowed a separate existence. In *their* embrace a working class was formed as labour.

Not so in England, where only the institutions of the residence community were available to workers through which to put demands to employers and to the state. Pressed together by the exigencies of law, repression, state organization, and public policy, the locality-based voluntary organization fused the separate facets of working-class life into a common, deeply felt consciousness of class.

Notes

1. One of the problems this approach to English working-class formation poses is worthy of comment in passing. By taking the class orientations of workers for granted, debates about reformism and militancy are oddly divorced from the actual content of the society's discourse, organizations and competing capacities of classes. The result, as Eley and Nield acutely observe, is an imitation by Marxist historiography of the liberal 'intellectual schematization – if workers go on the barricades they are "revolutionary", if they do not they are "reformist" or "integrated",' a perspective that 'misses the realities that drive workers to action or condemn them to inaction'. In accepting this dichotomy much Marxist historiography has appended to it the assumption that a formed working class *should* develop in certain ways. If it does not, a 'theoretical alibi' for the working class as a whole has to be found (Geoff Eley and Keith Nield, 'Why does social history ignore politics?' *Social History* 5 (May 1980), pp. 258, 260–61).
2. Henry Pelling, 'The concept of the labour aristocracy', in *Popular Politics and Society in*

Late Victorian Britain, ed. Henry Pelling, (London: Macmillan 1968), p. 41. Rooted in an article by Engels in 1885 and in Lenin's treatment of imperialism, the concept of a labour aristocracy was introduced into contemporary historical scholarship by Eric Hobsbawn. Work in this tradition has examined wages and conditions of work (including the divide between craft and factory workers), urban neighbourhood differentiation (emphasizing spatial segregation, housing conditions, voluntary organizations, and leisure activities – the focus I find most congenial), and politics (with a look at the positional location and world views of labour union and party leadership). For the development of the concept of the labour aristocracy, see Friedrich Engels, 'England in 1845 and 1885', in *On Britain*, ed. Karl Marx and Friedrich Engels (Moscow: International Publishers, 1934, pp. 67, 99; and E. J. Hobsbawn, 'The labour aristocracy', in *Labouring Men*, ed. E. J. Hobsbawn (London: Weidenfeld & Nicolson, 1964).

3. This division between employers and workers in space was accompanied as well by another division: between workers themselves. With the separation of labour and housing markets as a concomitant of the division between work and community, workers with different capacities to consume goods and services (the hallmarks of class for Max Weber) came more and more to be segregated from each other in different areas of the city. The result, Foster argued, was the development of a geographically segmented working class that produced a tendency toward fragmentation and, in his terms, false consciousness. In this view, the ties of occupation, income, and space conjoined to make possible the development of a distinctive privileged stratum of the working class, an aristocracy of labour, whose propensity for alliances with the bourgeoisie undermined the 'revolutionary consciousness' that had prevailed in the age of Chartism.

4. The spatial dimensions of a labour aristocracy approach have also been developed suggestively by Geoffrey Crossick and Robert Gray. Crossick's study of artisans segregated in space from industrial workers in mid-nineteenth-century Kentish London illuminates the contradictory elements of the values and language structure of these 'aristocrats' whose emphasis on sobriety, thrift and respectability seemed to imitate dominant middle-class Victorian values yet who also asserted an independent, even insular, working-class culture. Gray's work likewise stresses the corporate class consciousness (here he borrows from Gramsci) of the spatially separate 'superior' artisans, whose neighbourhoods, housing conditions and styles of life reflected 'feelings of exclusiveness and superior social status' intertwined with 'a strong sense of class pride'. There followed, in this view, a complicated pattern of implicit negotiated accommodations between this stratum of the working class and the middle classes that established the terms of incorporation of the working class into social and political life. Geoffrey Crossick, 'The labour aristocracy and its values: a study of mid-Victorian Kentish London', *Victorian Studies* 20 (March 1976), pp. 301–28; Geoffrey Crossick, *An Artisan Elite in Victorian Society* (London: Croom Helm, 1978); R. Q. Gray, *The Labour Aristocracy in Victorian Edinburgh* (Oxford: Oxford University Press, 1976).

5. Harold Perkin, *The Origins of Modern English Society* (London, Routledge & Kegan Paul, 1969), p. 177.

IV.2

Factory politics in Britain and the United States: engineers and machinists, 1914–1919

JEFFREY HAYDU

The priorities of British and American trade unions centre predominantly on the economic rewards received by union members. Collective bargaining and strikes typically focus on how much employers must pay for labour (in wages, pensions, and other benefits) rather than on how the labour, once purchased, may be used. Basic decisions regarding the organization of production are not considered by most unionists as legitimate issues for negotiation. Disputes over working conditions do arise, of course, but rarely concern securing for labour the rights of management. They involve instead efforts to protect jobs and work practices from encroachment by employers or poaching by other unions. In short, labour's goals are largely economistic, defensive and sectional.

Why, for most of this century, have labour's aims and struggles at work – what may be termed 'factory politics' – been little informed by broader visions of workers' control? Was this pattern inevitable, either because of the natural impulses of workers or the requirements of modern production for centralized control exercised by professional managers? It will be argued here that the current state of factory politics in Britain and the United States was not natural or inevitable but the outcome of contention between proponents of rival programmes and forms of organization. That outcome needs to be explained.

This article focuses on an industry where alternatives were clear and conflict sharp – the machine trades – and on a period in which radical programmes both commanded their widest support and suffered defeat – the First World War. The strategic importance of this industry for economic growth and wartime mobilization, combined with the prominence of skilled metal-trades unions in the national labour movements, give the struggles of engineers and machinists (the British and American names respectively for workers who make machinery) a special significance. The containment of workers' control movements was particularly clear in two

Originally published in *Comparative Studies in Society and History*, 27 (1985), pp. 57–85.

centres of munitions productions: Bridgeport, Connecticut, and Coventry, England. A comparative study of Coventry engineers and Bridgeport machinists shows that the economistic and sectional orientation of factory politics did not emerge uncontested; more important for the present purpose, the comparison demonstrates why these alternatives eventually triumphed.

Historically, the existence of competing agendas for labour is rooted in a particular period. For the machine trades, it was from roughly 1890 to the end of the First World War that management sought to win control of production from relatively autonomous craftsmen. During these years, the respective rights of labour and employers in implementing new methods of manufacture were unsettled and in dispute – particularly since the besieged craftsmen retained power and remained indispensable at work. The assault on craft control, moreover, forced skilled workers to reappraise traditional strategies of industrial action, and produced conflict within the labour movement over the proper goals and organization of workers. Every proposal had its partisans. It was unclear which faction would win the support of rank-and-file metal workers – especially while craft traditions remained alive and sustained a potential audience for programmes of workers' control. This study shows how the crisis was resolved in favour of management control and a factory politics centred on economic and sectional issues. As David Montgomery rightly emphasizes, conflict over work practices occurred well before the First World War and remains widespread.[1] Yet movements for workers' control during the war were both more ambitious and more specific than this. They represented not just opposition to particular employer policies and encroachments, but a comprehensive assertion of alternative standards for industrial government. They were rooted, moreover, in the transformation of craft traditions and production. The conditions which made these movements possible would not occur again.

Analytically, engineers and machinists seeking broad support for workers' control shared two basic dilemmas. First, issues of control frequently divided workers along craft and skill lines. Unity was more easily forged on behalf of common economic interests. Second, existing metal-trades unions were exclusive and conservative. Radical engineers and machinists could not pursue new alliances and programmes through formal union channels. The prospects of a broadly based movement for workers' control thus hinged on the development of new forms of rank-and-file organization which united workers regardless of craft or skill and were relatively independent of established trade unions. Herein lies the significance of institutions that skilled workers had created before, and extended during, the war: local amalgamation committees, metal-trades councils and shop committees. Through these bodies the divisive impact of control issues and the sectional influence of craft unions were tenuously overcome. Joint organization in the shops and cities gave radicalized craftsmen vehicles for broadening the constituency for workers' control. Explaining the fate of radical factory politics thus directs attention to the rise and (especially) fall of solidary, independent rank-and-file organization.

In explaining the absence of working-class opposition to capitalist control, scholars [. . .] have emphasized employee attitudes that are produced at work. Thus internal labour markets are seen to favour individualism and attach employees' interests to the firm, while mass production techniques and bureaucratic organization makes management authority appear inevitable. A different approach is taken here. The interests of individual metal workers varied and could be mobilized in different kinds of collective action. The explanations offered for changing patterns of factory politics thus focus less on subjective orientations than on structural conditions – especially rank-and-file organization – which favoured or inhibited concerted movements for workers' control.

The present account considers the influence of the labour process,[2] industrial relations, and union and government policies on the form and viability of rank-and-file organization. Comparative analysis also suggests the need to refine theories concerning the effects of trade unions and the labour process on factory politics. The article begins with a survey of pre-war challenges to craft control and the ways that engineers and machinists met them, focusing on the comparative development and limitations of solidary, independent organization. This survey sets the stage for a more detailed examination of Coventry and Bridgeport during the First World War. The impact of the war in these cities – introducing new workshop practices, increased rank-and-file bargaining power, union restraint in the national interest, major departures from pre-war industrial relations procedures, and unprecedented government intervention – is typical of munitions centres throughout Britain and the United States.

In one important respect Coventry is not representative of national conditions. As the home of Britain's most progressive engineering sectors (automobiles and motorcycles), Coventry experienced wartime changes in production techniques and organization that were less abrupt than elsewhere.[3] The radical potential of craft traditions was thus less fully expressed in Coventry. Yet the relative degree of wartime militancy (within or between countries) is not of primary concern. Rather, this article examines the contrasting structural bases of that militancy and the corresponding differences in the containment of radical factory politics. For these purposes, struggles over the status and organization of shop committees in Coventry and Bridgeport are unusually clear examples of conflicts occurring throughout the two countries. The resolution of these struggles also helped set the pattern for the industries as a whole. The settlement of Coventry's 1917 shop stewards' strike was national in scope and subsequently incorporated into the 1922 industry-wide agreement. Similarly, the system of works committees established for Bridgeport by the National War Labour Board in 1918 reflected general government policies and paved the way for company unionism in the metal trades during the post-war period.

THE PREWAR CONTEXT

Challenges to craft control

The traditional workshop roles of engineers and machinists were increasingly undermined in the twenty years before the First World War. Employers sought to introduce more specialized, semi-automatic machines and to subdivide production tasks in order to increase output and utilize workers who were less skilled and less expensive. Various systems of payment by results were designed to increase effort while cutting unit labour costs. Managers also became increasingly impatient with rule-of-thumb procedures in the shops. They sought control over the techniques, times and sequences of operations, often enlisting the aid of experts to calculate machine speeds, fix piece rates, prepare instruction cards, and monitor the men more closely.

These innovations were subjects of contention between managers and skilled workers. Deskilling (or dilution) undermined apprenticeship restrictions and the craftsman's monopoly on essential tasks and machine tools. At stake, however, were not just jobs and income, but the right to decide how work should be allocated and performed. Skilled metal workers considered incentive pay to be a backhanded method of extracting more work for lower wages and of undercutting collective bargaining and standard day rates. Moreover, payment by results encouraged men to think only of their own earnings, which was believed to destroy both individual craftsmanship and camaraderie among workmates. Finally, skilled workers resented being watched, driven, timed, and ordered about. Such conditions violated their sense of manhood and justice, and curtailed the autonomy and discretion at work to which their skills entitled them.

Alternative responses

The most common responses, particularly in well-organized districts, were sectional and defensive. Here engineers and machinists sought to enforce union work rules at the expense both of management prerogatives and of the interests of other workers. The manning of certain machines by unapprenticed men and women or by members of other craft unions, for example, was resisted, and craftsmen refused to accept piecework. Where organization was weaker, many union officials found a different policy more realistic: unionists should exchange the substance of craft control for a privileged economic position. In Coventry, for example, instead of defending traditional occupations, district officials claimed a minimum rate for a job, regardless of who performed it or the real skill involved. National executives of the Amalgamated Society of Engineers (ASE) and the International Association of Machinists (IAM) sanctioned incentive pay schemes, provided that employers guaranteed the men a minimum wage and offered safeguards against rate cuts. These policies often facilitated co-operation with other crafts and skills. In order to enforce wage rates. Coventry engineers made efforts to recruit less skilled specialists and joined with other craft unions in district-wide negotiations. Such alliances and strategies helped defend the economic position of engineering workers, but at the expense of traditional craft rules and customs.

A vocal minority advocated a third strategy – unity with other trades and grades without sacrificing workers' control. At a minimum, this alternative gave all workers a voice in the implementation of new techniques of production, methods of remuneration, and shop discipline. Such goals appealed to craftsmen accustomed to considerable autonomy in their work. Modest proposals for joint consultation between management and representative shop committees shaded gradually into more ambitious programmes. At the extreme, workers' control was to be built from the shop floor up, at the expense of private ownership as well as control of production. These were the goals of industrial unionists and syndicalists among the British engineers, many of them active in amalgamation committees and local branches of socialist parties. They were shared by radical machinists sympathetic to the Industrial Workers of the World (IWW) or active in dissident locals in New York, Chicago, Detroit, Schenectady, and elsewhere. In both countries they were in a minority; in both, their programmes faced considerable obstacles.

One difficulty was that in the workaday world the immediate impact of control issues was divisive. Among individual craftsmen and the various metal-trade unions, conflicts over dilution, piecework, and authority had an idiosyncratic quality. The same dispute was unlikely to affect workers of different departments, plants, or localities at the same time. Piecework, moreover, proved a fertile ground for conflict among workers over desirable jobs or the appropriate work pace; dilution, by eroding craft boundaries, produced frequent disputes between trade unions over jurisdiction. Divisions were more acute between different grades of workers; while dilution and piecework threatened craftsmen, they offered less skilled operatives opportunities for upward mobility. Control issues were thus not a promising basis for united action.

The established institutions of craft protest posed a second obstacle. National metal-trades unions were sectional, exclusive, and conservative, especially with regard to issues of workplace control. While in part an historical product of trade unionism's development in both countries, these conditions also reflect reasonable considerations on the part of national leaders. Officials were often unwilling to risk union funds and reputation in idiosyncratic local strikes – particularly when many of the prospective beneficiaries were not even dues-paying members.

Some progress in overcoming these obstacles was made before the war. Everyday conflicts at work prompted the formation of city-wide metal-trades councils, joint trade committees, amalgamation committees, and shop committees. Joint organization among city officials of different unions enabled them to meet representatives of local employers' associations on a more equal footing; joint organization within the factories enabled members of different crafts and union branches to present a united front; and shop committees acted to enforce union work rules, negotiate piece rates, and carry grievances to management. These institutions had a larger significance, however. Within joint organizations, diverse workers were able to choose common representatives, prepare collective demands, and act together in strikes. In conflict with union constitutions, they also assumed powers to negotiate with employers and initiate disputes.

By thus eroding boundaries of craft and skill and giving the rank and file some independence from sectional union authority, joint organization offered a potential base for the united pursuit of workers' control. The distinctive strengths and limits of solidary organization form the essential background to wartime factory politics and reflect the interacting influences of the labour process, union policy and industrial relations.

Solidary organization in Britain

The strength of joint organization among British engineers before the war reflects a long tradition of local autonomy and shop-floor activism. Union policy and structure contributed to this tradition. For want of concerted national trade policies, district committees and shop-floor bodies assumed responsibility for making and enforcing work rules. Joint committees at the city and plant levels, moreover, enabled engineers divided among different trade unions and residentially based branches to present a united front and take prompt action against employers. Such committees often pre-empted the authority of union officials and cut across traditional craft divisions.

Industrial relations reinforced these conditions. Under the Terms of

Settlement which concluded the 1897–8 national lockout, the ASE conceded management's right to man machines and introduce piecework as it chose and agreed not to strike pending the outcome of a total grievance procedure. Vigilant shop committees promptly assumed the burden of defending craft privileges and engineers' freedom of action. Under the Terms, moreover, shop-floor activism and resistance to management control entailed a growing worker hostility toward union officials – officials who at times seemed more committed to employer rights and constitutional action than to rank-and-file interests. This antagonism to union officialdom would prove important during the war. It broadened the appeal of alternative forms of working-class organization that could at once by-pass conservative unions and regain local initiative for rank-and-file engineers.

These developments laid an organizational basis for wider challenges to capitalist control of production. They were bound up with the ideological appeals of syndicalism, industrial unionism, and the Amalgamation Committee movement, which explicitly aimed to transcend exclusive and defensive action, and to unite all crafts and skills in opposition to capitalist control. It remained an open question, however, how far the radicalized craftsmen could extend their influence through shop committees. Independent, solidary organization had its limits. A strong union and the Terms provided at once a protective and a restrictive shell for shop-floor organization. Despite hostility of the rank and file to union policies and the Terms, the engineers clearly benefited from both. The ASE successfully defended union activists and stewards from victimization, while the Terms legitimated certain grievances and established basic rules for handling them. The price was union discipline and procedural constraints. It was not always paid, especially during prosperous times when engineers were in a position to win disputes quickly, without benefit of union strike funds or fear of the sack. But at other times, the prospect of union censure, denial of financial benefits, and forfeiture of the opportunity to invoke binding grievance procedures were powerful obstacles to unconstitutional action. To the extent that engineers agreed to play by the rules of the game, factory politics remained more or less routine and circumscribed by sectional union priorities.

Solidary organization in the United States

Solidary organization among machinists in the United States appears similar to that in Britain: vigilant shop committees, local co-operation among crafts through metal-trades councils, and joint committees to manage sympathetic strikes. Such organization, however, offered a less effective base for radical factory politics. In the broad view, united action faced greater obstacles in the United States, including the overlap of ethnic with occupational cleavages and a populist tradition that emphasized political democracy more strongly than working-class solidarity. Of more immediate importance, though, were the more advanced production organization, weaker unions, and open-shop conditions.

Compared to Britain, production and management techniques weakened shop-floor organization in the United States. The greater progress of dilution made militant machinists more vulnerable to being fired. More extensive use of payment by results and scientific management's reliance on individualized wage rates rather than union scales intensified divisions in the workplace as machinists competed for desirable jobs and promotions. Such changes were already under way in the 1890s, before the IAM was on its feet. The union was thus rarely in a position to prevent victimization or to offset divisions at work with strong shop committees and collective bargaining.

The resulting isolation and vulnerability of shop committees was reinforced by open-shop conditions. Where British employers preferred to deal with official union representatives rather than defiant shop stewards, most American managers would meet *only* with deputations from their own employees. Machinists of necessity relied on shop committees in lieu of collective bargaining. Such committees owed their autonomy not to a position of independent strength but to an enforced isolation from formal union organization. And while the IAM's freedom from restrictive trade agreements (like the Terms) minimized antagonisms between the rank and file and union leaders, it also left shop committees more at the mercy of management.

Compared to the case in Britain, then, shop committees in the United States presented a less effective base for bridging divisions at work and a less viable alternative to sectional unionism. Radical initiatives focused instead on the lower levels of trade unionism – metal-trades councils and militant union branches. Rather than constructing joint organizations and fighting for control at the point of production, local militants concentrated on securing the amalgamation of national craft unions and opening their ranks to the less skilled; on expanding the powers of city-wide metal-trades councils at the expense of national union leaders; and on organizing sympathetic actions among craft unions or between the IAM and IWW. Yet without strong roots in the shops these initiatives and their leaders were especially vulnerable to conservative counter-offensives. The American Federation of Labor (AFL) Metal Trades Department successfully circumscribed the powers of the metal-trades councils, and IAM leaders expelled IWW sympathizers and dissident locals.

At neither the shop nor the local level, then, did joint organization overcome decisions or provide alternatives to sectional unions. Battles over control were typically confined to particular grievances, in particular departments, and among single crafts, with little continuity over time. Strikes uniting broader constituencies usually did so by concentrating on the most readily shared grievances – wages and hours.

Summary

More advanced techniques of production and management in American machine shops weakened and divided machinists. This is an interpretation advanced by numerous students of American labour politics. A comparative perspective, however, emphasizes that the joint organizations at the shop and local levels – through which machinists might have gained the unity and strength to rectify workplace debilities – were relatively fragile. The containment of radical factory politics was thus hostage to the continued isolation and vulnerability of the shop committees within the factory gates and the radicals outside them, or, more concretely, to continued open shops and weak unions.

In Britain, by contrast, the labour process afforded engineers a stronger, more unified position. The development of control struggles, as many have argued, pitted rank-and-file organization against national union leaders and the rules and procedures laid down in the Terms of Settlement. The comparative view, however, suggests the dependence of shop-floor militancy on protective unions and well-established industrial relations. With dependence came constraint, and prewar protest remained largely confined by the priorities of sectional, unions and the routines of collective bargaining. But this stability was hostage to continued union control over shop committees and the continued effectiveness of union and industrial relations sanctions against unofficial organization and action.

THE WAR

The First World War altered the context of factory politics, expanding solidary organization and overcoming its prewar limitations. At work, war production both intensified the grievances and increased the bargaining power of skilled men. Yet in Britain, labour scarcity, union support for war programmes, and government labour policies undercut the restraining influence of sectional unions and industrial relations procedures on unofficial organization. In the United States, tight labour markets, combined with less restrictive union and government policies, strengthened local union and shop organization at the expense of open shops. War conditions thus fostered structural conditions favourable to radical factory politics: in Britain, workshop organization relatively free of sectional constraints, and in the United States, unprecedented co-ordination of strong shop committees by militant local unionists. While differing in form, both organizational shifts enabled radicalized craftsmen to expand their constituencies.

These developments will be reviewed for each case before proceeding to the key task of explaining the containment of radical factory politics. The reimposition of sectional and economic priorities required undercutting radicalism's structural roots and thus renewing the isolation of militants. In Coventry, this involved channeling shop-steward organization through craft unions and new industrial relations procedures, and in Bridgeport, breaking the links between union locals and shop-floor institutions.

Coventry: the impact of war

A city of 115,489 in 1914, Coventry's pre-war economy was dominated by automobile and motorcyle production. The war made the city a leading munitions centre. By 1918, local population reached 151,507 and Coventry had produced 25 per cent of the country's aeroplanes and large quantities of machine tools, army vehicles, and armaments. Local ASE membership increased by 50 per cent (to 4,000) by the end of 1916, with similar growth in other craft societies. The principal organization for less skilled engineering workers in Coventry, the Workers' Union, swelled from fewer than 3,000 members before the war to 8,590 in late 1916.

Coventry's leading firms were, by British standards, technically progressive even before 1914. Deskilling and payment by results associated with war production thus did not break with local customs as abruptly in Coventry as they did elsewhere. Yet here, too, engineers greatly resented the introduction of incentive pay contrary to pre-war practices. And amid the importation of 20,000 women in the first three years of the war, conflict intensified over the recruitment of women and unqualified men and the operation by a single operative of two or more machines. Munitions manufacture appeared to favour the less skilled workers over engineers. Indeed, craftsmen paid by the hour to equip and set up machines for repetitive routine often earned less than the dilutees whose work depended on the craftsmen's skill. When, in 1917, dilution became bound up with grievances over military exemption and restrictions on labour mobility, the combined threats to skilled engineers were to prove explosive.

War production simultaneously increased the leverage of the engineers while challenging their traditional status. At the same time, the government and the engineering unions sanctioned workplace changes and limited the right of the men to fight them. Union leaders agreed in March of 1915 to abandon pre-war trade restrictions and strikes on government work, and the Munitions of War Act in June made these concessions mandatory. By renouncing craft privileges and strikes, the ASE both incurred the further enmity of its members and ceased to be a useful instrument for rank-and-file militancy. War conditions, moreover, minimized the force of union sanctions against unofficial action. Strike benefits were unnecessary, for strikes did not last long; unemployment benefits were superfluous, because jobs were easily found; and the negotiating acumen of union leaders was dispensable, because the government settled disputes.

State intervention in wartime labour relations created further grievances, some of which were divisive. Engineers resented the government's involvement in dilution and restrictions in the mobility of skilled men, while less skilled workers opposed the preferential exemption of craftsmen from the draft. Other grievance cut across skill and craft lines, however, and facilitated broader alliances. The intrusion of the state into workshop discipline was commonly felt to buttress the power of employers, to the detriment of the men. There was a widespread sense that government and national union leaders were in league, in opposition to the interests of the rank and file and their chosen representatives. And regardless of trade or skill, patriotic sacrifices seemed to be all on one side: wage increases were delayed and lagged behind the cost of living, while the profits of landlords and manufacturers were large and assured.

Development of factory politics

With no effective official outlet for their grievances, rank-and-file engineers in Coventry turned to alternative forms of organization to defend their positions. These forms shared two key characteristics: they tenuously unified workers despite divisions rooted in the labour process, and they did so independently of sectional union authority. Most important was the expansion of workshop organization. Stewards assumed functions formerly reserved for district union officials – negotiating with management over dilution and piece rates and calling strikes despite union policy and the Munitions of War Act. In time, they came to be elected by the men in their departments rather than appointed by the District Committee. Particularly after 1916, moreover, their constituencies included workers of different crafts and skills, and stewards of different unions formed works committees to deal with the general grievances and enforce awards.

The Coventry Engineering Joint Committee (CEJC) represented another, moderate alternative. Through the CEJC, representatives of fourteen craft unions assumed an increased role in negotiating with the local employers' association and in formulating joint policy, often overstepping national and district officials of individual unions. The CEJC also consulted with the Workers' Union despite objections of the District Committee of the ASE. More ambitious was the formation of the Coventry Workers' Committee (CWC) early in 1916. The CWC united stewards in a city-wide body entirely independent of, and hostile to, trade unions. Workers' Union militants, Amalgamation Committee leaders, and local Socialist Labour Party officials were well represented. While smaller than workers' committees in some other cities, the CWC caused craft union officials considerable concern, and the events of 1917 were to demonstrate its appeal to both skilled and semi-skilled Coventry workers.

If there was anything on which craft society and Workers' Union stewards, progressive CEJC officials, and CWC militants could agree, it was the demand for shop steward recognition, raised in 1917. For much of that year this issue overshadowed sectional concerns over dilution and military exemption. And for each group, shop committees were crucial to the practical implementation of workers' control – however differently this goal was defined. The evolution of factory politics in Coventry is a story of the shifting fortunes of these contending factions.

For CWC partisans, shop committees were to form the basic unit in building workers' control, beginning at the plant and local levels and eventually rising to the National Administrative Council of the shop stewards' movement. This organization was designed to by-pass reactionary craft unionism and ultimately pre-empt capitalist ownership and control of production. The (limited) power of the CWC in Coventry was demonstrated in April and May of 1917. On 6 April, a CWC committee at a machine gun factory (Hotchkiss-et-Cie) ordered a strike over payment for toolroom work done in the production shop. Denounced by officials of the ASE District Committee and the CEJC, the strike quickly became a struggle for recognition of the shop committee. The antagonism of employers and union officials alike was overcome only by intervention of the Ministry of Munitions to establish a shop committee whose 'functions were to be advisory only, and were not to encroach upon the powers of the management or of the union executives'.

Later in the month, the government announced plans to extend dilution to private work and to withdraw from craft unions the authority to protect their members from conscription. Rumours that the post-war restoration of trade-union customs would be delayed heightened tensions. Proclaiming labour's right to local control over manpower, the CWC once again led the fight. On 8 May 30,000 Coventry engineering workers, ignoring District Committee warnings to remain at work, answered the call for strike action by the CWC and Amalgamation Committee.

At this point leadership of local militancy passed, not to individual district committees, but to the CEJC. On 9 May, the CEJC chairman secured formal government assurances that skilled men would retain draft exemptions and that the Dilution Bill was purely a war measure. The same day CEJC officials ordered affiliated members back to work, and on 11 May they called a mass meeting and persuaded the nearly 20,000 workers who attended to condemn the strike. The CEJC's success did not, however, mark a retreat into craft sectionalism. CEJC officials knew that the complacency of trade union leaders could restore the influence of the CWC, and they recognized both the general appeal of shop committee recognition and the weakness of traditional craft divisions. Over the summer, CEJC leaders accordingly developed a new shop steward system. They did so without the sanction of national union leaders and, much to the annoyance of the ASE District Committee, in consultation with the Workers' Union.

The proposed scheme moved away from the principle of direct democratic control from the shop floor, which was embodied in city-wide workers' committees, by making the CEJC (whose delegates were elected on a residential basis) the executive committee over all shop stewards. Stewards were denied authority to initiate industrial action, and, pending the outcome of a local grievance procedure, there were to be no strikes. These principles made the proposal unacceptable to the CWC. On the other hand, the CEJC rules gave shop stewards and works committees (composed of the chief stewards from each department) considerable power to negotiate with employers, and provided that 'any changes in the Shop or Works must receive the consent of the Joint Engineering Committee before being accepted by the men concerned'. Nor were sectional boundaries left intact. Stewards were to be elected by all members of a particular shop, regardless of union affiliation – a provision that left open the door for participation by the Workers' Union. Further, stewards and works committees were responsible to the CEJC, not to the district committees of individual unions. In these respects the CEJC programme was more radical than anything envisioned by district officials, much less national ones.

The CEJC had little success in securing recognition for its plan from individual firms. A strike at White and Poppe in November won from the Coventry Engineering Employers' Association only the concession that deputations to member firms might include a spokesman 'not necessarily a party to the dispute', with the larger question of shop steward recognition referred to national negotiations. This satisfied neither stewards nor CEJC leaders. In particular, they knew that the CEJC scheme would not fare well in conferences between national union and employer representatives. On

21 November 1917, the CEJC, meeting with shop stewards, resolved to strike for immediate recognition of its plan. From 26 November to 4 December, 50,000 Coventry workers – including members of the Workers' Union – took a holiday.

Containment

Industry-wide conferences soon pre-empted local conflict over the CEJC plan. Under pressure from the government above and insurgence below, on 20 December 1917, the National Engineering Employers' Federation and executive committees of all major engineering unions – save the still wary ASE – signed the Shop Stewards' Agreement. That document was designed to buttress both trade union authority over the rank and file and managerial control at work, in the hope 'that the constitution of officially approved works committees, with functions more or less clearly defined, would help check the more revolutionary tendencies of the shop stewards' movement by bringing it into an ordered scheme'. Unlike the CEJC scheme, this plan made the shop stewards subject to the authority of individual trade unions and limited their electorate to members of their own union. No recognition or facilities were granted for works committees by which stewards of different unions or departments could co-operate. Stewards were denied the power to negotiate with management over dilution and piecework, as proposed by the CEJC. Instead, their roles were incorporated into an industry-wide grievance procedure, with their functions closely regulated and circumscribed, and with disputes quickly passing out of their hands to district and national union officials. While the ASE was not formally included in this scheme until 1919, district officials of all major craft unions endorsed it in practice.

The Shop Stewards' Agreement aimed to reimpose sectional organization, isolate radical leaders, and restore trade union authority over the rank and file. The events of 1918 suggest that it succeeded. In January the government again proposed extending dilution to private work and the withdrawal of its schedule of draft-exempt occupations. Unrest was compounded by some local unemployment, in which it appeared that skilled men were the ones discharged while dilutees remained at work. In the ensuing crisis, local ASE officials were unable to secure co-operation from the CEJC to fight government measures. Not surprisingly, the Coventry branch of the Workers' Union – members of which had no desire to restrict their entry into skilled jobs on private work, or to see the ASE membership protected from the draft at their own expense – resolved to stay at work if any dispute arose. With the support of its stewards and many members, the ASE District Committee accordingly resorted to sectional action. Officials called for the creation of recruiting tribunals, composed equally of skilled men and employers, to review military exemptions. The ASE stewards agreed to provide lists of all dilutees in their shops, so that these men would be drafted first and promptly removed at the end of the war. In the meantime, ASE members insisted that they should not be laid off before less skilled men had been discharged.

These divisions intensified in July. At that time, in an effort to ensure an equitable distribution of scarce skilled labour, the Ministry of Munitions applied to four Coventry firms an 'embargo' on hiring additional skilled men without Ministry approval. Once again, this was a battle the Workers' Union had no interest in fighting. The CEJC at first resolved to strike on 22 July – a resolution supported by the district committees of local craft unions. However, government threats to conscript strikers, when combined with the lukewarm response accorded the strike plans by other cities and the National Administrative Council of the shop stewards' movement, persuaded CEJC officials to defer action.

This decision produced a decisive split between the CEJC and individual unions. Twelve thousand members of the ASE and three other craft societies went ahead and struck on 23 July, voicing confidence in their respective district committees. Appeals by the CEJC for a return to work were rejected, and a local union leader declared that 'anything that emanates from the Engineering Joint Committee is quite unofficial'. After the government agreed to negotiate (and announced its intention to draft strikers) the Coventry engineers, acting through their individual unions, returned to work. With these events craft militancy passed entirely from the hands of the CEJC to the sectional leadership of Coventry's craft unions.

The disputes of 1918 were very much concerned with issues of control – with the battle focused on fighting dilution and securing the right of workers to a voice in wartime manpower policy. The radical programmes of 1917, however, were no longer on the agenda. The dominant goals were to preserve the privileges of craft unionists, to the detriment of the less skilled. Such strategies continued after the armistice, as craft militancy concentrated on the discharge of wartime dilutees and the restoration of trade union customs. This outcome was in part the product of particular issues raised during 1918 – the draft, deskilling on private work, embargoes on skilled men, doubts concerning post-war restoration of craft rights – which highlighted the conflicts of interest between skilled and less skilled workers. Perhaps more important, however, was the reform of trade union structure and industrial relations sponsored by the government and embodied in the Shop Stewards' Agreement. The new structure of workshop representation completed the isolation of CWC radicals and began that of progressive CEJC leaders. By restricting the constituency of shop stewards to individual unions and departments, the agreement undermined the cross-craft and cross-grade solidarities developed earlier in the war. And by reimposing union authority over stewards and incorporating them into formal union-management grievance procedures, the agreement affirmed the priority of sectional craft interests in factory politics.

Bridgeport: the impact of war

The principal industrial base of Bridgeport, Connecticut, was metal working of all kinds: machine tools, electrical products, motor vehicles, and small arms and ammunition. Large employers were well organized, and the open shop prevailed. War orders transformed Bridgeport into a boom city. Headed by Remington Arms and the Union Metallic Cartridge Company, held under common ownership, city firms by mid-1915 were producing two-thirds of all small arms and ammunition supplied from the United States to allied powers. City population grew from 100,000 in 1914 to 150,000 by late 1916 and 173,000 in 1917. The wartime demand for labour finally gave machinists the security they needed to organize. In 1915, the membership of local IAM lodges increased from about 450 to 1,900, reaching perhaps 4,000 before the war ended. Bridgeport had no Workers' Union, however, and the vast majority of the less skilled munitions workers remained unorganized.

As in Coventry, the war's most dramatic effect on working conditions in Bridgeport was the great acceleration of deskilling. The lighter draft demands of the United States military meant that fewer women were recruited to factories in America than in England. The recruitment, training, and upgrading of less skilled men for repetitive work, however, increased enormously. Machinists assumed responsibility for setting up and equipping the machines and were increasingly confined to the toolroom. Yet, even there, the huge demand for tools and fixtures led to factory methods of production, and many skilled men found themselves assigned to single machines, 'working continuously, week after week, upon the same part of the same tool'. Like their British counterparts, skilled time-workers also faced a decline in wages relative to semi-skilled pieceworkers.

As in Coventry, then, war production both strengthened the hand and eroded the status of Bridgeport machinists. Yet, until America's entry into the war, machinists faced neither trade union impotence nor government constraint. Even after mid-1917, restrictive policies never went so far as in Britain. The AFL's renunciation of strikes and its disavowal of the closed shop and *new* restrictions on production were largely voluntary and left IAM lodges free to defend such prewar advantages as had been achieved.

State intervention, too, was relatively limited and discriminated less obviously against skilled men. The government opposed, but did not legally ban, strikes; nor did it formally lend its authority to shop-floor discipline or actively promote dilution. Indeed, by affording protection for unionists, organizing, and collective bargaining, and by requiring that outstanding disputes be settled by the War Department, government intervention strengthened the IAM and undercut the open shop. State regulation thus did not reinforce the grievances of craftsmen as strongly in Bridgeport as in Coventry. Bridgeport metal workers of *all* grades, however, shared with their Coventry counterparts an acute sense of the inequities of war policy. Patriotism for workers seemed to mean tighter budgets, longer hours, more crowded housing, and delays in grievance settlement, while for employers, landlords, and good suppliers, patriotism and profits went hand in hand.

Development of factory politics

Over the summer of 1915, fifty-five strikes swept Bridgeport. What unified craftsmen of different unions and machinists of different plants were their shared economic interests – specifically, the demand for an eight-hour day with no reduction in pay. As before the war, only in isolated firms were such questions as the abolition of piecework or the recognition of shop committees raised. Continuing divisions between grades were demonstrated in August when machinists, having won the eight-hour day for themselves, took no part in a wave of strikes among the less skilled.

These limitations were rooted in the weakness and isolation of shop committees. By mid-1917, new forms of organization overcame such limitations by strengthening shop committees, co-ordinating their activities under militant local union leadership, and bridging divisions of skill and craft. With labour scarce and machinists in a strong bargaining position, manufacturers were increasingly forced to negotiate with shop committees on overtime, unfair dismissals, piecework, and observance of the eight-hour day. Contrary both to the pre-war norm and to the situation in Coventry, these shop committees were closely tied to Lodge 30 or to the newly formed District 55 (incorporating all local lodges) of the IAM. Local union officials were not significantly constrained by national union or government policies. They were thus able to achieve an unprecedented co-ordination of machinists on a city-wide basis by promoting shop committees and working with them to recruit members, evaluate factory conditions, prepare demands and organize strikes. Finally, the broadened solidarities which in Coventry had been expressed only outside of and at odds with the ASE District Committee found a home within the IAM's local organization. Lodge 30 admitted to full membership many less skilled workers not eligible under the IAM constitution, and, beginning in 1916, it initiated efforts to organize women. In many shop meetings convened to vote on demands or strikes, all those attending participated, regardless of union affiliation, skill or sex. Similar procedures may have been adopted in the election of shop committees.

These tendencies were consolidated in May of 1917. In that month's election, a rank-and-file organizing committee headed by Sam Lavit, an industrial unionist and former IWW member, won control of District 55. The election tentatively united the machinists under radical local leadership, and it appeared to be a mandate for the concerted pursuit of demands for control. If in Coventry local militancy pitted independent workshop organization against the authority of craft unions, in Bridgeport insurgence was led by local union officials. Yet similar conflicts with trade union authority appeared in Bridgeport once the local branch began allowing less skilled workers and members of other crafts to participate in shop meetings and making semiskilled operatives the beneficiaries of union demands. This tension was heightened during 1918 as District 55 defied the IAM's renunciation of strikes and the closed shop.

The demands presented to employers in August of 1917 reflect these organizational shifts. They emerged from shop and union meetings over the summer and were advanced by the entire machinists' organization rather than by individual shop committees. The machinists' key goal was the classification of occupations into a relatively small number of job categories (toolmaker, machinist, specialist, etcetera), each with a minimum wage rate. Classification challenged the prevailing system of organizing employees and incentives into narrow classes and pay scales, and it aimed to eliminate much of management's discretion in job assignment and payment. Guaranteed minimum rates and restrictions on 'reclassification' to lower job titles and on substitution of cheaper labour appealed to skilled workers. But the same protections were extended to less skilled machine operators and helpers as well, and were soon joined by claims for equal pay for women on 'men's' work. District 55 also sought the recognition of shop committees and the closed shop. These two demands were designed to consolidate the machinists' organization in Bridgeport. More important, it seems to have been assumed that shop committees would play a role in administering the classification scheme. The programme thus sought not only to limit employers' prerogatives but to secure for representative shop committees a voice in factory management.

While solidarity on behalf of demands for control persisted through 1918, the break with craft-consciousness among highly skilled men remained an ambiguous one. Frustrated by employer and government procrastination, craftsmen were willing to use their strategic power for sectional benefit. Strikes by toolmakers and machinists at Remington and other firms in March, May, and June retained a commitment to classification and equal pay for women, but extended classification only to specialists. When the representatives from the National War Labor Board (NWLB) arrived in late June to restore peace, however, an all-grades programme was once more ascendant: District 55 asked the board to grant classification and minimum rates for specialists, operatives and helpers as well as for skilled men.

Containment

At the outset of the NWLB hearings, employers persuaded the board to include in its award all of the more than 50,000 Bridgeport workers in the fifty-three firms represented, on the grounds that a sectional award would create unrest among those excluded. The inclusion of all crafts and grades helped define the board's task as addressing the *economic* needs of *all* munitions workers. Under this agenda, the machinists' peculiar workplace concerns over dilution, piecework, and arbitrary authority were given short shrift. Employers further claimed that District 55's programme would disrupt war production. On 28 August, a NWLB umpire denied classification in favour of establishing a scale of wage increases, with the highest-paid bracket receiving the smallest raise. Two days later, 7,000 machinists – reiterating the demand for classification and minimum rates for all grades of metal workers – struck in defiance of the board. The decision to strike was made in 'open meetings where munitions workers, regardless of their affiliation with local 55, participated in the debate and voting'. Suggestions from IAM officials that members secure their back pay under the award in lieu of classification were 'jeered'; threats that their charter would be revoked were met with cries of 'take it'. The walkout ended only with President Woodrow Wilson's 13 September proclamation that strikers would lose their draft exemptions and be blacklisted from all city munitions work.

If presidential power won the battle, more subtle methods won the war. The NWLB sought a permanent solution for labour unrest by establishing a system of collective bargaining through shop committees and a local board of mediation. The plan required shop committee elections in every plant – elections not just by members of particular unions or crafts, but by all department employees. Union committees already established were replaced by NWLB committees over the winter of 1918–19, while employee representation schemes initiated by management at five firms won NWLB approval. Shop committees were explicitly denied any 'executive or veto powers' over hiring, firing, wages, or the way in which work should be done. Disputes not settled between committees and management were passed on to the Local Board of Mediation and Conciliation. While this boards' three labour representatives were IAM leaders (including Lavit), at no point was any union formally involved in adjusting grievances or administering other aspects of the award. Of more obvious importance, a permanent chair with a tie-breaking vote was never appointed; labour delegates resigned in March 1919 to protest the local boards' purely decorative role.

The NWLB's reform of workshop organization undercut solidarity around demands for control in two ways. First, the links between shop committees and radical unionists in IAM locals were broken. Second, union organization within the plants was replaced by independent shop committees elected by all workers, regardless of craft or union status. The fact that shop committees, thus constituted, both shut out the union and diluted the influence of craft interests put radical leaders in a dilemma: while NWLB committees were nominally democratic and cross-sectional, they were ineffective for the pursuit of classification and other demands rooted in the craft tradition. Lavit could push these issues, and strengthen the union's power in the factories, only by demanding exclusive craft committees and abandoning the less skilled and the unorganized – a step he did eventually take. By expanding the constituencies of non-union shop committees, the government diluted the social base for control struggles and blocked the co-ordination of such protest by a radical union local.

Employers were not, however, merely the passive beneficiaries of NWLB intervention. During the war, leading manufacturers showed increased concern to secure the willing co-operation of workers in order to reduce labour turnover, improve productivity, and lessen the influence of 'outside agitators'. In some plants this took the form of welfare programmes. Workers' compensation, life insurance and pensions were often contingent on loyalty to the firm, and in some cases were bound up with schemes of employee representation. Employers also made more conscientious efforts to rationalize wage grades and job ladders, partly to soothe unrest and partly to meet the unprecedented need to recruit, train, and upgrade inexperienced workers. Under these schemes workers were assigned to one of a large number of narrowly defined job categories. Each category offered a finely graded scale of wage rates – with as many as sixteen grades in each, spaced as little as one half cent per hour apart. Workers were to move up the scale, and from one classification to the next, according to the efficiency, skill, and discipline of the individual.

In the long run, such systems may have eroded the occupational solidarity of machinists and created divisions among them – divisions within firms, as workers competed for promotion, and across firms, as the diversity of employment schemes reduced the specific grievances *shared* by workers at different plants. Conflicts of interest between grades of workers were accentuated as firms formalized the promotion of less skilled workers, thereby undermining union apprenticeship and privilege. Clearly these factors were not themselves decisive, and, in fact, many of these innovations spurred the unified struggles of 1917–18. Effective opposition to management control, however, presupposed joint organization capable of bridging divisions among workers within and between the city's factories. It was precisely that organization which the NWLB's shop committee scheme broke.

The clearest evidence of the success of this two-pronged offensive – by employers and by the NWLB – is to be seen in the strike wave of 1919. Beginning at the end of July, a series of disputes, involving more than 10,000 skilled and less skilled workers, swept the city. The strikes demonstrated a considerable unity among skilled workers and, to a lesser extent, across grades. But the basis for this unity was the economic demand for a 44-hour week and a 25 per cent wage hike. Demands for classification, equal pay for women, or the recognition of shop committees appear only in isolated disputes, tacked on to the basic goals by individual strike committees. Even within these limits, moreover, solidarity across skill lines was tenuous. Many semi-skilled and unskilled workers belonged to the radical Workers' International Industrial Union, with which AFL and IAM leaders refused to co-operate.

The strikes further demonstrated the significance of the NWLB's collective bargaining system. In several strikes IAM officials sought to make good the losses inflicted the previous winter by demanding the establishment of *union* shop committees. The Manufacturers' Association of Bridgeport countered that the committees set up under the NWLB were the only ones recognized and approved by management. Employers had good reason to defend NWLB shop committees. In several firms the employee representatives had persuaded workers not to strike, and in others shop committees resolved disputes without union involvement. Less decisive evidence suggests the success of new employment systems and welfare programmes in containing militancy: union officials were unable to get men out on strike at two of the most progressive firms, the Bullard Machine Tool Company and the Crane Company.

Increasingly isolated from the shops, radical leaders were once again vulnerable to national censure. In August 1919 the IAM expelled Lavit on charges of unconstitutional action and irresponsible leadership. When a diminished constituency voted its confidence in Lavit, the charter of Lodge 30 was withdrawn. Detached from constraints of the IAM, Bridgeport's radical leadership was free to join the Amalgamated Metal Workers of America in a programme of socialism, industrial unionism, and workers' control. Their support in the shops was negligible.

CONCLUSION

Wartime factory politics, seen here in the cases of Coventry and Bridgeport, represents an alternative to the sectional and economic priorities that now dominate the British and American labour movements. Skilled metal workers then expressed an intense concern with issues of workplace control as war production speeded the demise of craft traditions. Insofar as radicalized craftsmen broadened their support through new types of organization, militancy moved beyond the defence of craft privilege to class-conscious assertions of workers' control. The structural foundation for radical factory politics were achieved quite differently in Coventry and in Bridgeport. In the former, the key was the development of workshop organization independent of sectional union branches; in the latter, it was the strengthening of shop committees and their co-ordination by militant local union officials.

In the first instance, the defeat of radical strategies involved the reimposition of union discipline over Coventry shop stewards and the breaking of union influence over Bridgeport shop committees. In both cases the effect was to isolate radicals – on the shop floor in Coventry, in local union offices in Bridgeport – from rank-and-file metal works. In both, the government was instrumental in securing that end. David Montgomery points out that, by 1923, unemployment, employer counterattacks and (in the United States) government repression had effectively checked labour militancy of any kind. Yet even before these factors proved decisive, a retreat from the broadly based radical movements of 1918 was evident in Bridgeport. The demands that unified strikers in 1919 no longer included a challenge to management's control of production.

Taking a broader view, an exclusive and economistic orientation for factory politics was assured in Coventry by the authority of sectional unions and the constraints of rules and procedures of industrial relations, and in Bridgeport, by the effects of the labour process and, to a lesser degree, employer paternalism. The Bridgeport case, however, casts some doubt on conclusions reached by students of the labour process. Far from fragmenting and subduing workers, as Stone and Edwards argue, piecework, job classification and mass production techniques acted for a time to spur solidary struggles for radical goals. Divisions and accommodation generated within the factory gates, then, were not necessarily decisive; these effects were contingent on the destruction of countervailing joint organizations. Weak unions and isolated shop committees made the difference.

The reform of workshop organization is of singular importance in these outcomes. In Coventry, the co-optation of shop stewards was crucial to undermining radical initiatives among the rank and file. Yet, in comparative perspective, the experience of the Bridgeport machinists is a forceful reminder that independent shop-floor organization is not a sufficient condition for rank-and-file militancy. A strong union and industrial relations safeguards, as well as propitious economic conditions, afforded rank-and-file organization some immunity from employers. Without that immunity, shop committees could not become a medium for solidary opposition to management control. Nor, however, did the evolution of protest in Bridgeport display a direct shift from the militancy of union shop committees to the quiescence of company unions, as Montgomery suggests. The strikes of 1919 show how an imposed separation of plant committees from radical local leadership blocked unified struggles for workers' control – but did not contain the widespread industrial conflict over wages and hours. The immediate significance of new patterns of local and shop organization lies less with the eventual decline of workers militancy in general than with specific changes in the character of factory politics.

Skilled metal workers subsequently raised issues of control largely to defend sectional privileges. This was especially characteristic of Britain, where the workshop apparatus for enforcing union rules and industrial relations agreements remained intact during the immediate postwar years. To the extent that labour struggles united workers of different crafts and skills, solidarity was based on common economic goals. This was particularly true in the United States, where the relative weakness of craft traditions, the comparatively greater obstacles to unity at the plant and local levels, and the frailty of organizational vehicles for concerted control struggles all favoured an emphasis on the issues most easily shared and mobilized – wages and hours.

By 1920, the distinctive radical potential in the craft tradition had come and gone. That potential was mobilized – and subdued – in a transitional period when machinists and engineers were under siege but retained both their power and their memories of autonomy and control at work. The resurgent working-class militancy of the 1930s featured new actors, issues, and forms of organization; the character and limits of that revival reflect the successful containment of radical craftsmen in the period before 1920.

Notes

1. David Montgomery, *Workers' Control in America: Studies in the History of Work, Technology, and Labour Struggles* (Cambridge: Cambridge University Press, 1979), esp. chs 4–5. Montgomery is well aware that craftsmen had a special interest in workshop control (e.g., p. 106). But given his more general interest in labour's resistance to management authority, the defeat of movements for workers' control after the First World War appears more as a temporary setback than a significant turning point.
2. For my purposes, the 'labour process' refers to the social and technical organization of production and how this organization influences relations of workers to their work, their workmates, and management. Especially relevant here are the skill levels 'required' by production techniques, how workers are assigned to specific tasks or machines, how they are supervised, and how they are paid.
3. This peculiarity is convenient for comparative purposes. The analysis emphasizes how contrasting union, industrial relations, and government conditions shaped engineers' and machinists' responses to challenges at work. It is thus useful to exmaine a British case where workshop practices more closely resemble those in the United States.

V Gender, Citizenship and Welfare

In a series of lectures delivered in Cambridge in 1949 T. H. Marshall defined citizenship as consisting of three principal elements: civil rights (such as freedom of speech, equality before the law and the right to own property), which were largely achieved by the end of the eighteenth century; political rights, generally won during the nineteenth century; and social rights, namely welfare and education provided by the state, which have been, broadly speaking, a feature of the twentieth century. Our final section treats citizenship with this definition in mind.

We begin with David Morgan's comparative study of the achievement of political rights, in the form of the franchise, by women on both sides of the Atlantic early in the twentieth century. The author proceeds from a summary of the origins of feminism to a consideration of the campaign for the vote and thence to a comparison of Suffragist strategies, organization and leadership and concludes with an analysis of the differing contexts in which American and British feminism had to operate.

Subsequent contributions move from the political to address the social dimension of citizenship. A key issue in respect of the development of welfare policy in early twentieth-century America concerns the emphasis given by some scholars to an alleged commitment to individualism in the United States in contrast to England, and the resulting hostility, even among American union leaders, to welfare provision. The cultural values approach and its emphasis upon the relative strength of traditional liberalism to explain variation in the timing of new welfare programmes in Britain and the USA, is criticized on both empirical and conceptual grounds by Ann Orloff and Theda Skocpol. In their exploration of the origins of modern pensions policy, they found that the conventional theories of welfare state development – emphasizing industrialization, liberal values and demand by organized labour – existed in both Britain and America, but only in Britain were programmes of public social protection enacted.

221

Searching for additional causal factors that could differentiate between the two cases, they argue that variation in the character and capacity of state and political institutions was connected with the different policy outcomes.

The relative salience of maternalism in social politics in the USA is the subject of a nuanced essay from Theda Skocpol and Gretchen Ritter. The significance of state-centred explanations of comparative welfare programmes and policies is taken up by Anthony Badger who, taking a stand against both radical and free market interpretations of the New Deal, applies a series of elegant cross-national comparisons to account for innovation and limitation in the creation of anti-Depression policies in Britain and the United States.

V.1

Woman suffrage in Britain and America in the early twentieth century

DAVID MORGAN

We who have come down from the last generation are reformers, but reformers are poor politicians.

(Carrie Chapman Catt, December 1916)

What a ridiculous tragedy it would be if this strong Government and Party . . . was to go down on Petticoat Politics.

(Winston Churchill, December 1911)

Women first voted in a British parliamentary election in December 1918. By ensuring in America a Republican-led 66th Congress the mid-term elections a month earlier had made it almost certain that women would vote in the presidential election in 1920. Elsewhere women were enfranchized at this period only in revolutionary conditions in Soviet Russia and defeated, newly republican Germany. Victorious France and Italy did not participate in this flood of the feminist tide; both were free of the Marxist necessities of Russia and the German desire to emulate the victors: neither had had strong suffrage movements. Only in Britain and America had there been a long political campaign and large-scale organizations, the leaders of which were the acknowledged pace setters of worldwide political feminism.

The general outline of the rise of feminism in these two leading countries has been the object of several studies. The final, climactic years when the question was before Congress and Parliament are now more clearly understood. It may, therefore, be possible to attempt a more systematic comparison of elements of the final campaign than has hitherto been possible. It is acknowledged, of course, that such comparison between significantly different societies, economies and policies is fraught with difficulties. The patterns of mass and elite expectation contrasted considerably in the

Originally published in H. C. Allen and R. Thompson (eds), *Contrast and Connection: Bicentennial Essays in Anglo-American History* (London, Bell, 1976), pp. 272–95.

nineteenth century and, indeed, continued to do so after 1900. Yet it was in the early twentieth century that Britain converged more quickly with America in the granting of political rights at the same time as both countries took important steps in the direction of ameliorating gross inequalities in the distribution of political, social and economic resources. In terms of Louis Hartz's analysis,[1] women suffrage was granted in both countries precisely at the time when the 'fragment' society returned to 'confront' the parent society and culture. It was granted at a time, moreover, when the political preoccupations of both societies were becoming more similar. Most particularly, it was granted when both countries were deeply involved in a war which forced them, formally at least, to deepen and clarify their attachment to participatory and egalitarian norms. Despite their differences both societies showed similarities in the range and speed of their responses to feminist demands. Suffragists, in both countries, could not fail to notice the similarities in the values lying behind the different political façades. Comparison, then, may be a more valid exercise in this period than in the nineteenth century.

It is already possible to regard the woman suffrage campaigns as the first *feminist* revolution. Revolution in the sense that a significant, if not fundamental, redistribution of power between the sexes took place; first in that we are now in the middle of a second feminist revolutionary impulse which might well be more thoroughgoing in its effects than the first. The second revolution like the first will need, eventually, further legislation and regulation, that is, its outcome will be political actions directly involving the state. Thus, while the suffrage campaign may be intrinsically interesting to study, it may also be of some interest to examine how such legislation in the past impacted on the political system and how it was moulded by it. In the first revolution the lead was clearly taken by feminists in the United States and Britain and, thus far, the second revolution seems likely to be similarly characterized. In neither country has the political system changed in most critical respects. There may, then, be clues from the suffrage campaign as to the interaction of Women's Liberation and the political systems in the two countries. More of that later, however.

Feminism came out of eighteenth-century philosophical radicalism, was embodied in nineteenth-century liberalism, and carried to its first major victory by early twentieth-century 'progressivism'. Britain provided the leading spokeswomen in the first phase, and the most 'militant' activists in the third phase.[2] America had the first real national organization, could show the most widespread and sustained political activity in the second phase, and closely paralleled the British campaign in the third phase.

Feminist ideas spread most widely when feminism and feminists were seen as part of larger causes. Thus, despite the powerful intellectual case made by Mary Wollstonecraft in the 1790s, feminism had to wait a further half century before an organization was created among American women who had come to see feminism as significant, if not vital, to their other causes. Similarly, in England an organization for women's rights came out of the mobilization of radicals and liberals for, *inter alia*, the Reform Act of 1867. In both countries the movements split in the 1870s as the reformist tide ebbed, and reformers, women included, had to establish their priorities. In America, the ostensible cause was the refusal of radical Republicans to include women in the *post bellum* settlement. The movement there split, and the dabbling of some eastern feminists in more general revolutionary ideas tailed off. Feminism, thereafter, took on a more western, homogeneously American, conservative hue. Hence in the 1890s many populists were sceptical of feminism and refused to endorse it. Not until the movement began to attract women who were 'progressive' did it advance steadily in the west and then, later, in the east. In general, feminism came to be attractive to the 'clean government' school of thought, the Americanizers of immigrants, the declared enemies of corrupt boss-ridden city politics. Woman suffrage, like prohibition, *could* be portrayed as part of a backlash, a last attempt of native Americans to retain their control over American politics and life. But, along with measures allowing voters the initiative, the referendum, primaries, the recall and the short ballot, woman suffrage could, by suffragists and 'progressives', be set in the context of attempts to refurbish American democracy. For this growing school, only by breaking the grip of party organization could the allegedly flagging faith of voters in their political competence be restored. Thus, while the 1890s gave the feminist cause only two states, Colorado 1893 and Idaho 1896, to add to their former territories Wyoming and Utah, the short period from 1910 to 1912 saw the cause triumph in Washington in 1910, California 1911, Arizona, Kansas and Oregon in 1912. Together, this meant that the women of nine states and a territory (Alaska) voted by the time Woodrow Wilson took office, a significant number in the very section where the party battle was at its keenest precisely because it was becoming the area whose choice was decisive in national elections.

The subsequent campaign may, briefly, be outlined. Wilson's inauguration marked a resurgence of suffragist interest in pressing for a constitutional amendment prohibiting state sex discrimination in setting franchise qualifications. This in turn helped split the National American Woman Suffrage Association (NAWSA), leading in 1913 to the expulsion of the Pankhurst disciple Alice Paul and her followers and the creation of the Southern States Woman Suffrage Conference, which was hostile to the proposed amendment. In 1914, after the Democrats in caucus had declared woman suffrage to be a state matter, and only two out of seven state referenda – Montana and Nevada – had succeeded, the NAWSA embraced a state-orientated policy symbolized by the proposed Shafroth–Palmer constitutional amendment. This overcame the problem of securing suffrage referenda in the states by allowing referenda upon petition of only 8 per cent of the vote cast at the last presidential election. This position was, in effect, endorsed by both parties right up to August 1916 when the Republican presidential candidate, Charles E. Hughes, came out for the original Susan B. Anthony amendment, which positively prohibited state discrimination and gave Congress power to enforce the prohibition. One month later the NAWSA changed both its officers and its policy and, until 1920, conducted an enormous campaign aimed at securing state victories for the express purpose of enacting the Susan B. Anthony amendment.

Until 1916 Woodrow Wilson had refused to involve himself in the campaign. From his re-election onward, nevertheless, he became steadily entangled. Not, however, until the United States was at war could he be persuaded to press Congress to allow a vote on the amendment, only to find that his own party was principally to blame for the failure to secure the two-thirds vote in the Senate of the 65th Congress. In the November 1918 elections the Republicans became the majority party and hence the amendment passed Congress quickly in the summer of 1919. The ratification campaign was successful in just over a year and Tennessee, the thirty-sixth state, ratified in time to allow both presidential candidates to appeal to the new women voters in time for the November 1920 presidential election. In both the Congressional and ratification campaigns the sectional characteristics of Southern hostility and Western enthusiasm were very clear.

In Britain the nineteenth century saw the franchise extended to men on an instalment basis and, after 1867, to women for local elections if they were qualified, but unmarried or widowed. By 1904 this process of enfranchisement was complete for local government and marriage had long ceased to be a bar. But anomalies and inequities abounded and liberals, particularly, gave vent to considerable concern. Suffragists, chiefly organized in the National Union of Women's Suffrage Societies (NUWSS) had strong reason to hope that the next government would be Liberal and would have to face up to franchise reform quickly. In that process they could hope to persuade or coerce a Liberal government into granting woman suffrage. The appearance after 1906 of a *Labour* wing of the Liberal party merely increased these expectations.

The Liberal party at large, however, had other priorities and the clash between the two opposed sets of expectations was the stuff of the violent campaign that followed the Liberals taking office. The party was moving steadily away from the old Gladstonian mould – a half of those elected in the huge majority of 1906 were in Parliament for the first time. Neither the old guard nor the new men put woman suffrage anywhere but low on their list of priorities and to this the Liberal–Labour members assented. Campbell-Bannerman, the prime minister, though generally sympathetic – as seven-eighths of Liberal MPs were – knew that the party was preoccupied with other questions and would not agree easily on a bill. In 1908 on his retirement he was replaced by H. H. Asquith whose strong opposition was intensified by the kind of campaign waged against his government. By 1909 the government had authorized the forcible feeding in prison of Pankhurst 'suffragettes' – organized in the Women's Social and Political Union (WSPU).

Only after the Parliament Act of 1911 was on the statute book was there any possibility of woman suffrage, and then only a slight one. The government's proposed Franchise Bill – which supposedly could take a suffrage amendment – added to the growing stress being felt inside the government. The debacle of January 1913 when the speaker forced the withdrawal of the bill, the subsequent 'suffragette' fury, the 'Cat and Mouse Act' and a general stalemate on the question were the results. Not until the war broke up this impasse was any advance possible. The question of votes for soldiers bought up general franchise reform and, in turn, woman suffrage. The replacement of Asquith by Lloyd George at the head of a broad coalition government created the bipartisan situation in which, *inter alia*, a suffrage solution was possible. In the event the actual bill went through its stages speedily and women over 30 years of age were enfranchised before the Armistice gave them the chance to vote in their first parliamentary election.

So much for the familiar outlines of the campaigns. What now may be said by way of comparison both of the operations of the political systems, and of the suffragists? First, it is clear that reactions of political leaders to the issue in both countries were more conditioned by constitutional and party political considerations than they were by considerations of justice, or even the needs of women. More will be said later of Wilson and Asquith personally on this question, but it is idle to see the reactions of either out of the context of, for example, the ramifications of the question of the Lords for Asquith, or the South for Wilson. These and other inhibitions were direct products of the constitutional situations and need elucidating.

In Britain the unitary constitution meant that women must be given the parliamentary vote all over the kingdom, or not at all. In America, under a federal system, western states might grant full suffrage but, at first, this meant little in the east or south. In Britain where, after 1906, the Liberals controlled the Commons and the Unionists the Lords, any government suffrage bill stood to be rejected by the Lords, given the political context. In America the actions of the federal government were conditioned, constitutionally, by state control of franchise qualifications and, politically, by the special tie between that and the racial question in the south. The eleven former Confederate states, if they opposed solidly, would need only two allies to prevent the ratification of an amendment to the constitution. The task of securing two-thirds majorities in Congress, and thirty-six ratifications was a huge test of political organization and pressure even without any concerted sectional opposition.

In Britain, the failure to settle the Irish question before 1906 meant that there was something of a British equivalent of the American sectional vote. After 1910 this was of great significance since it fostered the myth among Unionists that the absence of an *English* majority behind the Liberals plus the 1911 curb of the Lords, put the constitution in abeyance and left them free to oppose government measures by virtually – as the Curragh seemed to prove – all means. Again, the American constitution fixed the timing of elections and this contributed directly to the frustrating of some of Wilson's legislative intentions after 1916. Thus woman suffrage may be regarded as a failure for Wilson in the last days of the 65th Congress. On the other hand, in Britain, while the constitution gave the government the choice of election dates and issues – within limits – the Parliament Act of 1911 at once narrowed these limits from seven to five years and – via the Lords' two year delaying power – made a legislative log jam inevitable after 1912. The suffrage position was worsened by this.

Conversely, however, the constitutional and political situations provided compensations. In America, if it was sectional fear that inhibited federal action, it was also sectional pressure in the west that kept the issue before the dominant party and ultimately secured the Nineteenth Amendment. When both parties were bidding for the control of the west, both would have to pay – eventually – part of the west's price of support. In Britain a sectional vote existed – the Irish – and this was largely hostile to suffrage in the key period from 1911 to 1913, principally to prevent a cabinet split and preserve the Home Rule Bill. The cabinet system, however, provided something of a sectional equivalent to the American situation in Congress. While in America the president's cabinet was secondary, in Britain the decisive struggle lay in the Liberal cabinet where Asquith opposed most of his principal colleagues. By 1912 the fact that Grey, Lloyd George and Haldane were ready to press Asquith very hard on the question meant that suffrage was 'in the swim', would be before Liberals and the country at the next election, and could not be ignored by Asquith thereafter. The pressure of powerful friends in the cabinet made up – to an extent – for the fact that, lacking a federal system, British women voted nowhere in parliamentary elections and lacked the leverage of *voters*.

The power of a Prime Minister was great, especially when rivals and not he were hurt by scandal, but it was not overwhelming and Asquith could not have stood indefinitely against a majority of his cabinet and party. It is interesting to note that, assuming there had been no war, an Irish settlement, and a Liberal victory in 1914 or 1915, Asquith would have had to be 'converted' to suffrage by 1916, anyway, in order to ensure that – under the Parliament Act – the issue would be ready for an election in 1918 or 1919.

Suffrage could not be made a party issue in either country. A large majority of the Liberals were for it, but until 1911 the Lords would have certainly rejected a Liberal measure. Thereafter, parliamentary time and the sheer weight of legislation told heavily against suffrage when added to the fears of a cabinet split held among Irish Nationalists and the Liberals. In America the Democrats controlled the presidency throughout, and Congress until 1919, but they alone could not provide the two-thirds vote required for an amendment. Both parties had large programmes and resented the forcing of suffrage on them by a militant direct action policy. Mrs Pankhurst first appeared to Liberals as something of a Labour ginger group and then, later as a Unionist Trojan Horse. Democrats from south and north could rightly regard suffragists as more a Republican than a Democratic phenomenon. For both parties the issue became a danger when re-election had to be considered. For Liberals this period was around 1912–13 when – because of the Parliament Act – the 1914 or 1915 manifesto had to be envisaged. For Democrats it was during 1916 when Wilson realized that the price of western support in November entailed some gesture towards suffrage. The declarations of Roosevelt and Charles Evans Hughes only made the point more explicit. In 1912 Asquith's government could plead the problem of time, while in 1916 Wilson could plead the south. Neither plea had indefinite validity.

For parties and politicians the war was the catalyst forcing conversions to suffrage, and giving both a way to save face. In Britain, with the Irish question in abeyance, the war issue of 'votes for soldiers' carried suffrage explosively back into the political swim and, by helping, cost Asquith his position, put an active suffragist in office as Prime Minster of a coalition government; producing, in short, the conditions most likely to produce a successful conclusion to the campaign.

In America the impact of the war strengthened the President's hand in relation to Congress in general, and his own party in particular. It also weakened the capacity of anti-suffragists of all shades and, as in Britain, highlighted the role and status of women war workers. In both countries the extension of political, social and economic democracy became part of the rhetoric of politicians concerned to boost morale and prepare for postwar reconstruction. It is well to note, nevertheless, that in both countries the war would not have been the catalyst it was had there not been the large-scale campaigns of pre-war days. Suffrage was at the edge of the pre-war spectrum of practical politics – the war hastened its move towards the centre. In that process both Irish and Southern objections were dis-regarded, the Irish having an immediate political price to pay in the destruction of the Nationalists. An irony of the 1918 election in Britain in consequence was that the only woman elected – the Countess Markievicz – could not take her seat, not because she was a woman, but because she was a Sinn Feiner.

On suffrage the constitutional and party political systems pivoted im-portantly around the president and prime minister, certainly after 1916. The attitudes of both were of great importance. Asquith made no secret of his hostility, while Wilson only very slowly moved to further suffrage and was never an ardent champion. Asquith was converted too late to be in charge of the Suffrage Bill, but did include the issue in the Speaker's Conference after he had declared for it. Wilson bowed to the South in 1916, but not thereafter and paid the price in his own failure and that of his party in the 65th Congress. Subsequently he did his best to repair the damage both in Congress and during the ratification process. In Britain, after the departure of Asquith, Lloyd George had no real difficulty in securing suffrage via the speedy passage of the Representation of the People Act. Both Asquith and Wilson had fond memories of essentially non-political first wives and lived with second wives who enjoyed their voteless state when it went along with power and influence. Both resented militancy – Asquith with his 'want of imagination' concluding militants to be criminal and unbalanced, while Wilson saw their activities as a direct slur upon his good intentions. Had Asquith swung over in 1912 – and insisted on Irish support – it is likely that the Reform Bill could have gone under the Parliament Act and have been ready for implementation in 1914 – unless the Lords passed it in an attempt to force an earlier election.[3] Likewise had Wilson been more vigorous in 1916 he might have pre-vented the solidifying of the Southern position. By being so fearful he allowed racists and 'wets' to make the running and thus hurt the Democrats in 1918, and even in 1920. Fear and lack of vision in 1916 forced him to work very hard hereafter merely to avoid further damage.

The two cases were not really contemporary. The Americans had before them the example of what could happen should frustration among women boil over into Pankhurst militancy and by 1917 this was beginning to hap-pen. Neither Wilson nor the run of politicians in Congress and the states were ready to accept this – and refused to believe that what had occurred in pre-war Britain simply could not happen in America. In addition to fear, emulation and rivalry had a place. The success of the movement during

1917 was a precedent that Americans might follow. There was a traditional rivalry with monarchical Britain and the fact that the constitutional monarchy stood to look more 'democratic' was an incentive to action in wartime America both among suffragists and politicians who were unimpressed by Australian, Scandinavian and even their own western precedents. This was especially true when, in November 1917, the New York state referendum on suffrage was carried by the suffragists – just as the Commons was sending the Representation of the People Bill to the Lords. The New York victory was a turning point of Wilson, who swung his influence immediately in favour of a successful House vote. America could hardly lag behind when Britain was preparing to admit that votes for women was necessary for victory and reconstruction. The British victory was, then, of some importance coming when it did. The militancy of the Pankhursts and Alice Paul had shaken American politicians and suffragists alike – the success of the British movement reassured the politicians and strengthened the suffrage cause in America.

A noticeable difference between the campaigns was, of course, the overt political machinations of certain business interests in America. Both the liquor and textile industries opposed suffrage because each felt directly threatened by a female vote which was presumed to be 'moral' in its outlook. It seems clear, nevertheless, that in Congress when the two industries were counter-attacked in force, they were only successful where their cause coalesced with a more strictly political opposition, namely Southern fears of the Negro. British suffragists were less joined in the public mind with the image of a specifically moral, crusading temperance vote. Mrs Pankhurst, especially, drove home the notion that suffragists were, overwhelmingly, people who sought the vote as a right. In America corrupt politics and business saw its enemy in the vengeful native American matron, certainly in 1916 when there was less likelihood of a successful Socialist party. The parties there were more vulnerable to dedicated groups of strategically placed voters. In Britain a Labour party existed and was growing. It, rather than militant women, was cast in the role of nemesis.

Finally, among the political factors, it is worth noting the similarities between the two dominant parties which faced the demand for suffrage. Both had become more sectionally based and both were at the time facing a backlog of demands for measures of adjustment and compensation for sectional inequalities. They shared a distaste for big business, war and overseas commitments, though both had wings favouring the latter. Within their areas of strength there were 'town and country' parties – outside them they were seeking to be the parties of the lower classes of the growing cities. They were more loosely organized than their opponents and this meant that a question like Suffrage which at first lacked a powerful sectional thrust, or faced a sectional veto, stood little chance of becoming party policy. Both parties had staunch Protestants and Catholics in their ranks – both groups cool or hostile to female emancipation. Both had to face the violent opposition of opponents who had come to see governing as their prerogative and who were not favourably inclined to suffrage. Both had strong factions who had seized the ground of 'reformism' and resented the fact that their party's treatment of the suffrage question seemed to make them less 'reformers' than sectional, social, economic 'outs on the make'. It is only fair, then, to add that this was more apparent than real. The two parties were coerced and cajoled into overcoming their sectional preju-dices, and it is very doubtful if either opposing party would have acted more quickly or easily in power. Democrats and Liberals alike were much preoccupied with other questions and it is of great importance to realize that suffrage impinged unfavourably on two very important sources of pre-occupation, namely the Irish question for Liberals, and the race question for Southerners.

The suffragists themselves have been written up more than the poli-ticians they sought to influence. Even so, there are still comparisons and contrasts which can be usefully made in face of the changing political situ-ations the suffragists dealt with. Again, the connections between the British and American movements after 1905 are worth some clarification.

There are some immediately obvious similarities in the movements. By 1905 both had a history of more than fifty years, both had survived major splits, and both had seen the first generation of leaders give way to younger, more organizationally minded leaders. Both movements were weak in popular support but both entertained high expectations, the British especially. In Britain the rise of the Labour party encouraged some of the older leaders to believe that future gain lay in working for its suc-cess, and using its rise to force the other parties to act. Likewise, in America the faith of many suffragists was put in the Progressive movements of the west and the urban reformers of the eastern cities.

The time lag in the incidence of militancy is, equally, an obvious con-trast. Almost twelve years separated the beginning of American from British militancy – and even then it was initiated by conscious disciples of the Pankhursts. This contrast is somewhat lessened, however, by the fact that militancy *did* occur in America at that moment when, to suffragists at least, the political context was as promising for them as it had been in England in 1906. Both groups seized their main chance – the Americans twelve years after the British.

The appearance of militant, competing organizations had somewhat comparable effects on both parent movements. In America, after 1913, Alice Paul speeded up the process by which the old movement abandoned its Southern incubus, and proclaimed itself ready to use western women voters to coerce northern and Border Democrats and Republicans alike. Likewise, in the same year that Alice Paul appeared on the national scene in America, the older British movement opened negotiations with the Labour party thus signalling its disillusionment with the Liberal party. One movement abandoned a section, the other embraced a party – or so it seemed.

Two features of this change of political alliances may be compared. First, the change for both was largely a matter of legislative tactics and not of ideology. Accepting new allies in the campaign for the vote did not involve any commitment to the political programme of those allies. Thus, when the position in the legislature changed, there was nothing to prevent a return to former allies. Therefore, the American movement by 1919 was ready to gain any Southern support it could get by ignoring Southern women if they were black. Equally, the British movement was quite prepared to ignore the Labour party – as a party – once Lloyd George was Prime Minister and ready to enact its demands in 1917.

Secondly, both leaderships worked very hard to resist the logic inherent in the militant position. The Conciliation Bills of 1910–12 in England and the Shafroth–Palmer amendment of 1914 in the United States were both efforts to obtain suffrage via a consensus of parties unable, and unwilling, to make the issue a party one. Both moves traded on the influence and power possessed by the older movements within high political circles. In America Mark Hanna's daughter, the Republican Mrs Medill McCormick, and the Tory Lord Lytton in Britain – the respective agents – were both the victims and proponents of the delusion that there must and could only be a bipartisan solution. Formally, at least, they appeared to have been proved correct – both measures were enacted in bipartisan votes. In Britain, however, the old party lines had been transformed into those for and against the Lloyd George government while, in America, the Republicans took care not to provide the necessary votes in the Senate and during Ratification until Democrats had been seen resisting their leader and President in the 65th Congress. Woman suffrage was put through by those in the executive in Britain and out of it in America. In neither case was its intrinsic factors and qualities of greater importance than the political gain seen in it by its chief sponsors. Women were being recruited by parties rather than accorded 'justice' as such. The component of expediency can be overstressed but, seen from the perceptive of party leaderships, it appears to have been the dominant motif.

So much for the movements in general in the final period of their history. Some valid comparisons may also be made of the leaders produced after 1905. First, the two non-militant leaders – Mrs Millicent Fawcett of the NUWSS and Mrs Carrie Catt of the NAWSA. Both were widows and both, by the standards of their societies, were upper-middle class and of independent means. Both had served long apprenticeships in the movement and appeared at its head at about the same time. Both were internationally minded and both retained this outlook through and after the war. As leaders, both were single-minded in the pursuit of the vote and refused to allow other gestures to entangle their campaigns. Hence both resisted their pacifist wings after 1914, and urged war service as a duty which properly used could provide the desired reward. Both, nevertheless, saw the vote as more than a symbol of status, and neither had much of the bitterness towards men apparent among many of their militant co-Suffragists.

Both leaders resisted militancy through conceding that it made political sense at least in the early period from 1906 to 1908 in Britain and early 1917 in America. Both acted decisively when it was clear – by 1912 in Britain and 1915 in America – that persuasion of politicians must give way to party coercion. Both cultivated those who had access to leading politicians – for example Mrs Helen Gardener in America, a friend of Wilson's and the influential and well connected Ladies Frances and Betty Balfour in Britain – and, while retaining their independence, tried hard to accommodate politicians who were genuinely trying to promote suffrage.

Mrs Catt and Mrs Fawcett may be justly accused of not giving enough attention to the conversion of male voters who stood behind the male politicians they worked so hard to convert. Yet Mrs Catt in her distance from immigrant males and Mrs Fawcett in hers from working-class men were hardly alone among their social kind. The American middle classes were in this period reacting sharply against the immigrant vote, while their British counterparts could still view Labour MPs as a wing of the Liberal party. Formally, at least, so far as the working classes were concerned their chief organizations were in favour of suffrage. If suffragists seemed to concentrate too much on the middle-class voters this was surely because they realized that these needed converting and were – because of their education – accessible to the printed and spoken word. To expect that suffragists should have foreseen the power of organized labour is to ignore the fact that this was not obvious before 1905 when the basic suffrage strategies were laid down in both countries. Moreover, it is to ignore the fact that, as ardent feminists, both women saw the political advent of voting women as of greater importance than any conceivable Labour faction or political party.

Mrs Catt, unlike Mrs Fawcett, set up in the League of Women Voters, an organization designed specifically to press for feminist objectives using the newly enfranchised voters. That it largely failed, as did both leaders' pleas for women to become active in political parties, may hardly be said to be entirely the fault of the two suffragist leaders. Both, until their deaths, strove to lead their erstwhile followers in the cause of sex equality and opportunity and also to urge them to participate in the quest for international harmony.

In their dealings with both governments and legislatures both women were sanely realistic. Wilson, Mrs Catt understood, had to overcome the hesitation of the very Southerners he needed for the rest of his programme. Asquith, as Mrs Fawcett saw, had some cause for asserting that after 1911 the Liberal burden was heavy enough until the Home Rule and Welsh Church Bills were safely out of the way. Both women realized that party leaders were busy men who were personally affronted by militant unladylike behaviour and politically affronted by tactics which smacked of outright blackmail. More importantly they realized that such men had legitimate party concerns. Might there not be a higher Republican than Democrat turnout among women voters? Likewise in England would not Tory women be more likely to vote, and could a Liberal government really believe that a limited property-based extension of the franchise would not favour Tories? In disowning militancy, Mrs Fawcett after 1909 and Mrs Catt after 1917 performed the negative function of pressing their cause and the positive one of offering inducements to politicians who would join it.

The militants by comparison performed a complementary function, namely that, however much detested by politicians, their activities made too spectacular a subject for both hostile and friendly newspapers to ignore and thus kept the movement in daily contact with the public. Non-militants made friends, militants made news – both were needed. Woman suffrage was an issue which, since they could not adopt, parties would prefer to ignore. It had to have the means of gaining publicity, and that frequently. Soothing ruffled politicians became a routine task which non-militants were well placed to carry out. This task, anyway, was easier for them than the one which would have faced them had there been no militancy, namely that of preventing suffrage from being ignored through the fears, uncertainties and sheer preoccupations of politicians.

Newsworthiness, however, had its limitations. The militants in both countries found themselves misreported and misrepresented. More, they found themselves tempted constantly to change their tactics in order to keep their publicity. They had, again, the parallel task of controlling the increasingly desperate element recruited by the chance of personal publicity and possible martyrdom. Hence picketing and heckling gave way to attacks on property and this, in turn, to assaults on politicians and threats of worse. In Britain the cycle of militancy–repression–more militancy was fully developed by 1912. The separation of Mr and Mrs Pethick-Lawrence from the Pankhursts meant that there was no check on where Christabel Pankhurst was leading, or not leading, the movement. In America victory came before the pattern included major assaults on property and persons. It is almost certain that there would have been a similar development – Christabel could after all be distracted by the war; Alice Paul was not so distracted in April 1917 and the fury and exasperation engendered in wartime America was as great as anything seen in pre-war Britain.

On balance, however, no accusation that militancy retarded suffrage will stand. As was noted, the only real chance in Britain of success before 1914 was marred more by Asquith's personal opposition, Lloyd George's political weakness, and the election of the Speaker than by Mrs Pankhurst. Likewise the Negro problem and the prohibition campaign slowed suffrage more than did Alice Paul and her activities. Politicians who claimed to be alienated by both would have overlooked much had political considerations allowed or forced them to do so, Southern gentlemen notwithstanding.

The formal leader of the Women's Social and Political Union was Mrs Pankhurst, but the real moving spirit became her daughter Christabel, and it is she who must be compared with Alice Paul. While Christabel was a fluent, forceful platform speaker the charisma of both was seen more in committee than on the platform. Both acquired an impressive personal following and were quite ready to use this to overawe any opposition in their organizations. Christabel Pankhurst, the more overtly autocratic, felt sure enough of her position virtually to expel both the Pethick-Lawrences and her own sister Sylvia, all the while running the organization from Paris. Both women shared the conviction that the weakness of the suffrage movement and the hostility of politicians alike, testified to the need for new tactics. The readiness of the press to report their activities was, they realized, of far greater significance than condemnatory editorials and biased reporting.

Militant tactics in 1906 may have stemmed directly from the personal frustrations of the Pankhursts, but they were continued and later used in America because they were seen as the only way of securing publicity and forcing action on the suffrage question. Both women realized that militancy had a certain boomerang effect, but they judged this to be less politically important than continuous publicity, and might be allowed for when the reasons for opposition to suffrage had been exposed and neutralized. The superpatriotism of the Pankhursts during the war, and the absence of militancy during the American Ratification campaign were in part such allowances. Both may be seen as gestures towards politicians then in process of conversion or actively bent on helping suffrage.

The career of Alice Paul is the most significant example of the interaction between the British and American movements. Arriving in Britain in 1908 as a student at the Quaker Woodbrooke Settlement School in Birmingham, she departed two years later as a fully-blown Pankhurst militant with imprisonments and forcible feedings to her credit. Arriving as a young American Quaker and social worker convinced of the need for suffrage as a right and social necessity, she left having been fully exposed to the charisma of the Pankhursts and their non-Quaker methods of political agitation. Arriving a believer that men as voters and politicians were indifferent, she left having seen how a dedicated group, ready to accept imprisonment and personal indignities, might seize national publicity and convert male amazement and hostility into passive or even active support.

The Pankhurst policy of continuous opposition to the party in power, to Alice Paul, made political sense in England since that party, if converted, could put the issue through the legislature. The policy was modelled on the Irish Nationalist tactics which Mrs Pankhurst believed her husband had been an electoral victim of in the 1886 election. The British system of *party* government encouraged groups and small parties to believe that within a party in power the way to force factions – even leaderships – hostile to their aims, was to set against such groups their own party colleague whose policy proposals – related or not – were actually or potentially in jeopardy because of external or internal opposition or instability. The Irish had used this 'across the board' opposition successfully. The Pankhursts, in short, set out after 1906 to push Liberal ministers into conflict with their back-benchers.

After 1912 Alice Paul was accused of blindly trying to follow this tactic in the different constitutional setting of America where there was a separation of powers, and where no one party had ever secured two-thirds of the seats of both Houses; where in fact a bipartisan policy seemed the *sine qua non* of success. Politically, however, the policy had some justification. So long as both American parties competed for the allegiance of the West, so would they have to be sensitive to the demands of that section. This necessary sensitivity was their Achilles heel to Alice Paul for, after 1912, in the West many women voted. In Britain, opposing the party in power after 1906 meant asking Liberal *husbands* and *brothers* to abstain or vote Conservative. In America, the policy meant asking western *women* to vote Republican in 1916 and 1918 – and this at a time when Wilson was a minority President needing the West for re-election. The possession of the vote by women of the section which decided elections was the crucial element making for success once it was exploited.

As states granted the presidential vote after 1913, Mrs Catt herself was quite ready to use this increasing weight in Washington. She did not, however, go among western voters and ask them to coerce Democrats. It was left to the Pankhurst-trained Alice Paul to show her that politicians had to be as sensitive to hostility as to co-operation. Western Democratic politicians were grateful to Mrs Catt, but they feared Alice Paul and their fear was as potent a political force as their gratitude.

Much of Alice Paul's success stemmed from the fact that she was well backed from the beginning of her rebellion against the National American Woman Suffrage Association. Prominent among her backers was the imperious Mrs O. H. P. Belmont. She provides an example of an American contribution to British success, since it was she who had helped support Christabel Pankhurst during her exile in Paris in 1912. In Alice Paul she clearly saw an American version of Christabel and backed her forcibly despite her own close connections with the parent organization. Mrs Belmont thus played the American equivalent of the Pethick-Lawrence role in the Pankhurst organization, namely that of the wealthy, well-connected, zealous backer. She was familiar with the Pankhurst organization and not merely via press reports – a familiarity which may be put down as a further British contribution to success in America. For this to be understood it is necessary to turn to the background of the suffrage victory in New York State in 1917, to the work of Elizabeth Cady Stanton's daughter, Harriet Stanton Blatch.

Mrs Blatch lived in England from 1882 to 1902, met Mrs Pankhurst in the circle of Jacob and Ursula Bright, and participated in the work of the Equal Franchise Committee after it split off from the parent organization in 1889. In addition, she was active in the Women's Liberal Federation, became a Fabian, and was a friend of the Peases and the Webbs. On her return she immediately moved into women's trade union circles in New York, and by February 1907 was appearing at Albany as a labour spokeswoman. In December 1907 she sponsored a visit from the militant daughter of Richard Cobden, Mrs Cobden-Sanderson, and in October 1909, from Mrs Pankhurst herself. Eight months later she organized the first suffrage parade and, helped by Mrs O. H. P. Belmont and Mrs Mary Beard, she launched the Women's Political Union. Unlike the Pankhursts, seven years earlier, she did not insert 'Social' into the title in order to attract those fearful of its trade union overtones.

Mrs Blatch continued to organize Suffrage parades and, in 1912, took agitation a step further when she set up silent pickets outside the New York State Legislature when it debated a Suffrage proposal. In this same year Mrs Blatch introduced Alice Paul to Jane Addams and helped Miss Paul to gain the chairmanship of the Congressional Committee of the National American Woman Suffrage Association.

From this position Miss Paul went on to an independent and larger status – and a policy of attacking Democrats. This may have been second nature to a Philadelphian, but Mrs Blatch had made Democrats her allies against upstate Republicans and had secured, in 1912, a promise from 'Commissioner' Murphy of Tammany to allow a woman suffrage amendment to the state constitution to come to a referendum. National political necessity, as seen by Miss Paul, dictated threatening Democrats. Murphy, happily, resolved the dilemma by ordering the defeat of all amendments, including suffrage, in the referendum of 1914. Mrs Blatch merged her organization with that of Alice Paul in January 1916, though she kept up her personal contact with Tammany. By 1917, when New York State again voted on suffrage, Tammany saw fit to stay neutral and this allowed a New York majority to swing the whole state, crack open the reluctant East and lead directly to the successful January 1918 vote in the House of Representatives.

Mrs Blatch was a minor figure in the national suffrage picture but, in several respects, she was important. She had pioneered both the suffrage parade and suffrage picket – both used heavily by Alice Paul. In 1912, when she still had influence in the National Association, she helped Alice Paul to become its congressional chairman and stimulated Mrs Belmont to take an interest in the new beginning being made in Washington by a disciple of Mrs Pankhurst. Being the daughter of Elizabeth Cady Stanton gave her a certain standing with the press and she capitalized on all of this, when, on 5 October 1916 after Hughes had been 'converted', she revealed Wilson's reasons for refusing to follow as being concerned essentially with the Negro question in the South.

Mrs Blatch can hardly be described as a Pankhurst disciple. Rather, both had shared in the same educational experience at the hands of the Brights, the Fabians and later in the women's trade unions. Mrs Blatch herself, however, remained more as she had begun – the war did not make her bellicose and the peace found her still a socialist. In her role in the suffrage movement she bore a close resemblance to her old friend and former colleague, Mrs Pankhurst. Both were politically sophisticated widows who, from a sense of frustration in suffrage organizations, formed separate groups, pioneered new methods of agitation and then saw their movements pass into younger hands. Though Mrs Blatch, unlike Mrs Pankhurst, did not gain a national or international reputation, she yet deserves a mention as a significant figure in the Anglo-American aspects of the suffrage movement.

The woman suffrage campaign lasted seventy-two years in America and fifty-one years in Britain. On the face of it, this was a long campaign. In fact, the time lapse after the issue had come before Congress and Parliament as a serious question was relatively short – less than ten years in both cases. Partly this was because the suffrage movement had helped create and sustain an elite and engineered some favourable sentiment in educated, middle-class circles. Much more so this was owed to the fact that the rate of economic and social change had created for this elite a mass of potential followers who might be mobilized not for woman suffrage or notions of justice for women but for what might be done with the support of women voters. Inevitably the prior political commitments of such people could give rise to disputes over both the principle and priority of woman suffrage. The Irish in England and the Southern Democrats in the United States were very visible in their opposition but there were others, too, who questioned the priority of woman suffrage, even among those supposed to be friendly. The delay caused by such factors outweighed any due to the opposition of Asquith, the vacillation of Wilson or the folly of some suffragists. Woman suffrage, then, was delayed by potential political issues. In both countries it required the political consequences of war to break the log jam of party inhibition. Yet broken it was. Legislation deemed to be of considerable social consequence was enacted notwithstanding supposedly potent objections on divine, family, industrial and short-run party political and special interest grounds.

In that process much light was cast on the two political systems. The decentralized nature of American politics, the interaction between levels and the constraints on presidency and Congress alike were all too visible. Visible also, however, were the forces making for a degree of 'unitariness' and cohesion so that a carefully orchestrated and timed campaign at local, state and federal levels produced a fairly rapid result as opposition within parties was outflanked or eroded. The deadlock resulting in Britain with its unitary system when the leadership of the governing party was split, and the prime minister in particular was opposed, is in obvious contrast. Less obvious, however, was the *inability* of Asquith to prevent the erosion of his position of strength so that by 1914 he was forced to hint at change.

In this must lie grounds for hope for feminists. The political systems of both countries, which have not changed in critical respects, showed themselves responsive to sustained pressure by feminists if these could find allies in society. Grounds, too, for some concern. The price of allies was a public muzzling of questions which had been deemed vital in nineteenth-century feminism, e.g. the place of women in the family and society. To win the vote required hierarchic organizations which worked best when directed towards a simple goal – the vote – and which were not friendly environments for feminists who questioned the fundamentals of society. 'Organization women' could win the right to vote but seemed less able to infuse women with enthusiasm for making feminist use of the vote.

In retrospect it may be possible to assert that political rights, anyway, may be easier to extract than social or economic rights. The assertion of the 'emptiness' of political rights is still not, thankfully, beyond argument and would certainly have struck early twentieth-century Americans and Britons as simply not true. Suffragists, then, were certainly women of their time in their over-estimation of the impact of narrowly defined political rights and privileges but they can hardly be faulted for that. What they did do was to lay the foundations for their feminist successors, and what they did demonstrate was that their political systems were responsive to changes which, at the time, were seen as far reaching.

The suffrage campaign must give pause to those who assert the immutability of the Anglo-Saxon *status quo*. The political consequences of voting women are nowadays seen by feminists as minimal. It may well be that this is so because those consequences are defined in terms of the *personnel* of politics, i.e. the failure of women to 'surface' politically. If [. . .] we see the consequences in terms of party political agendas, for example in the steadily increasing emphasis on social policies, then the impact of women might be said to be considerable. Whether, of course, this is the proletarianization or modernization of politics, rather than its feminization, is a question which cannot be answered here.

Notes

1. Louis Hartz, *The Founding of New Societies* (New York, 1964).
2. The term militant connoted principally a follower of the Pankhursts in the Women's Social and Political Union in England after 1906 and those of Alice Paul in the National Woman's Party in America after 1916. The label came to connote those who picketed, went to prison, hunger struck, etc. In both cases, as will be seen, the differences between militant and non-militant were not merely over tactics, but also over strategies for gaining and using the vote.
3. By precedent enfranchising acts were followed by legislation redistributing seats and, more, by a general election as soon as the new register of voters was ready.

V.2

Why not equal protection? Explaining the politics of public social spending in Britain, 1900–1911, and the United States, 1880–1920

ANN SHOLA ORLOFF AND THEDA SKOCPOL

In 1919, a number of years after the initiation in Great Britain of all of the key programmes of what would later come to be called a modern welfare state, a poignant cartoon appeared in a pamphlet put out by the American Association for Labor Legislation (AALL), the leading association of US social-reform advocates in the Progressive Era. Two equally brawny workmen were portrayed holding umbrellas for protection against those 'rainy days' that inevitably come in capitalist industrial societies. The British workman's umbrella had a full set of panels, symbolizing industrial accident insurance promulgated in Britain in 1897 and 1906, disability coverage instituted in 1906, and the major breakthroughs in old age pensions in 1908 followed by health and unemployment insurance in the National Insurance Act of 1911. Building upon these pre-World War I foundations, during the 1920s Britain would become (according to a measure developed by Flora and Alber), the world's leader in overall 'welfare state development'.

In contrast, before the 1930s the United States took only small steps towards a modern welfare state. In the 1919 AALL cartoon the unfortunate American workman held an umbrella with only one panel, representing the laws requiring employers to have industrial accident insurance which had been passed in thirty-eight states of the United States by 1919. Between 1911 and 1919, thirty-nine states also passed mothers' pension laws, which mainly targeted respectable working-class widows, so another panel would have appeared in a still very skimpy umbrella for the American workingman's wife.

This article aims to explain why Great Britain was among the world's pioneers in launching social insurance, while the early twentieth-century United States failed to adopt old age pensions and health and unemployment insurance, settling only for workers' compensation and mothers' pensions. The skimpy existing literature on the emergence of modern wel-

Originally published in *American Sociological Review*, 44 (1984), pp. 726–50.

WHY NOT EQUAL PROTECTION ?

American workman's social insurance protection
compared with British workman's.

Figure 1. A cartoon about British and US social insurance, 1919.

fare states focuses almost exclusively on periods of major positive breakthroughs, and does not sufficiently explore why breakthroughs that might
well have happened did not occur at relevant points in nations' histories.
Yet an excellent case can be made for looking at the United States in comparison to Britain in the early twentieth century.

During the two decades following Bismarckian Germany's pioneering
institution of social-insurance programmes in the 1880s, reformers and
politically active leaders in all of the major industrial-capitalist nations of
the West investigated and debated how similar or alternative measures
might be devised to meet the needs of their own countries. In both the
United States and Britain, innovators of similar class and occupational
backgrounds participated in this transnational reform ferment. In due
course, similar legislative proposals for social insurance and public pensions

emerged in both countries. The early twentieth-century United States, in short, was part of the same community of policy discourse as Britain, and the US Progressive Era of about 1906–20 roughly coincided with the British 'Liberal reform' period of about 1906 to the First World War. So it seems obviously appropriate to ask why these two nations did not respond in the same way.

The need to take a close look at the failure of major modern social-spending reforms in the United States during the Progressive Era becomes even more apparent once we take account of some important but usually ignored facts about social spending by the federal government in the late nineteenth century. Historians and social scientists have long assumed that the US federal government had no major social-welfare role before the 1930s, but the remarkable expansion of 'Civil War' pensions after the 1870s utterly belies this assumption.

Figure 2 helps to show what happened to the Civil War pension law as it evolved from a provision for compensation of combat injuries into a de facto system of old age and disability protection. Benefits under the original 1862 law were extended only to soldiers actually injured in combat or to the dependants of those disabled or killed. As one might expect, the numbers of beneficiaries and total expenditures were falling off in the late 1870s. Subsequently, however, legislative liberalizations occurred, the most important in 1879 and 1890. The 1879 Arrears Act allowed soldiers who 'discovered' Civil War-related disabilities to sign up and receive in one lump sum all of the pension payments they would have been eligible to receive since the 1860s! Then the 1890 Dependent Pension Act severed altogether the link to combat-related injuries. Any veteran who had served 90 days in the Union military, whether or not he saw combat or was injured in the Civil War, could sign up for a pension if at some point in time he became disabled for manual labour. In practice, old age alone became a

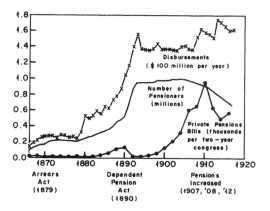

Figure 2. The expansion of Civil War pensions, 1866–1917.

sufficient disability, and in 1906 the law was further amended to state explicitly that 'the age of sixty-two years and over shall be considered a permanent specific disability within the meaning of the pension laws'.

Given that a considerable proportion of men then in their twenties and thirties served in Civil War regiments, and given that these men were in their sixties by 1890 to 1910, it is not surprising that at least one out of two elderly native-born white men in the North, as well as many old and young widows, were receiving what were in effect federal old age and survivors' pensions during this period.[1] Between the 1880s and 1910s the total cost of these pensions sopped up between one-fifth and one-third of the federal budget and constituted the largest item of expenditure, except for interest on the national debt, for every year from 1885 to 1897. Meanwhile, social expenditures in Britain – expenditures of all kinds at all levels of government – amounted to only 21 per cent in 1890 and 18 per cent in 1900, and rose to only 33 per cent in 1910, after the passage of old age pensions and at a time when Britain was not at war. Of course, in 1890 and 1902 US federal expenditures were only 2.4 per cent of GNP, and total US government expenditures were 6.8 per cent of GNP, while total British governmental expenditures went from 8.9 per cent of GNP in 1890 to 14.4 per cent in 1900 and 12.7 per cent in 1910. Still, in terms of the proportional effort devoted to public pensions, the American federal government was hardly a 'welfare laggard'; it was a precocious social-spending state.

The post-Civil War pension system was uneven in its coverage of the American population. Southerners were left out, unless they received help from state pensions for Confederate veterans. Also excluded were most blacks and all post-Civil War immigrants, which meant most unskilled workers. Middle-class native whites and the more privileged industrial workers were disproportionately helped. Yet precisely such people, not the very impoverished, were the ones targeted by early European social-insurance measures. For the idea was to keep 'respectable' working people out of demeaning and repressive poorhouses.

During the Progressive reform period, some politicians, reformers, and social scientists believed that the United States might move easily from the liberalized post-Civil War pension system toward a modern welfare state. When Representative William B. Wilson, a former labour leader, introduced the first national pension plan into Congress in 1909, he made a creative symbolic connection to the Civil War system, proposing 'to create an "Old Age Home Guard of the United States Army", in which all Americans sixty-five and over were invited to "enlist" as privates, if their property was less than $1500, or if their income was under $20 a month. Their duty was to report once a year to the War Department on the state of patriotism in their neighbourhoods.' At least as far as protection for the

245

aged was concerned, Wilson seemed to bear out the hopeful projection of University of Chicago sociologist Charles Henderson that 'the logic of national conduct' on military pensions would lead 'straight toward a universal system for disability due to sickness, accident, invalidism, old age, and death'. Moreover, social-insurance advocate I. M. Rubinow used economic reasoning to argue that Civil War pensions would serve as 'an entering wedge' for a modern welfare state: the steadily declining numbers of older Civil War survivors meant that 'a large appropriation will ... become available', permitting 'the establishment of a national old-age pension scheme without even any material fiscal disturbance – something which no important European country has been able to accomplish'.

Why did Henderson and Rubinow – both able social analysts – turn out to be so incorrect in their assessments? Scholars today need to take this question seriously. Thus the issue to be faced in this article is not simply why Britain and the United States responded differently in the early twentieth century to similar proposals for modern pension and social-insurance legislation. We must also ask why the United States allowed an extraordinary system of publicly funded old age and disability pensions for many working- and middle-class Americans to pass out of existence with the Civil War generation without immediately launching modern pensions and social-insurance programmes in its place.

EXPLAINING THE EMERGENCE OF MODERN WELFARE STATES

We plan to make sense of the contrasting trajectories of social reform in Britain and the United States during the early twentieth century by first providing comparative historical evidence questioning the sufficiency of some major existing explanatory approaches, and then offering a new explanatory approach of our own. Before we plunge into detailed historical evidence, though, it makes sense to introduce the major alternative lines of argument that will be at issue.

Logic of Industrialism arguments about the development of modern welfare states emerged from cross-sectional, aggregate-quantitative studies of large numbers of nations. Although specific arguments vary, such studies argue that thresholds or processes of industrialization, decline of labour-force participation in agriculture, and/or urbanization, demographic dependency ratios, and the sheer longevity of programmes are far stronger variables for explaining cross-national variations in social spending and programme coverage than regime types or political or ideological variations within regime types. Despite their ahistorical research designs, extrapolations about causes of welfare-state origins and the likely sequences of modern social programmes have been put forward in some of these studies. Breakthroughs toward modern social insurance are expected to come as nations develop economically; and as development proceeds, subsequent policies are expected to build upon and 'fill out' early beginnings.

Scholars have had to contend with the fact that both Britain and the United States launched their modern welfare states only after they were at comparatively high levels of industrialization and urbanization. Often, this difficulty has been handled – especially for the US case, where the gap between industrialization and the start of most modern pensions and social insurance was extreme – by stressing the unusual strength and historical persistence of *Liberal Values* in these nations. Indeed, so normal has it been for investigators to treat the United States as an 'exceptional case' due to the strength of its liberal values that rigorous efforts have not been made to incorporate US social politics before the 1930s into the same analytic frameworks as those used to account for the emergence of European welfare states, Britain included.

Working-Class Strength explanations of welfare-state development have emerged since the 1970s as the most prominent of various sorts of 'political economy' arguments made in critical response to the Logic of Industrialism school. Scholars developing these arguments have concentrated on explaining variations among twelve to eighteen rich capitalist democracies. At this intermediate range of comparison, levels of economic development and demographic variables no longer account for so much of the explained variation. Taking off from a certain understanding of Swedish Social Democracy as an ideal type, working-Class Strength theorists view the welfare state as shaped by class-based political struggles. According to the boldest variant of this line of reasoning, [...] 'the welfare state is a product of the growing strength of labour in civil society', and the way to explain its historical origins as well as its subsequent growth is to examine variations in the emergence of trade unions and variations in the strategic ability of trade unions to create – or reorient – electoral political parties into tools for the acquisition and use of state power to effect welfare measures.

Despite their obvious disagreements, proponents of the Logic of Industrialism, Liberal Values, and Working-Class Strength perspectives all share basic assumptions. They all understand the development of the modern welfare state as an inherently progressive phenomenon, perhaps launched and completed sooner by some nations than by others, yet appearing and growing in recognizable stages in all national societies as a necessary and irreversible concomitant of fundamental social and economic processes such as urbanization, industrialization and demographic change –

or else capitalist development and the emergence of the industrial working class. Moreover, at the root of these perspectives lies a way of thinking about government activities that has been shared by pluralists, functionalists, Marxists, and others: government activities are understood to be expressions of – or responses to – social demands. Organized groups, including political parties, are conceptualized as vehicles for the expression of such demands, which are seen as socioeconomically or culturally rooted. After groups or parties weigh in at the political arena, some perhaps more effectively than others, governments generate policy outputs to meet the social demands. The overall process therefore looks something like this:

SOCIOECONOMIC AND ⟶ CHANGING CLASS/GROUP FORMATION
CULTURAL CHANGES AND PERCEIVED NEW SOCIAL NEEDS

SOCIAL⟶ WHAT POLITICALLY⟶ WHAT GOVERNMENTS
GROUPS ACTIVE GROUPS DO
& NEEDS PROPOSE

A different view of the process by which social policies emerge is more historical, structural, and state-centred. This frame of reference draws on ideas from Heclo, Skocpol, and Shefter.

From Heclo's (1974) perspective on 'political learning' comes the insight that policy-making is an inherently historical process in which all actors consciously build upon, or react against, previous governmental efforts dealing with the same sorts of problems. This means that the goals of politically active groups and individuals can never simply be 'read off' their current social positions. Instead, the investigator must take into account meaningful reactions to previous policies. Such reactions colour the very interests and goals that social groups or politicians define for themselves in struggles over public policies.

Skocpol (1984) argues that social scientists need to 'bring the state back in[to]' their explanations of social change and policy developments. States are first and foremost sets of coercive, fiscal, judicial and administrative organizations claiming sovereignty over territory and people. According to this conception, states independently affect politics in two major ways. First, *states may be sites of autonomous official action*, not reducible to the demands or preferences of any social group(s). Both appointed and elected officials have organizational and career interests of their own, and they devise and work for policies that will further those interests, or at least not harm them. Of course, elected or appointed officials are sensitive in many ways to social preferences and to the economic environment in which the state must operate. Yet politicians and officials are also engaged in struggles among themselves, and they must pursue these struggles by using the capacities of the organizations within which they are located. If a given state structure provides no existing (or readily creatable) capacities for implementing a given line of action, government officials are not likely to pursue it, and politicians aspiring to office are not likely to propose it. Conversely, government officials or aspiring politicians are quite likely to take new policy initiatives – conceivably well ahead of social demands – if existing state capacities can be readily adapted or reworked to do things that they expect will bring advantages to them in their struggles with political competitors.

Secondly, states matter not only because officials and politicians can be independent actors but also because *the organizational structures of states indirectly influence the meanings and methods of politics for all groups in society.* This happens in various ways, only some of which can be highlighted here. One way can be understood as an extension of Heclo's argument about 'political learning': not only do groups react to existing public policies when they formulate their political demands, they also react to existing state structures. Definitions of what is feasible or desirable in politics depend in part on the capacities and the qualities that various groups attribute to state organizations and to the officials and politicians who operate them. Especially in periods when the very structure of the state is at issue and in transformation, particular policies may be advocated or opposed for reasons other than their perceived relevance to socioeconomic needs or cultural ideals. The appeal of particular policies may also depend on how well groups think that they could be officially implemented or how new policies might affect the fortunes of particular kinds of politicians and political organizations.

Historically changing state structures also affect the modes of operation of the very political organizations through which policies can be collectively formulated and socially supported. Martin Shefter's (1977) work on political parties is especially relevant here. Shefter investigates why it is that some political parties – and, indeed, *systems* of competing political parties – operate by offering followers 'patronage' jobs and other kinds of divisible payoffs out of public resources, while other parties and party systems offer ideological appeals and collectively oriented programmes to groups, classes, or 'the nation' as a whole. The traditional answers to this question refer to the inherent cultural proclivities and socioeconomic preferences of given nationalities or social classes: e.g., Irish people and peasants or first-generation ex-peasants want patronage, so that is what their governments and parties offer. But Shefter provides evidence against such answers and instead highlights the effects historical sequences of state bureaucratization and electoral democratization have on parties' modes of operation.

In some European absolute monarchies state bureaucratization preceded the emergence of electoral democracy (and even the emergence of parliamentary parties in some instances). When electoral parties finally emerged in such countries they could not get access to the 'spoils of office', and therefore had to make programmatic appeals based on ideological world views and (if their prospects of forming governments with some authority were good) promises about how state power might be used for policies appealing to organized groups in their targeted constituencies. But, in countries where electoral politics preceded state bureaucratization – as it did in both Britain and the United States – parties could use government jobs and policies as patronage. Later, there might be struggles over how to overcome 'political corruption' in order to create a civil service free of patronage. If bureaucratic reform succeeded before full democratization – as happened in Britain – political parties might then change their operating styles toward more programmatic appeals. However – as happened in the United States – if patronage was established in (or survived into) a fully democratic polity, it was, according to Shefter, extraordinarily difficult to uproot thereafter. Mass electorates and the party politicians appealing to them had continuing stakes in using government as a source of patronage, and reformers had to wage uphill, piecemeal battles to overcome democratized 'political corruption' in government and party politics.

Ideas from Heclo, Skocpol, and Shefter alike will figure in due course in the historically grounded and politically macroscopic explanation that we will offer for British and American social policymaking in the early twentieth century. At this point, let us simply summarize the theoretical frame of reference we will use, one which amalgamates emphases from the traditional frame of reference outlined above with the more state-centred ideas we have just discussed.

STATE FORMATION ⟶	HOW OFFICIAL ⟶	POLICY
(SEQUENCE OF	ORGANIZATIONS AND	POSSIBILITIES
BUREAUCRATIZATION	PARTIES OPERATE	SELECTED
AND DEMOCRATIZATION)		FOR
		STATE
CHANGING ⟶	WHAT POLITICALLY ⟶	ACTION
AND SOCIAL NEEDS	ACTIVE GROUPS	
	PROPOSE	

Overall, we maintain that the politics of social-welfare provision are just as much grounded in processes of statebuilding and the organization and reorganization of political life as in those socioeconomic processes – industrialization, urbanization, demographic change, and the formation of classes – that have traditionally been seen as basic to the development of the modern welfare state. Before we develop this argument for Britain and the United States, however, we shall present the comparative historical evidence for the insufficiency of explanations derived from the Logic of Industrialism, Liberal Values, and Working-Class Strength perspectives. In the process, we highlight specific patterns for Britain and the United States that have to be explained when we apply our own theoretical frame of reference to these cases.

Some brief words should be added about the sources of evidence for the comparative historical arguments of the following sections. Many points are documented with secondary evidence – that is, references to specific sections of books and articles by historians of Britain and the United States. Our contribution in these instances is the careful juxtaposition of findings that the historians themselves have usually presented without awareness of cross-national patterns. This can often make a major difference in the interpretation of the facts. In addition, we have drawn evidence from such primary sources as government statistics, records and reports, periodical publications, and the writings and speeches of contemporary public figures. We try to convey some of the texture of historical events, but place more emphasis on presenting systematic juxtapositions of British and US patterns in order to test or elaborate causal arguments.

CAN SOCIOECONOMIC DEVELOPMENT EXPLAIN THE EMERGENCE OF MODERN SOCIAL POLICIES IN BRITAIN AND THE UNITED STATES?

Logic of Industrialism arguments about the *relative timing* of the emergence of modern welfare programmes in various nations have not fared well in recent research. Nevertheless, Britain did become an industrial and urban nation much sooner than the United States, and one might suppose that factor straightforwardly accounts for the earlier emergence of a modern welfare state in Britain. In our study we have devised ways to control for the overall socioeconomic differences between the two nations in the early twentieth century.

First, we not only examine federal policy-making in the United States, but also probe possibilities for parallel legislative developments across states, especially the more industrial states. This approach addresses an objection often made to comparing the pre-1930s United States to other nations. The United States is a federal not a unitary polity, and before the 1930s most social policies were enacted at local and state levels, not at the level of the federal government. During the Progressive Era, cities and states were the major sites of policy innovation, and such 'national' changes as occurred – including the laws establishing workers' compensation and mothers' pensions – did so in the form of waves of similar legislation across many states.

Secondly, in addition to examining the US case at the federal and 'multiple-state' levels, we also draw on detailed evidence about the particular state of Massachusetts. This is the best single state to investigate for a comparative study of social politics in Britain and the United States before 1920, since it enables us to control for important social and economic characteristics that might be invoked in a pure Logic of Industrialism argument. As the first state in the United States to industrialize and urbanize in forms and tempos close to Britain throughout the nineteenth century, Massachusetts, more than the United States as a whole during the period of interest, very closely resembled Britain on a series of important socioeconomic and demographic measures. Table 1 summarizes relevant data on workforces in agriculture and industry, urbanization, and proportions of the population over 65 years of age for Britain, Massachusetts, and the entire United States.

Massachusetts is ideal for our purposes for other reasons as well. It is well known that this state's upper social classes and professionals closely

Table 1. Socio-economic characteristics of Britain, Massachusetts, and the United States, 1870s–1920s.

Percentage of population aged 65 and over					
England and Wales		Massachusetts		United States	
1881	4.6%	1880	5.0%	3.4%	
1901	4.7%	1900	5.3%	4.3%	
1921	6.0%	1920	5.4%	4.7%	

Percentage of population in towns of 2,500 and above					
1871	65%	1870	66.7%	25.7%	
1901	78%	1900	86.0%	39.7%	
1911	79%	1910	89.0%	45.7%	

Percentage of labour force in agriculture					
United Kingdom		Massachusetts		United States	
1890–99	15%	1895	7.2%	1890–99	42%
1910–19	12%	1915	4.8%	1910–19	31%

Percentage of labour force in manufacturing, mining, and construction					
1890–99	54%	1895	50.5%	1890–99	28%
1910–19	43%	1915	48.4%	1910–19	31%

resembled – and constantly communicated with – their counterparts in Britain. Moreover, Massachusetts was the pioneer in economic regulation, labour statistics, and social legislation in the nineteenth century, often serving as the 'gate-way' for British-style reforms to pass into the United States. From the mid-nineteenth century onward, there were strikingly close parallels in the *regulatory* labour legislation actually passed in Britain and Massachusetts. As we shall document below, only when *social-spending* measures came onto the public agenda after the turn of the century did the two polities diverge, despite their striking socioeconomic similarities.

CAN LIBERALISM EXPLAIN AMERICAN IN CONTRAST TO BRITISH SOCIAL POLITICS?

One way to explain why Britain moved decisively toward modern pensions and social insurance before the First World War, while the United States took only minor steps, is to maintain that although both countries were classically liberal in the nineteenth century, liberal practices and/or ideals actually became more strongly entrenched – and therefore remained more persistent – in the United States. If such an explanation is to be something more than a tautology, it has to be validated through precise definitions and comparative testing showing that 'liberalism', however defined, really was stronger and really did obstruct breakthroughs to new forms of public assistance and social insurance in the United States as contrasted to Britain. In our survey of various authors who invoke the 'Strength of Liberalism' to explain turn-of-the-century (non)developments in the United States, we have found that some refer to economic laissez faire and others place more stress on attitudes and cultural ideals of individualism and voluntary group action free from state controls. Yet neither of these approaches properly distinguishes the United States from Britain.

Liberalism as economic laissez faire

Some scholars argue that modern social-spending programmes were difficult to establish in the early twentieth-century United States because the nation was committed in the nineteenth century to 'self-adjusting' laissez-faire market capitalism. Supposedly, this ruled out positive national-state interventions for economic purposes, thereby discouraging social-welfare interventions as well. In fact, however, under its regime of 'free trade' Britain came closer to this ideal type, and when British Liberal politicians proposed pensions and social insurance after 1906, they did so partly in order to *maintain* free trade by heading off Conservative proposals for new protective tariffs on British industries. In contrast to the situation in Britain, US public policies in the nineteenth century were quite interventionist – for distributive purposes. Tariffs, of course, were the prime example of economic interventionism, but there were also major governmental distributions of public lands, economic charters, and regulatory privileges. And in the area of social intervention, as we have seen, Civil War pensions were distributed ever more widely as the nineteenth century moved toward its end. There simply never was a 'night watchman state' in US capitalism or in American society.

Liberalism as individualism and voluntarism

Most arguments about the United States as a 'welfare laggard' discuss American liberalism as an unanalysed amalgam of attitudes, cultural ideals and ideological or intellectual developments. Value commitments to individualism and voluntarism stand out in these presentations. Americans, it is said, emphasize the freedom and responsibility of individuals so much that virtually any kind of collective provision for individuals' needs becomes suspect as 'socialism' or 'tyranny'. As Gaston Rimlinger puts it: 'In the United States the commitment to individualism – to individual achievement and self-help – was much stronger than ... in England. ... The survival of the liberal tradition, therefore, was ... stronger and the resistance to social protection more tenacious.' And Roy Lubove's well-known history of the US social-insurance movement before 1935 posits that the long-delayed US acceptance of the modern welfare state can be attributed to the persistent faith of Americans not only in rugged individualism but also in *voluntary associations* rather than governments as instruments for the pursuit of collective purposes.

To validate such lines of reasoning, one would need to demonstrate that popular or elite attitudes were different between Britain and the United States and/or that the two countries experienced markedly different cultural and intellectual trends around the turn of the century, making possible collectivist departures from Victorian liberalism in the one case, and leaving nineteenth-century liberal values virtually unchanged in the other. By drawing systematically upon the available secondary literatures for Britain and the United States, we can tentatively conclude that existing arguments about the unusual strength of US liberalism are open to serious question.

In the absence of attitude surveys, the best evidence we have about popular attitudes toward state social spending refers to the orientations of voluntary social-benefit associations in Britain and the United States. It was in England that the most spectacular instance of voluntarist resistance to the coming of the modern welfare state occurred. Resistance from the British friendly societies, which enrolled over half the adult male population by the end of the nineteenth century, delayed the passage of public old age pensions for over two decades. Veritable bastions of 'the Victorian ethic of providence and self-help', the friendly societies collected contributions from respectable British workmen (and lower-middle-class people) and offered sick pay, medical care, and benefits to cover funeral expenses among their members. Even though their finances were being terribly strained, as by the late nineteenth century workers unexpectedly lived longer, the societies fiercely opposed contributory, state-run old age pensions because these would compete for the workers' savings and subject the affairs of the societies to increased government interference. Until just a few years before the 1908 pension legislation, when *some* societies retreated into cautious acquiescence, the friendly societies also refused to accept – let alone champion – non-contributory, public old age pensions. These would have relieved them of the unmanageable burden of caring for older members unable to work, but as Bentley Gilbert puts it, the societies 'preferred insolvency to immorality'.

In the United States various voluntary benefit societies may have enrolled up to one-third of the voting population (i.e., adult males minus most southern blacks), yet they did not vociferously oppose public social provision, and in some cases supported it. During the last third of the nineteenth century the Grand Army of the Republic – which seems to have functioned not only as a lobbying group but in many localities as a fraternal association and voluntary benefit society as well – championed the extension of Civil War pensions. Later, during the 1910s and 1920s the Fraternal Order of Eagles, a mainstream voluntary benefit association (with a white, predominantly native-born middle- and working-class membership of about 500,000 in 1924) waged campaigns in many states not only for workers' compensation and mothers' pensions but also for public old age pensions as an alternative to the almshouse for the elderly poor.

The clearest case in the United States of voluntary-group resistance to public social spending came in the fierce battle that most US charity societies put up against the passage of state-level mothers' pension laws during the Progressive Era. Despite the very broad political support for these laws, the charity societies argued on old-fashioned liberal grounds that the task of providing for – and supervising – worthy widows and their children ought to be left in the hands of private voluntary agencies run by middle- and upper-class people like themselves. This US reform, however, passed in spite of such principled resistance.

The evidence of British history suggests that Victorian ideals of individualism and voluntarism could remain strong among the people at large (as well as conservative elites) without preventing the coming of a modern welfare state. This was true because the cultural and ideological trends that mattered most were those affecting well-educated minorities of upper- and middle-class people. In this respect, British and American trends were remarkably parallel from the 1870s onwards – obviously in part because there was constant communication back and forth.

Initially, Charity Organization movements – launched in Britain in 1869 and imitated in American cities from 1877 on – tried to put individualist ideals about the poor, charity, and relief on a 'scientific' basis. These movements advocated the firm separation of the 'deserving' needy, who should be helped by the 'friendly visitors' of voluntary associations, from the 'undeserving' poor, who should be left to the discipline of the market-place to force them to take responsibility for themselves. In time, however, investigations by charity reformers led some of them – as well as their critics – toward the discovery of environmental and economic causes for mass poverty in the urban centres of Britain and America. From the 1880s, celebrated pieces of muckraking and early empirical social surveys undermined the earlier elite consensus that poor individuals were personally responsible for their troubles.

The awakening of social awareness and social conscience was further spurred in both countries through 'settlement house' movements. University or college-educated young people moved into urban neighbourhoods to live with, bring cultural improvements to, and learn about the working classes and the poor. Toynbee Hall was established in the East End of London in 1884, and by 1911 there were 46 settlement houses in Britain. Meanwhile, some Americans travelled to English settlement houses and carried models home; others arrived at similar ideas without such direct contact. US settlements sprang up in New York, Boston, Chicago, and many other cities, especially in the Northeast and Midwest. 'In 1891 there were six . . .; in 1897 there were seventy-four . . . and by 1910 there were more than four hundred' American settlement houses.

Varieties of 'socialist' notions about how the collective needs of industrial-capitalist Britain and America should be met were spreading in the late nineteenth and early twentieth centuries, and some settlement-house people as well as other reformers became socialists or maintained close working contacts with fellow reformers who were socialists. The really important story, however, was not the spread of socialist doctrines in either Britain or the United States.[2] It was, instead, the reworking of liberal ideals away from pure self-help and distrust of state intervention toward 'new' or 'progressive' liberal conceptions. Industrial society, more and more educated Britons and Americans were recognizing, makes people interdependent, and in such a society government becomes an indispensable support for individual dignity, providing security and regulating competition to undergird responsible personal initiatives. Thus cultural and intellectual resources were present in both England and the United States to justify new public-welfare efforts in terms of redefined liberal ideals.

Nor was this just a theoretical potential. Precisely such justifications actually were invoked by the progressive liberals in Britain who sponsored the old age pensions and social insurances of 1908 to 1911. Similar arguments were used by the social progressives in the United States, ranging from settlement workers and environmentally minded social or charity workers, to the reformist social scientists and other professionals who worked through the American Association for Labor Legislation and then the Progressive Party.

We are certainly not arguing here that elites and new middle-class people in Britain and the United States held, overall, exactly the same attitudes toward state action for social-welfare purposes. As we will soon show, American reformers as well as elites and middle classes in general were more fearful about 'political corruption' and concomitantly less willing to accept *social-spending* measures. The point is simply that new liberal understandings of the uses of state action to support the dignity of individual citizens were sufficiently well developed in both nations to allow new public welfare departures to be discussed and legitimated in liberal terms.

CAN 'WORKING-CLASS STRENGTH' EXPLAIN DIFFERENCES BETWEEN BRITAIN AND THE UNITED STATES?

If turn-of-the-century Britain and the United States were both sufficiently industrial and urban that new social protections for citizens were potentially needed, and if both nations experienced cultural and intellectual reworkings that made it possible to legitimate such changes, nevertheless it is possible that politically expressed working-class demands for pensions and social insurance were significantly different between the two nations. Was the British industrial working class 'stronger' – did it more effectively demand public social benefits than the US industrial working class?

Trade unions and social-benefit programmes

British friendly societies delayed the advent of a modern welfare state in the name of Victorian self-reliance and voluntarism, and throughout the period before the First World War the membership of this type of 'working-class organization' exceeded British trade-union membership by threefold. Nevertheless, analyses of British social politics in the early twentieth century highlight the demands of rapidly growing unions for social protections especially old age pensions, outside the cruel restrictions of the New Poor Law. In 1899, trade unions helped to launch a campaign through the National Committee of Organized Labour on Old Age Pensions, calling for non-contributory public pensions to cover all British citizens over 65 years of age. Later that same year the Trades Union Congress endorsed universal pensions for all citizens at age sixty. By 1908, the British government partially satisfied this extraparliamentary campaign by legislating pensions.

Arguably, therefore, union pressures were pivotal in triggering the entire set of major social-spending breakthroughs in Britain from 1908 to 1911. In contrast, many students of social politics during the Progressive Era in the United States portray unions, led by the craft-dominated American Federation of Labor, as weak, defensive, and strongly opposed to all kinds of public social provision. Our research shows, however, that matters are much more complex than the conventional portraits of British versus American unions suggest.

During the relevant periods of the early twentieth century, British and American unions of not such different organizational strength took similar

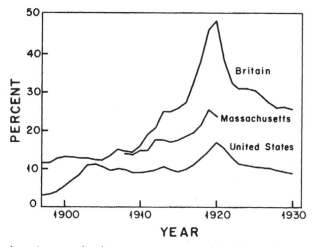

Figure 3. Trade union membership as a percentage of the labour force in Britain, the United States and Massachusetts.

Note: For the United States and Britain, trade union membership is calculated as the percentage of the labour force (including unemployed, but excluding proprietors, self-employed, unpaid family workers and armed forces) who are members of trade unions. For Massachusetts, it is calculated as the percentage of employees who were members of trade unions. To determine the number of employees in Massachusetts, it was necessary to use Massachusetts and US Census data on the 'gainfully employed' (anyone who worked, including proprietors and self-employed), along with the estimate of Keyssar that 79 per cent of men and 100 per cent of women in the Massachusetts workforce were employees. Workforce data for the years between the censuses of 1905, 1910, 1915 and 1920 are linear extrapolations.

if not identical stands toward possibilities for new public benefits. Figure 3 shows trends in 'union density' – proportions of the total labour force unionized – for Britain, the United States, and Massachusetts. The data show that, while British unionization exceeded US unionization throughout our time period, the percentages of the labour force unionized were comparable – from 9 to 16 per cent – during the respective periods of greatest reform ferment, between 1900 and 1910 in Britain and between 1906 and 1920 in the United States. The imperfect data we have been able to develop also show that unionization in Massachusetts more closely paralleled the British trends – and indeed quite a few of the most industrialized US states must have been much more similar to Britain than was the United States as a whole.

Not only was unionized American labour more weighty in the more industrialized states, it was also the case that labour unions and the Federation of Labor exercised most of their political influence at local and state levels. Especially at those levels, stances toward unemployment and health insurance were much more positive than conventional generalizations about the national AFL suggest. During the Progressive Era, labour organizations – including the state federations of labour in such leading industrial states as Massachusetts, New York, California, Ohio, New Jersey, Missouri, and Pennsylvania – joined reformers to support either proposals for health insurance or unemployment insurance, or both.

Even more to the point, *British developments reveal that it was not necessary for unions (or any working-class groups) to initiate or demand health and unemployment insurance in order for them to come about.* In the words of C. L. Mowat, these contributory social insurances – which taxed workers as well as providing benefits to them – 'owed their introduction to the fruitful collaboration of minister and civil servant'. As the detailed historical studies of both Gilbert and Heclo spell out, the key policy initiators operated from within the Liberal government and the British state, and they persuaded many reluctant – or uninterested – labour unions to accept their proposals through delicate negotiations about specific methods of implementing insurance taxes and payments.

Given that US state and local labour groups were at least as willing to accept social-insurance programmes as their British counterparts, it seems probable that comparable co-optive efforts directed at them by state-government leaders would have succeeded. Yet in the United States, in contrast to Britain, governmental leaders did not make efforts to devise social-insurance programmes and coopt organized working-class support for them, and it was surely this lack, rather than the lack of demands or acquiescence from the unions, that pinpoints a crucial mechanism by which the social insurances succeeded in Britain and failed in America.

As we move from contributory social insurances to non-contributory old age pensions, it becomes still easier to pinpoint that the important contrast between Britain and the US did not lie with the unions. Pensions were advanced by a cross-class alliance in Britain which had no US counterpart. In Britain, the extraparliamentary National Committee that agitated for universal old age pensions from 1899 on was initiated by upper- and middle-class reformers and flourished through the cooperation of reformers and some trade-union leaders. Moreover, the Liberal pension programme passed in 1908 did not simply concede to union-backed demands. In the United States, meanwhile, the missing ingredient was not the willingness of AFL unions to support proposals for non-contributory public old age pensions. That willingness came a little later than in Britain, but the Federation endorsed a need-based national pension scheme in 1909, and reiterated its support for national pension plans in 1911, 1912, and 1913. Indeed, AFL President Samuel Gompers was more willing to go along with old age pensions than with unemployment and health insurance and state-level AFL leaders often supported both pensions and social insurance.

During the Progressive Era, it was not US trade unions but rather many social reformers – and, in general, the upper and professional strata from which they came and to which they oriented their arguments – who were reluctant to push for or accept public old age pensions. Events at the elite level in the United States make a telling contrast to Britain. In Britain, from the 1880s onward, social investigators and national commissions acknowledged the problems of the elderly poor and grappled with various solutions, leading increasingly toward broad acceptance within the British establishment of the inevitability, if not the desirability, of some sort of public support outside the Poor Law. In America, however, exactly the opposite happened.

The first serious official investigation of old age poverty occurred in Massachusetts and dealt a virtual death blow to what had previously been a promising movement toward old age pensions in that state and beyond. An investigatory commission staffed predominantly with professionals and upper-class Bostonians gathered data on the elderly poor in Massachusetts, considered various pension policies and alternatives to them, and reported back that public pensions were neither needed nor morally desirable. A labour representative, Arthur M. Huddell, dissented from commission arguments about the preferability of contributory as opposed to non-contributory pensions and cited Civil War pensions as a favourable precedent. He did not call for state-level old age pensions, arguing instead in favour of Representative William B. Wilson's 1909 bill proposing national-level legislation for an 'Old Age Home Guard'.

In 1916 yet another Massachusetts commission, appointed by a progressive Republican governor, reconsidered non-contributory old age pensions. This happened only after the state Labor Federation supported pensions and voters in eight towns and urban districts endorsed them in referenda by almost a four-to-one margin! Even so, the commission members did not unite in support of old age pensions (or unemployment or health insurance), and it was not until 1930 that Massachusetts established old age pensions for the needy.

Across the nation, old age pensions were downplayed throughout the Progressive Era even by the reform-minded elites who worked through the American Association for Labor Legislation (AALL). In 1913–14 – just as the commitment of the American Federation of Labor to old age pensions was solidifying – the AALL moved toward promoting not old age pensions but health insurance as the 'next great step' after workmen's compensation in the 'inevitable' progress toward a full-scale modern welfare state in America. From 1915 onwards, the AALL also advocated a model bill for unemployment insurance as part of an overall plan for dealing with the problems of the unemployed. Not until the 1920s, when the upsurge of Progressive social reform was over and the Association was willing to associate itself with virtually any positive effort that remained, did the AALL finally begin to push for public old age pensions.

In sum, the comparative picture of Britain and the United States looks like this: Encouraged by elite reformers and building on a climate of broad elite and governmental acknowledgments of a problem requiring new public action, British union leaders were able to campaign effectively for non-contributory old age pensions. British unions also went along with contributory unemployment and health-insurance measures devised and pushed forward by intragovernmental elites, politicians and civil servants. In the United States, many union leaders, especially at state levels – and also at the national level in the case of old age pensions – supported social-benefits programmes, but for unemployment and health insurance, intra-governmental leadership was missing. American elites, including most of the prominent reformers, did not coalesce with unions to campaign for old age pensions; nor did they pave the way for them through official investigations.

The working class in electoral politics

Perhaps looking only at trade unions is too narrow a way to investigate 'working-class strength'. Working-class pressures for public social protections may have been registered not simply, or primarily, through trade unions, but more broadly through the processes of democratic electoral politics.

As both the British and the US cases reveal, modern social programmes do not come as automatic by-products of electoral democratization. The American electorate was fully democratized for white males by 1840, and the key phases of British working-class enfranchisement occurred well before 1908–11, when better-off workers got the vote through the reforms of 1867 and 1884, and later, when everyone except women under 30 received the franchise in 1918. Yet far from stressing the sheer fact of working-class enfranchisement, many proponents of the Working-Class Strength perspective argue that modern welfare programmes arise from the *combined* efforts of trade unions and a political party based in the industrial working class and programmatically oriented to furthering its interests. From this perspective, the slow arrival of a modern welfare state in the United States is basically attributed to the absence of a working-class-based socialist or labour party, while the British Labour Party, along with some of the trade unions, is given the basic credit for developing the British welfare state.

Obviously, such an argument cannot tell us how or why the US democratic polity of the late nineteenth century extended social benefits to many working-class and middle-class Americans under the reworked rubric of the Civil War pension system. Yet it is also misleading about the origins of the British welfare state. By the end of the First World War, the Labour Party overtook the Liberals and became thereafter the chief defender and extender of public social benefits in Britain. But the original legislative breakthroughs of 1908–1911 were *not* the direct achievement of the fledgling Labour Representation Committee (LRC) founded in 1900 to elect worker representatives to Parliament. It was a Liberal government, newly invigorated in 1908 by a strong progressive faction under Herbert Asquith, that proposed and put through pensions and social insurance.

At the juncture in question, the still tiny LRC, though increasingly successful in elections and by-elections, remained dependent for its electoral and parliamentary prospects on an alliance with the much stronger, established Liberal Party. Meanwhile, the progressives within the Liberal Party were looking for ways to appeal to working-class voters. British voter turnout was increasing in the early twentieth century, and the Liberals were pressed by competition from the Conservatives. Between the 1906 and 1910 elections, the Liberals lost significant ground to the Conservatives. For progressively minded Liberals, social benefits and pro-trade-union measures, besides being morally desirable according to new liberal values, were a way to keep working-class voters loyal to their party, with its free-trade priorities, rather than allowing Conservatives to woo them with a combination of tariffs and social spending.

In contrast to the causal emphasis placed by Working-Class Strength proponents on pressures from labour organizations, we view pensions and social insurance as grounded in cross-class alliances and as tools of politically mediated social control within industrial capitalism. Thus we have highlighted the greater willingness of British elites to co-operate with, or co-opt, industrial labour in furthering social insurance and (especially) non-contributory old age pensions.[3] To explain why British and American elites took different stances, the analysis of labour's strength or demands is not sufficient. We must understand the overall structures of the British and US states, and analyse the sequences of democratization and bureaucratization that transformed the two national polities from the nineteenth century into the early twentieth. Then it will become apparent why the British Liberal party and government was able and willing to launch modern pensions and social insurance in 1908–11, while America's extraordinary post-Civil War pension system could not serve as an 'entering wedge' for a similar modern welfare state.

STATE STRUCTURES AND SOCIAL POLITICS IN TWO INDUSTRIALIZING LIBERAL DEMOCRACIES

When the international ferment over modern social insurance and pensions spread to Britain and the United States around the turn of the century, it caught these nations and their social and political elites at very different conjunctures of political transformation. Essentially, these were two liberal polities that had moved from patronage-dominated politics toward public bureaucratization at different phases of industrialization and democratization. Britain already had a civil service, programmatically competing political parties, and legacies of centralized welfare administration to react against and build upon. Modern social-spending programmes complemented the organizational dynamics of government and parties in early twentieth-century Britain. The United States, however, lacked an established civil bureaucracy and was embroiled in the efforts of Progressive reformers to create regulatory agencies and policies free from the 'political corruption' of nineteenth-century patronage democracy. At this juncture in American history, modern social-spending programmes were neither governmentally feasible nor politically acceptable.

From oligarchic patronage to a modern welfare state in Britain

Britain's polity in the nineteenth century started out as a liberal oligarchy ruled by and for landlords. During the course of the century this polity underwent several intertwined transformations which laid the basis for the

Liberal welfare breakthroughs of 1908–1911: the expansion of national administrative activities, especially in the realm of social-welfare policy; the reform of the civil service; the step-by-step democratization of the parliamentary electorate; and transformations in the modes of organization and electoral operation of the major political parties.

For quite some time British historians have recognized the 'Victorian origins of the welfare state', in an administrative sense. Laissez faire may have been the charter myth of nineteenth-century British government, but despite the reality of free-market and free-trade economic policies, in the realm of domestic social-welfare policy the implementation of the New Poor Law called for administrative supervision and social planning on a national scale. The 1834 New Poor Law was radical not only in its substantive precepts embodying the ideals of market capitalism, but also because it established a central authority, the Poor Law Commission, to supervise local poor-relief institutions, and substituted elected boards of guardians governing groups of parishes for the local magistrates who had formerly monopolized supervision of the poor. The very structure of welfare administration in the unitary British polity meant that tensions generated by the workings of the local workhouses, asylums, and sick wards, and by the implementation of other policies to deal with the poor, inevitably and recurrently generated pressures for *national* debates, investigations and policy changes.

Meanwhile, important changes also occurred in the workings of the British civil service. In the eighteenth and early nineteenth centuries, oligarchic patronage predominated and 'the public services were the outdoor relief department of the aristocracy'. Industrialization and urbanization – along with the geopolitical exigencies of maintaining British imperial domains and coping with growing international economic competition – generated pressures for the British government to become more efficient and technically competent than patronage would allow. Governmental change did not come automatically: reform advocates were initially frustrated by those with a vested interest in the existing system. Yet, finally, proposals for civil-service reform succeeded politically in the 1870s. Prior changes in universities made them plausible as agencies for training and credentialing civil servants. Once it became clear that working-class political influence might grow as the electorate expanded, the landed and business groups and the existing governing elites of Britain came together in order to maintain the elite civil service on a new basis.

Civil-service reform in Britain did *not* ensure that bureaucrats would subsequently become policy innovators. At both the Local Government Board and the Home Office, two of the departments most concerned with questions of domestic social policy, there developed after 1870 a 'general inertia and disinvolvement from reform', accompanied by a view of the civil service 'as a source of income and status'. In this period, however, the British state structure was not administratively monolithic. The Board of Trade, a competing agency outside of the control of the LGB and the Home Office, was able during the 1880s and 1890s to develop independent capacities in the collection and use of labour statistics. The Board's activities expanded rapidly and it recruited a remarkable core of young, progressive-minded officials, eventually including William Beveridge, an expert on labour markets and issues of unemployment, who had gone from Oxford into settlement-house activities, journalism and unemployment-relief work before coming into government service under the Liberals in 1908.

Finally, and perhaps most important, civil-service reform along with step-by-step electoral democratization had important implications for the organization and operation of the political parties. With the credentialization of the civil service, the parties had to stop relying on elite patronage and develop new methods of raising funds and rewarding activists and new ways of winning votes in an expanding electorate. In the 1870s and 1880s, both the Liberal and Conservative parties created constituency organizations and began to formulate programmes to appeal through activists to blocks of voters and financial subscribers.

We are now in a position to see how the historical legacies of the New Poor Law, along with the state structure and party system in place in Britain by the early twentieth century, facilitated the Liberal welfare breakthroughs of 1908 to 1911. From the 1890s onward, there was widespread elite and popular disgruntlement with the way members of the respectable working class who became impoverished due to old age, ill health, or unemployment were handled by poor-law institutions. National politicians, Conservative and Liberal alike, became interested in reforming or replacing the New Poor Law to deal better with the problems of the 'worthy poor'. Some of their concerns were generated from administrative dilemmas within established programmes as well as by the threat to the whole edifice of local government finance posed by the rising and uneven costs of the poor law. Other concerns arose from the obvious political fact that the votes of working-class people – and the support of their organizations, the unions and friendly societies – had to be contested by parties engaged in increasingly programmatic competition.

During the 1890s, the voluntarist resistance of the friendly societies to old age pensions helped to delay new welfare breakthroughs, and then the Boer War of 1899 to 1902 provided political diversion and temporary financial excuses for avoiding new domestic expenditures. After the war, the Liberal welfare reforms – which bypassed the New Poor Law without abolishing or fundamentally reforming it – crystallized along two routes. In the face of the cross-class campaign waged by the National Committee of Organized Labour and Old Age Pensions, the Liberals devised their non-contributory and need-based old age pensions as a tool of programmatic competition with the Conservatives. The Liberals hoped to retain the loyalty of working-class voters and reinforce their party's alliance with the Labour Representation Committee. After the passage of pension legislation, proposals for contributory unemployment and health insurance came through initiatives from Liberal Cabinet leaders allied with civil administrators at the Board of Trade and the Treasury. For unemployment and health insurance alike, intragovernmental elites took the initiative in persuading both working-class and business interests to go along. Once this persuading was done and the Cabinet was set on its course, the discipline of the Liberal Party in Parliament ensured passage of the National Insurance Act, and there were no independent courts to which disgruntled parties could appeal.

Stepping back to put these policy departures in broader context, we must emphasize the fact that in this period the administration of social spending as such was not fundamentally problematic for British elites. The 'corruption' of patronage politics was behind them, and disputes were now focused on levels and forms of spending, and especially on direct versus indirect taxation. The Labour Party was not yet a major actor in British politics, and both Liberal and Conservative leaders were concerned to attract or retain working-class electoral support through programmatic party competition. Parts of the British state bureaucracy had the capacities and the personnel to take the initiative in devising new social policies. In this context and conjuncture, pensions and social insurance looked like good ways to circumvent for the respectable working class the cruelties, inefficiencies, and costs of the New Poor Law of the nineteenth century. Such policies also looked like appropriate programmes to appeal to – and, in the case of the social-insurance measures, newly *tax* – the working class, involving them more fully in the life of a united nation, yet under the hegemony of enlightened, professional, middle-class leadership.

The struggle against patronage democracy and the limits of social spending in the United States

America's polity in the nineteenth century has been aptly described as a polity of 'courts and parties' operating in a multi-tiered federal framework. The courts adjudicated rights of contract and private property. Meanwhile, highly competitive political parties provided a modicum of integration across the various levels and branches of government. Crucially, US electoral politics was fully democratized for white males in the Jacksonian era. Thus, political parties were able to rotate the 'spoils of office' to reward their cadres and followers as the parties swept into and out of office in the constant rounds of close-fought elections characteristic of nineteenth-century American democracy. The entire system worked best at all levels when governmental outputs took the form, not of programmes devised to appeal to functionally organized collectivities, but of politically discretionary *distributional* policies, such as financial subsidies or grants of land, tariff advantages, special regulations or regulatory exceptions, construction contracts and public-works jobs.

Ideal sets of distributional policies combined measures that raised revenues – or created jobs – with those that allocated them. Especially from the point of view of the Republicans, the post-Civil War pension system was an excellent example of a policy generated by the distributional proclivities of nineteenth-century patronage democracy. It allowed the Republicans to confer on individuals in many localities pensions financed out of the 'surplus' revenues from the constantly re-adjusted tariffs they sponsored to benefit various industries and sections of industries. Not surprisingly, Civil War pension laws and practices were transformed from the late 1870s to the 1890s (refer to Figure 2), when electoral competition between the Republicans and the Democrats in the North was especially intense. A few hundred votes could make the difference in states like Ohio, Illinois, and New York, so in addition to supporting recurrent legal liberalizations of the terms of eligibility, Congressmen intervened with the Pension Bureau to help people prove their eligibility and sponsored thousands of special pension bills tailored for individual constituents. Moreover, the Republicans were known to time the dispatch of pension commissioners into states and localities to coincide with crucial election battles!

In significant contrast to Britain, there was no national poor law in the nineteenth-century United States, either in theory or in administrative fact. Instead, mixtures of Elizabethan and New Poor Law practices were institutionalized in diverse forms in thousands of local communities, where the prime responsibility lay both financially (as in Britain) and legally. Reactions against poor-law practices would not so readily converge into a series of national debates as they did from the 1830s on in Britain, although the final decades of the nineteenth century did witness the emergence of state-level administrative supervision and policy debates in places such as Massachusetts.

At all levels of government there were, however, growing reactions against the 'inefficiency' and 'corruption' of nineteenth-century patterns of patronage democracy. As the United States became a truly national economy and society in the decades after the Civil War, problems faced by public policymakers challenged the distributional style of patronage democracy, and vociferous demands emerged for civil-service reform. The initial proponents were 'Mugwumps', mostly upper- and upper-middle-class reformers located in the Northeast, especially Massachusetts. Like the successful British civil-service reformers of the 1870s, the Mugwumps wanted public administration to be taken out of patronage politics, so that expertise and predictability could prevail. At first, however, the Mugwumps' reform proposals made only limited headway, for American party politicians had secure roots in the fully democratized and tautly mobilized mass white-male electorate. In contrast to the situation in Britain, there was no impending threat of further electoral democratization to prod political as well as social elites into civil-service reform.

Not until the Progressive Era of the early twentieth century did administrative reform really make significant headway in the United States, and then more at municipal and state levels than at the national level. Social demands for new kinds of collective policies 'in the public interest', and for reforms in government to ensure their proper implementation, broadened out from the very elite ranks of Mugwumpry to include the growing ranks of the educated, professionalizing middle class and (in many places) farmers and organized workers as well.

The legacies of nineteenth-century patronage democracy and the conjuncture of its crisis in the Progressive Era created a much less favourable context for advocates of old age pensions and social insurance in the early twentieth-century United States than the one enjoyed by their counterparts in Britain. Most basically, there was the sheer weakness of public administration, due to the original absence of state bureaucracy in America, the limited achievements of civil-service reform in the nineteenth century, and the dispersion of authority in US federalism. In contrast to the situation in Britain, there were in the early twentieth-century United States no influential high-level public officials strategically positioned to formulate new social-benefit policies with existing administrative resources, press them on political executives, and work out firm compromises with organized interest groups. Typically, reforms in the Progressive Era were not autonomous initiatives from either civil servants or politicians. They were usually urged upon state legislatures by broad coalitions of reform and interest groups.

This made sense, not only because of the weakness of public administration, but also because this was a period when party organizations as such were weakened, even though the Republicans and Democrats remained jointly dominant.[4] Moreover, US political parties operated differently from British parties. They were democratic, patronage-oriented parties that found their established ties to electoral constituents and business interests under attack by reformers. They were not programmatic parties looking for new policies to attract organized labour. The challenge for elected US politicians was to find ad hoc ways to propitiate reform-minded pressure groups while still retaining the loyalty of working-class supporters.

New social-spending measures did not fit this formula. For such policies, politicians could not get support or acquiescence from broad coalitions including middle- and upper-class groups. Throughout the Progressive Era, the common denominator of all reform remained the struggle against political corruption. People doubted that social-spending measures could be implemented honestly, and feared that they might well reinforce the hold over the electorate of patronage politicians. We have found some direct evidence that such fears were strongest and most openly expressed on the issue of old age pensions, which would have been non-contributory governmental handouts very much like the post-Civil War pensions.

Back in 1889, leading Mugwump and President of Harvard Charles Eliot Norton had denounced the Civil War pensions as 'a crime ... against Republican institutions' because they 'foisted ... perjured pauper[s] ... upon the public treasury'. Echoes of this revulsion reverberated into the Progressive Era and made even leading social-insurance advocates wary of pensions. For example, Charles Henderson, who wanted to believe that the logic of the Civil War pensions pointed toward more universal social protections, was forced to acknowledge that the 'extravagance and abuses of the military pension system have probably awakened prejudice against workingmen's pensions'. And Henry Rogers Seager, a professor at Columbia University and a prominent member of the American Association for Labour Legislation, pointed out in public lectures and a book advocating social insurance that 'our experience with national military pensions has not predisposed us to favor national pensions of any kind'.

Seager simultaneously made a strong case for publicly run disability, health, and unemployment insurance. Such modern social policies would be less risky than old age pensions because they would tax workers as well as providing benefits to them. Seager did not seem to realize, however, that broad political alliances between reformers and popular groups would be much harder to form around contributory measures as opposed to non-contributory old age pensions. And he did not take note of British developments, which demonstrated that contributory social-insurance measures had come in 1911 only *after* a broad cross-class alliance had supported the non-contributory old age pensions of 1908.

Social politics in Massachusetts

In Massachusetts the fight against political corruption raged throughout the Progressive period and reinforced tendencies to keep the state out of new realms of social spending. Fortunately for comparative purposes, the same kinds of legislative proposals came up for debate in Massachusetts as in Britain. A regulatory measure that actually passed, the Workmen's Compensation Act of 1911, was partly inspired by Britain's laws of 1897 and 1906. In the area of social spending, pioneering US legislative proposals and investigatory commissions on old age pensions, referring explicitly to British precedents, came in Massachusetts from 1903 onward, and an Unemployment Insurance Bill directly modelled on the British 1911 Act was introduced in Massachusetts in 1916 as the first such bill in the United States. Finally, a 1916 Massachusetts commission also investigated British-style health insurance. Of course, old age pensions, unemployment insurance, and health insurance failed to pass in Progressive-Era Massachusetts. This state, which had heretofore paralleled or followed Britain closely in social and labour legislation, stopped short when social spending as opposed to regulatory measures came on to the agenda.

Much evidence points to the centrality of upper- and middle-class fears about political corruption. Testifying before the 1907 Massachusetts commission that ultimately killed the first US campaign for potentially popular old age pensions, reformer John Graham Books stressed that:

> the condition of our politics is the first difficulty in the way of the working of a pension scheme.... We have no end of illustrations of the way that we pension off all sorts of persons in the army; while there are a large number of deserving, there are many thousands who are not – and pensions are given on account of politics. I do not see how we can save any pension system in this country from running into politics.

Moreover, Massachusetts reformers were already attempting to cope with needs for old age protection through Louis Brandeis's 'Savings Bank Insurance Plan'. This interesting plan attacked the vested interest of insurance companies in their profits on life-insurance schemes, thus indicating a willingness on the part of reformers to oppose big business. Yet in order to avoid relying on government action, the law passed in 1907, and later reindorsed by the *Report of the Commission on Old Age Pensions*, mandated savings banks to market low-cost old age and/or life-insurance policies to Massachusetts citizens. The author of the Savings Bank Insurance Plan wanted to avoid public social insurance because he believed that 'our government does not now grapple successfully with the duties which it has assumed, and should not extend its operations at least until it does'.

During the life of the commission to investigate pensions Massachusetts' 'good government' reformers were engaged through an investigatory Financial Commission in denouncing the extravagant practices of patronage politicians in Boston. With dissent coming only from a labour representative, the 1909 Financial Commission Report censured Boston Mayor John F. ('Honey Fitz') Fitzgerald for expanding public employment, letting out public contracts without competitive bidding, and hiring patronage workers. The commission's solution was to propose strict controls on public spending.

Ethnic tensions between the Anglo-Saxon Protestant Massachusetts establishment and the predominantly Irish Catholic Boston lower strata obviously underlay the happenings just discussed and one might wonder whether such ethnic conflicts account for US versus British patterns of social policymaking. Ethnic conflicts in politics were not simply primordial givens, however. They crystallized especially in struggles over the role of political patronage. These struggles, rather than the more often cited ethnic divisions within the US working class, are the primary mechanism by which ethnic variety in America adversely affected the prospects for modern social-benefits programmes. Floods of Irish poor also immigrated into industrializing England, creating sharp sociocultural tensions there as well, but without preventing the emergence of a modern welfare state in a British polity *not* wracked with quarrels over patronage at the turn of the twentieth century.

Some important social-welfare innovations did occur in Massachusetts during the Progressive Era. Labour regulations were strengthened, especially for women and children, and mothers' pensions were enacted. The state also joined many others in passing workers' compensation and – despite the cries of business that the state's competitively pressed industrial economy could be hurt – the 1911 Massachusetts law had the broadest workforce coverage (fully 80 per cent) of any such American law. This helps to make a point more broadly true of Progressive reform: even with business and other powerful and mobilized interests opposed, purely regulatory reforms often passed. They fit well into the Progressive proclivity to create new regulatory agencies, a kind of 'fourth branch' of government beyond the direct control of politicians which employed middle-class professionals to watch over the behaviour of business and workers in 'the public interest'. In contrast to measures calling for large-scale social spending, regulatory measures and the independent agencies ideally established to implement them were not seen as likely to reinforce 'political corruption'.

Why workers' compensation and mothers' pensions?

Indeed, it would not do for us to explain how America's early twentieth-century political context frustrated prospects for old age pensions and social insurance without at the same time underlining why it allowed laws to pass establishing workers' compensation and mothers' pensions, each in almost forty states. The ultimate pressure that pushed through both of these new social-welfare programmes came from the wide publicity magazines and investigatory commissions gave the issues and from the lobbying of state legislatures carried on by broad coalitions of reform and interest groups. This pressure could never have built up in the first place had not elites and the political public generally been broadly receptive to these ideas – receptive through forms, such as official commissions, that were simultaneously used to denounce or delay pensions and social insurance.[5] Why was this?

One feature of both types of laws that recommended them to reformers, elites, and Progressive Era political publics was that they involved little or no public spending, certainly not of the order that would be required for old age pensions or partially state-funded, British-style social insurance. Workers' compensation laws merely required businesses to insure their employees against injuries; in all but a few states this could be done through private carriers or even through self-insurance. Mothers' pension laws largely restricted themselves to helping morally 'worthy' widows; only 25 per cent of the states provided any of the financing; and all the laws were 'local option', leaving it to individual counties or towns to decide whether to help mothers, exactly which ones, and at what levels of aid.

Equally significant, neither workers' compensation nor mothers' pensions constituted a wholly new departure for public action in America. They did not mandate (as pensions and social insurances would have done) new fiscal functions for barely established civil administrators or for potentially 'corrupt' party politicians. Rather, *these laws reworked activities already being handled in the American polity by the courts.* Workers' compensation laws removed disputes over compensation for injured workers from the common law and the courts, and typically placed settlements under the supervision of regulatory agencies that were set up to monitor payments by businesses to injured workers or the dependants of deceased workers. No brand new public jurisdiction was established; the venue was simply changed from common-law courts to regulatory agencies.

Mothers' pensions also involved the courts, this time, interestingly enough, both as proponents of change and as loci for trustworthy administration of social spending. As things were, judges – including those of the new-style juvenile courts established in the Progressive Era – had to decide about the removal of the children of poor women when mothers could not adequately provide for their offspring. Especially where respectable widows were concerned, removal from the home was coming to be a heinous decision, for the idea was growing that children needed maternal care. Juvenile-court judges in Illinois and Missouri helped to initiate the nation-wide movement for mothers' pensions. Private charity organizations strongly opposed the pensions as encroachments upon their voluntary sphere, and some reformers worried, as did Charles Henderson, that even the small sums involved in mothers' pensions might become 'another kind of spoils for low politicians'. Most of the new laws, however, obviated this worry by putting juvenile-court judges in charge of deciding who should receive pensions and supervising the performance of the recipients thereafter. Thus, not politicians or bureaucrats, but new kinds of judges operating with 'expert' discretion took charge of administering most of these tiny new flows of social spending instituted in the United States during the Progressive Era.

CONCLUSION

Far from finding socio-economic development, the rise of the industrial working class, and new liberal values irrelevant, this study has repeatedly referred to them in accounting for British and US social politics around the turn of the century. Yet these tendencies were comparably present in both countries. Thus they cannot sufficiently explain why Britain launched a full range of modern pension and social-insurance programmes before World War I, while the United States resisted the possibility of launching modern social-spending measures and, in fact, actually allowed a popular system of old age and disability pensions for many working- and middle-class Americans to pass out of existence without replacement.

To explain these contrasting trajectories of British and US social politics, we have invoked a state-centred frame of reference to complement the society-centred factors more usually invoked in the literature on modern welfare states. We have highlighted both the autonomous actions of officials and politicians and the ways in which state structures and their transformations affected the policy preferences of politically influential social groups. Our findings and arguments here dovetail with [. . .] recent state-centred arguments about the determinants of social policy in Israel, and with broader comparative findings about the autonomous role of the state in social-welfare policymaking in authoritarian-bureaucratic or late-developing nations. By demonstrating the relevance of variables about state structures and state/society relationships for two liberal-democratic countries that ought, if any do, to fit traditional socio-economic and cultural theories of welfare-state development, we believe we have under-lined the need – and the opportunity – for continuing analytic reorienta-tion in the literature on the emergence and development of modern social policies.

It will not do to imagine public social policies as inevitable and irre-versible by-products of industrial or capitalist development, even with class struggles and value orientations introduced to account for variations and possible delays along the march. Welfare policies are also directly ground-ed in the logics of state-building, in the struggles of politicians for control and advantage, and in the expectations groups have about what states and parties with specific structures and modes of operation could or should do. Our theories will serve us poorly for understanding the past, present, and future of public social policies in the United States and across the world if we do not redesign them to take better account of the macro-political de-terminants of the making and un-making of measures that are, after all, thought to add up to 'the modern welfare *state*'.

Notes

1. I. M. Rubinow correctly estimated that in 1913 half the native white men over 65 in the entire United States were receiving pensions. However, his guess that two-thirds of the native white men of the North were pensioners was an overestimate. From our examination of data in *Historical Statistics of the United States* and in the *Statistical Abstract of the United States, 1913*, we estimate that in 1910 56 per cent of the native-born white men of the North (i.e., outside the Confederate South) were pensioners. This was 30 per cent of all men over 65 in the entire nation. We also estimate that about 36 per cent of all men then between 15 and 44 years old in the Northeast and the Midwest served in the Union armies during the Civil War.
2. Socialists were a modest presence in both British and US politics in the pre-First-World-War years. The American Socialist Party peaked at 6 per cent of the presidential vote in 1912, while in Britain Labour, which had socialist along with non-socialist components, gained 5.9 per cent of the parliamentary vote in 1906 and 7.6 per cent in 1910. Some interpreters cite 'the socialist threat' as an impetus to liberal reform in Britain or America. We doubt this interpretation, but in any event the socialist presence was com-parable in the two nations before the First World War.
3. Why are we talking about 'elites' rather than 'capitalist classes' or 'business'? Some inter-preters of welfare developments in the early twentieth century have emphasized partial business support for public initiatives in Britain in contrast to the preference of even the most 'progressive' American capitalists for corporate rather than public action in the social welfare area. We do not deny those realities, but propose to explain them in pol-itical rather than economically determinist ways. Capitalists or business leaders have no fixed attitudes toward public welfare measures, as comparisons across times, places, industries, and enterprises will readily attest. Business leaders were part of broader elite networks that included professional experts, reform advocates, and middle-class politi-cal activists in both Britain and America, and their attitudes toward the possibility or

desirability of state, as opposed to private, solutions to welfare problems were shaped by the same forces that determined balances of preference among all such groups.

4, Finegold (1981) analyses the failure of the Progressive Party between 1912 and 1916 in terms that complement our argument. Advocates of social welfare in the party hoped to organize a constituency base and develop programmatic discipline among party leaders. But the most prominent electoral politicians wanted immediate victories at the polls, and returned to the major parties when quick victories did not come. Progressives rarely attempted, and less often succeeded in appealing to working-class voters or collaborating with organized labour, and they shared general middle- and upper-class preoccupations with the need for regulatory reforms free of 'political corruption'. Only one wing of the Progressive Party advocated social insurance, and the party platform did not promise non-contributory pensions.

5. For example, in Massachusetts, where the Commission on Old Age Pensions (1907–10) chaired by Magnus Alexander reported strongly against state action, a 1910–11 Commission on Compensation for Industrial Accidents (on which Alexander also served) proposed and drafted the state's Workmen's Compensation Act of 1911. And a 1912–13 Commission on the Support of Dependent Minor Children of Widowed Mothers recommended and drafted the state's mothers' pension legislation, enacted in 1913.

REFERENCES

Finegold, Kenneth (1981) 'Progressivism and the party system, 1912–1916', paper presented at the annual meeting of the American Political Science Association, New York.
Heclo, Hugh (1974) *Modern Social Politics in Britain and Sweden* (New Haven: Yale University Press).
Shefter, Martin (1977) 'Party and patronage: Germany, England and Italy', *Politics and Society*, 7, pp. 403–51.
Skocpol, Theda (1984) 'Bringing the state back in: strategies of analysis in current research', in Peter Evans, Theda Skocpol and Dietrich Rueschemeyer (eds), *Bringing the State Back In* (New York: Cambridge University Press).

V.3

Gender and the origins of modern social policies in Britain and the United States

THEDA SKOCPOL AND GRETCHEN RITTER

Comparative research on the origins of modern welfare states typically asks why certain European nations, including Great Britain, enacted pensions and social insurance between the 1880s and the 1920s, while the United States 'lagged behind', that is, did not establish such policies for the entire nation until the Social Security Act of 1935. To put the question this way overlooks the social policies that were distinctive to the early twentieth-century United States. During the period when major European nations, including Britain, were launching paternalist versions of the modern welfare state, the United States was tentatively experimenting with what might be called a maternalist welfare state. In Britain, male bureaucrats and party leaders designed policies 'for the good' of male wage-workers and their dependants. Meanwhile, in the United States, early social policies were championed by elite and middle-class women 'for the good' of less privileged women. Adult American women were helped as mothers, or as working women who deserved special protection because they were potential mothers.

Both Britain and the United States had liberal, electorally competitive polities, whose publics engaged in similar debates about potential social policies around the turn of the century. Consequently, a comparison between paternalist social policy accomplishments in Britain and contemporary maternalist policy breakthroughs in the United States can be very enlightening. This comparison sharpens our sense of what was distinctive about American social politics prior to the New Deal, and it also allows us to explore various explanatory approaches that should be applicable to developments in the United States compared to other nations.

In this essay [...] we analyse the political activities of women's groups, exploring the reasons for the special impact of certain women's associations and outlooks on early modern social legislation in the United States [...]

Most comparative studies of the origins of modern social policies have

Originally published in *Studies in American Political Development*, 5 (1991), pp. 36–7, 48, 74–93.

ignored gendered dimensions of politics as well as the roles that women's organizations may have played in bringing about particular sorts of measures. 'Public' life is typically presumed to have been an exclusively male sphere, with women regarded as 'private' actors confined to homes and charitable associations. Debates have centred on the relative contributions of male-dominated unions, political parties, and bureaucracies to the shaping of labour regulations and of social spending laws targeted on male breadwinners. Established approaches often overlook maternalist social policies directed at mothers and potential mothers (as well as children); and they fail to notice the contributions of female-dominated modes of politics, some of which were not dependent on action by parties, trade unions, or official bureaucracies.

Unfortunately, the unconsciously gendered premises of cross-national research on welfare state origins have blinded scholars to patterns of politics and policy that were especially important in the United States. If bureaucratic initiatives and class-conscious politics were largely absent from the Progressive Era, certain styles of women's politics were central to the period's reform agendas and actual legislative accomplishments, especially across the states. Meanwhile, during the construction of the British paternalist welfare state, there were socialists and women's groups who advocated even more far-reaching maternalist policies than those enacted in America. But British advocates of a universal 'endowment of motherhood' were defeated by civil servants and the Labour movement; and benefits to women increasingly flowed to 'dependants' on account of male breadwinners' 'contributions' through waged labour.

The historically evolved positions of American and British women in relation to political institutions, higher education, and turn-of-the century possibilities for different styles of politics can help us to understand the early triumph of a range of maternalist social policies in the United States, in contrast to the failure of the campaign for the 'endowment of motherhood' in Britain.

CONDITIONS FOR WOMEN'S POLITICS: THE UNITED STATES IN CONTRAST TO BRITAIN

In nineteenth-century America, women – above all, middle-class married women – were relegated to a 'separate sphere' of domesticity and morality, charged with protecting the sanctity of home life and raising their children to be Godfearing, solid citizens. Meanwhile, after the suffrage was extended to all white males, and once mass-based parties were organized in

277

the Jackson era, formal politics became as strictly a male sphere as home life was a female sphere. This was true not only because women were excluded from voting, but more importantly, because rituals of male fraternalism were central during 'the party period' of US governance. At the grass roots, partisan supporters associated in Democratic, Whig or Republican clubs. The party faithful staged marches and parades replete with military trappings as 'officers' mobilized the 'rank and file' for electoral 'battles'. Campaigns 'culminated in elections held in saloons, barber shops, and other places largely associated with men'. Voting rights and party loyalties tied men together across class lines in nineteenth-century America – so much so that partisan political participation was part of the very definition of American manhood.

Despite their exclusion from electoral and party politics – or perhaps we should say, in part because of such exclusion – American women became deeply involved in civil affairs. For 'separate spheres', as ideology and practice simultaneously encouraged nineteenth-century American women to further domesticity and morality not only by staying at home but by participating in community matters that had to do with religion, morals, and (as we would say today) social welfare. Throughout the nineteenth century elite and middle-class women, sometimes joined by working-class women, built organizations to promote virtues assigned as ideally feminine. Prior to the Civil War, such women's organizations became involved in church and charitable work, evangelical movements, moral crusades against prostitution, and the struggle to abolish slavery. During the Civil War many women contributed in service efforts, and afterwards continued their activities in new ways.

From the late nineteenth century, the transdenominational Women's Christian Temperance Union (WCTU) again expressed the will of many American Protestant women to reform society on feminine moral terms. Launched during 1873–4, the WCTU expanded to 27,000 members in over a thousand locals in twenty-four states by 1879, to reach over 168,000 dues-paying members in some 7,000 locals in every state of the union around the turn of the century. With a motto declaring that 'Woman will bless and brighten every place she enters, and will enter every place', the WCTU adopted a 'do-everything policy'. The organization's various departments fought against prostitution, campaigned for female wardens and police matrons, worked for temperance propaganda in the schools, ran kindergartens for working mothers, and even supported labour reforms that might sustain respectable working-class homes. The WCTU, writes historian Barbara Epstein, 'pushed the women's culture of its time to its limits', turning women's subordination in a separate sphere into a resource for seeking political reforms of the nation as a whole.

Significantly, organized temperance activities in the United States were much more female dominated than contemporary temperance activities in England.

Probably the largest proportion of married American women between the 1870s and the early 1900s confined their community participation, beyond church attendance, to literary clubs promoting what was known as 'self culture'. Before long, however, these originally locally based and inwardly-oriented literary clubs became nationally organized and civically assertive, following the route of earlier groups in parlaying women's separate sphere into political power. After 1890, these clubs coalesced into a national network, the General Federation of Women's Clubs (GFWC), which by 1911 claimed over one million members in locals spread across all 48 states, each of which also had its own state federation. Clubwomen made the transition from cultural to reform activities not by abandoning the Victorian conception of women's special domestic sphere but by extending it into what came to be called 'municipal housekeeping'. In the words of Rheta Childe Dorr, author of a 1910 book about clubwomen in politics entitled *What Eight Million Women Want*: 'Woman's place is in the home. This is a platitude which no woman will ever dissent from.... But Home is not contained within the four walls of an individual home. Home is the community. The city full of people is the Family. The public school is the real Nursery. And badly do the Home and the Family and the Nursery need their mother.' Having decided that 'all clubs, as bodies of trained housekeepers, should consider themselves guardians of the civic housekeeping of their respective communities', turn-of-the-century women's clubs worked for better libraries and schools, for measures to promote public health and consumer safety, and for new laws to ensure social welfare – above all, for mothers and children.

In this new set of endeavours, the GFWC often worked in tandem with the National Congress of Mothers, which was founded in 1897 to 'carry the mother-love and mother-thought into all that concerns or touches childhood in Home, School, Church, State or Legislation'. By 1910 the Congress had 50,000 dues-paying members in twenty-one state branches; and by 1920, the Congress was organized in thirty-seven states and had 190,000 members. Obviously, this was a much smaller and somewhat less widespread association than the General Federation. Yet the National Congress could be extremely influential on matters of social legislation, because it had excellent relations with the newspapers and certain women's magazines, and because its leaders in the early years – like the leaders of the GFWC – tended to be social elites well connected in their communities and regions.

Not only were large numbers of married, domestically based American women well organized and civicly active in the late-nineteenth and early-twentieth centuries, a hefty minority of American women also achieved higher education and college degrees. And a fraction of these went on – especially via the social settlement movement – to become leaders of reform efforts during the Progressive Era.

Despite the ideology of domesticity, the United States led the world in offering higher education to women through its decentralized and fast-growing system of colleges and universities. By 1870, some 11,000 women constituted over one-fifth of all American students in institutions of higher learning; and by 1880, some 40,000 women constituted a third of en-rollees. Women's share increased to about 37 per cent in 1900, with 85,000 enrolled, and rose to nearly half of all enrollees at the early twenti-eth-century peak in 1920, when some 283,000 women were in institutions of higher learning. Some perspectives can be gained on American women's considerable educational achievements, when we note that contemporary British women lagged far behind. In 1880, 'only London University granted degrees to women scholars. The handful of students in the women's colleges of Cambridge and Oxford (less than 200 in 1882) took the same examinations given to men, but were not allowed to receive degrees until after World War I.' Around 1890, there were more women students at Smith College alone than at all Oxford and Cambridge colleges. According to a list compiled by the Women's Institute, the total number of British women enrolled in women's colleges in 1897 was only 784 – a minuscule number compared to the tens of thousands of American women.

Those higher-educated American women who took jobs went over-whelmingly into school teaching; and many worked only for a few years prior to marriage. Nevertheless, the sheer extent of female higher edu-cation in America did produce large numbers, spread throughout the country, who could appreciate Progressive reform efforts justified in terms of both feminine values and the need for greater 'professional expertise' in politics. This was important, even if most educated women simply served as rank-and-file supporters through such bodies as the American Association of University Women, professional associations, and the General Federation of Women's Clubs.

Higher education for American women also led a critical minority to become active reformers by way of the settlement movement. Significantly, from the 1870s through the 1920s, when only 10 per cent of all American women did not marry, between 40 and 60 per cent of women college graduates remained single. Among those who obtained PhDs between 1877 and 1924, fully 75 per cent in this group remained single. From the ranks of these mostly unmarried, educated women, including the elite few with graduate degrees, came the founders of many 'social settlements' in American cities.

Settlement houses were a British innovation. The first one, Toynbee Hall in the East End of London, was founded by Canon Samuel Barnett and Henrietta Barnett in 1884, and by 1911 there were 46 such houses in British cities. Some British settlements were staffed by college women, but none of these became a leading centre of reform; women were attracted to them as routes toward specialized types of charity work and, in due course, social work.[1] The more prominent British settlements, and especially Toynbee Hall, were mostly staffed by male graduates of Oxford and Cambridge who spent a few years engaged in social investigation and urban reform en route to careers in journalism, the universities, and the civil service. Nearly a quarter of the men who resided at Toynbee Hall between 1884 and 1914 went on to become civil servants, and the proportion taking this career path increased with time. In due course, four men who became prime ministers had close connections to Toynbee Hall. As one observer commented sarcastically, 'men who went in training under the Barnetts ... could always be sure of government and municipal appointments ... [They] discovered the advancement of their own interests and the interests of the poor were best served by leaving East London to stew in its own juice while they became members of parliament, cabinet ministers, civil servants.'

A telling instance was William Beveridge. After graduating from Oxford, Beveridge became subwarden of Toynbee Hall in 1903, writing to reassure his parents that 'Toynbee Hall is not a cul de sac. It is known among men of position.' While at the settlement, Beveridge did economic research, served on private and public bodies dealing with unemployment in London, and became a regular writer on social issues for the *Morning Post* prior to joining the newspaper's regular staff. All of this, of course, was prelude to Beveridge's achievement of many important national governmental assignments during a lifetime of shaping the British welfare state, including as the Board of Trade official behind the Liberal Party's plans for social insurance in 1911.

Although early social settlements in the United States were directly modelled on Toynbee Hall, the American movement departed from the British settlement movement in a number of ways. The American movement became much larger, encompassing over 400 houses by 1910. Continuing to expand even as the British movement levelled off with the emergence of the official welfare state, the US social settlement movement also developed a more democratic philosophy. And if Canon Barnett and William Beveridge, leaders of Toynbee Hall in the British capital of London, were the exemplary leaders of the British settlement movement, it is not accidental that Jane Addams, founder and long-term resident of Hull House in the midwestern US city of Chicago, is the best known American settlement leader. Women settlers predominated numerically in the US movement; higher-educated, unmarried women like Addams were the most persistent American settlers, the ones who gave the houses and the movement staying power over time. While the median number of years spent by all residents of US social settlements was three, unmarried women spent a median of ten years there, and many remained for their entire adult lifetimes. The United States had numerous successful mixed-gender settlements in which women were leaders, while Britain had only six such in 1913 and these were not considered to work well.

Perhaps most important, in contrast to the situation in Britain, many American women settlers were highly influential reformers and public figures – that is, leaders outside as well as within the settlement movement. The balance of opportunities offered to male and female reformers in the British versus the US polity can help us to understand why these American women became prominent. Whereas British male graduates of Oxford and Cambridge could use settlement work as a predictable and quite direct route to elite careers in the political parties and the civil service, given the nature of parallel American institutions these opportunities were not regularly available to American male college graduates who went into settlement work. In the British settlements, women either operated in sex-segregated environments or else were treated as 'helpers', without the establishment futures of their male counterparts, sporting Oxford and Cambridge degrees. In contrast, American settlement houses – such as Hull House in Chicago and Henry Street in New York – became settings from which talented women could create and pursue careers combining social research, public education and civic activism. American men were not in a position to preempt all of the possibilities along this line, because, again, the kinds of institutions that in Britain increasingly took up the relevant 'civic space', as we might label it – institutions such as expert bureaucracies, programmatic political parties, and in due course the 'welfare state' itself – simply weren't there to the same extent in the United States. Through the settlements, intellectual American women at the turn of the twentieth century could pursue long-term careers as professional reformers, supporting one another and cooperating with some male co-workers, without being crowded out by an official, male-dominated social policy establishment.

Because American reformers, including the social settlement people, could not pursue reforms through programmatic parties and national bureaucracies as the British social policy establishment did, they built eclectic political coalitions capable of civic education and legislative lobbying. Settlement leaders were especially adept at knitting together coalitions – on the one hand among women from different classes, and on the other hand among women in the middle and upper classes.

Founded in 1903 by an alliance of women's trade union organizers, settlement house leaders, and some upper class matrons active in charity work, the US Women's Trade Union League (WTUL) provided critical resources, including money and strike support, for women workers attempting to unionize. In addition, to help make up for the weakness of women workers in labour markets and trade unions, the WTUL agitated for new laws to limit their hours of work, improve their wages, and regulate working conditions that might threaten women's health. It also brought working women into alliances on behalf of female suffrage. Significantly, the American WTUL was more devoted to legislative causes than was its British counterpart. Operating in a national setting where unions were steadily gaining organizational and political strength, the British WTUL actively guided female unions into the national labour confederation. Indeed, in 1921 the British WTUL dissolved and became instead the women's section of the Trades Union Congress. Meanwhile, the American WTUL persisted as a basically gender-based and fully cross-class organization devoted to legislation and the cause of women's suffrage, as well as to unionization. For American WTUL members, the rhetoric of 'sisterhood' was more meaningful than the language of class.

Another small gender-based policy organization was the National Consumers' League (NCL), which involved many upper-class as well as middle-class women in economic boycotts and legislative struggles on behalf of working women. Some prominent male academics and reformers were titular officers of the NCL, but they often failed to show up for meetings, and the organization was clearly both run and energized by women. The NCL – which had no British counterpart – was founded during the 1890s by Mrs Josephine Shaw Lowell, Mrs Maud Nathan and other elite women who came together to agitate for better working conditions for shop girls. Although the Consumers' League's membership never grew beyond a few thousand nationwide, the organization did claim 64 local leagues in 20 states in 1905. After that, the number of states organized dropped, with 15 states still claiming one or more local leagues by 1917. Members of the Consumers' League were well connected socially in their states and communities and thus often strategically placed to press for legislative reforms. Moreover, the NCL took the bold step of hiring the remarkable socialist reformer and settlement resident Florence Kelley as its Executive Secretary. Under her politically principled and technically expert leadership, the National League became an effective advocate of child labour legislation as well as protectionist legislation for women wage-workers. Thus, even more than the WTUL, the National Consumers' League was a pure embodiment of gender politics, with a maternalist agenda, engaging women career reformers from the settlements and upper- and middle-class matrons on behalf of reforms deemed beneficial to working-class women and their children.

Settlement leaders also co-operated on many political issues with the larger and more widespread associations of elite and middle-class married women, especially the General Federation of Women's Clubs. Partnership between social settlement leaders and organized married ladies was possible during the Progressive Era in large part because both sides shared beliefs about women's roles in society and about the morally justifiable reforms needed in industrializing America. Ironically, although women leaders from the social settlement movement were often unmarried and childless, they thought of themselves as 'public mothers'. Seeing mothers and children especially worthy of public help, they also believed that women had special proclivities for moral decision-making and civic activity; thus women were the logical ones to lead the nation toward new social policies. In sum, intellectual women from the American settlement movement ended up functioning as a kind of political vanguard of organized womanhood on reform issues understood to be part of women's special sphere of concern.

VICTORIES FOR MATERNALIST POLICIES IN THE UNITED STATES

Because American women did not have the vote in a polity where white men of all classes did, they viewed themselves as separate from the 'corrupt' male realm of partisan politics. In contrast to contemporary British women, American women were not tempted to operate as auxiliaries of a strong working-class movement. Instead, reacting against a cross-class patronage democracy, American women developed an alternative style of politics emphasizing public education and moralistic lobbying for allegedly disinterested and nonpartisan legislative goals. During the Progressive Era, alliances that included women's groups and reformers from the social settlement movement used this political style to advocate social benefits for mothers and children. Many women's groups also promoted protective regulations for women workers, on the grounds that being positioned in the labour market they needed special help as potential mothers.

Viewing matters from an equal-rights, feminist perspective that became prominent from the 1920s on, some scholars have argued that protective labour laws were detrimental to women workers. Scholars argue that such measures were often promoted by trade unions trying to exclude women from competition with male breadwinners. Certain kinds of protective labour laws do fit this profile, particularly those intended to exclude women altogether from narrowly defined craft occupations. But it should be remembered that, during the 1910s, groups such as the Women's Trade Union League advocated both limited hours and minimum wages for women workers, viewing such joint legal protections as ways to help vulnerable, non-unionized wage earners. Not until the 1920s did it become clear that hours laws without minimum wages would have the effect of hurting many women by reducing their pay cheques and shutting them out of some jobs. Moreover, as we discussed above, many reformers who supported protective labour laws for women during the Progressive Era saw them as an 'entering wedge' for more general laws to protect all workers from low wages and too many hours of daily work.

Whether in the end they were really good for women or not, protective labour laws were enthusiastically supported by middle- and working-class women's groups. Enacted in virtually all states during the 1910s, new or improved women's hour laws were often supported by state Federations of Labor, yet they were also advocated nationally and in the states and localities by the National Consumers' League, the Women's Trade Union League, the General Federation of Women's Clubs, and various other women's groups. Minimum-wage laws for women were usually opposed by both organized labour and organized business, which helps to explain why they did not pass nearly as often as hours laws. Still, cross-class alliances of women's groups did manage to get such proposals on the agenda in most stages, and fifteen legislatures actually enacted minimum-wage laws. In the state of California, a broad alliance of women's groups in 1913 persuaded the legislature to enact a minimum-wage law, and they successfully defended it the next year in a state-wide referendum against concerted opposition from both business organizations and the California State Federation of Labor. The women's organizations used the slogans, 'Let us be our sisters' keepers' and 'Employed womanhood must be protected in order to foster the motherhood of the race'.

Women's politics during the Progressive Era achieved new public social spending for mothers, as well as protective legislation applying to women workers. Although in practice they were woefully underfunded, mothers' pensions would never have become the one kind of social spending measure to squeak through the Progressive Era's general bias against such policies had it not been for the early and persistent advocacy of women's voluntary associations. The National Congress of Mothers took up the cause in 1911. At its 1912 Biennial Convention, the General Federation of Women's Clubs also endorsed the idea of mothers' pensions; and at least twenty state Federations of Women's Clubs lobbied state legislatures for the enactment of these measures between 1913 and 1919. Despite opposition or lack of enthusiasm from other progressive reformers, the cause of mothers' pensions was also supported by leading women social settlement figures and aided by a series of vivid muckraking articles written for a women's magazine, *The Delineator*, by William Hard, a former social settlement worker and close friend of Jane Addams and Julia Lathrop.

Even though women were not able to vote in most states during the 1910s, feminine advocates of maternalist social policies were surprisingly effective at getting bills through state legislatures. The widespread federated associations such as the General Federation and the National Congress of Mothers were skilful at highlighting a policy issue simultaneously across much of the nation. They mobilized local opinion makers to put pressure on legislators – not just in state capitols, or in Washington DC, but in their own home districts. The women's organizations could link local efforts to programmes shaped nationally by their own leaders in conjunction with the social settlement reformers. Organized US women were much better at using such tactics to shape public opinion and set legislative agendas than were the unionized workers of the AFL and the various state Federations of Labor. Women's politics in the early twentieth-century United States crossed class lines, linked local to supralocal efforts, and tied intellectuals to ordinary people much more effectively than contemporary US labour politics did any of these things.

Whatever their party affiliations, members of state legislatures found women's moral rhetoric hard to publicly deny. Thus, when educational tactics and lobbying succeeded in getting proposals on to the legislative agenda, bills often passed by huge, lopsided majorities. Of course, given the way US politics operates, this might not have been enough to ensure victories for maternalist protective labour regulations – had not gender-based rhetoric also held sway in the American courts during the Progressive Era. As they revealed in their landmark 1908 ruling in *Muller* v. *Oregeon*, the Justices of the Supreme Court were likewise persuaded that women as potential mothers were worthy of special public protection.

This 1908 decision, so crucial to the progress of women's protective legislation at a time when similar laws could not be passed for male workers, was partially shaped by the efforts of American women's organizations. At one level this is the case because the brief presented by Louis Brandeis on behalf of the Oregon hours statute at issue was initiated by the National Consumers' League and researched by its staff member, Josephine Goldmark. Yet turn-of-the-century US women's politics also figured more tacitly in *Muller*'s ideological background. Judges did not simply accede to expert opinions from doctors and social scientists; in other cases they demonstrated the ability to ignore or legally controvert such 'evidence'. Rather, as profoundly rhetorical institutions, courts were bound to be affected by moral understandings deeply embedded in political discourse. Thus, as Mr Justice Brewer saw it, the expert opinions presented to the Supreme Court in *Muller* v. *Oregon* were:

> significant of a widespread belief that woman's physical structure, and the function she performs in consequence thereof, justify special legislation restricting or qualifying the conditions under which she should be permitted to toil. Constitutional questions, it is true, are not settled by even a consensus of present public opinion.... At the same time, when a question of fact is debated and debatable, and the extent to which a special constitutional limitation goes is affected by the truth in respect to that fact, a widespread and long continued belief concerning it is worthy of consideration. We take judicial cognizance of all matters of general knowledge.

In short, the justices of the Supreme Court, who unanimously decided in 1908 to treat women workers as a special class deserving public protection, were strongly affected by contemporary public understandings of gender differences. We can hypothesize that the justices saw women as mothers especially worthy of help from innovative public policies, because organized American women had taught civic leaders – and the educated public in general – to think in this way. If governmental paternalism was still suspect, maternalism had become much more acceptable by the Progressive Era, even to crusty judges still largely wedded to individualistic doctrines of free contract.

In both the legislative and the judicial realms, therefore, turn-of-the-century American women's politics – a politics based on extending rather than contravening ideals of separate spheres for the genders – was well suited to overcoming the obstacles that the US polity placed in the way of advocates of new social policies. There was, for a time, an especially good fit between what politically active American women wanted and could do, and what the changing American state structure could accommodate. Thus, women's hour and minimum-wage laws were widely enacted, along with mothers' pensions, in a polity otherwise inimical to labour regulations and social spending measures.

BRITISH COUNTERPOINT: THE FAILURE OF AN ENDOWMENT FOR MOTHERS

Like their American sisters during the nineteenth century, British women also organized for civic action, inspired in many cases by similar Protestant values and by an analogous desire to extend ideals of Victorian domesticity into community service. But turn-of-the-century British women holding ideas about the moral superiority of their gender did not initially claim, or ever achieve, the same degree of influence in shaping social policies that such American women did.

Doctrines of women's moral superiority were initially weaker among British women, while Enlightenment-bred ideals of equal rights and ideologies combining working-class and women's concerns were stronger. More consequential over time, there were differences in social movements as well. British temperance activities as a whole were not female-dominated as were American temperance activities; nor did the female British temperance association endorse women's suffrage or promote such a wide range of social reforms as did the US Women's Christian Temperance Union. Before the First World War, there were no true British counterparts to those nation-spanning US associations, the General Federation of Women's Clubs and the National Congress of Mothers. Nor was there any British version of the National Consumers' League. Finally, even though there certainly was a British Women's Trade Union League, its reform agenda converged with that of the trade unions, and the British WTUL eventually dissolved as a separate organization, transforming itself into the women's arm of the Trades Union Congress. Indeed, those British women who became politically active on behalf of political changes favouring women tended to do so either as equal-rights feminists or as socialists active in the labour movement.

The social and political context in which civicly engaged British women and women's organizations operated was very different from the US. As we have seen, very few British women received higher education, so they could rarely follow the established path from Oxford and Cambridge into the British social and political establishment. Nor did British women become national leaders in or through the social settlements. Instead, British women active in charitable or political affairs typically gained prominence through individual ties of marriage or friendship to men, even moderate socialists, who were part of the British establishment. Beatrice Webb is the most celebrated example of a woman who gained access this way – and made the most of it, yet normally in ways that meshed with the viewpoints of labour leftists and administrative reformers.

Seen more broadly, the major obstacles facing British women in any quest to translate separate gender concerns into political issues were the prominence of paternalist competitors who took up most of the 'space' for reform efforts. American women were excluded from a cross-class male democracy, in which bureaucratic agencies were weak and unions and politicians remained entangled in patronage politics, but such a setting was ideal for mobilizing middle-class women representing the distinctive morality of their gender through non-partisan styles of locally rooted politics – exactly the styles that paid off well during the Progressive Era. In contrast, British women's organizations had to operate in a polity where, from the 1850s through the 1920s, working-class men (as well as all women) were collectively seeking initial political access through the vote, thus polarizing British politics along class lines. British women also had to relate to a strong and growing trade union movement. And they faced a political structure in which, especially after the 1870s, programmatic party politicians and civil administrators increasingly claimed to speak 'in the public interest' about social welfare issues. As individuals and as local organizations, British women may often have spoken the same 'maternalist' messages as their American sisters, but their voices tended to be absorbed into other choruses or simply drowned out in a national polity where male working-class leaders, politicians and administrators were calling the tunes.

Developments from the nineteenth century onward were thus not propitious for any hegemonic British women's politics based on ideals of the separate, domestic sphere, even though particular movements and local women's groups often effectively used maternalistic ideas. What is more, social policies targeted on mothers and – especially – children were pushed forward by women working with and through other politically active forces. After the Boer War raised concerns about the physical fitness of the population, the Conservatives implemented some measures for children in the name of 'national efficiency'. The 'new' Liberals supported the cause of female suffrage and also initiated many welfare measures, including the 1911 National Insurance Act which provided some maternity benefits for wives of covered male workers. Yet the Labour movement was most important for British women. As Olive Banks explains:

[W]hether because of its sympathy for feminist ambitions [including the suffrage] or its democratic basis, there is little doubt that women's groups and auxiliaries had much more influence on the policy of the Labour Party than similar groups within the other two main parties. . . .

The most strongly feminist of the women's auxiliaries, at least in the early years of the Labour movement, was the Women's Co-operative Guild. Ardent suffragists, they were also active campaigners for a number of other issues concerned specifically with women and children. In the years immediately before the First World War they ran influential campaigns for equal divorce laws for men and women, for better maternity and infant welfare and for maternity benefits to be paid to mothers. . . . The Women's Labour League, founded in 1906 with the object of persuading women to take an active interest in political affairs, also concerned itself with issues affecting women and children. There were lengthy campaigns on school meals, medical inspections in schools, the provision of nursery schools, and pit-head baths. The League also played a major role in the passing of the Maternity and Child Welfare Act of 1918....

The consequence of this pressure from within their own ranks was to make the Labour Party receptive to many policies that were also of importance to the feminists. Maternity and infant welfare, for example, which in the United States was almost entirely a feminist issue, was a significant aspect of Labour Party policy.... This alliance between feminism and the Labour Party was not paralleled in the United States until Roosevelt's New Deal, which ended the isolation of feminist reformers and social workers.[2]

Matters might have rested in the early British welfare state with piecemeal measures for mothers and babies had it not been for the impact of the First World War on gender relations, particularly within the working class, and on organized women's politics, especially among middle-class feminists. During the War and the 1920s, calls for the 'endowment for motherhood' reached the centre of official welfare policy debates in Britain. At stake was a truly maternalist policy proposal much more sweeping than anything American women achieved − or even widely debated − during the Progressive Era. It is interesting to see how and why the possibility of this radically maternalist policy came up in Britain, even after the foundation stones on the paternalist welfare state had been laid in 1906–11. Yet the 'endowment for motherhood' idea failed to become law, and actually paved the way for the extension and consolidation of the paternalist welfare state. So this telling failure reveals, once again, the power of the bureaucratic and working-class political forces that successfully shaped British social policies through the 1920s, and afterwards.

In 1917, Eleanor Rathbone and other British feminists organized a 'Family Endowment Committee', which a year later proposed to give regular allowances to all British women with young children. This measure sought to make universal and permanent the 'separation allowances' that had been paid to the wives and children of British soldiers and sailors during World War I. These wartime allowances had given working-class wives new economic independence, and the wartime experience had also helped to move British feminist thinking in the direction of advocating direct economic support for motherhood rather than just the equal wages or legally guaranteed share of male wages that had been feminist demands before the war. Such 'new feminism', based on separate spheres ideals, gained ground in organized British women's politics during the 1920s, after Eleanor Rathbone became President of 'the most powerful feminist organization, the National Union for Societies of Equal Citizenship' in 1919. Significantly, separate spheres ideals came to the fore in British women's politics just after all British males were finally enfranchised in 1918, while many women remained without the vote until 1928.

Despite widespread feminist support, however, a universal endowment for motherhood was not enacted in Britain, because the Labour Party and British civil servants, working from somewhat different paternalist premises, transmuted this demand into the contributory social insurance benefits for widows that were enacted in the Widows', Orphans', and Old Age Pensions Act of 1925. Advocates of the universal endowment could not get full support from the Labour Party. Even though Labour women's organizations were very interested in the endowment possibility, '[t]hrough the mediation of the women labour leaders themselves, the demands of the Labour women's organizations were scaled down to mesh with the traditional family policy of the Trades Union Congress', which called for protecting the male 'family wage' and channelling all benefits to married women through that wage. Labour was prepared to support direct public payments to women only when the male breadwinner was absent. Conservatives and civil servants, meanwhile, wanted to keep down the state's direct cost of social benefits, so they favoured contributory pensions paid out of earlier collections from male wageworkers; they also believed that elderly widows without children should receive support.

When Widows' Pensions were enacted in 1925 by a Conservative government, civil service preferences completed 'the metamorphosis of "mothers' pensions" from a step toward payment for motherhood to a necessary component of a welfare system constructed around men's right to maintain [their wives] ... [T]he decision to finance pensions through insurance linked them both administratively and ideologically to the working man. Since eligibility turned on the man's insurance status and not [on] the woman's need, the system would exclude those women whom men had been least willing or able to support – deserted and separated wives, wives of uninsured casual labourers, and unmarried mothers.' The original British feminist proposals for endowment of motherhood had explicitly intended to include all such women when they were caring for children. It is worth pointing out that many or all of these categories of women *could be covered* by contemporary US mothers' pension laws, depending on the precise provisions of statutes in individual states.[3]

As historian Susan Pedersen sums up the British developments from 1917 to 1925, 'in the end ... maternalist, "separate but equal" ideology was pressed into service in the creation of policies encoding dependence, not the value of difference'. The unsuccessful British women's 'campaign for the endowment of motherhood exposed where the real policy-making power and political influence lay: with the civil service and the trade union movement.'[4]

CONCLUSION

Organized labour, reformist intellectuals and officials, and women's groups all worked to launch modern social policies in Britain and the United States between the 1880s and the 1920s. But in the two nations such groups devised policy ideals and political strategies – and contended or allied with one another – in the context of very different governmental institutions and party systems. The result was that distinctive kinds of politics flourished, leading to the enactment of contrasting sorts of social policies in Britain and the United States.

In Britain, social spending and labour regulations were furthered by civil service bureaucracies and by programmatic political parties competing for organized trade union support. In a unitary polity with a sovereign parliament, such forces were able to enact and implement social policies covering workers in general, regardless of gender. Over time, as the initial foundations of the British welfare state were laid in the teens and twenties, bureaucratic and organized working-class forces converged on social policies that reinforced and depended upon the ideal of the male-breadwinner, family wage. Meanwhile, radical maternalist demands for a universal endowment of motherhood were shunted aside in Britain.

In the United States during this period, bureaucratic forces and electorally involved trade unionists were too weak to push forward old age pensions or social insurance benefits for all workers. This was especially the case because of middle-class and elite hostility during the Progressive Era toward the precedent of public social spending created by the earlier expansion of Civil War pensions. Progressive public opinion favoured regulations rather than public social spending. Even so, reformers and labour groups were unable to enact public regulations setting limited hours or decent wages for all US workers, because of the unwillingness of the independent and powerful U.S. courts to accept such 'interferences' in contractual freedom for adult males.

Even as America's federal state of weak bureaucracies, patronage parties, and strong courts obstructed possibilities for paternalist labour regulations and social spending for the working class in general, it left space for forces advocating maternalist benefits and regulations targeted on women and children in particular. The courts were willing, for some time, to accept legal hours limits and minimum-wage regulations for adult female workers as the potential 'mothers of the race'. And at the turn of the century, higher-educated women reformers and widespread associations of married ladies, both inspired by normative ideals of women's separate sphere of domesticity and motherhood, were able to shape public discourse and put effective simultaneous pressure on many state legislatures at once, encouraging bipartisan support for women's labour regulations and mothers' pensions. Some tentative beginnings toward a distinctively maternalist American welfare state were thus made at a time when the prospects were dim for an early paternalist welfare state along British or European lines.[5]

In ways that go beyond what we can describe and explain here, later policy developments in both Britain and the United States transformed as well as built upon the early paternalist, in contrast to maternalist, beginnings analysed in this article. Our purpose here has not been to identify unchanging national essences. Rather, by contrasting these two liberal nations at a watershed period in their political histories, we have aimed to demonstrate the value of analysing the politics of social policy-making from an historically grounded institutionalist perspective. Class and gender differences existed 'in themselves' in both Britain and the United States. But class and gender identities and outlooks were expressed differently in British and US social politics around the turn of the twentieth century. This happened in significant part because the British and US polities selectively facilitated contrasting ideologies and political alliances. A paternalist social politics for and by the industrial working class was encouraged in the British polity. Meanwhile, the changing US polity called forth and temporarily rewarded a non-electoral style of social politics for and by women. These turn-of-the-century American maternalists were understood, by themselves and others, as members of a 'separate sphere' charged with safeguarding family, morality and community within US capitalism and democracy. In the name of such values, American women sparked most of the social policy innovations that occurred at all during a time when the United States was refusing to follow Britain on the road toward a paternalist welfare state.

Notes

1. We do not mean to argue that British women settlers never became prominent reformers. Some did; for example, Eleanor Rathbone, who started out at the Liverpool Women's Settlement.
2. Olive Banks, *Faces of Feminism* (Oxford: Martin Robertson, 1981) pp. 165–6.
3. For example, the very liberal Michigan law allowed aid to any needy mother who was widowed, deserted, divorced, or unmarried, or 'whose husband is insane, feeble-minded, epileptic, paralytic, or blind and confined in State hospital or other state institution; incapable of work because of tuberculosis; or inmate of State penal

institution.' [. . .] To be sure, lack of fathers' economic support for children was the bedrock criterion here, so the 'male breadwinner' norm was upheld. But as policy developments unfolded in contemporary Britain, that norm was adhered to by tying benefits to the absence of, specifically, a former wage-earning husband. Analysts of social policies for women need to investigate not only whether particular measures emphasized male breadwinning versus women's labour-force participation. Analysts should also look for alternative ways that policies may embody male-breadwinner norms. In this instance, the Michigan statute placed the emphasis on mothers' needs due to the absence of fathers for various reasons (including unwed parenthood), not on the wage-earning status of husband-fathers.

4. S. Pedersen, 'The failure of feminism in the making of the British welfare state', *Radical History Review*, 43 (1989), p. 105.
5. In the end, a maternalist welfare state did not fully crystallize in the United States. See chapters 10 and 11 in Theda Skocpol's *Protecting Soldiers and Mothers: The Political Origins of Social Policy in the United States* (Cambridge, MA: Belknap Press, 1992).

V.4

State capacity in Britain and America in the 1930s

ANTHONY BADGER

New Deal historiography has followed a cycle of celebration and lamenta-tion, rather than explanation. The New Deal has been consistently cele-brated by liberal historians for extending the responsibility of the federal government to cover the economic security of individual citizens without succumbing to the ideological extremes of contemporary mass movements. Recurrently it has been savaged from the right: in the 1940s for leading the country down the path of socialistic regimentation, in the 1970s and 1980s for decisively distorting the free market and launching America on the road to the dead hand of Big Government. In the 1960s the New Deal was mauled from the Left for missing the greatest opportunity for substantial reform and, instead, sustaining the hegemony of corporate capitalism.

British historical writing on the New Deal may have been rather con-ventional – but I have argued that we escaped this cycle of celebration and lamentation by leaving out the lamentation. British historians have tended to a judicious, liberal, consensus view of the New Deal familiar enough to the mainstream of American historiography. This approving tone was shaped by historians who grew up in the 1930s and, despairing of the alleged feebleness of British governments and the onset of fascism in Europe, saw the New Deal as a beacon of democratic hope. To British historians after the war who had long experience of social welfare pro-vision, a genuine Marxist left, and the nationalization programmes of the post-war Labour government, the American conservative denunciation of the New Deal as an instrument of socialistic regimentation and a seedbed of communist subversion made little sense. Equally, in the 1960s and after, British historians eschewed a New Left interpretation of the New Deal. They doubted that there were radical roads not taken in the 1930s. Familiar with powerful twentieth century European states, they were sceptical that the United States had the state capacity in 1933 to

An earlier version of this essay was presented as a paper at the conference of the European Historians of the United States, Middelburg, Holland, in April 1993.

embark on detailed centralized planning of the economy. Their awareness of the British and continental experience reminded them that the alternatives to the New Deal were as likely to be on the right as on the left. Their knowledge of an ideologically based, centralized, and accountable party system made them realize the enormity of the task of securing the party realignment in the United States necessary to secure the enactment of liberal reform in a society where localism was so powerful.[1]

Running through this argument is the explicit assumption that the British state had a more highly developed capacity for social and economic intervention. But British historians of the New Deal have not in fact actually carried out comparative history. The lively debate in American historical sociology between state-centred and society-centred theorists, which takes the 1930s in the United States as its empirical testing ground but also draws on British neo-Marxist political theorists for many of their insights, has not really found an echo in British work on the New Deal. This essay is a highly tentative effort to make some comparison between Britain and America in the 1930s.

What I want to do is first to compare the state capacity for social and economic intervention in Britain and America on the eve of the New Deal in order to suggest, on the one hand, that America did not have the capacity for more radical reform in 1933 that New Left historians imagined and that, on the other, the emergency of 1933 did not cause the unequivocal permanent expansion of federal government power that a free market economic historian such as Robert Higgs sees as so decisive in his history of the growth of Big Government, *Crisis and Leviathan*.

Second, I want to ask why the British with their apparently much more highly developed capacity for state economic intervention failed to adopt policies of large-scale public works spending in the 1930s.

Third, I want to use the British comparison to question whether the national state-building that took place in the United States in the 1930s really produced the 'gargantuan' government that historians like Robert Higgs imagine and lament.

In recent years historians have cautioned against too exaggerated a contrast between an American minimal state in the early twentieth century and a highly developed British state.

On the American side, Stephen Skowronek has charted the development of national administrative capacity; William Brock has documented the variety and extent of local state government commissions and agencies in the years before 1920; Theda Skocpol recently has reminded us of just how much welfare the American government provided for soldiers and mothers before the New Deal. Barry Supple and Mary Furner in their 1990 collection *The State and Economic Knowledge* have stressed the similarities, as much as differences, in state development in both Britain and America, especially in contrast with some more statist continental European societies. On the British side, there is always a danger reading the undoubted state capacity of the British government post-Beveridge and post-Second World War back into the earlier period.[2]

Nevertheless, the contrast in the early 1930s is still, I believe, stark. Britain provided welfare benefits for citizens unmatched in the western world: unemployment insurance for all its industrial workers, old age pensions and health insurance. It had already nationalized the electricity industry which employed almost a third of a million workers and had operated both the railroads and the mines as nationalized industries during the war. It sponsored low-cost public housing – between the wars local authorities built 38 per cent of the new houses constructed – and extracted substantial tax revenue from an income tax, proportionately twice as much as the United States. It possessed a highly educated elite professional bureaucracy and in the Treasury had an agency that, in close alliance with the Bank of England, exercised tight control over the key levers of economic policy – tax rates, levels of government spending and levels of interest rates. Unlike the US government it was not constrained by federalism or the courts. Statute was supreme: judicial review in Britain meant the judicial review of executive and bureaucratic procedures, not the constitutionality of legislation.

In the United States, neither the federal, nor, for the most part, state governments provided unemployment insurance, unemployment relief, pensions or health insurance. Less than 5 per cent of the population paid federal income taxes throughout the 1930s. The civil service was largely neither professional nor expert. The government's ability to influence macro-economic policy was limited both in terms of public institutions and in terms of economic knowledge. One striking contrast with Britain was the American inability to deliver accurate unemployment figures during the Depression. William Leuchtenburg has summed up by arguing that 'the United States in the 1920s had almost no institutional structure to which Europeans would accord the term "the State" '.[3] He noted that Washington was a sleepy, rather inconsequential Southern town that nobody would have thought of calling the centre of anything very important. For most citizens their only contact with the federal government was the post office.[4]

It was this feeble state that had to confront the economic emergency of 1933. Left-wing critics argued then and since that the complete collapse of the economy created a golden opportunity for radical reform with a desperate population willing to vest dictatorial powers in Roosevelt and his new administration. Robert Higgs has argued that the economic crisis of 1933, in part artificially created by the incoming administration, and deliberately cast as an emergency justifying wartime powers, was one of the key crises, like both world wars, that ratcheted up federal government power, leaving it as each crisis subsided bigger than before. I think these views underestimate the obstacles to substantial change that the lack of state capacity threw up and misunderstand the inhibiting, rather than liberating effect, that the economic emergency and the overarching need for speedy action had on the development of state economic intervention.

It was not surprising that the New Dealers should turn to the war for their models of government intervention in 1933. The wartime analogy gave a justification for emergency government powers that would otherwise be of dubious constitutionality, but also the war was the one model of large-scale state economic intervention that the underdeveloped American government could turn to. It is important, however, to remember that that wartime model was not the model of a command economy: the government exercised much of its wartime powers on a voluntaristic basis (as it would in the Second World War). In the economic emergency of 1933 the need for speed and the inadequacy of the existing state capacity in the United States also meant that, despite the government's supposedly new and vast powers, New Deal programmes had to depend on the consent of those who were being regulated and often had to be administered by the very people who were being regulated.[5]

The banks had to be reopened quickly – it was only the bankers themselves who knew which banks could be safely reopened and which could not. If the NRA was going to have to kick start the economy into recovery and provide jobs quickly – rather than restructure American industry on a long-term basis – it would require the consent of the businessmen themselves, who held a monopoly of information about their industries. As Mordecai Ezekiel remarked in 1939 it would have taken ten years to develop the trained people and the data base to make the NRA work. No government could police the production of millions of individual farmers – it was inevitable that the domestic allotment plan in 1933 should be a voluntary programme and that it should be administered by the farmers themselves, especially as the AAA had to move quickly enough to sign contracts with over a million cotton farmers in a matter of weeks to plough under a cotton crop that was already in the field. Agriculture is a particularly illuminating example of the way in which the emergency of 1933 constrained, rather than released, the government. Theda Skocpol has noted that in agriculture, as distinct from industry, the state capacity existed for successful government programmes. The agricultural state was 'an island of strength amidst an ocean of weakness'. The Bureau of Agricultural Economics had developed a disinterested bureaucracy of professional economists who had clear policy prescriptions for the current crisis and had built up considerable statistical data on the operation of the rural economy. But even those clear-sighted policy-makers had, in order to get their programmes launched, to rely on mechanisms of grass-roots democracy which strengthened the position of larger farmers and the Extension Service and, in the long-run, ensured that the intellectuals' hopes for the planning of agriculture and the tackling of rural poverty would be thwarted.[6]

In order to get relief to the unemployed immediately, the New Deal did not have time to create a new federal bureaucracy in Washington – it had to franchise out relief operations to the states and state relief administrations. It is notable that in the emergency the government in providing relief also had to turn to the one agency of the state whose capacity was unchallenged – the army. The army administered the Civilian Conservation Corps camps. The Army Corps of Engineers provided many of the personnel who ran the public works and work relief programmes of the New Deal. It is interesting that Robert Higgs, who is so anxious to see the role of war crises in expanding the power of government, has failed to note this military participation.

There were two government agencies in 1933 that did invoke unprecedented power. The first was the Reconstruction Finance Corporation, which presided over a credit revolution, and strove to refinance debt and to finance New Deal programmes. By 1935 it had lent over $10.6 billion dollars – it underpinned the economic rescue of homeowners, farmers facing foreclosure, banks and thousands of businesses – it provided what has been described as the 'socialization of credit'. Yet it is important to remember that the RFC was a creation of the Hoover administration and that Jesse Jones resolutely refused to use the RFC to make macro-economic decisions and to facilitate planning of the economy through government direction of investment. The second was the Tennessee Valley Authority, which acquired vast powers for regional planning, land allocation, public power generation and flood control. The TVA was perhaps the New Deal agency that aroused greatest interest in Britain: many hoped that its regional planning could be a model for development programmes for Scotland and Wales. It sometimes seemed that for Labour politicians in the 1930s, such as Hugh Dalton, the TVA was the only programme they had heard of. In the 1940s, despite the paper shortage in Britain, a number of American accounts of the TVA were published under British imprints. In the first major British history of the New Deal, Denis Brogan devoted a whole chapter to the dazzling TVA. Yet it has to be remembered that the TVA backed off coercive, overhead planning in favour of mechanisms of grass-roots democracy and that Roosevelt's efforts to replicate the TVA experience by creating seven little TVAs in other river basins was defeated in Congress.[7]

In short, because of the lack of state capacity in 1933 the economic emergency did not actually create great radical opportunities for the New Deal. Nor did it, using the model of wartime powers in an emergency, provide for a dramatic and revolutionary expansion of that state capacity to distort the free market. The emphasis because of the need for speed was on voluntarism and consent. As Alger Hiss once commented to me, 'Rexford Tugwell thought we could have nationalized the banks using the post offices. Well, in Britain you might have been able to use the post offices, but can you imagine using the American post office for that? We would have still been trying to get the banking system opened again at the end of 1933.'[8]

But paradoxically the feebleness of existing state capacity in the United States, and its relatively highly developed nature in Britain, helped explain why the United States spent billions on public works and job creation programmes in the 1930s and the British government spent almost nothing. Under the Works Progress Administration the United States employed up to 40 per cent of the unemployed; in Britain the government employed none. In the United States the New Deal adopted modified versions of Keynesian remedies to tackle the Depression; in Britain, where Keynes had provided the economic rationale for a massive public works programme which was advocated by the out-of-office Lloyd George and Oswald Mosley, the government did not.

In part, the discrepancy reflected the less damaging nature of the Depression and the timing of political change in Britain. Unemployment was more regionally specific in Britain: it did not affect all classes and regions as it did in the United States. The Labour Government was in power at the time of the financial collapse of 1931 and bore the opprobrium of that disaster. The National Government, soon a Conservative government in all but name, benefited from a steady recovery from 1932 onwards.

The resistance to work relief in Britain also reflected the policy legacy of the 1920s and the existence of much more generous welfare provision in Britain. For the Left, the political battles of the 1920s, culminating in the Second Labour Government, 1929–31, were to secure the extension of the coverage of unemployment benefits and to make them more generous. These benefits were the primary tool the Labour Party used to alleviate the impact of unemployment and it was the cut in unemployment benefit that divided the party and brought the government down in the summer of 1931. By contrast, work programmes smacked of the old Poor Law requirements of punishing the idle poor. Politicians like Prime Minister MacDonald and Chancellor of the Exchequer Snowden also argued that public works were a short-term 'reformist' delusion that would prevent the long-term implementation of genuine socialist remedies. By contrast, New Deal policy-makers saw work relief as a means of providing cash and dignity to the unemployed, a vast improvement on means-tested and inadequate relief benefits that were degrading and all too often provided benefits in kind, not in cash.[9]

But above all, the failure to adopt Keynesian solutions in Britain reflected the powerful organization of the British state under Treasury control. Treasury economists adhered to a rigidly orthodox view linking a balanced budget, the gold standard and Free Trade. The essence of this orthodoxy was that economic policy should be knave-proof, i.e. not subject to the irresponsible actions of demagogic politicians seeking short-term popularity or selfish special interests. The Treasury managed to impose this orthodoxy even after the discipline of the gold standard had to be abandoned in 1931. Public works were unremunerative. 'Experience has taught us that they (relief works) do less good in the direct production of work than harm in the indirect increase of unemployment by depleting the resources of the country which are needed for industrial restoration.'[10]

Of course, orthodox economists held such views in the United States. What was different in Britain was that the leading officials in the Treasury held these views particularly tenaciously. They were not trained economists but, as Peter Clarke has described them, they were 'a self-conscious elite, largely self-taught in economics, but owing intellectual deference to nobody'. What was also different was that the Treasury in Britain could impose its views on the government as a whole. It exercised close control over individual department's spending programmes – those departments did not have the independent political support of organized pressure groups and Congress that bolstered individual government agencies in the United States. The Treasury also dominated the civil service – British civil servants were imbued with the Treasury orthodoxy and followed a career path, especially after 1919. The government bureaucracy was not therefore open to powerful experts with unorthodox views who might take a government job in mid-career. It was only the war that would bring heterodox economists like Austin Robinson, James Meade, and other students of Keynes out of the academic worlds and into government. Meade, later a Nobel prize-winner in economics, recalls working in 1944 for the Second Secretary at the Treasury, who sent him 'a most disarming letter saying that he had no training in economics but he was trying to master the subject. . . . When one looks at it objectively, what a state of affairs it is when a man chiefly responsible for internal and external policy has had no technical training. I am sure that in our grandchildren's day this will be considered very odd.'[11]

The contrast with the American state under the New Deal could not have been more striking. Amid the plethora of emergency agencies and established departments with their own power bases, no government department could exercise the control the Treasury exercised in Britain. Each programme had its own economists and its own lawyers and could call on congressional support. Above all, the New Deal opened up government service for a new breed of academics and intellectuals – the 'service intellectuals' described by Richard Kirkendall. Hoover had tried through the 1920s to bring such people into government. The emergency programmes of the New Deal brought them to Washington in droves. William Barber has described the 1930s as a 'government laboratory for economic learning'. One consequence was the dramatic improvement in the statistical base of economic knowledge. The Americans pioneered national income estimates. It would not be until the post-war Labour government, that Meade would attempt these for the government in Britain.[12]

Thus, the more fragmented and diffuse nature of state capacity in the United States enabled the Americans to adopt more imaginative anti-Depression programmes than the highly developed state capacity in Britain allowed.

That the decade of the 1930s was a time of intense national state-building in the United States is unquestioned. As William Leuchtenburg observed, 'the federal government became an institution that was directly experienced'. In the 1930s the government had told farmers what they could and could not grow, told employers whom they could and could not fire, what they could and could not pay their workers. It had expanded welfare provision out of all recognition from 1929, and had introduced effective and direct regulation of the banks, the stock exchange and private utilities. In every community citizens could see tangible evidence of the federal government's involvement in their daily lives – a housing project, a park, a library. To Robert Higgs this development was the decisive shift to the Big Government of modern America:

Institutional legacies of those fateful years stand all around us: federal lending for a multitude of purposes, federal production and sale of electricity, federal manipulation of agricultural production, prices and marketing, federal regulation of virtually every aspect of labor markets, the

vast federal social insurance system, a plethora of anticompetitive federal laws, and an uncountably large variety of federal subsidies – the list
goes on and on. The most important legacy of the New Deal, however,
is a certain system of belief, the now dominant ideology of the mixed
economy, which holds that the government is an immensely useful
means for achieving one's private aspirations and that one's resort to this
reservoir of potentially appropriable benefits is perfectly legitimate. To
take – indirectly if not directly – other people's property for one's own
benefit is now considered morally impeccable, provided that the taking
is effected through the medium of the government.... The commitment of both masses and elites to individualism, free markets, and
limited government suffered a blow in the 1930s from which it is unlikely ever to recover fully. In place of the old beliefs there now prevails
a greater toleration of, and even a positive demand for, collectivist
schemes that promise social security, protection from the rigors of market competition, and very often – to be blunt – something for nothing.[13]

To a British observer this does not seem quite to fit. One is more
impressed by the persistence and resilience of anti-statist sentiments and
traditions of individualism in the 1930s. The American state in the late
1930s did not provide its citizens with health insurance. Its system of social
security was purely contributory: participants certainly did not get something for nothing. The federal government did not use general tax revenues for social insurance benefits. Distinctions between the undeserving
and the deserving poor were maintained. The deserving would contribute
to social security. The undeserving would receive nothing. The Federal
government had got out of the business of relief. New Dealers expected
welfare or relief to fade away as recovery came. In the meantime the able-
bodied unemployed not covered by social insurance would receive work
relief or be left to the tender mercies of local states. Such was the hostility
to the spending of tax dollars on assistance, on providing 'something for
nothing', that, as James Patterson noted, it was amazing that Congress
agreed to provide matching funds for state programmes to assist those who
could not look after themselves – the needy aged, the blind, and single-
parent families. It was an entirely unintended consequence of the New
Deal that the latter ADC programme designed to help poor widows should
mushroom into the central welfare programme of today.[14]

Rather than Higgs's apocalyptic vision of the gargantuan New Deal
state, it is surely more accurate to take the viewpoint of Theda Skocpol and
Alan Brinkley that the New Deal state was founded on the idea of 'commercial' rather than social Keynesianism, a rationale that did not require
an elaborate capacity for state intervention. Many New Deal liberals did

advocate a social Keynesianism in which the state would intervene to ensure that government spending policies would be effective. Such intervention would involve a commitment to full employment, redistributive taxation and the extension of social security to protect mass purchasing power, the disciplining of corporate behaviour to prevent monopolistic price rises, the protection of trade unions to safeguard workers' incomes. Given the fragile nature of the state capacity that I have argued for at the end of the 1930s, it is not surprising that this social Keynesianism did not triumph. Rather it was the 'commercial' variant of Keynesianism that won through during the war and after: stimulating the economy through fairly automatic adjustments of government income and expenditure, particularly through tax cuts, but otherwise not extending the capacity of the state to intervene socially and economically. As Alan Brinkley has argued, Keynesian ideas 'provided a way to manage the economy without directly challenging the prerogatives of capitalists. Growth did not necessarily require constant involvement in the affairs of public institutions, . . . it did not require a drastic expansion of the regulatory functions of the state.'[15]

The war highlighted this contrast with the British experience.

In the United States the war brought unprecedented economic controls but the economy was not a command economy. Where possible the government relied on incentives, the profit motive and voluntarism. There was little prospect of the extension of state-sponsored reforms. The emergency programmes of the New Deal were dismantled, never to be revived again. Defence housing was, at the end of the war, to be sold off or dismantled. The social Keynesian agenda of the National Resources Planning Board in its report *Security, Work and Relief*, which called for government guaranteed minima for all American citizens, health care and low-cost housing, was ignored, except for returning GIs. After the war, the commitment to full employment was emasculated, health insurance was defeated, attempts to combine decent farm incomes and low food prices for consumers in the Brannan plan lapsed, only an attenuated low-cost housing bill passed Congress. Anti-statist and individualistic values triumphed. As the Office of War Information had told Roosevelt, the American people's post-war aspirations were 'compounded largely of 1929 values and the economics of 1929, leavened with a hangover from the makeshift controls of the war.' These attitudes scarcely fitted the picture Robert Higgs portrays of a fundamental shift in belief systems about the role of the state.[16]

By contrast, Britain did fight the war with a command economy. At the same time, a political consensus developed that the participation of the whole country in the war effort needed to be rewarded. The government provided substantial social services to enable women to join the work force: there was only occasional and minuscule official child care assistance in the United States. The financing of the war in Britain saw a dramatic shift in income distribution in favour of those earning less than £300 a year. Whereas the American National Resources Planning Board report sank without trace, the Beveridge Report in Britain became part of an all-party consensus. That report provided for universal, not means-tested benefits, notably family allowances, rationalized and made comprehensive social insurance, and called for the thoroughgoing overhaul of health care provision. Benefits which in the United States were restricted to GIs were to be made available in Britain to all citizens. The post-war Labour government put these reforms on the statute book, obliterating the final traces of the old poor law, and launched the National Health Service. At the same time, the government nationalized the railroads, air transport, the coal mines, the gas and electric utilities, and the steel industry.[17]

The development and extent of state capacity before 1930 in Britain, and its dramatic further expansion in the 1940s, stands in stark contrast to the restricted and circumscribed role of the federal government of the United States during the New Deal. Such a comparison offers a useful corrective to glib interpretations, both radical and free market, of America in the 1930s.

Notes

1. I developed these arguments in a paper, 'Roosevelt and the New Deal: the view from Britain', given in Chicago at the Organization of American Historians' meeting in April 1992.
2. Stephen Skowronek, *Building a New American State: The Expansion of National Administrative Capacities, 1877–1920* (Cambridge: Cambridge University Press, 1982); William R. Brock, *Investigation and Responsibility: Public Responsibility in the United States, 1865–1900* (Cambridge: Cambridge University Press, 1984); Theda Skocpol, *Protecting Soldiers and Mothers: The Political Origins of Social Policy in the United States* (Cambridge, Mass.: Belknap, 1992); Barry Supple and Mary Furner, 'Ideas, institutions and the state in the United States and Britain: an introduction', in Barry Supple and Mary Furner (eds), *The State and Economic Knowledge: The American and British Experiences* (Cambridge: Cambridge University Press, 1990), pp. 3–39.
3. William E. Leuchtenburg, 'The "Europeanization" of America, 1929–1950', *The FDR Years: On Roosevelt and his Legacy*, p. 284.
4. Robert Higgs, *Crisis and Leviathan: Critical Episodes in the Growth of American Government* (New York: Oxford University Press, 1987), pp. 159–95.
5. Leuchtenburg, 'The New Deal and the Analogue of War', *The FDR Years ...*, pp. 35–75.
6. Otis L. Graham, *Toward a Planned Society: From Roosevelt to Nixon* (New York: Oxford University Press, 1976), p. 30; Theda Skocpol and Kenneth Finegold, 'State capacity and economic intervention in the early New Deal', *Political Science Quarterly*, 97 (1982), pp. 255–79; Richard S. Kirkendall, *Social Scientists and Farm Politics in the Age of Roosevelt* (Columbia: University of Missouri Press, 1967), pp. 11–192.

7. James S. Olson, *Saving Capitalism: The Reconstruction Finance Corporation and the New Deal, 1933–1940* (Princeton, NJ: Princeton University Press, 1988); Jordan Schwarz, *The New Dealers: Power Politics in the Age of Roosevelt* (New York: Knopf, 1993), pp. 59–95. John Dizikes, *Britain, Roosevelt and the New Deal. British Opinion, 1932–1938* (New York: Garland, 1979), pp. 259–60; Ben Pimlott, *Hugh Dalton* (London: Cape, 1985), p. 217; Ben Pimlott (ed.) *The Political Diaries of Hugh Dalton* (London: Cape, 1986), p. 387; Denis Brogan, *The Era of Franklin D. Roosevelt: A Chronicle of the New Deal and Global War* (New Haven and London: Yale University Press, 1950), pp. 161–72.

8. Alger Hiss interview with the author, 26 January 1976.

9. James T. Patterson, 'Comparative welfare history: Britain and the United States, 1930–1945', in Wilbur J. Cohen (ed.), *The Roosevelt New Deal: A Program Assessment Fifty Years After* (Lyndon B. Johnson School of Public Affairs, Virginia Commonwealth University, and the Lyndon Baines Johnson Library, 1986), pp. 125–43; Margaret Weir and Theda Skocpol, 'State structures and the possibilities of "Keynesian" responses to the Great Depression in Sweden, Britain and the United States', in Peter Evans *et al.*, *Bringing the State Back In*, pp. 107–63.

10. Peter Clarke, 'The Treasury's analytical model of the British economy between the wars', in Barry Supple and Mary Furner, *The State and Economic Knowledge*, pp. 171–207. See also Peter Clarke, *The Keynesian Revolution in the Making, 1924–1936* (Oxford University Press, 1988), pp. 27–69.

11. Clarke, 'The Treasury's analytical model . . .' pp. 176–205; Weir and Skocpol, 'State structures . . .' pp. 120–9.

12. Richard S. Kirkendall, 'Franklin D. Roosevelt and the service intellectuals', *Mississippi Valley Historical Review*, 49 (1962–3), pp. 456–71; William J. Barber, 'Government as a laboratory for economic learning in the years of the Democratic Roosevelt', in Barry Supple and Mary Furner, *The State and Economic Knowledge*, pp. 103–37.

13. William E. Leuctenburg, *Franklin D. Roosevelt and the New Deal, 1932–1940* (New York: Harper & Row, 1963), p. 331; Higgs, *Crisis and Leviathan*, pp. 194–5.

14. Patterson, 'Comparative welfare history . . .', p. 133.

15. Weir and Skocpol, 'State structures', p. 108; Alan Brinkley, 'The New Deal and the idea of the state', in Steve Fraser and Gary Gerstle (eds), *The Rise and Fall of the New Deal Order* (Princeton, NJ: Princeton University Press, 1989), pp. 85–129; Alan Brinkley, *The End of Reform: New Deal Liberalism in Recession and War* (New York: Columbia University Press, 1995).

16. Brinkley, *The End of Reform*, pp. 175–271; Weir and Skocpol, 'State structures', 142–8; John Morton Blum, *V was for Victory: Politics and American Culture in World War II* (New York: Harcourt Brace Jovanovich, 1976), p. 104.

17. Jose Harris, 'Britain: The People's War' in David Reynolds, Warren F. Kimball and A. O. Chubarian (eds), *Allies at War: The Soviet, American and British Experiences, 1939–1945* (New York: St Martin's Press, 1994), pp. 233–60.

Index

AALL, *see* American Association for Labor Legislation
Addams, Jane 238, 282
AFL, *see* American Federation of Labor
Africans, as slaves in the US 28, 31, 32
agriculture 246
  in the UK 51, 53, 66
  in the US 49, 52, 55, 61–2, 65–6, 69, 76, 78, 80–1, 107, 252, 298–9
Alaska, woman suffrage 225
Albany plan of union 39
Allegheny 105
Allen, Theodore 171
Allis Company of Milwaukee 93
Amalgamated Society of Engineers (ASE) 200, 202, 205, 206, 207, 208, 209–10, 212
American
  as an identity (mentality) 1, 21, 26–47
  use as a term 32–4
American Association for Labor Legislation (AALL) 242, 257, 261
American colonies xi, 1, 3–25
  and British culture 28–9
  emergence of identity 26–47
  first settlers 27
  promotional literature for 39–40
  women colonists 30
American Federation of Labor (AFL) xiii, 121, 203, 211–12, 216, 258, 259, 260, 261, 286
American Philosophical Society 33
American Protective League 126
American Revolution 1, 4, 5, 6–7, 11, 13, 19, 20–1, 23–4, 30, 32
American United Shoe Machinery Company 83

American Socialist Party 274 n. 2
Ames, Nathaniel 29–30, 35
Ammanford, Battle of 120
Anglo-American Brush Electric Light Corporation 92
Anthracite strike 1902 (US) 124
Arizona
  copper miners 126
  woman suffrage 225
arms manufacture 64, 66, 69, 82, 85, 205, 211
Arrears Act 1879 (US) 244
ASE, *see* Amalgamated Society of Engineers
Asquith, H. H. 227, 228–9, 230, 235, 236, 240, 262
Atbara bridge, Sudan 84
automobiles, *see* cars and car industry

Babcock & Wilcox 92
Balfour, Lady Frances and Betty 234
ball bearings 85
Baltimore 109
Barnett, Canon Samuel and Henrietta 281
Bedford, Duke of 35–6
Belmont, Mrs O. H. P. 238, 239
Berkeley, George 29
Beveridge, William 265, 281, 305
bicycles 85–6, 87
Birmingham, UK 104, 134
  debating society 171, 177
  gatling gun works 85
  GEC works 94
  police 118
  population 180
  street railway 162